BRIDGING THE INTERPRETIVE ABYSS

SEMEIA STUDIES

Jacqueline M. Hidalgo, General Editor

Editorial Board:
Rhiannon Graybill
Suzanna Millar
Raj Nadella
Emmanuel Nathan
Kenneth Ngwa
Shively T. J. Smith
Wei Hsien Wan

Number 105

BRIDGING THE INTERPRETIVE ABYSS

Reading the New Testament after the Cultural Studies Turn

Luis Menéndez-Antuña

PRESS

Atlanta

Copyright © 2025 by Luis Menéndez-Antuña

All rights reserved. No part of this work may be reproduced or transmitted in any form or by any means, electronic or mechanical, including photocopying and recording, or by means of any information storage or retrieval system, except as may be expressly permitted by the 1976 Copyright Act or in writing from the publisher. Requests for permission should be addressed in writing to the Rights and Permissions Office, SBL Press, 825 Houston Mill Road, Atlanta, GA 30329 USA.

Library of Congress Control Number: 2025931630

Cover art: *Zoociedad*, by Richard Peralta. Used by permission.

CONTENTS

Acknowledgments vii
Abbreviations ix

1. New Testament Studies: An Epistemological Critique 1

2. The Gospel of Cultural Studies: An Intercontextual Approach 35

3. The Gospel of Queer Love (Matthew 25:31–46) 65

4. The Gospel of Torture (Mark 15:1–39) 97

5. The Gospel of Social Death (Luke 8:26–39) 129

6. The Gospel of Love in Times of Coloniality (John 13:1–20) 161

7. The Gospel of HIV (Acts 9:1–8) 191

    Conclusion 227

Bibliography 235
Ancient Sources Index 279
Modern Authors Index 282
Subject Index 290

ACKNOWLEDGMENTS

This book is in debt to a multitude of people and institutions. People first.

Thanks to Jin Young Choi and Jacqueline Hidalgo for their caring and challenging feedback on the manuscript. Your scholarship remains an inspiration for my own, and I am honored to have you as conversation partners.

Thanks to Jonathan Calvillo, Rebecca Copeland, Filipe Maia, and Nicolette Manglos-Weber for being integral to this professional journey and for generously reading different parts of this contribution. Thanks to Shively Smith for being a partner in crime, and so much more.

Thank you to Mary Elizabeth Moore, Sujin Pak, and Bryan Stone for always saying yes to my petitions for support. Thank you, Shelly Rambo, for being a beautiful colleague.

Thank you, Samantha Reilly, for tidying up my writing messes and for modeling what living graciously in the academy looks like. Thank you, Lindsay Donnelly-Bullington, for your generosity.

My research for this book greatly benefited from conversations that took place worldwide. Too many names to name: Xochitl Alvizo, Ellen Armour, Debra S. Ballentine, Tat-siong Benny Liew, Karen Bray, Mark Brettler, Kent L. Brintnall, Greg Carey, Manuela Ceballos, Cavan Concannon, Leonard Curry, Benjamin Dunning, Sarah Emanuel, Emily Filler, Constance M. Furey, Jennifer Glancy, Warren Goldstein, Meghan Henning, Chris Hoklotubbe, Janna Hunter-Bowman, Andrea Jain, Martin Kavka, Jill Hicks-Keeton, Mark Jordan, Joel B. Kemp, Herbert Marbury, Méadhbh McIvor, Candida Moss, Halvor Moxnes, Roger Nam, Jorunn Økland, Wongi Park, Jennifer Quigley, Erin Runions, Ethan Schwartz, and Mitzi Smith, Ekaputra Tupamahu, and Carmen Yebra. I remain indebted to your brilliance across multiple venues at the Society of Biblical Literature, the American Academy of Religion, at our institutions, at professional symposia, or over coffee.

Elena Olazagasti-Segovia and Fernando F. Segovia continue to inspire me professionally and personally. I truly love you.

Part of chapter 3 is adapted from an article published in the Journal of Religious Ethics 45 (2017). Part of chapter 4 is adapted from an article published in the Journal of the American Academy of Religion 90 (2022). Part of chapter 5 is adapted from an article published in the Journal of Biblical Literature 138 (2019). Part of Chapter 7 is adapted from an article published in Critical Research on Religion 6 (2018).

This research would not have been possible without the generous support from the Louisville Institute. Obtaining a Sabbatical Grant for Researchers and participating in an enlivening Winter Retreat—amid a pandemic—gave me the air I needed to breathe.

My pedagogical and professional vocation has been nourished over these writing years by the generous support from the Wabash Center for Teaching and Learning in Theology and Religion and from the Hispanic Theological Initiative. I can only hope to give back a small portion of what I have received from both institutions.

Tim, let our laughs, love, and lives be enduring. Thank you for understanding and supporting this crazy life of the mind. Equipo!

ABBREVIATIONS

Primary Sources

4 Regn.	Dio Chrysostom, *De regno iv* (*Or.* 4)
A.J.	Josephus, *Antiquitates judaicae*
Amat.	Plato, *Amatores*
Ant. rom.	Dionysius of Halicarnassus, *Antiquitates romanae*
B.J.	Josephus, *Bellum judaicum*
Doctr. chr.	Augustine, *De doctrina christiana*
Fact.	Valerius Maximus, *Facta et Dicta Memorabilia*
Fin.	Cicero, *De finibus*
Flacc.	Philo, *In Flaccum*
Flor.	Stobaeus, *Florilegium*
Gal.	Julian, *Contra Galilaeos*
Hist.	Polybius, *Historiae*
Ios.	Philo, *De Iosepho*
Leg.	Cicero, *De legibus*
Off.	Cicero, *De officiis*
Pol.	Aristotle, *Politica*

Secondary Sources

ABR	*Australian Biblical Review*
AcBib	Academia Biblica
AJBI	*Annual of the Japanese Biblical Institute*
AYB	Anchor Yale Bible Commentaries
ACW	Ancient Christian Writers
AugStud	*Augustinian Studies*
AYBRL	Anchor Yale Bible Reference Library
BAR	*Biblical Archaeology Review*

BETL	Bibliotheca Ephemeridum Theologicarum Lovaniensium
Bib	*Biblica*
BibInt	*Biblical Interpretation*
BibInt	Biblical interpretation Series
BibSem	The Biblical Seminar
BTB	*Biblical Theology Bulletin*
BW	Bible and Women
BZNW	Beihefte zur Zeitschrift für die neutestamentliche Wissenschaft und die Kunde der älteren Kirche
CBQ	*Catholic Biblical Quarterly*
CurBR	*Currents in Biblical Research*
CurTM	*Currents in Theology and Mission*
DDD	Toorn, Karel van der, Bob Becking, and Pieter W. van der Horst, eds. *Dictionary of Deities and Demons in the Bible*. 2nd ed. Leiden: Brill, 1999.
EC	*Early Christianity*
ECL	Early Christianity and Its Literature
EstEcl	*Estudios eclesiásticos*
ETL	*Ephemerides Theologicae Lovanienses*
ExpTim	*Expository Times*
GPBS	Global Perspectives on Biblical Scholarship
HvTSt	*Hervormde Teologiese Studies* (*HTS Teologiese Studies/HTS Theological Studies*)
JAAR	*Journal of the American Academy of Religion*
JBL	*Journal of Biblical Literature*
JECS	*Journal of Early Christian Studies*
JFSR	*Journal of Feminist Studies in Religion*
JRE	*Journal of Religious Ethics*
JSNTSup	Journal for the Study of the New Testament Supplement Series
JSOTSup	Journal for the Study of the Old Testament Supplement Series
JTS	*Journal of Theological Studies*
LNTS	Library of New Testament Studies
LS	*Louvain Studies*
Neot	*Neotestamentica*
NovT	*Novum Testamentum*
NTL	New Testament Library

NTS	*New Testament Studies*
PRSt	*Perspectives in Religious Studies*
PzB	*Protokolle zur Bibel*
RAC	Klauser, Theodor, et al., eds. *Reallexikon für Antike und Christentum: Sachwörterbuch zur Auseinandersetzung des Christentums mit der antiken Welt.* Stuttgart: Hiersemann, 1950–.
RBS	Resources for Biblical Study
ResQ	*Restoration Quarterly*
RevExp	*Review and Expositor*
RevistB	*Revista bíblica*
SBLDS	Society of Biblical Literature Dissertation Series
SBLTT	Society of Biblical Literature Texts and Translations
SBS	Stuttgarter Bibelstudien
SEÅ	*Svensk exegetisk årsbok*
SemeiaSt	Semeia Studies
SR	*Studies in Religion/Sciences religieuses*
TCS	Text-Critical Studies
TNTC	Tyndale New Testament Commentaries
TS	*Theological Studies*
WUNT	Wissenschaftliche Untersuchungen zum Neuen Testament
ZKT	*Zeitschrift für katholische Theologie*
ZNW	*Zeitschrift für die neutestamentliche Wissenschaft und die Kunde der älteren Kirche*
ZTK	*Zeitschrift für Theologie und Kirche*

1
NEW TESTAMENT STUDIES: AN EPISTEMOLOGICAL CRITIQUE

How is it possible that the canon of thought in all the disciplines of the social sciences and humanities in the Westernized university is based on the knowledge produced by a few men from five countries in Western Europe (Italy, France, England, Germany and the USA [sic])? How is it possible that men from these five countries achieved such an epistemic privilege to the point that their knowledge today is considered superior over the knowledge of the rest of the world? How did they come to monopolize the authority of knowledge in the world? Why is it that what we know today as social, historical, philosophical, or critical theory is based on the socio-historical experience and world views of men from these five countries?[1]

Geopolitical Locations, Epistemological Mappings, and Historiographical Foundations

Biblical studies as an academic field suffers from what I would call an epistemological crisis.[2] The New Testament is a historical document, a set

---

1. Ramón Grosfoguel, "The Structure of Knowledge in Westernized Universities: Epistemic Racism/Sexism and the Four Genocides/Epistemicides of the Long 16th Century," *Human Architecture: Journal of the Sociology of Self-Knowledge* 11 (2013): 74.

2. This book centers mostly on the New Testament texts. Chapters selectively pick up texts from the gospels, Acts, and Paul's letters, and most secondary sources cited belong to the field of New Testament studies. Notwithstanding the focus on this part of the canon and the subsequent scholarly discourse, much of the methodological and theoretical considerations equally apply to the world of the Hebrew Bible, and different parts of the argument frequently refer to secondary literature in that field. Many of the metatheoretical considerations in this chapter and the methodological moves in the subsequent chapters have parallels in the way the field of Hebrew Bible stud-

of texts produced in the first century, no less than it is a religious and theological archive with enduring social, political, and cultural influence. These texts center religious liturgies weekly around the globe, belong in the museums through countless visual representations of their motifs, pop up regularly in political debates, influence the ways contemporary citizens understand themselves, and constitute an essential component of the educational curriculum across the widest variety of institutions. The epistemological crisis issues, I argue, from a mismatch between this plurality of identities—biblical texts exceed their historicity to morph into cultural entities of their own—and the ways professional critics have made historicism the lingua franca of biblical studies.[3]

This introductory chapter offers a tentative diagnosis of such a plight, offering a genealogy of the dominance of historicism and suggesting an alternative framework, via cultural studies, to broaden our epistemological options. My set of arguments, despite their seemingly impassioned take, aim at criticizing a certain hegemony, not at disqualifying its epistemological credentials. All knowledge is necessarily contextual, but not all knowledge occupies the same contexts. Knowledge production originates in political contexts with deeply rooted epistemological assumptions.[4] When certain contexts, with their sets of assumptions, claim privileged access to truth while disregarding alternative frameworks, hegemony ensues. In a nutshell, this introductory chapter argues that historicism constitutes a hegemonic mode of knowledge production in biblical studies

---

ies currently operates. For these reasons, I use *biblical studies* as an umbrella concept that refers mostly to the New Testament but reaches out to the Hebrew canon. This rationale, furthermore, is consistent with most critics' use of the term biblical studies.

3. See Anna Runesson, *Exegesis in the Making: Postcolonialism and New Testament Studies* (Leiden: Brill, 2010), 17–50; Elisabeth Schüssler Fiorenza, *Democratizing Biblical Studies: Toward an Emancipatory Educational Space* (Louisville: Westminster John Knox, 2009), 51–84; Caroline Vander Stichele and Todd Penner, "Mastering the Tools or Retooling the Masters? The Legacy of Historical-Critical Discourse," in *Her Master's Tools? Feminist and Postcolonial Engagements of Historical-Critical Discourse*, ed. Caroline Vander Stichele and Todd Penner, GPBS 9 (Atlanta: Society of Biblical Literature, 2005), 1–30; George Aichele, Peter Miscall, and Richard Walsh, "An Elephant in the Room: Historical-Critical and Postmodern Interpretations of the Bible," *JBL* 128 (2009): 383–404.

4. Walter D. Mignolo, *The Darker Side of Western Modernity: Global Futures, Decolonial Options* (Durham, NC: Duke University Press, 2011); Mignolo, *The Politics of Decolonial Investigations* (Durham, NC: Duke University Press, 2021).

that has resulted in an impoverishment in the vocabularies, theories, and methods available to interpret biblical texts.

The introduction of an epistemological critique, a debunking of historicism as hegemony, represents both an exercise in epistemic justice and an essay on utopian thinking. On the one hand, Western notions of truth have relegated contextual knowledges to the margins of our discipline; on the other, the hegemony of historicism has hindered attempts at moving biblical studies toward creative intellectual paths. On this front, this introductory chapter grounds an ethos of biblical interpretation that materializes in a series of exegetical and hermeneutical exercises in the ensuing chapters. A critical genealogy of knowledge production as practiced in the Global North entails a questioning of the telos of our discipline. Is biblical studies an exclusively historicist discipline, a project of reconstructing a bygone past or distilling an ancient document's meanings, whether literary, cultural, or political? As I hope to show, the project of summoning cultural studies to the center of biblical hermeneutics has the potential to renew research agendas beyond the hackneyed roads of studying old topics with new methods. Most likely, some scholars will argue that my analysis overstates the case. There are innumerable counterexamples—many of them cited in the chapters that follow—and still, I insist, the hegemonic core of our discipline remains tied to a set of historicist assumptions.[5]

To ignore the multitude of new approaches that have emerged in biblical studies over the past fifty years would be oversimplifying the matter. Each chapter in this book relies heavily on these interpretive operations. However, it would also be simplistic to overlook the continued dominance of historicism as the standard for intellectual rigor and scholarly quality.

---

5. Let me offer on this front two sets of examples. Consider first the tables of contents of the most prestigious journals in our field: *Journal of Biblical Literature*, *Journal for the Study of the New Testament*, *New Testament Studies*, *Theological Studies*, *Harvard Theological Review*, *Catholic Biblical Quarterly*, *Zeitschrift für Neues Testament*, or *Estudios Biblicos*. Recent book contributions that survey the field of New Testament studies include Scot McKnight and Nijay Gupta, *The State of New Testament Studies: A Survey of Recent Research* (Grand Rapids: Baker Academic, 2019); Delbert Royce Burkett, *An Introduction to the New Testament and the Origins of Christianity* (Cambridge: Cambridge University Press, 2002). Some exceptions to the rule of historicism include Todd Penner and Davina C. Lopez, *De-introducing the New Testament: Texts, Worlds, Methods, Stories* (Chichester: Wiley-Blackwell, 2015); Mitzi J. Smith and Yung Suk Kim, *Toward Decentering the New Testament: A Reintroduction* (Eugene, OR: Cascade, 2018).

Recent advancements in critical and contextualist biblical hermeneutics can be seen as building upon the fundamental questions of epistemology: How do we acquire knowledge? What type of knowledge? What are the historiographical assumptions underlying our exegetical arguments? Which research agendas and topics are prioritized? Which primary and secondary sources guide our interpretive task? Which theories, methods, approaches, and perspectives are favored? Ultimately, what is the purpose of our work? While the epistemological crisis in the Global North stems from the predominance of historical criticism, the crisis in the Global South is further complicated by the close connection between biblical knowledge and theological institutions. In the North, our academic community is predominantly characterized by historicism, objectivism, and a scientific mindset.[6] This triad, one that fuels secularism, as I show in this chapter's last section, feeds on the fact that demographically, methodologically, and in terms of the sources cited, biblical interpretation is in the hands of white, male scholars, in the grasp of a white method, and, almost exclusively, referential to white sources.[7] In the Global South, although epistemologically colonized, the task of biblical critique remains closely tied to contextual analyses, deeply concerned with a series of political, ethical, and cultural crises. The production of knowledge here springs from theological centers that have close ties with ecclesial communities. Demographically, methodologically, and in terms of the sources cited, biblical interpretation is in the hands of confessionalism.

This introduction offers no definite answers to the questions posed above, but it rehearses some theoretical and methodological explorations concerning the task of biblical critique, its epistemes and its heuristics, its concerns, and its *teloi*. The first and second chapters form a diptych: chapter 1 displays a tentative diagnosis of dominant and subjugated epistemes in our field, adventuring a theoretical armature that takes specific exegetical forms and shapes in the ensuing chapters; chapter 2 is an exercise in imagination in that it foregrounds a thematic fugue that reintroduces contemporary cultural and political crises into the field of New Testament studies. Both goals, the first eminently critical and the second predominantly constructive, are intimately connected. Concerning the first objec-

---

6. Elisabeth Schüssler Fiorenza, *Rhetoric and Ethic: The Politics of Biblical Studies* (Minneapolis: Fortress, 1999), 17–30.

7. Wongi Park ("Multiracial Biblical Studies," *JBL* 140 [2021]: 435–59) terms the field as "monoracial" and drowning in whiteness.

tive, this chapter roots biblical hermeneutics in the West, with its investment in historicism, as part of colonial knowledges. As we unearth the connections between historicism and colonialism, we discover some of the defining features of the historicist task, such as its extractivist ethos and objectivistic monopoly. Regarding the second objective, my purpose is to put theory to work not as a vain exercise in intellectualism but as an entryway to broach, within but at the discipline's margins, unattended topics in our guild. If historicism creates a series of asphyxiating circumstances for the flourishing of new areas of investigation, then cultural studies offers some inspiring alternatives for an ethically responsible production of knowledge.

The epistemological crisis—an idea that I will explore in the following sections—issues from a demographical stasis that, in turn, results in a democratic standstill in terms of how scholars produce, disseminate, and consume knowledge. Heretofore I referred to epistemological crisis to name a critical deficiency in the production of knowledge and the ensuing setback in the ways biblical critics imagine possible futures. Whereas the first item pertains to a sociology of knowledge—that is, who produces biblical scholarship and how such production circulates—the second dimension refers to how the current demographic patterns impede how biblical scholars sketch the lines of the discipline's future. Although the ethos of biblical interpretation differs in the North and Latin America, both are essentially indebted to certain strands of historicism as it issues from putative scientific historiography. Subsequently, a probe into the origins, production, and dissemination of knowledges requires a geopolitical account of different epistemes, their ecosystems, and their contentious relationships. On this front, the intellectual project of Epistemologies of the South by Boaventura de Sousa Santos constitutes an impulse to develop a more contextualized idea of our historiographical goals, a lucid framework to grasp the field's investments in the reconstruction of the past and its influence in the theorization of our present.[8]

As found in the epigraph to this introduction, Ramón Grosfoguel's pungent and somewhat rhetorical questions about the sociology of knowledge in the Global North apply seamlessly to the field of biblical studies. The dominance of historicism does not ensue from its inherent

---

8. Boaventura de Sousa Santos, *Epistemologies of the South: Justice against Epistemicide* (Boulder, CO: Paradigm, 2014).

epistemological superiority nor from its ability to generate innovative research agendas. Rather, historicism benefits from a tradition of scientific knowledge that has effectively spread into the humanities. What does it mean to claim historicism dominance? Simply put: analyzing a biblical text involves retrieving its original meaning whether such meaning resides in the author's original intention, the text's rhetorical goals, or how the text works in a specific historical, cultural, or social context. Accordingly, I refer to this historiographical mode as *preterist* to express how scholars conceive the research agenda, the telos of hermeneutics, and the retrieval of textual meaning as the intellectual task of reconstructing the past as past.

In contrast, this book resorts to *presentism* as a historiographical style that conceptualizes biblical interpretation as the scholarly task of taking contemporary crises, topics, and traditions as the springboard to produce intellectual work. Whereas preteritism assumes that the "past" should inform the disciplinary domain, presentism argues that such a task is hegemonic and exclusionary and suggests that biblical scholarship should expand its scope to attend not only to the biblical past but also to the biblical present and future. Presentism and preteritism are not mutually exclusive options, but they have dramatically different purchasing values in the market of biblical studies. Given historicism's hegemonic role, even presentist-oriented studies consider preteritism as the sine qua non of intellectual rigor. Against views that naturally equate biblical interpretation to the past, what we call "exegesis," Vincent L. Wimbush forcefully argues that such an exegetical take represents "a high cultural practice and art…, a fetishization of text that in turn reflects a fetishization of the dominant world that the text helped create."[9]

---

9. Vincent L. Wimbush, *Black Flesh Matters. Essays on Runagate Interpretation* (Lanham, MD: Lexington/Fortress Academic, 2022), 106. Wimbush coins the term "scripturalization" to account for the process of making scriptures do things, "a semiosphere, within which a structure of reality is created that produces and legitimates and maintains media of knowing and discourse and the corresponding power relations" (*White Men's Magic: Scripturalization as Slavery* [Oxford: Oxford University Press, 2012], 46). See also Jacqueline M. Hidalgo, *Revelation in Aztlán: Scriptures, Utopias, and the Chicano Movement* (New York: Palgrave Macmillan, 2016). In a similar fashion, Steed Vernyl Davidson ("Postcolonializing the Bible with a Little Help from Derek Walcott," in *Present and Future of Biblical Studies: Celebrating Twenty-Five Years of Brill's Biblical Interpretation*, ed. Tat-siong Benny Liew, BibInt 161 [Leiden: Brill, 2018], 166) creates the term "to postcolonialize" to convey the notion that the hermeneutical

Different genealogies explain different elements of the current situation.[10] This chapter introduces a decolonial approach, seeking to reframe the terms in which preteritism and presentism relate to each other: instead of using the past as the template for the study of a biblical text, a decolonial approach situates the present as the framing narrative for the task at hand. Preteritism, as the critique goes, circumvents the colonial legacies of the biblical text because it conceives of the biblical past as a pristine historical moment,[11] impervious to the legacies of colonialism in the West. Preteritism, for instance, may claim that the biblical text is anti-imperialist, but only by resorting to ways of knowing that are indebted to colonial knowledges. Although presentism does not produce decolonial wisdom per se, it is better equipped to address the entanglement of knowledge production with coloniality because it unapologetically initiates the hermeneutical process with a theorization of current global realities.

In the Global North, the challenges to preteritism have mostly originated from identity-based critiques to the putatively objectivist scholarly

---

task, in the context of a postcolonial world, is called to tap "into the various domains around literature and the social to generate meaning from an ancient text to speak to the liberative needs of Mbembe's durées." These approaches share an understanding of the text not as a fixed entity that ought to be an interpretive object but rather a result of conflicting realities informing a conflictual world. From a queer perspective, see also Ken Stone, "Bibles That Matter: Biblical Theology and Queer Performativity," *BTB* 38 (2008): 14–25.

10. Hector Avalos, *The End of Biblical Studies* (Buffalo, NY: Prometheus, 2007); Stephen D. Moore and Yvonne Sherwood, *The Invention of the Biblical Scholar: A Critical Manifesto* (Minneapolis: Fortress, 2011); Fernando F. Segovia, *Decolonizing Biblical Studies: A View from the Margins* (Maryknoll, NY: Orbis Books, 2000); Henning Graf Reventlow and William Farmer, *Biblical Studies and the Shifting of Paradigms, 1850–1914*, JSOTSup 192 (Sheffield: Sheffield Academic, 1995); Craig Bartholomew, C. Stephen Evans, Mary Healy, and Murray Rae, *"Behind" The Text: History and Biblical Interpretation* (Grand Rapids: Zondervan Academic, 2003); Vincent Wimbush, ed., *Theorizing Scriptures: New Critical Orientations to a Cultural Phenomenon* (New Brunswick: Rutgers University Press, 2008); Elisabeth Schüssler Fiorenza, *Wisdom Ways: Introducing Feminist Biblical Interpretation* (Maryknoll, NY: Orbis Books, 2001); R. S. Sugirtharajah, *Exploring Postcolonial Biblical Criticism: History, Method, Practice* (Chichester: Wiley-Blackwell, 2012); Musa W. Dube, *Postcolonial Feminist Interpretation of the Bible* (St. Louis: Chalice, 2000).

11. The construction of the past as an authentic, clear, and stable entity is itself a part of the racialized discourse in the West; see Shawn Kelly, *Race, Ideology and the Formation of Modern Biblical Scholarship* (London: Routledge, 2002).

ethos. In Latin America, at least within the liberationist tradition, the critique springs from contextualist takes inspired by Marxism. In the first case, consider, for instance, Wongi Park's critique of the ways that whiteness suffuses historicism. A theoretical and methodological advocacy for multiracial criticism, Park's contribution, an anomaly itself in the publication record of the flagship journal, exposes whiteness as orchestrating, baton in hand, the disciplinary choir.[12] Whiteness provides the invisible but dominant slant that different interpretative strategies invested in historicism inadvertently trade in. Whiteness, an ethos of performing the critical task,[13] is then historically attached, methodologically wedded, and theoretically invested in historicism. Biblical studies' monoracialism, Park accurately determines, is the epiphenomenon of a complex historical disciplinary trajectory that understands itself tied to European, mostly German, roots (genealogy), invested in historical criticism (method), and committed to a research agenda issuing from such origins and methodological investments.[14] This is not just a high-theory analysis of cultural trends within our field. To the chagrin of those who deny or minimize criticism's investment in whiteness, Park reminds us of the statistics. If knowledge production, as the sociology of knowledge and the philosophy of science have amply demonstrated, is tied to its demographics, there is little wonder that biblical critique reproduces the interests of white, Anglo-Saxon, and German, cisgender males, straight, and upper-middle or middle-class researchers. Wongi Park's analysis instantiates in biblical studies what Ramón Grosfoguel diagnoses about the humanities writ large.

---

12. Park, "Multiracial Biblical Studies," 454.

13. Whiteness, at least in this version, is an episteme: a dominant ethos of doing biblical research, invisible as the air we breathe and for this reason informing every dimension of scholarship as scholarship. Whiteness, to say it with Michel Foucault (*Discipline and Punish: The Birth of the Prison*, trans. Alan Sheridan [London: Peregrine, 1979], 170; "Truth and Power," in *Power/Knowledge: Selected Interviews and Other Writings*, ed. Colin Gordon, trans. Colin Gordon et al. [New York: Vintage, 1980], 120–25), has disciplinary and capillary power: not as coming from above but as shaping who we are, what we do, and how we imagine. It is from this perspective that scholars of color are not immune to whiteness very much like queer scholars are likely to perpetuate heterosexism, etc. As Park ("Multiracial Biblical Studies," 447) points out, at stake here is whiteness's unexamined assumptions about history, knowledge, and hermeneutics.

14. Park, "Multiracial Biblical Studies," 440.

The epistemological crisis, however, transcends race and ethnicity because it evinces the close ties between the academic ethos and the concerns of marginalized populations, between intellectual inquiry for the sake of intellectualism and political activism geared toward transformative change.[15] Our field still considers, to name a few, queer theory, postcolonial critique, or disability studies a postscript rather than essential and formative components of its modus operandi. Significant historical and philosophical factors sustain the existing hegemonic episteme. Regardless of explanatory genealogies, including the one rehearsed in this chapter, the end result proves that professional biblical interpretation remains oblivious to contemporary political and cultural crises, ill-equipped to address the concerns of the majority world. Communities affected by such problems hardly make their voices present in the echo chambers of biblical scholarship. Furthermore, the hermeneutical theoretical traditions in the North have made it either impossible or unreputable to mix contemporary concerns and agendas with biblical texts and contexts. Such is the realm of historicism as preteritism.

The landscape in the Global South remains a bit more scattered and, for that reason, more inspiring. Numerous scholars and centers inaugurated and contributed to emancipatory hermeneutics, while many others adhere to the epistemologies imported from the North.[16] Rather than focusing on identity-based claims, Latin American exegesis has gravitated around the category of the impoverished, a socioeconomic category that informs hermeneutical methods as they bridge the historiographical gap.[17] Although "the option for the poor" grounds emancipatory hermeneutics,[18]

---

15. Miranda Fricker (*Epistemic Injustice: Power and the Ethics of Knowing* [Oxford: Oxford University Press, 2009], 7) makes a useful distinction between two forms of epistemic injustice: "testimonial injustice," in which someone is wronged as a producer of knowledge; and "hermeneutical injustice," in which someone is wronged in their capacity as subject of social understanding.

16. Osbert Uyovwieyovwe Isiorhovoja, Godwin Omegwe, and Sylvester Ese Ibomhen, "Quest for Africentric Biblical Reading among African Christians," *KIU Journal of Humanities* 8 (2023): 257–63, https://doi.org/10.58709/niujhu.v8i2.1676.

17. Miguel Ángel Ferrando, "La interpretación de la Biblia en la teología de la liberación, 1971–1984," *Teología y Vida* 50 (2009): 75–92, http://dx.doi.org/10.4067/S0049-34492009000100007; René Krüger, "Teología bíblica contextual en América Latina," *Acta Poética* 31 (2010): 185–207, https://doi.org/10.19130/iifl.ap.2010.2.351.

18. The question of the "poor and crucified" at the center of the theological task is at the heart of the methodological reflection. Thus bibliography here is extensive: see Jon Sobrino, *The True Church and the Poor* (Maryknoll, NY: Orbis Books, 1984);

biblical exegesis has been particularly slow to ground how such ethical-political commitments find their rationale in historiographical and philosophical theories indebted to the North. Biblical hermeneutics, on the one hand, has drawn from theological agendas determined by confessional interests and, on the other, has been slow to incorporate methodological insights from decolonial philosophies. On this front—on the importance of history—my contribution contextualizes a specific historical way of knowing as it is practiced in our field within a broader episteme. In the following section, I argue that historicism, inextricable from scientificism and objectivism, is best understood as part of colonial knowledges.

Historicism relies on inextricable links between exegesis, objectivism, and scientificism. As a virtual solution, from a global perspective, I explore what models of knowledge are available to scholars disinvested in the afterlife of the Enlightenment.[19] Historicism, a component of the modernist macro-episteme, forecloses in advance research topics (heuristics) and disbands the richness of reading strategies that readers bring to the table.[20]

Sobrino, *Witnesses to the Kingdom: The Martyrs of El Salvador and the Crucified Peoples* (Maryknoll, NY: Orbis Books, 2003); Sobrino, *No Salvation outside the Poor: Prophetic-Utopian Essays* (Maryknoll, NY: Orbis Books, 2008); Manfred K. Bahmann, *A Preference for the Poor: Latin American Liberation Theology from a Protestant Perspective* (Lanham, MD: University Press of America, 2005); José María Vigil and Leonardo Boff, *La opción por los pobres*, Presencia Teológica (Santander: Sal Terrae, 1991); Vigil and Boff, *¿Qué es optar por los pobres? Evangelio con rostro Latinoamericano* (Santa Fé de Bogotá: Ediciones Paulinas, 1994); María López Vigil, Jon Sobrino, and Rafael Díaz-Salazar, *La matanza de los pobres: Vida en medio de la muerte en El Salvador* (Madrid: HOAC, 1993); Jorge V. Pixley and Clodovis Boff, *The Bible, the Church and the Poor*, Theology and Liberation (Maryknoll, NY: Orbis Books, 1989); José M. Castillo, *Los pobres y la teología: ¿Qué queda de la teología de la liberación?* (Bilbao: Desclée de Brouwer, 1997); Castillo, *Escuchar lo que dicen los pobres a la iglesia* (Barcelona: Cristianisme i Justícia, 1999); José Ignacio González Faus, *Vicarios de Cristo: Los pobres en la teología y espiritualidad Cristianas; Antología comentada* (Barcelona: Cristianisme i Justícia, 2005).

19. A difficult task, since "biblical scholarship" is "still fundamentally predetermined and contained by the Enlightenment episteme" (Moore and Sherwood, *Invention of the Biblical Scholar*, 48).

20. Literary criticism outside biblical studies has now a long and rich tradition of moving beyond critical theory with its narrow focus on criticism as demystification and exposure. These debates have not touched the surface of biblical studies because, among other reasons, our field has never fully embraced critical theory. In a masterfully elegant book, Rita Felski (*The Limits of Critique* [Chicago: University of Chicago Press, 2015]) makes the rather simple but brilliant point that interpreting involves all

Consider, for instance, the plight that queer hermeneutics faces. This approach falls outside of the Northern side because it is not historical enough. Despite its contextual nature, it remains outside of the scope of Latin American approaches because of their confessionalism, clericalism, and political commitments. The irony should not be lost on us: biblical scholarship lacks the hermeneutical potency to address the seemingly most homophobic text—as performed in cultural debates about marriage equality, for instance. Historicism straitjackets virtually all approaches to the topic of sexuality by confining the types of questions that count for scholarly relevance. Even the most queer-friendly agendas remain thoroughly historicist: Is there "sexuality" in antiquity? Does Paul consider homoeroticism a moral fall? Is there "homosexuality" in the Bible?[21] Notice that these questions not only welcome historicist practices, but they are also posed—ironically, given queer theory's aversion to essences—in quite identitarian terms.[22]

---

kinds of affects, dispositions, embodiments, and goals and that literary critique has not developed an adequate vocabulary to convey all this wealth. See also Felski, *Hooked: Art and Attachment* (Chicago: University of Chicago Press, 2020). Eve Kosofsky Sedgwick and Bruno Latour are to be credited with this "postcritical" turn. See Eve Kosofsky Sedgwick, "Paranoid Reading and Reparative Reading, or, You're So Paranoid, You Probably Think This Essay Is about You," in *Touching Feeling: Affect, Pedagogy, Performativity* [Durham, NC: Duke University Press, 2003), 123–52; Bruno Latour, "Why Has Critique Run out of Steam? From Matters of Fact to Matters of Concern," *Critical Inquiry* 30 (2004): 225–48. For a helpful survey, see Tim Lanzendörfer and Mathias Nilges, "Literary Studies after Postcritique: An Introduction," *Amerikastudien/American Studies* 64 (2019): 491–513; and Herman Paul, "The Postcritical Turn: Unravelling the Meaning of 'Post' and 'Turn,'" in *Writing the History of the Humanities: Questions, Themes and Approaches,* ed. Herman Paul (London: Bloomsbury, 2022), 305–24.

21. One of the most interesting examples can be found in the discipline's flagship journal: *Journal of Biblical Literature*. Jeramy Townsley ("Paul, the Goddess Religions, and Queer Sects: Romans 1:23–28," *JBL* 130 [2011]: 728) uses the word "queer" to refer to all kinds of idolatrous practices and "to the gender and sex-variant practices of the goddess cults." Townsley can only conclude that Paul is not really referring to "contemporary queer relationships" by emptying *queer* of any nonheteronormative connotation. Given my argument's emphasis on the structure of the knowledge production, it should be noticed that this is the only time that *JBL* has published an article with reference to queer theory. There are, of course, multiple exceptions, and all of them will be cited in the following chapters. These exceptions, however, remain on the epistemic margins of our discipline.

22. As Moore and Sherwood (*Invention of the Biblical Scholar*, 73) observe, "in academia in the West, we cannot seem to get past a certain obstinate essentialism that lingers around the brute fact of being 'black' or 'Asian' or 'gay' or 'transgendered'

Queer historicism, as practiced in the North, inadvertently replicates a colonial framework because it centers the "history of sexuality" in the West. As the Foucauldian genealogy goes, sexuality is a Western invention that maps onto the past a set of arrangements that obscure how the Greco-Roman world lacked identitarian labels around sex. Whereas queer approaches illuminate first-century notions of sex "outside sexuality," they also reify the idea that we ought to take the origins of European history as normative.[23] On this front, queer historiography participates in the historical-critical principle that the present remains an obstacle to grasp the past. The plot thickens. Since the production of knowledge in the Global South is rooted in ecclesial institutions, topics around sex, gender, and sexuality remain underexplored or framed within enclosed theological agendas. My hope is that, by shifting the epistemological terms, we no longer rely on erasing the present as a condition of possibility to make claims about our past. Presentism on this front is not oppositional to preteritism but an ethos that expands and frames our study of the past. In the wake of Boaventura de Sousa Santos, whose initiative I present in the next section, I argue that, by relying on preteritism/historicism, biblical hermeneutics offers a nonabyssal solution to an abyssal problem. Such a metatheoretical approach—insofar as it scrutinizes conditions of knowledge production—leverages decolonial philosophy both in its critique and its proposal. My hope is that Epistemologies of the South incites new developments in liberation hermeneutics. Consequently, in the next section, inspired by a series of decolonial thinkers from the Global South, I situate historicism, secularism, and objectivism as practices of epistemicide. Modernity/coloniality, even in its postmodern iterations, obliterated, disparaged, and chastised nonscientific knowledge as faulty sapience. Coloniality hunted, strangled, and ultimately killed traditions that did not abide by its objectivist, allegedly universalistic, ethos.

The conceptualization of the abyssal line affects New Testament studies because it puts a magnifying lens on the fact that research agendas and exegetical inquiries find their ethos on this side of the line. Rather than

---

in a way that it does not around, say, being 'working class.'" In chapters 2, 6, and 7, I seek to move beyond essentialist claims by focusing on queer practices rather than on identities.

23. See Luis Menéndez-Antuña, "Bible and Sexuality Studies," in *The Oxford Handbook of Bible in Latin and Latinx America*, ed. Fernando F. Segovia and Ahida Pilarski (Oxford: Oxford University Press, forthcoming).

being natural, straightforward, and direct inroads into texts, the questions posed in the North issue from inherited genealogies of history, science, and hermeneutics. Admittedly, the same, in descriptive fashion, applies to the Global South. In the case of the Bible, the wedding of theologies and biblical scholarship, or rather, the insertion of biblical studies within theological disciplines, dependent on ecclesial contexts, results in a thematic production constrained by confessional interests. Epistemologies of the South creates a normative hermeneutical ontology that denaturalizes criticism on this side, unhinges exegesis from theology without necessarily erasing it, and ultimately foregrounds a presentist model that allows criticism to prioritize contemporary crises.

Ultimately, the drive behind this intellectual enterprise issues from a lament, a scholarly mourning of sorts, about the poverty, inadequacy, mostly scarcity, of our vocabularies, theories, concepts, and methods to convey the complicated relationships contemporary readers of all sorts keep with ancient texts. Despite historicist prejudices, the task of expanding how contemporary readers, whether professional, academic, flesh and blood, religious, and so on, embrace the historical archive entails neither endorsing confessional, political, or ideological agendas nor excluding them. In an academic example of "when you have a hammer, every problem looks like a nail," historicism closely monitors the standards of proper biblical knowledge: every issue ought to be historical. The result turns out to be a field dried out, ill-equipped to account for the obvious fact that the Bible is not *just* a historical document; it is a cultural device, a political composition, a theological understanding of reality, a witness of the myriad ways ancient actors interpreted reality, and, perhaps more prominently, a document that conjures very different types of cognitive, emotional, and communal reactions in the present.[24] All these elements belong at the core of biblical interpretation itself.[25]

---

24. See Eric D. Barreto, "Introduction" in *Thinking Theologically: Foundations for Learning*, ed. Eric D. Barreto (Minneapolis: Fortress, 2015), 1–6; Greg Carey, *Using Our Outside Voice: Public Biblical Interpretation* (Minneapolis: Fortress, 2020), 12–25.

25. The ethical vision on this front is distinct from John J. Collins's (*The Bible after Babel: Historical Criticism in a Postmodern Age* [Grand Rapids: Eerdmans, 2005]) call for an informed consensus and the need for a common ground for critical engagement because this project ultimately centers historicism as the criterion for scholarly rigor. Postmodernism's danger is "the disintegration of the conversation into a cacophony of voices, each asserting that their convictions are by definition preferred" (Collins, *The Bible after Babel*, 161). Notably missing in Collins's otherwise insightful

Epistemologies of the South and Epistemicide

Addressing hermeneutics in the Global North inevitably involves tackling historicism and its discontents. Dissatisfaction with the hegemonic episteme has a long tradition of its own. Although the knife has gotten sharper and the cutlers more numerous, historical criticism has morphed accordingly, becoming a moving target that repeatedly centers itself as offering criteria for establishing what counts as rigorous scholarship. By the time the surgeons have opened wide their object, the alleged patient has left the surgical table onto better things. A fascinating phenomenon indeed, considering that the practitioners come to the table with the most sophisticated tools. Fernando F. Segovia, Vincent L. Wimbush, Elisabeth Schüssler Fiorenza, Stephen D. Moore, and Tat-siong Benny Liew, to name a few, have tackled the tyranny of historicism from a wide variety of perspectives.[26] Most recently, building on such trajectory, Wongi Park has advanced the Multiracial Biblical Studies project as a multifaceted approach invested in exposing the white dominance attached to historicism.

---

analysis and conciliatory tone is an analysis of power in the production of knowledge. For what it is worth, this book is an essay in cacophonies in the sense that a multitude of theories, methods, approaches, and questions dialogue with each other without a clear methodological center. Zeba Crook's recent review of John Dominic Crossan's 2022 work (*Render unto Caesar: The Struggle over Christ and Culture in the New Testament* [New York: HarperOne, 2022]) epitomizes how historicism centers itself by way of discrediting theological takes as outside our discipline. Crook argues that this type of scholarship "is more biblical theology than biblical scholarship" ("Render unto Caesar," *BAR* 49.2 [2023]: 28).

26. Tat-siong Benny Liew, "What Has Been Done? What Can We Learn? Racial/Ethnic Minority Readings of the Bible in the United States," in *The Future of the Biblical Past: Envisioning Biblical Studies on a Global Key*, ed. Fernando F. Segovia and Roland Boer, SemeiaSt 66 (Atlanta: Society of Biblical Literature, 2012), 307–336. Also in the same volume, Elisabeth Schüssler Fiorenza, "Changing the Paradigms: Toward a Feminist Future of the Biblical Past," 289–306; Fernando F. Segovia, "Cultural Criticism: Expanding the Scope of Biblical Criticism," 307–36; Vincent L. Wimbush, "Signifying on the Fetish: Mapping a New Critical Orientation," 337–48; see also Stephen D. Moore, "A Modest Manifesto for New Testament Literary Criticism: How to Interface with a Literary Studies Field That Is Postliterary, Posttheoretical, and Postmethodological," in *The Bible in Theory: Critical and Postcritical Essays*, RBS 57 (Atlanta: SBL Press, 2010), 355–372.

The project of Multiracial Biblical Studies implicitly addresses the crisis as issuing from the dominance of whiteness.[27] Our guild, essentially "monoracial," drowns in whiteness; demographically, methodologically, and in terms of the sources cited, biblical interpretation, at least as it is practiced in the Global North, is in the hands of white scholars, in the grasp of a white method (historicism), and almost exclusively referential to white sources. Whiteness, ubiquitous and therefore invisible, argues, colors—plagues, really—trends, spaces, and institutions in biblical scholarship.[28] Monoracialism as whiteness infuses the production of knowledge: it centers and trades European and Euro-American sources globally. As the pithy title suggests, Park offers multiracial biblical studies as the cure for the monoracial disease, an enterprise, an ethos that provincializes and particularizes whiteness by locating it in a much wider landscape of ethnic identifications. The potential result yields, one can only hope, a broadening of the current epistemological limitations and a stretching of the boundaries of legitimate knowledge production. Briefly, if whiteness filters "rigorous scholarship," multiracialism would open the narrowly defined gates of scholarly flow.

Park acknowledges the pioneers in identifying the epistemological problems: per Randall C. Bailey, Tat-siong Benny Liew, and Fernando F. Segovia, "stretching conventional boundaries and borders of the field"; per Denise Kimber Buell, an "expansive definition of biblical canons"; per Tat-siong Benny Liew, a "citational invention of tradition."[29] Not a comprehensive inventory but an exemplary set of virtual proposals and strategies, not a focalized investment in any particular theory or method but an assortment of possible paths moving forward, the project of Multiracial Biblical Studies scaffolds a platform to move beyond historicism. The guild

---

27. Park, "Multiracial Biblical Studies," 435–59.
28. Park, "Multiracial Biblical Studies," 454.
29. Randall C. Bailey, Tat-siong Benny Liew, and Fernando F. Segovia, eds., *They Were All Together in One Place? Toward Minority Biblical Criticism*, SemeiaSt 57 (Atlanta: Society of Biblical Literature, 2009); Denise Kimber Buell, "Canons Unbound," in *Feminist Biblical Studies in the Twentieth Century: Scholarship and Movement*, ed. Elisabeth Schüssler Fiorenza, BW 9.1 (Atlanta: Society of Biblical Literature, 2014), 293; Tat-siong Benny Liew, *What Is Asian American Biblical Hermeneutics? Reading the New Testament* (Honolulu: University of Hawai'i Press; Los Angeles: UCLA Asian American Studies Center, 2008). All quotes from Park, "Multiracial Biblical Studies," 456, with the last one a quotation from Liew, *What Is Asian American Biblical Hermeneutics*, 8.

need not be—and these are my own words—an asphyxiating and tedious chamber for mainstream biblical scholarship, now turned into a declawed and defanged creature that discounts as edgy any creative and invigorating contribution.

A theoretical and methodological advocacy for multiracial criticism, Park's contribution exposes whiteness as orchestrating, baton in hand, the disciplinary choir. Whiteness provides the invisible but dominant slant that different interpretive strategies invested in historicism inadvertently reinforce. Whiteness, an ethos of performing the critical task, is then historically attached, methodologically wedded, and theoretically invested in historicism. Biblical studies' monoracialism, Park accurately determines, is the epiphenomenon of a complex historical disciplinary trajectory that understands itself tied to European, mostly German, roots (genealogy), invested in historical criticism (method), and committed to a research agenda issuing from such origins and methodological investments.[30]

Whiteness, despite cultural assumptions, goes beyond phenotypical traits and seeps into methodology. Historical-criticism dominance relies on whiteness and vice versa. As Park puts it:

> To be clear, the fact that a majority of scholars prefer historical criticism, in and of itself, is not the issue—just as the fact that a majority of scholars identify as male and White is not the issue either. The problem, at root, lies in the intricate relationship between the two. The way historical criticism functions in biblical studies as a universal, normative, unmarked method of interpretation is a telltale sign of its proximity to whiteness.... The underlying issue is that the dominant methodological center of biblical studies elevates Eurocentric models of history, epistemology, and social location—a process that is centered through the very methods of the field. In this sense, and only in this sense, White scholars enjoy a hermeneutical advantage insofar as their identities, locations, and methods are presumed as the norm.[31]

On this front, Park's diagnosis of biblical critique as monoracial constitutes a sharp analysis of biblical studies' infrastructure: its demographics and sociological conditions. Similarly, Park's proposed treatment in the shape of multiracial interventions promises to provincialize whiteness and historicize historicism. It is on this front—on the importance of history—

---

30. Park, "Multiracial Biblical Studies," 440.
31. Park, "Multiracial Biblical Studies," 447.

that my contribution contextualizes a specific way of knowing (history), as it is practiced in our field, within a broader episteme. In the following section, I argue that historicism, inextricable from scientificism, objectivism, and secularism, is best understood as part of colonial knowledges. Although the multiracial approach judges the field in terms of its tangled links between whiteness and historicism, I suggest that such a verdict replicates, at least partially, historicist assumptions, ironically renewing whiteness. It remains, to say it differently, too confined in Western and USA-based theorizations of race and ethnicity. As a virtual solution, from a global perspective, I explore what models of knowledge are available to scholars disinvested in historicism, objectivism, and scientificism. A particularization of whiteness, prescribed as the key remedy, remains an urgent need and a pressing project, but it leaves unaddressed and undertheorized whiteness as part of the colonial, capitalist, (post)modernist, and secularist projects, all of which suffuse biblical studies at a deeper level.[32] To use Santos's terminology, multiracialism offers a nonabyssal solution to an abyssal problem. Turning to different and more diverse sources remains a primordial task,[33] but it will leave the field untouched unless we interrogate the nature of such an approach and, more relevantly, unless we learn from those very same sources what constitutes knowledge in the first place. Consequently, in the next section, in the wake of decolonial theory issuing from the Global South, I explore how historicism, secularism, and objectivism manifest epistemicidal inclinations. "Subjugated knowledges," "decolonial epistemologies," or "unknown unknowns" refer, then, to the wisdom that modernity/coloniality, even in its postmodern iterations, obliterated, disparaged, and chastised as inadequate sapience.

The invention of race in modern science and the subsequent dominance of whiteness as the superior/default ethnic ascription stems from colonialism. The convergence of whiteness and historicism is not a mere historical accident; it is the product of the colonial project that, as postcolonial and decolonial thinkers have shown, did not end with the conquest of the land. Colonialism imposed a cosmovision, a reorganization of the world with European knowledges, anthropologies, and taxonomies as nor-

---

32. Park, "Multiracial Biblical Studies," 459.
33. "What would it mean, for example to develop an approach to biblical studies using Aboriginal, Ethiopian, Jamaican, Korean, Malay, Mestizo, Native American, or South Asia sources?" (Park, "Multiracial Biblical Studies," 459). See also Wimbush, *Black Flesh Matters*, 97–142.

mative. Such imposition erased indigenous ways of knowledge, resulting in an epistemicide of global proportions. As we will see, religious/theological knowledge played a fundamental role both in colonialism and coloniality. Contemporary historicism's roots grow deeper than its German origins; it is the epiphenomenon of the epistemological shift accompanying modernity/coloniality. Therefore, a critique and a constructive proposal ought to engage in decolonial thinking.

Decolonial epistemologies have taken modernity to task for its entanglement with imperialism. Theorists and activists from the Latin American subcontinent offer different narratives, but they all coincide in tracing contemporary (post)modernity to its colonial roots, mapping the power imbalances in the divide between North and South and its subsequent division between subjugating and subjugated knowledges. Enrique Dussel, Walter Mignolo, and Aníbal Quijano offer compelling accounts of the Enlightenment project from the "other side," exposing historicism, objectivism, scientificism, and secularism for their colonial abetment.[34] Although these theoretical projects have a broad influence in different fields in the humanities, their reach has barely touched biblical scholarship. Critical accounts of the genealogies of biblical criticism have drawn almost exclusively upon Western epistemologies. This is a theoretical development worth exploring itself. With such an objective in mind, I suggest that Boaventura de Sousa

---

34. Enrique Dussel, *The Invention of the Americas: Eclipse of the "The Other" and the Myth of Modernity* (New York: Continuum, 1995); Walter Mignolo, *The Politics of Decolonial Investigations* (Durham, NC: Duke University Press, 2021); Aníbal Quijano, "Coloniality of Power, Eurocentrism, and Latin America," *Nepantla: Views from the South* 3 (2000): 533–80. See also Arturo Escobar and David L. Frye, *Pluriversal Politics: The Real and the Possible* (Durham, NC: Duke University Press, 2020); Santiago Castro-Gómez and Ramón Grosfoguel, *El giro decolonial: Reflexiones para una diversidad epistémica más allá del capitalismo global* (Bogotá: Siglo del Hombre Editores, 2007); Jean Comaroff and John L. Comaroff, *Theory from the South: Or, How Euro-America Is Evolving toward Africa* (London: Routledge, 2016); Julie Cupples and Ramón Grosfoguel, *Unsettling Eurocentrism in the Westernized University* (London: Routledge, 2019); Paula D. Royster, *Decolonizing Arts-Based Methodologies: Researching the African Diaspora* (Leiden: Brill, 2021); José Romero Losacco, *Pensar distinto, pensar de(s)colonial* (Caracas: Editorial El Perro y la Rana, 2021); Nelson Maldonado-Torres, "Descolonización y el giro decolonial," *Tabula Rasa* 9 (2008): 61–72; Walter Mignolo, *The Politics of Decolonial Investigations* (Durham, NC: Duke University Press 2021); Aníbal Quijano, *Ensayos en torno a la colonialidad del poder* (Ediciones del Signo: Buenos Aires, 2019); Walter Mignolo and Catherine E. Walsh, *On Decoloniality: Concepts, Analytics, and Praxis* (Durham, NC: Duke University Press, 2018).

Santos, an exemplary theorist from the Global South, and his proposal titled Epistemologies of the South introduce a new epistemic paradigm that aids biblical scholars in disinvesting from objectivism, enabling them with the possibility of charting a different future for the discipline.

Epistemologies of the South, both the overarching philosophical project and the title of one of the works in which such a project is presented, relies on a series of key concepts (abyssal line, sociology of absences/emergences, ecology of knowledges, intercultural translation, and artisanship of practices) whose detailed presentation and examination exceed this chapter's goals. Here, I am interested in showing how Epistemologies of the South contributes to a clearer diagnosis of biblical studies' epistemological crisis. In such a diagnosis whiteness constitutes an important but not essential part of the epistemicide perpetrated in the abyssal line. Let us turn now to expound the concept.

In *The End of the Cognitive Empire*, Boaventura de Sousa Santos explains how the project of Epistemologies of the South is also an ontological exercise because it creates nonexistent knowledges about erased realities.[35] The distinction between abyssal and nonabyssal realities grounds the epistemological project, and it offers a heuristically rich idea for analyzing the distinctions between colonial and decolonial epistemologies, ethics, and politics. The project is political from the outset: whereas ontology allows us to excavate erased realities and epistemology animates us to invest in other ways of knowing, the political dimension, after the proper diagnosis, seeks to make sure that abyssal problems are handled by abyssal solutions. Moreover, whereas epistemologies in the North occupy themselves with what we can know and how we know it, the question from the other side of the abyss is: Is it worth knowing? Santos faults modern social sciences for having conceived of humanity as living on this side of the line when, in reality, there is an abyssal gap on both sides of the colonial reality (metropoly/colony). Modernity's inventions, such as the liberal state, the rule of law, human rights, and democratic rule are forms of deception that erase epistemological lines while papering over the abyss that separates both realities:

> the abyssal line is the core idea underlying the epistemologies of the South. It marks the radical division between forms of metropolitan

---

35. Boaventura de Sousa Santos, *The End of the Cognitive Empire* (Durham, NC: Duke University Press, 2018).

sociability and forms of colonial sociability that has characterized the Western modern world since the fifteenth century. This division creates two worlds of domination, the metropolitan and the colonial world, two worlds that, even as twins, present themselves as incommensurable. The metropolitan world is the world of equivalence and reciprocity among "us," those who are, like us, fully human.[36]

The discrete gap between the modes of socialization in the metropolis and the colony does not accurately map onto geographically distinct areas but rather corresponds to different worlds falling on opposite sides of modernity: both spheres interact but represent oppositional ontologies. The world of the metropolis thrives on the epistemology of the North: scientificism and objectivism, an understanding of knowledge as politically neutral, a staunch division between the subject and object of study, and a separation between theory and praxis (more on how these elements play in biblical studies in the last section). The abyssal line is definitional: on this side, the world of the metropolis; on the other side, the colonized world. This ontological distinction underlies an epistemological one: knowledge about the realities on the other side is nonexistent, reading reality on the other side as nonreality, therefore offering putatively global solutions that replicate the abyssal gap.[37] Santos faults European critical thought precisely for being "built upon a mirage," for thinking that "all exclusions are nonabyssal."[38]

How many scholars from the Global South are regularly cited as part of biblical criticism? How much allegedly liberatory hermeneutics relies on sources sanctioned in the Global North? Even when scholars from the Global South get to publish in what is considered the top journals in our field—supposedly known for their international appeal—the list of sources remains exclusively produced in the Global North. Knowledge produced on the other side of the abyss does not qualify as knowledge: presumably international biblical scholarship knows nothing about African or Latin American biblical scholarship.

The gap and the negation of reality (what lies on the other side of the abyssal line) constitutes Western scholarship, despite its selling appeal as global and international. As Santos puts it, "the sociology of absences

---

36. Santos, *The End of the Cognitive Empire*, 19–20.
37. Santos, *Epistemologies of the South*, 118–35.
38. Santos, *The End of the Cognitive Empire*, 25.

is the cartography of the abyssal line. It identifies the ways and means through which the abyssal line produces nonexistence, radical invisibility, and irrelevance."[39] Epistemologies of the South, acutely attuned to the intensification of global crises, strongly argues that the production, value, dissemination, and consumption of knowledge on this side of the abyssal line bypasses the aggravating conditions of the Majority World. More important, Western knowledge has equated the scientific problem-solving dimension with technocracy, generating a type of paradigmatic ethos that operates singularly on exclusionary binarisms such as subject/object, reason/emotion, individual/community, and so on. In sum, Santos's core contribution is as straightforward as it is overarching: epistemologies as valid knowledges prodigiously exceed the Western scientific paradigm, and such a paradigm has resulted in epistemicide (the destruction of rival knowledges deemed as nonscientific).[40]

Epistemologies of the South enacts a forceful critique of customary knowledge production in the Western academy. With its drive for epistemicide and its extractivist ethos, scholarship on this side of the abyss understands research as learning from rather than learning with. Extractivist methodologies vary in modes and figurations, but they share in the assumption that the scientist/interpreter stands in a position of superiority regarding her "object" of study.[41] Put differently, "nonextractivist methodologies aim at knowing-with instead of knowing-about, founding relations among knowing subjects rather than between subjects and objects."[42] Of course, this expansive view of the epistemological processes does not disqualify scientific knowledge; it fittingly contextualizes a specific type of expertise within an organic, ecological, and wholesome understanding of knowledge production. Epistemicide, then, refers not only to the disqualification of organic, postabyssal knowledges but also to the dismissal of the types of knowledges fit to address the issues that such epistemicide has created. We live in a world, Santos argues, created by modern science where the myth of progress—and its assumption that global crises have a

---

39. Santos, *The End of the Cognitive Empire*, 25.
40. Santos, *The End of the Cognitive Empire*, 296.
41. An object of study that is, in turn, gendered and racialized; see Yii-Jan Lin, "Who Is the Text? The Gendered and Racialized New Testament," in *The Oxford Handbook of New Testament, Gender, and Sexuality*, ed. Benjamin H. Dunning (Oxford: Oxford University Press, 2019): 137–156.
42. Santos, *The End of the Cognitive Empire*, 297.

technical solution—is partly responsible for the problems themselves. On the other side of the abyss, however, we are to explore "a vast landscape of postabyssal knowledges, postabyssal methodologies, postabyssal pedagogies whose main objective is to generate a radical demand for the democratization of knowledge, a demand for cognitive democracy."[43]

Biblical Hermeneutics and the Epistemologies of the South

Epistemologies of the South theorizes epistemology as a philosophical field traversed by ethical-political commitments. The value-neutral configuration of Western knowledge is both dispensable and impossible. Santos argues that "the epistemologies of the South conceive of indifference toward the struggles of the oppressed as one of the most deep-rooted kinds of ignorance produced by the epistemologies of the North in our time."[44] On the one hand, the ideologically impartial aspiration of Western knowledge covers its own colonialist roots; on the other, it constructs epistemological and ontological analyses of the abyssal divide as "not-knowledge/ignorance." Although Santos does not minimize race and ethnicity as markers of subjugation, as components of epistemicide, he subsumes racialization processes within the global historicized dynamics of colonialism, patriarchy, and capitalism. Epistemologies of the South shares this contextualization and theorization of racial/ethnic classifications with most decolonial theorists from the Global South.

In the Global North, there is a multidimensional connection between historicism and whiteness.[45] Such association between ethnic ascription and methodological preference belongs to a wider set of equations, with whiteness on one side and epistemological options on the other: historicism, objectivism, scientificism, and secularism, to name a few. In this section, I signal how these four prevalent dimensions on this side of the abyss dislodge theological/religious thought—a recurrent component in the Global South—of legitimacy within our field. Biblical studies, in its Euro-North American variant, regards theological commitments as inimical to biblical science. Of course, such implicit disavowal should not lead us to infer that scholarship is devoid of theological assumptions. On the contrary, it should be clear by now that mainstream biblical scholarship

---

43. Santos, *The End of the Cognitive Empire*, 295.
44. Santos, *The End of the Cognitive Empire*, 91.
45. Park, "Multiracial Biblical Studies," 445–50.

in the Global North is suffused with individualist notions of agency, will, or sin.⁴⁶ As Moore and Sherwood have compellingly demonstrated, Euro-American biblical scholarship's pledge to objectivism has, on the one hand, dismissed religious/theological investments as inimical to sound exegesis and, on the other, allowed unexamined Western theological foundations to slip through the cracks of most biblical exegetical arguments.⁴⁷

Secular critique on this side of the abyss thinks of theological commitments on the other side as parochial, contextualist, and subjective. Theology, as the argument goes, pollutes history. The relation between the epistemologies of the North, secularism, whiteness, and colonialism calls for further exploration.⁴⁸ For Aníbal Quijano, the processes of racialization in the colonies are determined by the need to determine labor divisions geared toward the extraction of resources.⁴⁹ Modernity/coloniality operates, then, on a series of shifting dichotomies that keep the abyssal line in place. Religion/secular plays a determinative role not least because the religious realm has come to stand in opposition to reason, enlightenment, civilization, liberalism, and the like. On this front, Nelson Maldonado-Torres offers a compelling analysis of the formative trajectories of religion as they interact with the forces of colonialism and the formations of race.⁵⁰ For Maldonado-Torres, coloniality/modernity allowed for indigenous religions to enter the category of religion at the precise moment when the subontological difference religion/nonreligion ceased being a major axis of differentiation:

> In this transition the idea of exorcising religion from public life also became important. In this context, the colonizer can afford having the colonized claim entry into the realm of the religious. But this is done under at least two presuppositions: (a) that European religiosity is still

---

46. See an evocative critique of this trend from a historicist framework in Katherine A. Shaner, "The Danger of Singular Saviors: Women, Slaves, and Jesus's Disturbance in the Temple (Mark 11:15–19)," *JBL* 140 (2021): 139–61.

47. Moore and Sherwood, *Invention of the Biblical Scholar*, 123–32.

48. See Eduardo Mendieta, "Imperial Somatics and Genealogies of Religion: How We Never Became Secular," in *Postcolonial Philosophy of Religion*, ed. Purushottama Bilimoria and Andrew B. Irvine (Berlin: Springer, 2009), 235–50.

49. Aníbal Quijano, "Coloniality of Power, Eurocentrism, and Latin America," *Nepantla: Views from the South* 1 (2000): 533–80.

50. Nelson Maldonado-Torres, "Race, Religion, and Ethics in the Modern/Colonial World," *Journal of Religious Ethics* 42 (2014): 691–711.

taken as the standard for defining acceptable religions, which means that the anti-colonial act of claiming religion in a context where such act is denied can also entail the assumption and incorporation of Eurocentric elements, and (b) that having religion no longer provides the ultimate or definitive concession of full humanity.[51]

Right when indigenous belief systems were admitted into "religion," religion became surpassed by autonomy, reason, and science. Decolonial thought shows how secularism did not replace theology; it surreptitiously attached it to new forms of legitimization.[52] An Yountae suggests that "the continuing regime of coloniality from the fifteenth century to today is in a way characterized by the replacement of one theology by another. The newly imposed theology of secularism places the notion of the human at its center—a particular conception of the human."[53] Like recent developments in biblical hermeneutics, where one method surpasses the previous one even as it leaves untouched grounding epistemological premises, knowledge on this side of coloniality evolves as it renders the abyssal line nonexistent.

If it is true that historicism has dismissed theological thinking as biased, anachronistic, or unscientific, the same applies to historicism's hegemonic fellow: literary analysis in the vein of critical theory, a modus operandi to which I have subscribed in my own scholarship.[54] Biblical studies' resort to postmodern theory has had a similar effect on the developments of the discipline: Foucault, Derrida, Butler, Said, or Spivak, to name a few of the high-theory inspirers, ratify the abandonment of any theological critique in biblical studies.[55] However, as decolonial thinkers from the South insist, the religious/theological realm constitutes an essential component of much biblical/theological production. For instance, José Carlos Mariategui, the Peruvian philosopher who would eventually inspire Gustavo Gutiérrez and serve as intellectual fodder to many revo-

---

51. Maldonado-Torres, "Race, Religion, and Ethics," 708.
52. Galen Watts and Sharday Morusinjohn, "Can Critical Religion Play by Its Own Rules? Why There Must be More Ways to Be 'Critical' in the Study of Religion," *JAAR* 90 (2022): 1–18.
53. An Yountae, "Decolonial Theory of Religion," *JAAR* 88.4 (2020): 956.
54. See a helpful discussion of the productive use of anachronism in Daniel R. Huebner, "Anachronism: The Queer Pragmatics of Understanding the Past in the Present," *The American Sociologist* 52 (2021): 740–61.
55. Maldonado-Torres, "Race, Religion, and Ethics."

lutionary movements (EZLN in Chiapas, MST in Brazil, or the Sandinista movement in Nicaragua), was a critic of the secularizing aspects of Marxism as much as the colonial dimensions of capitalism. Despite the brutal reality of colonization and the imposition of official religion "The Indian has not renounced his old myths. His sense of the mystical dimension has changed. His animism subsists.... he has not renounced his conception of life that does not question Reason but Nature. The three jircas, the three hills of Huánuco, weigh more on the conscience of the Huanuqueño Indian than the Christian afterlife."[56] An Yountae sees a religious critique of religion in this decolonial strand, but one that sees religion as an essential force for decolonial thought and praxis.

As Quijano has shown, colonialism is intrinsic to modernity.[57] Since Christian theology provided the ideology for the conquest, it is the task of the decolonial enterprise to account for the emergence of secularism in the process of coloniality. Maldonado-Torres offers here a critique that applies directly to the biblical studies episteme. He notes that "defenders of secularism have invested more time passionately attacking religion than critiquing the forms of subjugation that are constitutive of the modern state."[58] He also reads secularism's takeover of Christianity/theology as an intraimperial event, a shifting from the colonized as soulless to the subjugated as uncivilized. Maldonado-Torres argues that secularism/colonialism ended up rejecting religion not so much because religion was imperial "but simply because it was not imperial enough."[59] Admittedly, such a shift should not be interpreted as defending the idea that secularism left imperial religion behind; rather, secularism recasts its inherent division between the sacred and the profane as civility and uncivility, knowledge and opinion, reason and fanaticism, and so on. In the process, Judaism

---

56. "El indio no ha renegado sus viejos mitos. Su sentimiento místico ha variado. Su animismo subsiste.... No ha renunciado a su propia concepción de la vida que no interroga a la Razón sino a la Naturaleza. Los tres jircas, los tres cerros de Huánuco, pesan en la conciencia del indio huanuqueño más que la ultratumba cristiana" (José Carlos Mariategui, *Siete ensayos de interpretación de la realidad Peruana* [Barcelona: Linkgua ediciones, 1928]: 290). Unless otherwise noted, all translations are mine.

57. Quijano, "Coloniality of Power."

58. Maldonado-Torres, "Secularism and Religion in the Modern Colonial World-System: From Secular Postcoloniality to Postsecular Transmodernity," in *Coloniality at Large: Latin America and the Postcolonial Debate*, ed. Mabel Moraña, Enrique Dussel, and Carlos A. Jáuregui (Durham, NC: Duke University Press, 2008), 366.

59. Maldonado-Torres, "Secularism and Religion," 367.

is cast as a legalistic religion and Islam as embedded in violence: "only in Europe one finds the last and more complete expression of the religious, out of which a properly rational civilization can emerge."[60] Jürgen Habermas, on the side of modernity, and his model of communicative rationality epitomizes such a process. Gianni Vattimo, on the side of postmodernity, and his notion of "weak thought" would represent a reverse side and the death of a metanarrative that opens the door back to religion, one "that gave legitimacy and impetus to the imperialism of the first modernity."[61]

In light of such observations, historicism leaves unaddressed the complex links between (post)modernity and colonialism. An epistemic shift centered on expanding the primary and secondary sources, democratizing access to the guild's table, and particularizing historicism is indeed an urgent task. However, such an enterprise remains at the epiphenomenal level unless we interrogate the constitutive elements of what passes as valid and rigorous knowledge. In the words of Santos, historicism offers a nonabyssal solution to an abyssal problem. Since historicism has relegated religion/theology to a subepistemological dimension, biblical studies both feeds from and generates a type of secularism that reinforces its whiteness. Even in the case of postcolonial thought, religion has come to stand in opposition to rationality. Maldonado-Torres criticizes Said and Spivak for equating religion with the obscure. Once again Maldonado-Torres offers an insightful note: "My point is not that secularism is purely the West's invention, but that more often than not the accent on the secular helps to maintain the West's epistemic hegemony."[62] To bring it back to biblical studies, Western investment in secular critique—even as it surreptitiously infiltrates all types of theological assumptions into exegesis—functions as a gatekeeping device that reassures its own rigor and downgrades, ignores, or dismisses explicitly theological projects. Fascinatingly, secular critique in biblical studies further typecasts any type of nonhistoricist understanding as religiously grounded or theologically informed.

Biblical Ways of Knowing in the Global South

The philosophical and epistemological project drafted in Epistemologies of the South, with its engraved decolonial take on religious/theological

---

60. Maldonado-Torres, "Secularism and Religion," 369.
61. Maldonado-Torres, "Secularism and Religion," 375.
62. Maldonado-Torres, "Secularism and Religion," 378.

knowledge as an ethos of interpretation invested in political commitments, does not disqualify objectivistic/historicist paradigms hegemonic in the Global North. Rather, it contextualizes Western epistemological investments within a holistic approach to knowledge. In this vein, biblical scholarship would be global not for its virtual multiculturalism and/or multiracialism but because it would not filter knowledge through its Western lenses. Such a project, utopian as it might be, disrupts the temporal metanarrative that modernity and postmodernity in the West, and its subsequent investment in secular critique, have overcome confessional, religious, or theological commitments. Secular critique in its modernist version, with a callous investment in historicism, or in its postmodern variety, with an allegedly avant-garde resort to high critical theory, have expunged biblical criticism from confessional commitments: dogmatic ascriptions belong either to ecclesial settings or to ideologically invested scholars. Although I am the first to welcome the benefits of bracketing church influence from knowledge production, a decolonial approach suggests that, by denying theology a green card in the biblical country, we have impoverished the range of epistemological options. We throw away the baby with the bathwater.

A decolonial critique of epistemological commitments brings back into the fold the diverse ways in which scholars from the Global South have been doing and continue to perform biblical critique. On this front, Latin American liberation theology offers a fitting paradigm to explore how epistemologies of the South have been playing in what the Global North would consider its backyard. The term backyard here has several connotations. In terms of the sociology of knowledge, it refers to how the centers of production (reputable academic journals and presses) consistently ignore contributions from the Global South. In terms of citation politics, it signals how scholars in the West routinely overlook scholarship in the South. In terms of heuristical concerns, it points at how scholarly research agendas whitewash the political edge of emancipatory hermeneutics.

A recap of the theoretical journeys of Latin American liberation theology remains beyond the scope of the present chapter. My goal here, rather, is first to place other ways of knowing as foundational to the task of criticism and then to illustrate how the theological realm contributes to the ethico-political ethos that drives the hermeneutical task. This paradigm's main contribution consists of prioritizing "the eruption of the poor" in theological thought and exegetical analysis. Methodologically speaking, liberation theology embodies an epistemology that takes the material analysis of the impoverished conditions of the Majority World as its starting point. What does it mean, such research agenda asks, to interpret the Bible in a global context in which two-thirds of the population experience deprivation? Such an ethical impulse—constitutive at the heuristical, hermeneutical, methodological, and teleological levels—strips the political naïveté from the historicist's research agendas. To be specific, Western biblical scholarship bypasses authors such as Gustavo Gutiérrez, Leonardo Boff, Jorge Pixley, Jose María Castillo, González Faus, Elsa Támez, Ivone Guebara, Juan José Tamayo, and Marcela Althaus-Reid because their contributions do not fit the criteria set up by objectivism, scientificism, historicism, and secularism. The broader call for biblical studies, as Epistemologies of the South would have it, is to address pressing global problems such as the disarming of grassroots movements, the collapse of any alternative system to neoliberal dominance, the rise of far-right totalitarianism, the relentless advance of surveillance capitalism, the inevitable ecological crisis, the ascent of white supremacy, and so on. These issues are not merely political problems; they pose epistemological challenges. Subsequently, a decolonial approach has as its main impetus a questioning of the very foundations that we have taken for granted in knowledge production. [63]

Let me briefly consider two recent works in this vein. The goal here is not to deepen our knowledge of ancient contexts but rather to survey what are the likes of "a tone," "an ethos," "an episteme" that departs from historicism, embracing political enterprises, manifesting ideological commitments, and projecting utopian futures. In a recent collaborative effort, "La fuerza de los pequeños" seeks a communal reflection of theological realities issuing from the South:

---

63. As Gustavo Gutiérrez ("Expanding the View," in *Expanding the View: Gustavo Gutiérrez and the Future of Liberation Theology*, ed. Marc H. Ellis and Otto Maduro [Maryknoll, NY: Orbis Books, 1990)], 5) puts it, "Black, Hispanic, and Amerindian theologies in the United States, theologies arising in the complex contexts of Africa, Asia and the South Pacific, and the especially fruitful thinking of those who have adopted the feminist perspective—all these have meant that for the first time in many centuries, theology is being done outside the customary European and North American centers. The result of the so-called First World has been a new kind of dialogue between traditional thinking and new thinking. In addition, outside the Christian sphere, efforts are underway to develop liberation theologies from Jewish and Muslim perspectives."

1. NEW TESTAMENT STUDIES: AN EPISTEMOLOGICAL CRITIQUE 29

> To contribute to our people's transformational and liberating processes, interpreting faithfully and critically our historical present and rediscovering the mystical and prophetical elements in liberation theology, we seek to enact a systemic change and an ecclesial renewal from an intergenerational synergy.[64]

The authors locate their project as a political, ethical, theological—even ecclesial—enterprise through and through. This is a contemporary recasting of the original liberation theological project. Methodologically, as expected, it starts with an analysis of the historical, economical, and cultural situation of the Latin American continent. Historically defined by colonialism, economically determined by the North's expropriation of natural resources, and culturally informed by a population embedded in ecclesial structures, the material reality of the subcontinent centers the hermeneutical endeavor. Similar to how minoritized scholarship in the USA resorts to critical theory to disrupt historicism's sticky assumptions, the Global South—Latin America, in this case—renders mainstream distinctions, on this side of the abyssal line, between exegesis and hermeneutics, theology and critical analysis, historical research and political commitments inconsequential.[65]

The heuristical, hermeneutical, and methodological point of analysis is "the least of these" (Matt 25:40). On this front, let me quote Elsa Támez:

> Biblical scientism alone is not enough to account for the immensity and the absences we experience. In our hermeneutics there is passion and compassion, dimensions that the academy overlooks but that are impor-

---

64. "Contribuir a los procesos de transformación y liberación de nuestros pueblos, leyendo en clave creyente y critica el momento histórico que vivimos y redescubriendo los resortes místico-proféticos y metodológicos de la teología de la liberación, que pueden impulsar un cambio sistémico y una renovación eclesial desde una sinergia intergeneracional" (Pablo Bonavía, "Sinergia intergeneracional y teología de la liberación," in *La fuerza de los pequeños: Hacer teología de la liberación desde las nuevas resistencias y esperanzas*, ed. Francisco Aquino Júnior, Geraldina Céspedes, and Alejandro Ortiz Cotte [Montevideo: Fundación Amerindia, 2020], 11).

65. For instance, Isabel Iñiguez ("Construimos Teología de la Liberación desde las Nuevas Resistencias y Esperanzas," in Aquino Júnior, Céspedes, and Ortiz Cotte *La fuerza de los pequeños*, 173–83) names three fissures (*grietas*) as the starting point of analysis: (1) the structural fissure of the earth (ecological crisis); (2) the structural fissure of expropriation (geopolitically based appropriation); and (3) the fissure of the accumulation gap.

tant to capture truth. Words that are 'soaked in mystery' are like magic as they warm our hearts and minds and propel us to seek a life worth living for everyone.[66]

In Latin American and Caribbean biblical hermeneutics, the quotidian and concrete, lived out in different contexts, is our starting point for biblical analysis. This is where we find the light, our lamps that illuminate the biblical texts that, in turn, also become new lamps.[67]

Támez epitomizes how an epistemology of the South manifests in the biblical realm, both in its descriptive and normative dimensions.[68] Such an approach entwines the concrete and the abstract, the historical and the ethical, the theoretical and the practical, the critical and the theological, activism and scholarship. It yokes onto the exegetical enterprise what I would call the inescapable burden of reality. Historicism will likely object that such dimensional conflations obscure the study of original contexts, rehearse long-gone theological commitments, and reduce hermeneutics to politics and ethics. In this case, objectivism, secularism, and scientificism—a triad of value-laden investments undergirding historicism—turn into totalitarianism and, in the telling of Santos, evince epistemicidal inclinations because they invalidate any knowledge outside what they consider rigorous scholarship. These disciplinary prohibitions not only shore up whiteness; they also sanction coloniality, patriarchy, and classism.

Although Epistemologies of the South comes late in the game in the development of liberation theologies, it provides a strategic foundation to situate contextual emancipatory hermeneutics broadly understood

---

66. Elsa Támez, *Bajo un cielo sin estrellas: Lecturas y meditaciones bíblicas* (Sabnilla: Departamento Ecuménico de Investigaciones, 2001), 20: "La sola ciencia bíblica no es suficiente para dar razón de la inmensidad o de la ausencia que experimentamos. En nuestra hermenéutica hay Pasion y Compasion; dos dimensiones humanas marginadas en la academia, pero que también son maneras de penetrar la verdad de las cosas. Son esas palabras "húmedas de misterio" que como arte de magia calientan los corazones—y la cabeza—, y dan animo en la lucha por la vida digna para todos y todas."

67. Támez, *Bajo un cielo sin estrellas*, 22: "En la hermenéutica bíblica latinoamericana y caribeña, la vida concreta y sensual, vivida en los diferentes contextos particulares, es el punto de partida para el análisis bíblico. Y aquí descubrimos también luces, lámparas que nos llevan a la Biblia e iluminan textos que a la vez se convierten en lámparas."

68. Támez, *Bajo un cielo sin estrellas*, 26.

within global markets of knowledge. This framing further allows biblical hermeneutics to skip some of the methodological traps that await the critic as she navigates the interpretive relationships between past and present, text and interpreter, historical reconstruction and ethical relevance. And, since we are in the thick of it, the epistemological critique offers an open-ended model for the critics in the Global North—me being an assistant professor of New Testament at Boston University—to venture into a world beyond dominant epistemologies. As I understand it, the task here is broad in scope and wide in reach. Rita Felski wittingly notices that to "immerse oneself in the last few decades of literary and cultural studies is … to be caught up in a dizzying whirlwind of ideas, arguments, and world pictures."[69] Rather than flattening out these spiraling movements, I suggest we should run with them.

Let's face it: the inclination of the biblical scholar *as scholar* is inherently conservative.[70] As I show in the following chapters (especially chs. 3, 4, and 7), the academic—usually writing from her desk, cup of coffee in hand—is ill-equipped to think about contemporary crises as they affect the most vulnerable.[71] Although I have an extensive activist career in the areas of HIV, incarceration, immigration, and homelessness—paired with personal experience—I also have a comfortable tenure-track job at a research university. My point here is that critics ought to expand the experiences that become available to them. Cultural studies, with its attention to subcultures of meaning production and consumption, fits the task at hand. A partial solution to the epistemological crisis demands that interpreters tend to different types of experiences without appropriating and extracting from them.

---

69. Felski, *The Limits of Critique*, 20.
70. Wimbush, *Black Flesh Matters*, 1–19.
71. Despite notable contributions ranging from the 1990s into the early 2000s, autobiographical biblical criticism as such has mostly disappeared; see Janice Capel Anderson and Jeffrey L. Staley, eds., *Taking It Personally: Autobiographical Biblical Criticism*, Semeia 72 (Atlanta: Scholars Press, 1995); Fiona C. Black, ed., *The Recycled Bible: Autobiography, Culture, and the Space Between*, SemeiaSt 51 (Atlanta: Society of Biblical Literature, 2006); Ingrid Rosa Kitzberger, *Autobiographical Biblical Criticism: Between Text and Self* (Leiden: Deo, 2002); Philip R. Davies, ed., *First Person: Essays in Biblical Autobiography* (New York: Sheffield Academic, 2002); Robert Paul Seesengood, *Competing Identities: The Athlete and the Gladiator in Early Christianity* (New York: T&T Clark, 2006).

The Paths Ahead

No straight lines exist between a scholar's location and identity and her scholarly production.[72] The evidence, however, remains overwhelming: biblical scholarship has not even started to touch the other side of the abyssal line. The project of multiracial biblical studies proves that the vast majority of authors and sources cited in biblical scholarship are white. The epistemological crisis shows that scholars from the Global South are grossly underrepresented and that the current criteria for knowledge production disqualifies them as "less than" any hermeneutical approach disinvested in historicism, scientificism, and objectivism. Despite self-identified references to the "global" or the "international," biblical scholarship knows little about African, Asian, or Latin American knowledge production. On this side of the abyssal line, biblical studies mirrors the contexts and responds to the questions of white, Euro-American, cis, and straight male, middle-class interpreters.[73]

This book seeks to make a modest contribution by imagining New Testament studies otherwise. It rehearses a discipline concerned with contemporary problems, crises, and agendas, rather than with the traditional disciplinary concerns. In the always delicate balance of interpreting the past, New Testament studies has veered exceedingly toward understanding history on its own terms, forgetful that any reconstruction of the past inevitably assumes a working definition of the present, oblivious that the production of knowledge should tend to the concerns of its audiences and constituencies. As scholars, we are socialized into a discipline that rewards disinterest, objectivity, and disinvestment in the present, and we become oblivious to the fact that we belong in a world full of contradictions, crises, and on the verge of collapse.

---

72. On this front I find Madhavi Menon's (*Indifference to Difference* [Minneapolis: University of Minnesota Press, 2015], 2–24) denunciation of identitarian knowledge particularly convincing.

73. Francisco Lozada Jr., "New Testament Interpretation in the United States: Perspectives from a Cultural Observer," in *Reading the New Testament in the Manifold Contexts of a Globalized World: Exegetical Perspectives*, ed. Eve-Marie Becker, Jens Herzer, Angela Standhartinger, and Florian Wilk, Neutestamentliche Entwürfe zur Theologie 32 (Tübingen: Francke, 2022), https://doi.org/10.24053/9783772057656 209–225.

Contextuality may take several paths. In the Global North, contextual hermeneutics has tended to wed identity-based claims,[74] while the Global South has veered toward a problem-centered approach. Both tendencies are, of course, a matter of emphasis rather than exclusivity. As explained in the previous sections, this book centers on crises rather than identities, on problems rather than subjectivities. Nonetheless, the task at hand remains fraught. Most of us writing from the North-Western hemisphere have been socialized and disciplined in historicism (German roots) or literary criticism (high theory). Success in the academy entails mastering historical-critical methods of interpretation and producing a type of knowledge that is disseminated preferably in certain types of journals and academic presses.[75] There are, however, other disciplinary stories to be told. On this front, my contribution is nothing new. It simply draws from what I consider the nuclear contribution of Latin American liberation theology: interpretation starts with analyzing contemporary contexts.

Locating contemporary crises as the hermeneutical starting point impacts the book's layout. The book explores different sections of the New Testament following a canonical order (Synoptics, John, Acts, and Pauline letters). A cultural studies approach, however, nuances this traditional arrangement by underlining thematic connections rather than their sequential disposition. Although the book moves through the canon "as it is,"[76] it focuses on how such a canonical setup creates a constellation of reflections around contemporary political and cultural crises, showing

---

74. Stephen Moore and Yvonne Sherwood (*Invention of the Biblical Scholar*, 118) sharply notice how these approaches from the margins "can easily be accommodated to the democratic ethos of the discipline ... and accorded a place in it—precisely on its margins, where they can be both visible from the mainstream of the discipline and extraneous to it, and need have no deep or lasting effect on how mainstream practitioners of biblical scholarship go about their daily business."

75. Elisabeth Schüssler Fiorenza and Kent Harold Richards, eds., *Transforming Graduate Biblical Education: Ethos and Discipline*, GPBS 10 (Atlanta: Society of Biblical Literature, 2010).

76. This is one instance, among several, where I have felt the pull of historicism. By arranging the chapters following a canonical order, interpretation reifies the notion that biblical meaning shall remain contained, definable, and delimited. I am also aware of the disciplinary and institutional restrictions imposed on junior biblical scholars who ought to navigate staying recognizable as "biblical" in the job market and the guild even as they stretch the boundaries of what counts as recognizable scholarship. I thank Jacqueline Hidalgo for this insight.

how resonances in one passage echo meanings in other unrelated texts. Since literary and historical connections are brought together through cultural topics and works of art, the result is a cacophony/polyphony of intercontextual references, a vision of the New Testament as a soundboard reaching into our presents and futures. To say it with Santos, the interpretive task from the perspective of the Epistemologies of the South is to develop a postabyssal critical apparatus "in which the mixture of knowledges, cultures, subjectivities, and practices subverts the abyssal line that grounds the epistemologies of the North."[77]

The reader will notice that there are few to no references to issues that continue to frame our discipline's ethos: authorial intention, intended audience, implied author and reader, rhetoric as persuasion, visions of justification and righteousness, ethnicity, and gender in antiquity; nor are there reflections on the imperial or anti-imperial nature of the canon. These all are esteemed topics worthy of scholarly pursuit and deserving of further academic engagement. Still, I suggest that biblical scholars continue to diversify the discipline beyond its historicist moorings. To this end, let me now foreground the role of cultural studies.

---

77. Santos, *The End of the Cognitive Empire*, 107.

2
THE GOSPEL OF CULTURAL STUDIES: AN INTERCONTEXTUAL APPROACH

Different ghosts haunt different disciplinary houses. Literary studies, for instance, has been waging a war for several years now against the hegemony of critical readings. The dominance of suspicion, Rita Felski compellingly argues, has impoverished vocabularies of interpretation, dried out the rich experience of readership, and hampered the appreciation of artistic representations.[1] She finds "postcritical" to be a fitting label to encapsulate a wide range of interpretive strategies that account for the complex relationships that readers establish with literature. Texts are no longer, in this version, the epiphenomenon of subterranean historical, cultural, or political forces but unique artistic pieces that transcend original contexts through the types of networks they can create with other material forces and media. Although such diagnosis remains irrelevant to biblical studies—the subfields that have tended to critical theory remain modest—its remedy proves inspiring because it exposes how the sharp tools of a dominant episteme have turned out blunt, alienating readers and uninspiring interpreters. Considering the epistemicidal inclinations of historicism, the question-killing nature of objectivism, and the gatekeeping of scientificism, I suggest turning to cultural studies as a paradigm fitting to address some of the questions issuing from the epistemological challenges from the South.

Turning to cultural studies is both a remedial hermeneutical enterprise and a strategic political task. First, considering the previous diagnosis of the epistemological status quo, cultural theory opens historicism and literary criticism to a creative interpretative ethos with the potential to disentangle biblical studies from objectivism. Second, in the wake of the problems de-

---

1. Rita Felski, *The Limits of Critique* (Chicago: University of Chicago Press, 2015), 172–82.

fined around the abyssal line, cultural studies imagines a disciplinary field invested in political commitments, an interpreter attached to worldly matters, and hermeneutical practices in the service of contemporary crises.

As expected, cultural biblical studies originates outside the discipline, becoming strengthened by a renaissance in reception history, a field within a subfield that centers the next section. Specifically, cultural studies gained traction by presenting "how biblical scenes, themes, and stories have been represented in the traditional arts (visual and literary) and modern media (especially cinema)."[2] The rise of reception history, however, steered cultural studies as practiced in our field once again toward historicism: from historicizing the text's cultural milieu to historicizing its reception across time and space.[3] We see here a renewed colonization of historicist modes of operation as they shift their focus from the meaning of the text in its historical context to the significance of the biblical narratives as they play out in different periods and media. What version of cultural studies should we rehearse to attune our interpretive practices to worldly matters rather than historical circumstances? What would constitute a difference between historical explorations proper to reception history and the representational telos embedded in cultural studies?

The task at hand remains tortuous, not in the least because cultural studies itself has experienced and continues to go through several iterations of an identity crisis, struggling to identify its defining contours. Furthermore, were we to subtract reception history and literary studies from cultural studies in biblical interpretation, the remains would be scarce. Cultural studies constitutes a broader umbrella than the analysis of the reception of biblical topics throughout history and the study of biblical texts from the perspective of literary criticism. Michael Ryan argues that cultural studies is adjacent to literary studies, but "it also represents a broadening of concerns to include visual studies, popular music, advertising and magazines, subcultures, and the media."[4] Michal Beth Dinkler,

---

2. Stephen D. Moore, "Between Birmingham and Jerusalem: Cultural Studies and Biblical Studies," *Semeia* 82 (1998): 20.

3. Thomas Tops, "Transforming Historical Objectivism into Historical Hermeneutics: From 'Historical Illness' to Properly Lived Historicality," *Neue Zeitschrift für Systematische Theologie und Religionsphilosophie* 61 (2019): 490–515.

4. Michael Ryan, "Introduction to the Encyclopedia of Literary and Cultural Theory," in *The Encyclopedia of Literary and Cultural Theory*, ed. Michael Ryan (Chichester: Wiley-Blackwell, 2011), 1:xiii.

arguably one of the most sophisticated critics in the realm of literary biblical studies, makes a useful distinction on this front when she narrows the field of literary theory to the study of literature as *literature*, defined as "written poetry or prose that communicates through the use of specific linguistic techniques, and that is taken by society to be meaningful beyond its immediate context of origin."[5] Accordingly, literary theory "investigates the means by which humans make meaning through written poetry and prose."[6] Cultural studies reaches beyond textual exegesis, literary exploration, and historical contextualization,[7] although it resorts to these goals as it tends to meaning production in different subcultures.[8]

What variety of cultural studies would benefit our current episteme? How would cultural studies contribute to addressing the diagnosed epistemological crisis? Although scholarship addressing the tectonic shifts involved in paradigms remains scant, some of the critical concerns expressed heretofore sporadically populate contextual approaches located at the intersection of political criticism and ideological critique. Fernando Segovia, for instance, presumes cultural studies as a subfield that "seeks to integrate, in different ways, the historical, formalist, and sociocultural questions and concerns of the other paradigms on a different key, a hermeneutical key, with the situated and interested reader and interpreter

---

5. Michal B. Dinkler, *Literary Theory and the New Testament*, AYBRL (New Haven: Yale University Press, 2020), 6.

6. Dinkler, *Literary Theory*, 7.

7. Little surprise when Stephen D. Moore's charting of the field spends more than twenty pages on cultural studies and little more than four on its impact on biblical scholarship. More than a quarter of a century after Moore's assessment, the pages of cultural criticism have not grown much thicker; perhaps more worrying, there is scant reflection on how to decouple historicism from cultural studies. Historicism is let off the hook, and so it sneaks back in at the slightest chance. Consider, for instance, how reflections about the politicization of our field, the depoliticization of literary criticism, the telos of our critical task, or even the tools required to practice the interpretative craft have little disciplinary purchase. See Moore, "Between Birmingham and Jerusalem," 18–23; see also J. Cheryl Exum and Stephen D. Moore, "Biblical Studies/Cultural Studies," in *Biblical Studies/Cultural Studies: The Third Sheffield Colloquium*, ed. J. Cheryl Exum and Stephen D. Moore (Sheffield: Sheffield Academic, 1998), 19–45.

8. Chapter 4 will pay sustained attention to how literary studies *stricto sensu* might benefit from a thicker attention to realities beyond the literary realm. There I show how tending to the experiences of victims under the regimes of mass incarceration provides a thicker, richer, and more nuanced account of biblical characters such as the Gerasene (Luke 8).

always at its core."⁹ Cultural studies of this ilk surfaces across a series of axes crossing at the junction where texts and interpreters meet: interpreters "from within specific social locations with specific interests in mind."[10] Contextualization of texts and interpreters, their respective contexts, and their multifarious interactions constitute a modus operandi, an ethos, a drive for extending interpretation beyond textuality and hermeneutics beyond historicity.[11] The *cultural* dimension, Segovia suggests, implicates a localization of the interpreter in a cultural context beyond the traditional localization of the text within its own milieu. In other words, the goal here is to do unto us what we have been doing unto others.

We notice a shift of ontological proportions concerning the act of critique. The relation subject (usually an analytical interpreter) and object (a text of a bygone era) transmogrifies into two subjects of equal importance. This transition happens according to a continuum of relationality, for the text becomes more subject-like and the interpreter more object-like; because of their inequal starting points, the nature of the relationship humanizes the text in that it turns into a repository of the human experience and objectifies the interpreter in that she becomes an object of critical analysis herself. Let us unpack, then, the implications of this ontological shift for the critical task.

The category of the real interpreter, the flesh-and-blood reader—the professional critic, despite his resistance, being of this kind—speaks to the presentism of cultural biblical studies in that the critic no longer is the subject of interpretation but an object of analysis herself and, as such, part of a diverse community of interpretation,[12] with a fragmented and perspectival vision of reality. Such expansion of the interpreter's identity inevitably results in a move beyond the monopoly of historicism—the interpreter is never exclusively a historian—and the traditional theological agendas—the critic is no longer uniquely a theologian.[13]

A call of this order, a proposal for the thorough contextualization of texts and interpreters across the widest possible range of times and geog-

---

9. Fernando F. Segovia, *Decolonizing Biblical Studies: A View from the Margins* (Maryknoll, NY: Orbis Books, 2000), 41.

10. Segovia, *Decolonizing Biblical Studies*, 43.

11. Segovia, *Decolonizing Biblical Studies*, 43.

12. Francisco Lozada Jr., *Toward a Latino/a Biblical Interpretation*, RBS 91 (Atlanta: SBL Press, 2017), 1–20.

13. Segovia, *Decolonizing Biblical Studies*, 85–86.

raphies necessarily demands a series of theoretical optics, methodological armatures, drawing, in turn, from a wide range of complex and conflicted theoretical fields.[14] This concern—of a political, cultural, social, economic, and ideological nature—groups under its umbrella all types of context-mindful hermeneutics with a broadest task at hand: "the analysis of texts—the world of antiquity; the analysis of 'texts'—the world of modernity; the analysis of readers of texts and producers of 'texts'—the world of postmodernity."[15]

Segovia's pioneering proposal has progressively shifted from an interpreter-centered model to a systems-level paradigm.[16] Without abandoning the features of more traditional cultural studies, more recently Segovia has called for a systemic paradigm focalized on global crises rather than interpreters. Tentatively named "global-systemic," the focus of the paradigm is on bringing "the field [of biblical studies] to bear upon the major crises of our post–Cold War times, in both individual and converging fashion,"[17] calling for an expansive mutual interaction between previous models of interpretation and contemporary global crises. The role of the biblical critic, it would seem, consists of interpreting the past (biblical texts as they are produced, disseminated, and consumed) while considering a present that is, in turn, theorized in a series of planetary cultural, political, historical, economic junctures. The reverse is of equal importance: the interpretation of the present with the world of antiquity and its subsequent receptions in mind. Such a project is political to the core, an invitation to the critic to forge, paraphrasing Neruda, "a pact of blood with the world."[18]

---

14. Fernando F. Segovia, "Cultural Criticism: Expanding the Scope of Biblical Criticism," in Segovia and Boer, *The Future of the Biblical Past*, 307–36.

15. Segovia, *Decolonizing Biblical Studies*, 131.

16. In response to criticisms by Abraham Smith, Stephen Moore, and Elisabeth Schüssler Fiorenza, Segovia expands the realm of cultural studies to include contributions from nonacademic contexts, to honor religious-theological expressions, and to bridge our guild's insularity from cultural studies broadly understood. Cultural biblical criticism could be framed within a religious studies approach, "a valid extension of scope for a non-theological and humanist approach" (Segovia, "Cultural Criticism," 328). When addressing Smith's critique, Segovia expands his criticism to "the entire spectrum of social and cultural interpretation" in their cultural-discursive and social-material matrix (Segovia, "Cultural Criticism," 330).

17. Fernando F. Segovia, "Criticism in Critical Times: Reflections on Vision and Task," *JBL* 134 (2015): 26.

18. Segovia, "Criticism in Critical Times," 29.

With this much-welcomed transition from a focus on interpreters and interpretive communities to a contextual paradigm centered on global crises, the critical task becomes truly global. Biblical scholarship receives an invitation to interact with "by now well-established discourses regarding each crisis" and to exchange with "discourses addressing the convergence of crises, the global state of affairs, by way of world theories from the North and alternative theories from the South."[19] An unapologetic positioning of the present and its complexity, a professed global-systemic approach to biblical studies reorients the task of the cultural critic beyond the legacy of historicism insofar as it conceives the interpretative task as a history of the present.

Further, Segovia highlights, such biblical enterprise could materialize via two kinds of diversity: religious-theological and geographical-spatial. Such a normative proposal, were it to be accomplished, would result in a highly decentralized field. At the geopolitical level, it grounds the Global South—its epistemologies, concerns, trajectories, and so on—as an equal conversation partner. At the epistemological level, it reconfigures the telos, focus, and origins of our discipline by offering historicism a place among many other conversation partners. The centralization of a set of global crises in the contemporary world further sharpens the role of the biblical critic in the direction of an organic intellectual, a critic arising from underrepresented constituencies within the field and therefore attuned to marginalized concerns with the historicist realm.

Decentering does not equate delegitimizing. Hegemonic epistemologies entrench themselves into victimization whenever their dominance and exclusivism feel attacked, whenever their dominance gets questioned, and when their tyrannical ruling gets labeled as epistemicide. The politicization of hermeneutics, admittedly the staple of cultural studies,[20] perseveres on framing cultural productions of all types as manifestations and

---

19. Segovia, "Criticism in Critical Times," 26.

20. Cultural studies as a field suffers from an ongoing identity crisis. See Claire Alexander, "Stuart Hall and 'Race,'" *Cultural Studies* 23 (2009): 457–82. Cultural studies "does not actually occupy a territory of its own—at least not in the same way that 'real disciplines' do. Cultural studies is not a sovereign discipline-nation, nor is it a colony that belongs to some parent discipline's empire. Instead, it's a set of loosely affiliated—but widely scattered—nomadic groups that (at least in its academic manifestations) roam across the disciplinary terrain with a deliberate disregard for disciplinary borders" (Gilbert Rodman, *Why Cultural Studies?* [Chichester: Wiley-Blackwell, 2014], 24–25).

enhancers of social structures. This overarching scope affords biblical studies a sort of thematic fugue,[21] provincializing what has remained a singularly historicist agenda. In this book, cultural studies shows up in the analysis's attentiveness to crises of subjectivities among political exploitation and oppression. The stakes are high, for the questions at hand are unexplored but urgent: How do the HIV crises, the carceral state, the legacies of enslavement, or the torture of citizens in the midst of democracy speak to religious texts?

Attentiveness to the processes of interpretation as they emerge from the concerns of marginalized constituencies may take many forms, from ethnography to phenomenology, from ideological takes to artistic manifestations.[22] Lawrence Grossberg concludes that cultural studies is

> concerned with describing and intervening in the ways cultural practices are produced within, inserted into, and operate in the everyday life of human beings and social formations, so as to reproduce, struggle against, and perhaps transform the existing structures of power. That is, if people make history but in conditions not of their own making, cultural studies explores the ways this process is enacted with and through cultural practices, and the place of these practices within specific historical formations.[23]

In biblical studies, this type of approach has taken the shape of ideological criticism, a hermeneutical orientation tending to the political implications of the text, the interpreter, and the interaction between both. Ideological criticism has privileged a hermeneutics of suspicion in part as a reaction against naïve readings of the text that endorsed the point of view of the text as authoritative.[24] Under this umbrella, interpretations have resorted

---

21. Topics such as labor and precarities, decolonizing knowledge, refugee crisis in the Mediterranean, dance cultures, managing cities, urban imaginaries, securitization, popular affect online are but some of the many topics current in cultural studies.

22. Helen C. John, "Conversations in Context: Cross-Cultural (Grassroots) Biblical Interpretation Groups Challenging Western-Centric (Professional) Biblical Interpretation," *BibInt* 27 (2019): 36–68.

23. Lawrence Grossberg, *Cultural Studies in the Future Tense* (Durham, NC: Duke University Press, 2010), 8.

24. George Aichele et al., *The Postmodern Bible*, The Bible and Culture Collective (New Haven: Yale University Press, 1995); Tina Pippin, "Eros and the End: Reading for Gender in the Apocalypse of John," *Semeia* 59 (1992): 193–210; Pippin, *Death and Desire: The Rhetoric of Gender in the Apocalypse of John* (Eugene, OR: Wipf &

to postmodernist frameworks to underscore the instability of meanings, whether they are produced in ancient contexts, in contemporary realities, or at the intersection of both.

My contribution builds on these approaches because it remains attentive to power dynamics, especially as the text travels across time and space, but it conceives of cultural studies as a broader approach that considers that structures of power are both coercive and generative. Postmodern approaches as they draw from theory have taught us to what extent we remain entangled in a biblical past that reinforces the status quo, but they have been less fruitful in producing meaning-making readings to help us think through contemporary crises in emancipatory ways. Fernando Segovia captures this ethical ambivalence when he suggests that, ultimately, the task of cultural studies is to be of assistance "both positively and negatively, in pointing to and conjuring up a different world, globally as well as locally."25

History, Theory, and Culture

The New Testament contains a set of first-century texts. As a historical text, it invites the critic to explore the historical, political, and cultural contexts that originated it. Equally important, the New Testa-

---

Stock, 2021); Brook W. R. Pearson, "Method, Metaphor and Mammaries: the Ideology of Feminist New Testament Criticism," in *Religion and Sexuality*, ed. Michael A. Hayes, Wendy J. Porter, and David Tombs (Sheffield: Sheffield Academic , 1998), 226–39; as well as anthologies detailing an array of interests and perspectives. See, for example, Harold C. Washington, Susan Lochrie, and Pamela Thimmes, eds., *Escaping Eden: New Feminist Perspectives on the Bible* (Sheffield: Sheffield Academic, 1998); Shawn Kelly, *Racializing Jesus: Race, Ideology, and the Formation of Modern Biblical Scholarship* (London: Routledge, 2005); Robert M. Royalty, *The Streets of Heaven: The Ideology of Wealth in the Apocalypse of John* (Macon, GA: Mercer University Press, 1998); Jeremy Punt, "New Testament Interpretation, Interpretive Interests, and Ideology: Methodological Deficits amidst South African Methodolomania?" *Scriptura* 65 (1998): 123–52; Mark G. Brett, ed., *Ethnicity and the Bible*, BibInt 19 (Leiden: Brill, 1996); Richard T. Martin, "Ideology, Deviance, and Authority in the Gospel of Matthew: The Political Functioning of Performative Writing," *Literature and Theology* 10 (1996): 20–32; and Fernando F. Segovia, "'And They Began to Speak in Other Tongues': Competing Modes of Discourse in Contemporary Biblical Criticism," in *Social Location and Biblical Interpretation in the United States*, vol. 1 of *Reading from This Place*, ed. Fernando F. Segovia and Mary Ann Tolbert (Minneapolis: Fortress, 1995), 1–32.

25. Segovia, "Cultural Criticism," 336.

ment is a theological, cultural, and political script with unparalleled cultural import. In significant ways, these documents differ from other ancient documents: its contents are preached every Sunday across the globe, its verses appear in national constitutions, its stories get screened in motion pictures, its motifs painted across centuries and immortalized in prime museums, its political message reappropriated in the lives of world communities. For all their foundational and civilizational import, Aristotle, Plato, or Seneca come up short when we factor all these biblical legacies. A truism though frequently obviated: the Bible remains an unparalleled cultural artifact, and this "biblical exceptionalism" should be consequential for the discipline; it should shape its contours and inflect scholarship's arguments.

The cultural critic is positioned in an oblique relation to history: historical knowledges and agendas constitute one among many other elements shaping scholarly arguments. Biblical texts move from being repositories of history to conversation partners to reflect on structures of domination and subversion, meaning making in the crafting of subjectivities, inspirational elements in our representational politics, and so on. Grossberg advances that the goal of cultural studies is "to understand not only the organizations of power but also the possibilities of survival, struggle, resistance, and change. It takes contestation for granted, not as a reality in every instance, but as an assumption necessary for the existence of critical work, political opposition, and even historical change."[26] The political responsibility of the intellectual comes to the front.

Emphasis on the explicit political telos of critique sets cultural studies apart from theory-informed approaches invested in theory for the sake of theory. If it is true, as I have shown in the previous section, that critical theory has obfuscated the religious dimensions of texts, it has also, quite ironically, defanged their immediate political edge. Quite explicitly, cultural studies has no qualms in resorting to high theory as long as it strategically serves specific political ends. As Lawrence Grossberg puts it, the resort to theory aims at gaining "knowledge necessary to describe the context in ways that may enable the articulation of new or better political strategies. It takes what Marx called the 'detour through theory,' in order to offer a new and better description, moving from 'the empirical' to 'the concrete,' where the concrete is produced through the theoretical work of

---

26. Grossberg, *Cultural Studies in the Future Tense*, 19.

the invention of concepts."²⁷ Grossberg further refers to the importance of tending to the "empirical context" in a back and forth between theory and praxis of a dialectical nature: "based on the political demands and questions placed before it at the beginning."²⁸ Theory, to put it in a way speaking against the allegedly neutral nature of biblical studies, serves activist hermeneutics.

What about culture, then? So far, we have skipped this question, despite its explicit relevance. How are we to conceive of culture in the process of interpretation? By now, it should be clear that *culture* cannot refer to the cultural background of the Greco-Roman period, lest, disciplinary-wise, we throw cultural studies once again into the arms of historicism. Culture, equally, cannot exclusively refer to descriptions of how a contemporary group or class experiences and performs a way of life. The interpretive task would end unbalanced, the hermeneutical equilibrium truncated. Thick descriptions of cultures remain a gap in biblical studies, but we may only do that by remaining in the world of antiquity. My approach on this front consists of going back and forth between contexts, attentive to the ways in which they mutually illuminate each other, carefully scaffolding an intercontextual approach.

Tony Jefferson defines culture as "maps of meanings" that solidify in patterns of social organizations, creating structures and shapes of social relations.²⁹ The phrase "maps of meanings" captures the way in which specific subcultures navigate dominant cultures, readapting language, practices, customs, and embodiments. In this book, I will spend substantial energy teasing out how specific subcultures experience, navigate, and embody certain social conditions. An immediate consequence of swimming in the undercurrents of dominant cultures is that taken-for-granted tenets become exposed, even as they permeate dominant strategies of interpretation. For instance, theorizing the experience of solitary confinement brings forth a different type of subjectivity, relationality, and sociability of consequence to study the biblical past. Concerning the topic of culture and referring to queer subcultures, David Halperin writes:

---

27. Grossberg, *Cultural Studies in the Future Tense*, 25.
28. Grossberg, *Cultural Studies in the Future Tense*, 25.
29. Tony Jefferson, *Resistance through Rituals: Youth Subcultures in Post-War Britain* (London: Routledge, 2002), 10.

That distinctively gay way of being, moreover, appears to be rooted in a particular queer way of feeling. And that queer way of feeling—that queer subjectivity—expresses itself through a peculiar, dissident way of relating to cultural objects (movies, songs, clothes, books, works of art) and cultural forms in general (art and architecture, opera and musical theater, pop and disco, style and fashion, emotion and language). As a cultural practice, male homosexuality involves a characteristic way of receiving, reinterpreting, and reusing mainstream culture, of decoding and recoding the heterosexual or heteronormative meanings already encoded in that culture, so that they come to function as vehicles of gay or queer meaning. It consists, as the critic John Clum says, in "a shared alternative reading of mainstream culture."[30]

None of these elements, I show, is inconsequential to studying the biblical past, be it literary or historical. The unique perspective of being part of a subculture places the interpreter in an oblique relationship to hegemonic cultural norms. This perspective, shared by minoritized interpreters, offers intriguing insights into the tension between interpretation and historicism. It also sheds light on how one's position manifests in epistemological assumptions at odds with what has become the core of biblical studies. This understanding can spark new avenues of research and interpretation. It also explains a range of professional and personal dispositions—from alienation to rebellion and desperation to creativity—impacting research topics, hermeneutical strategies, and pedagogical practices.

Let me summarize before we elaborate further on the heuristic import of all these reflections: if meaning, as the consensus goes, hap-

---

30. David M. Halperin, *How To Be Gay* (Cambridge: Harvard University Press, 2012), 12. Here "culture" defines a way of being in the world characterized by resignification of customs, ideas, and beliefs and a creation of new meanings as creative resistance and livability. Queer subculture maps new meanings on culture, it creates maps of meaning. Halperin offers thick descriptions of how gay male culture creates a way of relating to gender and sexuality through resignification of cultural data such as Judy Garland, interior decoration, inappropriate humor, or dating culture. Inspired by Stuart Hall's contribution, in similar fashion, Tamura Lomax defines culture as a "signifying system that is simultaneously reflexive and lived, and that emerges from integrated cultural stimuli, practices, utterances, and interpretations" (*Jezebel Unhinged: Loosing the Black Female Body in Religion and Culture* [Durham, NC: Duke University Press, 2018], 7). Lomax understands cultural analysis as "analysis of language, customs, and practices of resistance, negotiation, accommodation, appropriation and consent" (Lomax, *Jezebel Unhinged*, 7).

pens in the complex interactions between text and interpreter, it is of the utmost importance to stay equal with both sides of the equation. Biblical studies tends to acknowledge this reality, paired with an equal inertia to dismiss its implications. It matters who the interpreter is, and it matters consequentially. Both dimensions, descriptive and normative, are of equal importance: first, cultural analysis unpacks the grammar of significations; and, second, it has a knack for underlining those resignifications that prove to have resistant valence. Cultural analysis, in sum, gravitates toward a critical understanding of semiotic components that resist cultures of dominance.[31]

The normative dimension in cultural studies brings forth a critical disposition with a utopian drive. On the one hand, it responds to the precarious situations of minoritized communities; on the other, it accounts for what has not been accounted for.[32] The acknowledgment of the abyssal line is both a recognition of historical and structural oppressive structures and an invitation to probe into unasked questions. Raymond Williams argues that, within the assortment of interpretive strategies lodged under its roof, cultural studies' ultimate ethos addresses a democratic deficit.[33]

---

31. Womanist thought can be approached as an enterprise of accounting for and enhancing the lived experience of black women. "A way to do this is by interrogating and unsettling old and new texts and embedded epistemes.... the critical cultural historicizing and theorizing of early texts on race, sex, gender, and representation helps explore, name, disrupt, reconfigure, and unhinge the pornotropic gaze in the latter chapters of this study" (Lomax, *Jezebel Unhinged*, 11). "As I read black liberation theology and black cultural criticism, I understand it to be hermeneutical in orientation. That is, it takes seriously the stories within black life and considers attention to black narratives necessary in approaching black religious and cultural life" (Roger A Sneed, *Representations of Homosexuality: Black Liberation Theology and Cultural Criticism* [Basingstoke: Palgrave Macmillan, 2010], 50–51).

32. "Thus, while Black feminists have worked primarily in the fields of sociology, literary studies/cultural studies, and history as a means to illuminate core themes impacting the agency of Black women, including work, family, motherhood, controlling images, and sexual politics, womanist scholars work primarily in the areas of ethics and theology, and draw on the disciplinary frameworks and methodological tools of literary studies, sociology, history, and anthropology in order to better demonstrate Black women's methods for creating ethical theological frameworks that they apply to such themes" (Laura Gillman, *Unassimilable Feminisms: Reappraising Feminist, Womanist, and Mestiza Identity Politics* [New York: Palgrave Macmillan, 2016], 62).

33. Raymond Williams, *Politics of Modernism: Against the New Conformists* (London: Verso 1989), 152.

Nick Couldry, similarly, specifies the nemesis of the cultural project: market values taking over democratic spaces and globalization infringement of progress, rationality, and democracy.[34]

Cultural studies constitutes, by nature, a progressive project. It is important, however, to qualify what we mean by this label within our disciplinary boundaries. The activist nature of the intellectual task, a non-negotiable in cultural critique, the belief "that an interventionist progressive project can never relent,"[35] sits at odds with the objective nature of historicism, always wary of contaminating history with stories. It is not uncommon for certain strands of historicism to label themselves as progressive, especially against the forces of evangelical fundamentalism, or as an antidote versus church-based theological readings. Although my approach does not directly enter such debates, it speaks against the idea that the only solution to historicism is more and better history. Cultural studies, with its unrelenting theorization of power, disowns how historicism claims to have a solution to every problem and advances new paths that do not respond to historicist concerns. In other words, cultural studies does not buy into a historicist agenda and therefore does not respond to historicist calls for engagement.

Consequently, cultural studies does not simply offer new answers to established questions; it creates new agendas. This heuristic innovation actively responds to current political, cultural, and social crises. In response to the often-hackneyed research agendas embedded in historicism,[36] cultural studies strives for democratization rather than elitism, queerness rather than a politics of inclusion, praxis rather than intellectualism. Stuart Hall defines this ethos within the realm of a "politics of theory," penned by "some kind of organic intellectual political work" and aimed at not defining theory as "the will to truth, but theory as a set of

---

34. Nick Couldry, "The Project of Cultural Studies: Heretical Doubts, New Horizons," in *The Renewal of Cultural Studies*, ed. Paul Smith (Philadelphia: Temple University Press, 2011), 11. Summing up and bringing together what he sees as trend in philosophy (Etienne Balibar), sociology (Ulrich Beck), political theory (Nancy Fraser), history (Pierre Rosanvallon), or economics (Amartya Sen), Couldry sees cultural studies' project as an investigation into the conditions of a new politics arising against "strong forces that would close it down" ("The Project of Cultural Studies," 13).

35. Melissa Gregg, *Cultural Studies' Affective Voices* (New York: Palgrave Macmillan, 2014), 155.

36. Mary Zournazi, *Hope: New Philosophies for Change* (New York: Routledge, 2003), 14–20.

contested, localized, conjunctural knowledges, which have to be debated in a dialogical way."[37] The consequence is clear, explicit, and wide ranging: theory is "practice which always thinks about its intervention in a world in which it would make some difference, in which it would have some effect."[38] The hermeneutical enterprise, in sum, seeks to illuminate "what keeps making the lives we live, and the societies we live in, profoundly and deeply antihumane in their capacity to live with difference."[39]

Cultural studies' prospective research agenda resists the hegemonic agendas set by historicism, which tends to see its interests as issues from the texts themselves. This putative straightforward relationship between contemporary research agendas and the texts' original intentions shapes a type of protectionism that favors the disciplinary status quo. Stephen L. Young critiques protectionism in New Testament studies, defining it as "the privileging of a source's own claims to such an extent that interpreters let them dictate academic analysis."[40] Young's critique ultimately seeks to expose a doxa legitimating the guild as male-dominated and conceptualizing its outer boundaries as niche or provincial. Young uses Bourdieu's coinage of doxa as theorized by David Schwartz to refer to "the fundamental assumptions and categories that shape intellectual thought in a particular time and place and which are generally not available to conscious awareness of the participants."[41] The field of the New Testament is dominated by the doxa of protectionism, defined, in turn, as "the collapsing of inquiry into description such that the perspectives of those being studied are privileged in scholarly analysis."[42] Young offers useful distinctions between "descriptive reduction" and "explanatory reduction" and between dominant and dominated protectionism. The main drive behind his analysis is to show that New Testament studies privileges the claims of its object of study, resulting in the artificial creation of a field that would welcome only those who follow (doctrinally, philosophically, etc.)

---

37. Stuart Hall, "Cultural Studies and Its Theoretical Legacies," in *Cultural Studies*, ed. Lawrence Grossberg, Cary Nelson, and Paula A. Treichler (New York: Routledge, 1992), 286.

38. Hall, "Cultural Studies and Its Theoretical Legacies," 286.

39. Hall, "Race, Culture, and Communications: Looking Backward and Forward at Cultural Studies," *Rethinking Marxism* 5 (2009): 17.

40. Stephen L. Young, "Let's Take the Text Seriously," *Method and Theory in the Study of Religion* 32 (2020): 328.

41. Young, "Let's Take the Text Seriously," 330.

42. Young, "Let's Take the Text Seriously," 330.

in the arguments of the New Testament authors. Protectionism collapses explanation into description, "such that insider claims become normative for scholarly analysis."[43]

I sympathize with Young's critique of the field, but I think the argument about protectionism already casts the debate in historicist terms, the dominant episteme, and thus, ironically enough, protects the dominant episteme. On this front, an *episteme* refers to a set of disciplinary assumptions that may include several doxai, an ethos of sorting out those assumptions and categories in a way of hermeneutical reasoning. Briefly put, historicism is an episteme in the sense that, no matter the types of categories and assumptions deployed, they are always geared toward historicizing. The hegemony of the descriptive, to use Young's expression, fosters a type of scholarship that relegates "text-decentering rediscriptive interests."[44]

Young offers two examples of how such protectionism works in recent debates. In the first one, he shows how John Barclay's critique of the ethnic analysis performed by Caroline Johnson Hodge reframes the debate in emic terms by creating a clear-cut distinction between God-made and human-made identities, advocating for the first and dismissing the second.[45] This protectionism, Young argues, relies on the idea that the text claims to support the first: "Paul's theological claims become normative for legitimate inquiry."[46] The second example draws from the debates around the boundaries between Judaism and Hellenism in the study of early Christian texts. Young shows again how mainstream biblical scholarship takes the texts' own claims as departing from Hellenism as normative and then proceeds to analyze the consequences of such assumptions.

For the purposes of this contribution, it is worth noticing that what appears as a radical critique of a doxa in New Testament studies reifies a dominant episteme. Whatever position the critic takes on the debates, the episteme is historicist. If the protectionist doxa "renders the field itself

---

43. Young, "Let's Take the Text Seriously," 332.
44. Young, "Let's Take the Text Seriously," 339.
45. See Caroline Johnson Hodge, "Apostle to the Gentiles: Constructions of Paul's Identity," *BibInt* 13 (2005): 270–88; Hodge, *If Sons, Then Heirs: A Study of Kinship and Ethnicity in the Letters of Paul* (New York: Oxford University Press, 2007); John M. G. Barclay, "An Identity Received from God: The Theological Configuration of Paul's Kinship Discourse," *EC* (2017): 354–72.
46. Young, "Let's Take the Text Seriously," 344.

seemingly natural, obvious, self-evident, or undisputed,"[47] the historicist episteme in which this doxa thrives renders the field essentialist colonialist, objectivistic, and positivist. As the critic contests protectionism, she is set to reinscribe the dominant forces of epistemic colonialism that sustain "sound biblical scholarship." Framing the debate in these terms, Young hopes, opens biblical criticism to "real criticism," because it dismantles a doxa where scholarship follows in the argumentation of the texts under analysis. Antiprotectionism, at least in this version, does not contest what traditional biblical scholarship has constructed as the main agenda in the studies of biblical texts. It continues to leave historicism's dominance unchallenged and relegates contextualist approaches to the margins.

Stuart Hall's clarion call, more than twenty years ago, still rings true in the echo chambers of contemporary cultural criticism: "time to return to the project of cultural studies from the clean air of meaning and textuality to the something nasty down below."[48] Hall, seemingly responding to the poststructuralism dominance that had invaded the shores of literary criticism, sought to return to the dirty soil of real history. For some biblical scholars, the postmodern turn offered a comforting siren call to escape the traps of historicism: the political drive in postmodernism brought the "present" into the "past" by exposing the ideological assumptions in allegedly impartial historicist and literary studies. However, the present was hardly ever a reality dictum, more like an abstracted atmosphere than dirty soil. If cultural studies, as David Harvey advocates, addresses the factuality of the past, the realism of the present, and the openness of the future, poststructuralism differs from cultural studies in that the realism of the present was constructed in its linguistic rather than materialist forms.[49]

---

47. Young, "Let's Take the Text Seriously," 355.
48. Hall, "Cultural Studies and Its Theoretical Legacies," 278.
49. David Harvey, "From Space to Place and Back Again: Reflections on the Condition of Postmodernity," in *Mapping the Futures: Local Cultures, Global Change*, ed. Jon Bird, Barry Curtis, Tim Putnam, and Lisa Tickner (New York: Routledge, 2016), 13. Examples of cultural studies in the theological realm are more common than in biblical studies. Consider, for instance, Frederick Douglass's invitation to hear spirituals as manifestations of a world. The "Negro spiritual" becomes a recognizable cultural form that is both a reflection and a builder of black culture and subjectivity. Jon Cruz notices how Frederick Douglass and William Lloyd Garrison amplified enslaved voices creating, in turn, a material cultural that expanded its significance. What had hitherto "been misunderstood as well as scorned, derogated, and dismissed" became

In this work, I have taken pains to illustrate how biblical critique can operate without necessarily buying into historicist tenets. Abraham Smith contends that the task of cultural critique involves unmasking the innocent, revealing "the ideologies or systems of thought that make otherwise historical constructions appear as timeless and neutral givens."[50] Historicism is in itself a historical construction with colonizing drives, keeping biblical scholarship circumscribed within a narrow set of epistemes. Thus it is no surprise that Schüssler Fiorenza portrays the field as a battleground over reading practices. The historicist king reigns supreme in such a contested kingdom. Smith, for instance, conceptualizes cultural studies in terms of an ideological cultural critique of history. The historicizing task enters biblical criticism through the back door of cultural studies: the biting probe into the hegemonic epistemologies that characterizes cultural criticism becomes a supplement to the dominant task of historicism. By a sleight of hand, postcolonial theory turns into imperial studies, queer critique into liberal hermeneutics, Marxist analysis into economic history, cultural criticism into history of reception. No matter what we eat, the disciplinary esophagus assimilates it to historicizing nutrients.

If cultural studies foreshadows historicist inertias, it does not embrace suspicion as its default optic. Rita Felski, in a pungent and lengthy commentary on the traditions of cultural studies in the United States, demonstrates how the advancement of high theory in literary departments gobbled up an intellectual tradition that aspired to a democratization of the culture rather than a critique of it, a valorization of the aesthetic rather than a dismissal of beauty itself. In an ironic turn of events, Felski complains, cultural studies shifted into ideological criticism, anti-aestheticism, suspicion, and

---

"culture" (Cruz, *Culture on the Margins: The Black Spiritual and the Rise of American Cultural Interpretation* [Princeton: Princeton University Press, 1999], 6–7). The reverse rings equally true: dominant stereotypes demand from cultural studies an exposé of their maligning effects. As Emilie Townes argues, Aunt Jemima, Sapphire, the Welfare Queen, the Tragic Mulatta, and Topsy necessitate a type of hermeneutics that teases out cultural production both as a symptom and as a disease. Thinking about the future, Townes adds: "If we refuse to engage in dismantling systemic and intentional structural evil, we only leave a parched and desolate land for generations to come" (Emilie Maureen Townes, *Womanist Ethics and the Cultural Production of Evil* [Basingstoke: Palgrave Macmillan, 2007], 6).

50. Janice Capel Anderson and Stephen D. Moore, *Mark and Method: New Approaches in Biblical Studies*, 2nd ed. (Minneapolis: Fortress, 2008), 183.

symptomatic reading.[51] In an interesting turn of events, cultural studies originated as a critique of ideological critique, as an invitation to undo distinctions between high and low culture. Cultural studies democratized the aesthetic value in that it saw culture worth studying everywhere. The curiosity for tending to learn how things mean beyond booking and elitist cultural manifestations animated a search for beauty, meaning, and significance *everywhere*. What started as a critique of ideology, a modus operandi geared toward the dissolution between high and low culture, evolved into a type of elitism performed by an adjuratory critic invested in exposing, revealing, probing, and dissecting the entanglements of literature and power. If cultural studies initially advocated for the study of culture everywhere, this curiosity for meaning mechanisms beyond bookish limits and a heed for the "culture in subcultures" swiftly became a demystification of all cultural expressions for their complicit attitude toward systems of oppression.[52]

Whereas cultural studies remains attentive to the mundane structures of power that shape and are shaped to a wide range of populations and subcultures, the Bible constitutes one among many axes of power in the configuration of people's lives. Jacqueline Hidalgo perceptively notices that "scriptures have been places of power, not just because they are 'sacred' but also because people have found ways to uncover, challenge, transform, and uphold the power regimes of the world around them with and through these texts."[53] Such an approach unearths hidden stories of interpretation that not only cast the biblical texts under new light but also cast the task of biblical interpretation under new interpretive strategies. Similarly, Erin Runions examines the role of the Bible in the theopolitical, how Babylon turns into a cultural motif deployed by the right and the left to refer to political ills, whether the "fracturing of the single Christian morality in the United States" or "the abuses of the capitalist system."[54] Sharon Jacob turns her attention to surrogacy in postcolonial India to unveil how the

---

51. "Cultural studies, once a name reserved for a specific intellectual tradition, is now being applied, often quite haphazardly, to any attempt to link literature, culture, and politics. A phrase that once identified a specific field of study originating in Britain is now being used as ammunition in America's own culture wars" (Michael Bérubé, *The Aesthetics of Cultural Studies* [Hoboken, NJ: John Wiley & Sons, 2008], 31).

52. Bérubé, *Aesthetics of Cultural Studies*, 33.

53. Hidalgo, *Revelation in Aztlán*, 24.

54. Erin Runions, *The Babylon Complex: Theopolitical Fantasies of War, Sex, and Sovereignty* (New York: Fordham University Press, 2014), 29–31.

Matthean and Lukan infancy narratives construct motherhood as a politically complex project promoting "self-slavery," in that a desire to be liberated is predicated on the condition of one's oppression.[55] These studies substantially contribute to the legacy of cultural studies within biblical hermeneutics and constitute a point of reference throughout this book. Unlike these monographic contributions, my approach seeks to extend the conversation in multiple directions, hinting at a wide variety of crises in conversation with a broad selection of texts.

Looking everywhere informs this project and constitutes one of the main contributions of cultural studies to biblical criticism: a thematic fugue of sorts, a heuristic exploration in uncharted directions, a runaway exercise into political fields. How does a thick theorization of present political and cultural concerns inform a disciplinary field invested in capturing the past? I should note that, rather than seeing the present as an obstacle to reach the past, the ensuing conversation between past and present contexts creates a fruitful interpretive space that disavows a linear/straight connection (from past to present and vice versa), adhering to circular/spiral connections. With a reluctance to staying on either side of the historiographical spectrum (present or past), different contexts converse with each other, mindful of connecting and dissimilar touch points. This intercontextual negotiation aims at informing ethically, politically, and culturally the present through the creative approach to the past and the past through the cultural opportunities of our times: the Bible, after all, represents our cultural past as much as our political present. This is an invitation to complexify the historiographical mandate by way of strengthening the weakest link of the hermeneutical processes: past and present, text and interpreter, history and culture.

Cultural Studies, Reception History, and Intercontextuality

In a mundane way, interpreting the New Testament always entails interpreting its reception. Any strict philological exegesis ought to engage with received questions, topics, and themes in the field.[56] Equally, any

---

55. Sharon Jacob, *Reading Mary alongside Indian Surrogate Mothers* (New York: Palgrave Macmillan, 2015).

56. Klaus Wachtel and Michael W. Holmes, eds., *The Textual History of the Greek New Testament: Changing Views in Contemporary Research*, TCS 8 (Atlanta: Society of Biblical Literature, 2011).

determined historical-critical approach is inevitably embedded in a scholarly tradition of historiographical assumptions.⁵⁷ In a more sophisticated fashion, reception history refers to a subfield attentive to how cultural manifestations draw from or have some type of relation to biblical texts and motifs. Reception history constitutes an intertextual approach insofar as it broaches comparatively two texts, one belonging to the canon, the other situated in time. In this sense, reception history, as the name gives away, is historical through and through.

Each chapter in this book is intertextual in that it links specific biblical texts to artistic representations that, directly or obliquely, relate to the biblical canon. The biblical textual world enters in close conversation with the artistic representational sphere. Every interpretive practice heretofore, however, acquires significance in the context of a political and cultural crisis. It is at the juncture of biblical texts, their reception, and their contemporary valence that this work seeks to intervene in biblical studies. Accordingly, I turn to the term *intercontextuality* to convey an ethos of interpretation where different contexts—past and present—converse with each other in dynamic fashion, enforcing a determinate drive to grant past contexts predominance.⁵⁸ Intercontextuality draws from intertextuality, but it also differs significantly from intertextuality.

---

57. Beth M. Sheppard, *The Craft of History and the Study of the New Testament*, RBS 60 (Atlanta: Society of Biblical Literature, 2012); Eve-Marie Becker, *The Birth of Christian History: Memory and Time from Mark to Luke-Acts* (New Haven: Yale University Press, 2018); Maia Kotrosits, *How Things Feel: Biblical Studies, Affect Theory, and the (Im)Personal* (Leiden: Brill, 2016).

58. Tat-siong Benny Liew pioneered a sustained use of the term "intercontextuality" to convey a back-and-forth directionality between texts and contexts. "Writing a text and writing about a literary text," he adds, constitute "rhetorical projects that help construct subject positions even as the projects themselves are constructed within concrete socio-political situations" (*Politics of Parousia: Reading Mark Inter(con)textually*, BibInt 42 [Leiden: Brill, 1999], 149). Despite Liew's productive theorization and application of the concept, its afterlife has been rather slim. Although some contributions have referred to "intercontextuality" and "intercontextual," they have tended to apply it exegetically without further theoretical developments. For instance, *Fragile Dignity: Intercontextual Conversations on Scriptures, Family, and Violence* includes the term in the title yet does not mention it again in the book (Juliana Claassens and Klaas Spronk, eds., *Fragile Dignity: Intercontextual Conversations on Scriptures, Family, and Violence*, SemeiaSt 72 [Atlanta: Society of Biblical Literature, 2013]). In the wake of Liew's contribution, a few scholars have theorized and used the term in terms similar to my contribution. See Jean Kyoung Kim, *Woman and Nation: An Inter-*

Intertextuality, a term first coined by Julia Kristeva to convey the idea that every text is in contact with other texts in transforming ways,[59] has inspired literary critics to look to the ways in which the art of reading always involves tracing relationships between texts. Initially offered as a challenge to stabilizing readings of text, leading into ideas about the death of the author with Barthes,[60] intercontextual approaches have reached beyond the world of the text into painting, music, sculpture, and even architecture and urbanism. Similarly, the concept has proven particularly fruitful in postcolonial and African American literary studies, where the intertextual relationship between the Western canon and subjugated traditions touches on questions of accessibility, intelligibility, and subject formation.[61] In New Testament studies, the development of intertextuality has been, as expected, less culturally attentive and more historically attuned.[62]

---

contextual Reading of the Gospel of John from a Postcolonial Feminist Perspective, BibInt 69 (Leiden: Brill, 2004); Sakari Häkkinen, "Developing Methods for Poverty Studies," Diaconia 4 (2013): 122–42.

59. Julia Kristeva, The Kristeva Reader, ed. Toril Moil (New York: Columbia University Press, 1986).

60. Roland Barthes, The Pleasure of the Text, trans. Richard Miller (New York: Hill & Wang, 1975).

61. The work of Henry Louis Gates Jr. (The Signifying Monkey: A Theory of Afro-American Literary Criticism [Oxford: Oxford University Press, 1988]) is illustrative on this point. African American literature, he argues, is consciously intertextual in relation to standard white literature and black vernacular discourses, and it has been deemed as "nonspeech" by the Western canon. The figure of the Signifying Monkey, a trickster character from African American folklore who uses wordplay, satire, and humor, emerges as a symbol to subvert authority and challenge dominant narratives. By referencing and deconstructing texts from the Western tradition, African oral traditions, African American slave narratives, and African American folklore challenge the notion of a fixed, universal meaning and highlight the multiplicity of interpretations and perspectives.

62. B. J. Oropeza, arguably one of the most prominent theorists of intertextuality in biblical studies, laments: "A disturbing trend I noticed when first chairing the Intertextuality in the New Testament sessions was that few of the presenters mentioned how they were going about interpreting the texts they claimed the NT authors were echoing or referencing (almost always from the OT). Some papers simply seemed to be doing a historical-critical study of a NT passage. For me, this resembled too much the mere study of 'New Testament Use of the Old Testament,' whereas intertextuality invites a wider constellation of sources and various approaches that is not limited merely to traditional historical-critical inquiry." See B. J. Oropeza, "New Studies in

Understood "as the presence of a text (or texts) in another text,"[63] intertextuality offers a pass to move beyond authorial intention and straightforward literary and textual influences.[64] But if one is to survey the most recent and sophisticated intertextual studies, one would be hard pressed not to consider intertextuality as historical intratextuality. Increasingly attentive to how meaning occurs within "the culture of a particular time as construed by social discourse,"[65] the context, whether cultural, social, or political, remains circumscribed to the context of antiquity, hardly ever to the contexts of contemporary interpretation. Intercontextuality, on the other hand, refuses to anchor context in any given temporal range, inviting the contexts of contemporary readers into the hermeneutical task.

The contours of intercontextuality come into sharp focus as we incorporate the abyssal line. Conversations across time and space create a sense of familiar and unfamiliar bonds grounded on thematic similarities, temporal connections, spatial affinities, and geographical coincidences. Most notably, such conversations reach beyond this side of the abyssal line to touch on the experience of those untouched by history. An intercontextual approach renders those affected by history, but hardly subjects in the production of knowledge, coprotagonists of the historical task. Whereas intertextuality continues to frame the issue of context in antiquity, often debating whether Jewish or Greco-Roman contexts make for a better case, intercontextuality suggests that contemporary contexts inform the construction of past contexts and that there are no solid reasons to privilege

---

Textual Interplay: An Introduction," in *New Studies in Textual Interplay*, ed. Craig A. Evans, B. J. Oropeza, and Paul Sloan, LNTS 632 (London: Bloomsbury, 2020], 4).

63. Oropeza, "New Studies in Textual Interplay," 3.

64. Steve Moyise, "Intertextuality and Historical Approaches to the Use of Scripture in the New Testament," in *Reading the Bible Intertextually*, ed. Richard B. Hays, Stefan Alkier, and Leroy A. Huizenga (Waco, TX: Baylor University Press, 2009), 23–32; The work of Richard Hays (*Echoes of Scripture in the Letters of Paul* [New Haven: Yale University Press, 1989]) has proved highly influential on this point for years. Hays's introduction of metalepsis (through John Hollander, *The Figure of Echo: A Mode of Allusion in Milton and After* [Berkeley: University of California Press, 1981]) and his criteria of availability, volume, recurrence, thematic coherence, historical plausibility, history of interpretation, and satisfaction (Hays, *Echoes of Scripture*, 29–32) continues to inform intertextual studies in New Testament.

65. Doosuk Kim, "Intertextuality and New Testament Studies," *CurBR* 20 (2022): 250, https://doi.org/10.1177/1476993X221100993.

one set of specific contexts over others, whether past or present, textual or visual, literary or political.[66]

In the following chapters, an intercontextual approach conceives artistic representations as thinking images. On this front, the question of how the visual interacts with the textual and vice versa remains at the center of a cultural studies approach. As in the field of reception history, an intercontextual approach shows how biblical motifs travel across time and space, illuminating the historical and cultural afterlives of canonical texts. Intercontextuality offers a significant addendum: once we decenter historicity as the dominant epistemological ethos, the connections between history and culture, past and present, and visual and textual proliferate. Whereas reception history tends to draw straight lines between sources, intercontextuality privileges spiraling forces.[67] Referring to feminist hermeneutics, Judith McKinlay vividly summarizes this syncretic approach:

> interpretive explorations likewise never come to an end. Historical-critical methodology, together with its more radical turn to the New Historicism, will continue as one voice among the many, but accompanied by new and sometimes highly experimental, if tentatively presented, ways to bring the text into meaningful dialogue with the world of the reader.... The quest for understanding the dynamics of texts may lead to drawing upon resources far removed from those of the more traditional approaches. Conversations about texts will spiral out and spill over into new contexts. A feminist reading works with this expectation, for it is inherently a committed reading, which refuses to leave texts in a closed world of the past. They are not to be locked up and examined only under the rubric of "what the text meant," but read with an eye open to the present and the future, with a concern for their political and ethical influence.[68]

---

66. Adam Winn, "The Good News of Isaiah and Rome in Mark 1:1," in Evans, Oropeza, and Sloan, *New Studies in Textual Interplay*, 95–108.

67. Schüssler Fiorenza resorts to the metaphor of a spiraling dance to visualize her proposed method of sociorhetorical interpretation: "an image of interpretation as forward movement and spiraling repetition, stepping in place, turning over and changing venue in which discrete methodological approaches become moving steps and artful configurations" (Schüssler Fiorenza, *Rhetoric and Ethic*, 101).

68. Judith E. McKinlay, "Sarah and Hagar: What Have I to Do with Them?" in Vander Stichele and Penner, *Her Master's Tools*, 176.

The biblical past shapes our cultural present and vice versa. Historically speaking, connecting biblical texts with their cultural effects involves interpreting textuality anew, inserting ourselves in a spiral of interpretation. How we interpret the past depends on where we stand in the present and vice versa. Unlike a traditional reception approach that considers "the history of how a text has influenced communities and cultures down the centuries,"[69] intercontextuality draws history close to our present, making both texts and images interlocutors in clarifying, theorizing, complicating, or illuminating the present. The metaphor of the spiral befits this ethos because it visualizes how where the interpreter stands at any point affects her perception of what lies ahead, what lies behind, and how close or far she stays from other concentric lines. The subjects and objects of interpretation, in this view, turn into moving targets.

How do we travel contexts across historical periods? What modes of knowledge become available as we bring in "the visual"? What new questions arise as we braid together seemingly unrelated contexts? How do images "cite" texts in a way that problematizes, in line with this book's fundamental drive, the historiographical gap? In what sense does art become a way of knowing, informing how we inhabit the present, casting our eyes onto the past, and imagining the future? What is art's research agenda? Or, mundanely put, how does a picture coin new questions?[70] How, ultimately, do we skip the historicist grasp that inevitably envisions art as an afterlife/afterthought of an allegedly original meaning? Reception history inevitably conjures up historiographical, epistemological, and heuristic concerns.

These questions trouble the foundations of reception history because they refuse to privilege origin over process, initiation over continuation. Timothy Beal argues that "biblical literature is not a fact but an event, a dialectic relationship of production and reception."[71] Beal sharply observes that reception history brings two important contributions to the field: it demonstrates that the Bible and its aftermath is all effective history, "always both production and reception"; and it shifts the focus from

---

69. John F. A. Sawyer, *Sacred Languages and Sacred Texts: Religion in the First Christian Centuries* (London: Routledge, 1999), 2.

70. For an example of how contemporary black art informs and nuances the study of antiquity, see Laura S. Nasrallah, "The Work of Nails: Religion, Mediterranean Antiquity, and Contemporary Black Art," *JAAR* 90 (2022): 356–76.

71. Timothy Beal, "Reception History and Beyond: Toward the Cultural History of Scriptures," *BibInt* 19 (2011): 364.

discovering textual meanings to meanings as they are constructed from texts. In other words, reception history problematizes the existence of the "other horizon of the 'text' to be received and understood within effective history."[72] The Bible "is not a thing but an idea, or rather a constellation of often competing, heterogeneous ideas, more or less related to a wide variety of biblical things."[73]

Grounded in the foundational insight that biblical texts hold no ontological priority, the interpretive task faces the challenge not of reaching into the text as "a thing" but "rather multiple, often competing, symbolic and material productions of them [relations] that are generated and generative in different scriptural cultures."[74] Beal suggests here a shift "from interpreting scripture via culture to interpreting culture, especially religious culture, via scripture."[75] Rather than traveling the historiographical gaps unidirectionally, an intercontextual approach travels back and forth between contexts that are being shaped as the interpretation proceeds.

This version of reception history chips away at the historicist spine that continues to vertebrate the field. Williams Lyons, one of the most prominent theorists in the area, insists on the nature of reception history as history.[76] His contribution reframes the traditional quarrel between historicists and postmodernists by assuaging the former in terms of the latter.[77] Historical criticism, defined as "the attempt to understand the Bible by setting it in the context of its time of writing, and by asking how it came into existence and what were the purposes of its authors,"[78] claims objectivity "in the sense that it tries to attend to what the text actually says and not to read

---

72. Beal, "Reception History and Beyond," 368.
73. Beal, "Reception History and Beyond," 368.
74. Beal, "Reception History and Beyond," 370.
75. Beal, "Reception History and Beyond," 371. For Beal, such an approach leads to locating biblical studies within religious studies "and, more generally, the academic humanities."
76. William John Lyons, "Hope for a Troubled Discipline? Contributions to New Testament Studies from Reception History," *JSNT* 33 (2010): 207–20.
77. Lyons defines the field as follows: "it is better defined as a pragmatic activity in which a historically located investigator is attempting to understand the dynamics of an interaction between a biblical text or a biblical text as rendered in some other media, a context, and an audience's response" (William John Lyons, *Joseph of Arimathea: A Study in Reception History* [Oxford: Oxford University Press, 2014], 2).
78. Lyons, "Hope for a Troubled Discipline?," 211.

alien meanings into it."[79] Reception history, similarly, "aims to understand the interaction between a text, a context, and an audience's response."[80] For many practitioners of reception history, historicism absorbs the hermeneutical task because, once again, historical circumstances monitor the textual meanings. Reception history here trades first-century contexts for operative historical periods, the deciding factor no longer being the Greco-Roman context but the Middle Ages, modernity, or postmodernity.[81]

It may not be coincidental that one of the most sophisticated theorizations of reception history stems from cultural studies itself. Mieke Bal's notion of "preposterous history" complicates the linearity of sources and receptions embedded in those subfield strands invested in historicism.[82] Bal frames the topic in epistemological terms: "Does ancient art have to be seen as having a foundational influence on everything that follows in its wake, to be seen as the source, as the traditional view would have it? The problem with this view is that we can only see what we already know, or think we know."[83] Such historiographical questioning not only targets history's straight lines but also further complicates the distinction between the subject and object of inquiry and signals the fetishization of sources. To bend history entails toying with the possibilities of coevalness across time and space, synchronicity of contexts, histories, stories, subjects, and motifs. Despite its rather sophisticated name, the historiographical insight is rather simple: "that the past should be altered by the present as much as the present is directed by the past."[84] Caroline Vander Stichele's application

---

79. Lyons, "Hope for a Troubled Discipline?," 211.

80. Lyons, "Hope for a Troubled Discipline?," 213.

81. Jon Morgan, "Visitors, Gatekeepers and Receptionists: Reflections on the Shape of Biblical Studies and the Role of Reception History," in *Reception History and Biblical Studies: Theory and Practice*, ed. Emma England and John Lyons (London: Bloomsbury T&T Clark, 2015), 63.

82. "Historians of art and literature have long been aware of the inevitable screen that later art puts between the historian's gaze and the older works. But instead of considering this a problem, a liability of history, I have decided to explore this inevitability as an enrichment of our cultural habitat as a whole" (Mieke Bal, *Quoting Caravaggio: Contemporary Art, Preposterous History* [Chicago: University of Chicago Press, 1999], 7).

83. Bal, *Quoting Caravaggio*, 3.

84. Caroline Vander Stichele, "The Head of John and Its Reception or How to Conceptualize 'Reception History,'" in England and Lyons, *Reception History and Biblical Studies*, 83.

of Deleuze and Guattari's image of the rhizome remains apposite: the conceptual image of reception history "as a dynamic and open-ended process, with multiple entries and exits, rather than linear trajectories. As a result, 'the Bible' is no longer conceived as origin or centre, but as a node from which its history unfolds in multiple directions"[85]

Blurring the boundaries between past and present, reception and creation, object and subject, Bal further complicates the relationships between textual and visual cultures by bestowing textuality to imagery. Artworks, obviously appraised for their aesthetic values, are also "theoretical objects that 'theorize' cultural history. This theorizing makes them such instances of cultural philosophy that they deserve the name theoretical objects."[86] On this front, the task of cultural studies presupposes an engagement with art pieces—and with texts—beyond their immediate historical circumstances. Like texts, images become meaning-producing entities as they interact with specific contexts in the present. Texts and images touch each other across time and space, dispelling the strictures of historical contextualism.

The following exegetical chapters follow a canonical order, so their sequential arrangement remains "straight." My hope, however, remains that the reader will get lost in the zigzag of history, textuality, and visuality that every chapter ventures. The meandering argumentative lines that connect contexts, texts, and images intend to illuminate, inspire, and question the way contemporary interpreters think about the stakes of interpreting the past in troubling present contexts. The syncretic articulation of theories, methods, testimonies, and experiences rehearses hermeneutical insights beyond the realm of the purely "intellectual."

At the end of the introductory chapter, I mentioned how the attitude of the biblical scholar is inherently conservative because the intellectual task of writing about the past demands bracketing a series of experiences that are usually disregarded as nonacademic. Minoritized scholars have long felt in their own bodies such disregard for other ways of producing knowledge. Fernando Segovia recounts this anecdote of presenting

---

85. Vander Stichele, "The Head of John and Its Reception," 85. See, for instance, Colleen Conway's take on Jael as an elastic girl, an "example of cultural history of biblical traditions once they stray from their scriptural origins" (Colleen M. Conway, *Sex and Slaughter in the Tent of Jael: A Cultural History of a Biblical Story* [New York: Oxford University Press, 2016], 5).

86. Bal, *Quoting Caravaggio*, 6.

at a professional conference on liberationist hermeneutics and a young German scholar approaching him and asking "in a tone of arrogance and disdain ... what all this had to do with him."[87] Angela Parker recently reflected on the implications for her subjectivity and scholarly formation of being trained in (Western) biblical studies as an African American woman: "I realize that asking proper questions was connected to how the professors who were training me were steeped in Western thought that considered anything 'other' as alien and corrupt."[88] The written and oral stories of minoritized scholars in biblical studies are countless. My own experience in the field resembles this plight. Let me share just one instance, particularly relevant given my previous arguments about epistemicide and the politics of knowledge production. On several occasions—I can remember at least three—I have received desk rejection from journal editors who have explicitly labeled my contribution as non-scholarly. In one particularly grievous instance, the journal editor felt "offended" that I would send "such a questionable piece of scholarship" for consideration. Of course, as academics, rejection is our business. My point, however, is that the politics of rejection/acceptance applies differently to different epistemes, resulting in a recentering of historicism, objectivism, and scientificism.

The objectivistic nature of historicism, its dominance and exclusionary ethics, bans explicitly contextual topics from scholarly inquiry and boycotts any intellectual disposition outside disembodied rationality. Listening to the experiences of those who have suffered the utmost cruelty in torture, tending to the lives destroyed in solitary confinement, or recounting the atrocity of enslavement demands a writer/interpreter attuned to embodied knowledge.[89] One cannot sit close to the Other's pain without being on the verge of the precipice of the human experience. While researching and writing on these topics, I had to stop numerous times to breathe and process the cruelty of our current social and cultural arrangements. By the same token, I had to pause and celebrate the resilience of

---

87. Segovia, *Decolonizing Biblical Studies*, 172.

88. Angela N. Parker, *If God Still Breathes, Why Can't I? Black Lives Matter and Biblical Authority* (Grand Rapids: Eerdmans, 2021), 21.

89. Jin Young Choi refers to "phronesis" as a type of embodied wisdom where "the interpreter's practice and engagement play a significant role in meaning creation" (Choi, *Postcolonial Discipleship of Embodiment: An Asian and Asian American Feminist Reading of the Gospel of Mark* [New York: Palgrave Macmillan, 2015], 31).

the human spirit, its creativity, and its utopian drive. I hope that this type of embodied knowledge continues to filter through our field to make humanities fully human.

3
THE GOSPEL OF QUEER LOVE
(MATTHEW 25:31–46)

A Representational Crisis

Liberation theologies have reified the gap between sexual desire and political transformation, between sexual and social justice. Marcella Althaus-Reid responds to theology's obliviousness to the sexual desires of poor women: we don't care only about children and food; "we must care a lot about our orgasms too."[1] Take, for instance, liberation theology's magnum opus. In a chapter devoted to sexuality, Antonio Moser equates sexual liberation to bourgeois ideology, "an instrumentalization of sexuality."[2] For Moser, sexual liberation, with its dismissal of virginity, marriage, and absolutization of sex, distracts the poor from the real problems. In this version, sex is the opium of the masses, and erotic drives sit at odds with agapic love.

The eruption of the "sexual subject" in theological reflection has resulted in a reconsideration of some anthropological assumptions: in queer theology, studying the sexual subject entails analyzing the processes of subjectification in relationship to religious and theological systems of power. Resorting to the sexual subject has resulted in the centering of identities over practices; such discursive intervention, on the one hand, has indeed introduced eros back into theological reflection and, on the other, has con-

---

1. Marcella Althaus-Reid, *Indecent Theology: Theological Perversions in Sex, Gender and Politics* (London: Routledge, 2000), 137. See also, from a cultural- and literary-studies perspective, Carlos Ulises Decena, *Circuits of the Sacred: A Faggotology* (Durham, NC: Duke University Press, 2023).

2. Antonio Moser, "Sexualidad," in *Mysterium liberationis: Conceptos fundamentales de la teología de la liberación*, ed. Ignacio Ellacuría and Jon Sobrino (Madrid: Editorial Trotta, 1990), 122.

ceptualized eros as an anthropological quality rather than a category to think about queer practices.³ As I show in chapter 6, this phenomenon expands to queer theologies in the Global North and, quite ironically, to queer theory itself. For all the identity-averse foundations of queer critique, sexual practices and the ethos of sexual subcultures remain underrepresented. If we understand, in good queer fashion, that *sexuality* names a *dispositif* that shaped contemporary sexual identities and *sex* names a set of practices that refers to bodies and pleasures, queer theology is sexuality intense and sex-averse. The interpretive question becomes urgent: How does biblical criticism enter into conversation with queer subcultures? What interpretive paths become available? How do we move the needle of queer biblical interpretation toward sex rather than sexuality? This chapter offers a contribution in this direction, weaving together a theorization of political *caritas* (agapic love) with queer sex practices (sexual eros).

Eros and Agape and the Task of Queer Critique

Matthew 25:31–46 encourages its audience to take care of the disenfranchised. Christian theology and pastoral practice have traditionally understood the pericope's injunctions to "feed the hungry," "quench the thirsty," "shelter the homeless," "clothe the naked," and "visit the imprisoned" to be emblematic examples of agapic love.⁴ Although the Greek text contains no word referring to love itself, this pericope plays a foundational role in Latin American liberation theology for its reference to ethics of love attentive to the needs of the impoverished. Jon Sobrino, elaborating on Gustavo Gutiérrez's argument that Matt 25 grounds liberation Christology, claims that "Matthew 25 is basic, both for doing theology from the point of departure in the poor and for understanding Jesus as he is to be

---

3. Genilma Boehler, "La visibilización de los sujetos invisibles: el método 'queer' para la Teología," *Pasos* 155 (2012): 2–9; Hugo Córdova Quero, "Risky Affairs: Marcella Althaus-Reid Indecently Queering Juan Luis Segundo's Hermeneutical Circle Propositions," in *Dancing Theology in Fetish Boots: Essays in Honour of Marcella Althaus-Reid*, ed. Lisa Isherwood and Mark D. Jordan (London: SCM, 2010), 207–18; Córdova Quero, "Queer Liberative Theologies," in *Introducing Liberative Theologies*, ed. Miguel de la Torre (Maryknoll, NY: Orbis Books, 2015), 210–31; Beatriz Febus Perez, "El sujeto sexual en las teologías queer: ¿Implicaciones para una teologia queer latinoamericana de la liberación?," *Conexión QUEER: Revista Latinoamericana y Caribeña de Teologías Queer* 1 (2018): 145–74.

4. All biblical translations are mine.

found in the poor."⁵ Matthew 25 infuses the notion of "caridad," the core of Christian life according to Gutiérrez, with consequential meanings in terms of political commitment.⁶

Liberation theology in the Global South covers a wide range of contextual topics except sex. This phenomenon results in an erotic crisis where the sexual desires, practices, and arrangements of the impoverished remain in the dark. There are several reasons for such development, but here I will name two. First, I have argued elsewhere that liberation theology resorts to Western notions of subjectivity, sex, and gender.⁷ Second, the call for political action and transformation relies on agape to exclude eros. Concerning the first topic, Breny Mendoza argues that "gender and patriarchy are social categories that have meaning only in Western epistemologies."⁸ Regarding the second, partly indebted to Marxist disregard for erotic life and partly due to the confessional setting of theological production, the realm of eros has been circumscribed to "vanilla sex."⁹ This chapter represents a modest attempt at blurring the hard lines between eros and agape, inviting queer sex into the realm of political love. I explore how specific queer practices satisfy the requirements of agape and how a queer reading of the biblical text offers a way to bridge the gap, pervasive in Christian ethics and philosophy, between eros and agape. Whereas the Matthean

---

5. Jon Sobrino, *Jesus in Latin America* (Eugene, OR: Wipf & Stock, 2004), 11; Gustavo Gutiérrez, *The Power of the Poor in History: Selected Writings* (Maryknoll, NY: Orbis Books, 1983), 142. Gutiérrez relates Matt 5 (the Beatitudes) with Matt 25: Jesus's teachings "begin with the blessing of the poor (Matthew 5); they end with the assertion that we meet Christ himself when we go out to the poor with concrete acts (Matthew 25). So the teaching of Jesus is framed in a context that moves from the poor to the poor" (Gutiérrez, "The Irruption of the Poor in Latin America and the Christian Communities of the Common People," in *The Challenge of Basic Christian Communities*, ed. S. Torres and J. Eagleson [Maryknoll, NY: Orbis Books, 1981], 121).

6. Gustavo Gutiérrez, *A Theology of Liberation: History, Politics, and Salvation* (Maryknoll, NY: Orbis Books, 1973), 5.

7. Menéndez-Antuña, "Bible and Sexuality Studies." See also chapter 6 below.

8. Breny Mendoza, "Colonialidad del género y epistemología del Sur," in *Ensayos de Crítica Feminista en Nuestra America* (Mexico: Herder, 2014), 57: "tanto el género como el patriarcado son categorías sociales que solo tienen sentido en las epistemologías occidentales." See also María Lugones, "Methodological Notes toward a Decolonial Feminism," in *Decolonizing Epistemologies: Latina/o Theology and Philosophy*, ed. Ada María Isasi-Díaz and Eduardo Mendieta (New York: Fordham University Press, 2011), 73.

9. Althaus-Reid, *Indecent Theology*, 52.

text stands as the exemplary scriptural text for agape, an intercontextual reading that focuses on how different texts and their contexts merge to produce contemporary meanings shows to what extent eros lurks in it. Is it possible for erotic practices to fulfill these ethical demands of agapic love?

At first sight, the answer to this question is no. Eros has played a marginal role in biblical exegesis in general and New Testament studies in particular.[10] The place of eros in Christian theology has always been contested,[11] not least because it is positioned as being at odds with agapic love, traditionally understood through Augustine's and Aquinas's rhetoric about *caritas*.[12] The relationship between different kinds of human and divine affection, love and sex, agape and eros, *philia* and *concupiscentia*, continues to flame debates on the origin, nature, and aims of love,[13] all the more so since contextual theologies have shifted the focus from the disembodied subject to the "desiring body."[14]

---

10. Eros occurs only twice in the Septuagint, where it is associated with unbridled passion (Prov 7:18; 30:16), and it is totally absent in the New Testament. See Pieter W. van der Horst, "Eros," *DDD*, 304–6. However, the Song of Songs has prompted important exegetical and theological work on the nature of erotic love. See Edmee Kingsmill, *The Song of Songs and the Eros of God: A Study in Biblical Intertextuality* (Oxford: Oxford University Press, 2009). Virginia Burrus and Stephen D. Moore, "Unsafe Sex: Feminism, Pornography, and the Song of Songs," *BibInt* 11 (2003): 24–52, has particularly inspired my arguments, my methodological moves, and my theoretical framework.

11. Origen seems to be an exception when in his *Commentary on the Song of Songs* he urges theologians to use eros to refer to God's love and Christians' love of God (R. P. Lawson, trans., *The Song of Songs: Commentary and Homilies*, ACW [Westminster, MD: Newman, 1957], 63–71).

12. Timothy P. Jackson, *The Priority of Love: Christian Charity and Social Justice* (Princeton: Princeton University Press, 2003), 1–2. Given the animosity toward and fear of eros, David McLain Carr sets as his goal "eros-positive reading of the Bible" (*The Erotic Word: Sexuality, Spirituality, and the Bible* (Oxford: Oxford University Press, 2003), 12).

13. Although I acknowledge that the definitional field of love and the taxonomies around the term are expansive and multidimensional, I focus exclusively on the contraposition between eros and agape as conceptualized in recent theological thought. See Paul J. Wadell, *The Primacy of Love: An Introduction to the Ethics of Thomas Aquinas* (New York: Paulist, 1992); Edward Collin Vacek, *Love, Human and Divine: The Heart of Christian Ethics* (Washington, DC: Georgetown University Press, 1994); and Timothy P. Jackson, *Love Disconsoled: Meditations on Christian Charity* (Cambridge: Cambridge University Press, 1999).

14. See Marcella Althaus-Reid, *The Queer God* (London: Routledge, 2003); Althaus-Reid, ed., *Liberation Theology and Sexuality* (Aldershot: Ashgate, 2006);

In Western Christian tradition, Augustine's distinction continues to frame the debate on love. In *Doctr. chr.* 3.10.15, Augustine argues that "scripture enjoins nothing except charity, and condemns nothing except lust" (trans. Shaw), then distinguishes between charity (*caritas*) and lust (*cupiditas*):

> I mean by charity [*caritatem*] that affection of the mind [*motum animi*] which aims at the enjoyment of God for His own sake, and the enjoyment of one's self and one's neighbor in subordination to God; by lust [*cupiditas*] I mean that affection of the mind [*motum animi*] which aims at enjoying one's self and one's neighbor, and other corporeal things, without reference to God. Again, what lust [*cupiditas*], when unsubdued, does towards corrupting one's own soul and body, is called vice; but what it does to injure another is called crime. And these are the two classes into which all sins may be divided. (*Doctr. chr.* 3.10.16 [Shaw])

For Augustine, concupiscence (*concupiscentia*) leads us away from God toward material things and inevitably to the soul submitting to the body's rule. Lust (*cupiditas*) is not merely a bodily desire; it is an affection that taints every sexual act.[15] Although Augustine is known for stressing the difference between vertical (divine) and horizontal (neighbor) love and for his distrust in human flesh, he offers a redemptive view of eros: it can be uplifted and become *caritas* or devolve into *cupiditas*.[16] The fallen erotic subject tends to turn the other into the self unless the always-divine agapic love aids her.[17]

Virginia Burrus and Catherine Keller, eds., *Toward a Theology of Eros: Transfiguring Passion at the Limits of Discipline* (New York: Fordham University Press, 2006); and LeRon Shults and Jan-Olav Henriksen, eds., *Saving Desire: The Seduction of Christian Theology* (Grand Rapids: Eerdmans, 2011).

15. John C. Cavadini, "Feeling Right: Augustine on the Passions and Sexual Desire," *AugStud* 36 (2005): 196. Timo Nisula further argues that for Augustine *cupiditas* and *concupiscentia* have similar meanings (Nisula, *Augustine and the Functions of Concupiscentia* [Leiden: Brill, 2012], 190–91).

16. See Hannah Arendt, *Love and Saint Augustine* (Chicago: University of Chicago Press, 1996).

17. For Augustine's doctrine on *caritas* and his subtle distinctions with *cupiditas*, see David Tracy, "The Divided Consciousness of Augustine on Eros," in *Erotikon: Essays on Eros, Ancient and Modern*, ed. Shadi Bartsch and Thomas Bartscherer (Chicago: University of Chicago Press, 2005), 91–106; and Nisula, *Augustine and the Functions*, 50. Nisula also points out that these terms are not deployed unequivocally and

In *Agape and Eros*, Anders Nygren dramatically recasts the distinction between both kinds of love: agape as the unconditional love from God and fully explained in the gospels, and eros as the love for the beautiful, "the love of desire."[18] Augustine, Nygren argues, set out to combine the incompatible, for *caritas* cannot subsume a type of love that cannot eliminate the self.[19] Only Luther achieved a complete theological understanding of the need to safeguard the agapic unconditionality of God as an expression of God's total sovereignty.[20]

Nygren's arguments rest on a simplistic opposition between pagan philosophy and Christian theology, body and soul, downward and upward movements, God- and human-centered love, and selfless and egocentric affection. Recent scholarship has thoroughly criticized these binaries by exposing Nygren's biased understanding of the gospels and the tradition. Christian theology, says Nygren, should be exclusively a theology of agape.[21]

---

that a diachronic study of Augustine's work shows an evolutionary semantics. For instance, *concupiscentia* and *cupiditas* do not always have, contrary to what Jackson's reading suggests, a negative connotation.

18. For a philological/exegetical distinction in the New Testament, see Ceslas Spicq, *Agape in the New Testament* (St. Louis: Herder, 1963). See also Anders Nygren, *Agape and Eros: A Study of the Christian Idea of Love,* trans. A. G. Hebert and Philip S. Watson (London: SPCK, 1932).

19. Thomas J. Oord, *The Nature of Love: A Theology* (St. Louis: Chalice, 2010), 35–38.

20. For a critique of Nygren's view on Luther's theology of love, see Tuomo Mannermaa and Kirsi Irmeli Stjerna, eds., *Two Kinds of Love: Martin Luther's Religious World* (Minneapolis: Fortress, 2010).

21. Nygren interprets Augustine's Platonism at variance with his Christianity. See John Burnaby, *Amor Dei: A Study of the Religion of St. Augustine; The Hulsean Lectures for 1938* (London: Hodder & Stoughton, 1938); Victorino Capánaga, "Interpretación Agustianiana del amor: Eros y agape," *Augustinus* 18 (1973): 211–22; Josef Pieper, *Faith, Hope, Love* (San Francisco: Ignatius Press, 1997). Despite Nygren's dichotomic approach, he continues to be the point of reference in contemporary debates on the implications of pitting eros and agape against each other (Timothy P. Jackson, *Political Agape: Christian Love and Liberal Democracy* [Grand Rapids: Eerdmans, 2015], 252–54, 259–62). See also Colin Grant, "For the Love of God: Agapē," *JRE* 24 (1996): 3–21; and the responses to Grant in Carter Heyward, "Lamenting the Loss of Love: A Response to Colin Grant," *JRE* 24 (1996): 23–28; Edward Collin Vacek, "Love, Christian and Diverse: A Response to Colin Grant," *JRE* 24 (1996) 29–34; and Gene Outka, "Theocentric Agape and the Self: An Asymmetrical Affirmation in Response to Colin Grant's Either/Or," *JRE* 24 (1996): 35–42. On the other side of the spectrum, defend-

Contemporary theologians and philosophers continue to reflect on the relationship between agape and eros as they construct a balanced theology capable of accounting for Christian love's horizontal and vertical dimensions. For instance, Timothy P. Jackson compares Freud and Augustine and concludes that agape is essential to Christianity because it is the condition of possibility for every other kind of love, whether it is eros or *philia*. Only the kind of love from God (agape) can offer a real beginning because only God's *kenosis* can foreground a "pathos-filled service of neighbor characteristic of Christian ethics."[22]

Freud's take on eros as the only type of love due to agape's delusional universality and unconditionality, Jackson argues, finds its Christian response in Augustine's schooling of natural desire (*amor*) away from investment in material things (*cupiditas*) and toward communion with God (*caritas*).[23] Eros, as Nygren and others show, is traditionally understood as a type of love that is partial toward the beautiful and attractive subject, whereas agape, as Jackson further explains, is unconditional and operates regardless of the subject's self-worth. Whereas eros is conditional and justice is neutral and inclusive, agape is "prejudiced in favor of everybody."[24] From these preliminary observations, one could easily conclude that, although agape and eros need not be opposite (contra Nygren), they hardly complement each other.[25] They might not be enemies, but they are not bedfellows either.

---

ing the sufficiency of eros, see Alan Soble, *The Structure of Love* (New Haven: Yale University Press, 1990).

Yet some philosophers envision eros as capable of helping the subject in overcoming personal, political, and economic obstacles. Marcuse theorizes eros as an energy that will develop as society allows for more phantasies and polymorphous sexualities. Once eros is freed, it will eroticize the entire personality, breaking free of a repressive, production-centered civilization. In such a utopia, eros and agape will become the same. See Herbert Marcuse, *Eros and Civilization: A Philosophical Inquiry into Freud* (Boston: Beacon, 1966), 49.

22. Jackson, *Love Disconsoled,* 90. For similar conclusions from an exegetical perspective, see James Barr, "Words for Love in Biblical Greek," in *The Glory of Christ in the New Testament: Studies in Christology in Memory of George Bradford Caird,* ed. L. D. Hurst and N. T. Wright (Oxford: Oxford University Press, 1987), 10.

23. Jackson, *Love Disconsoled,* 65.

24. Jackson, *Priority of Love,* 68–69.

25. The debate extends to philosophy. For instance, Jacques Derrida emphasizes that agapic love, in the form of the gift, ought to be unconditional, unacknowledged, and unreciprocated, so the act skips any possible economic calculation (Derrida, *The*

Augustine's conceptualization of *cupiditas* as a motion that can lead to *caritas* is riddled with ambiguities, for, as Jackson points out, it does not define the love for the neighbor or creation as an end in itself.[26] Only agape, Jackson further elaborates, as a supernatural virtue, can ground the love for the Other as unconditional.[27] For Jackson, then, whereas eros concerns itself with otherness based on its (perishable) excellence, agape evinces universality regardless of merit, hence its foundationalism.[28] The priority of agapic love over any other kind of love, including eros, derives from its unconditionality as much as its regard for the Other's well-being and openness to self-sacrifice.[29] Such priority is chronological in that such kind of care is the first thing we receive as infants; it is axiological in that, without it, we cannot develop into responsible individuals, lexical in that it gives us access to other human goods, and, finally, ethical because agapic care makes others caring.

Jackson's project is to account for agape as a metavalue, a virtue grounding any other "moral or nonmoral" good.[30] My argument does not contend against such an overarching account of love's origins and goals. Still, my contribution pictures, via a specific example, how it is virtually impossible to separate agapic love from its erotic undertones. In other words, by teasing out the erotic undertones of a supposedly pure caritative action, I point at the problematic nature of delinking agape from eros.[31] Although Jackson does not use Matt 25 to support his theological reflection on love, one can hardly find a better biblically based example to explore love as *caritas*/agape.

Jackson's multivolume theorization of the priority of agape fits within contemporary scholarship on love that accounts for the traditionally con-

---

Gift of Death, trans. David Wills [Chicago: University of Chicago Press, 1995], 97). Jean-Luc Marion critiques Derrida's unilaterality by proposing a phenomenology of love that takes reciprocity into account, blurring the distinction between agape and eros. For Marion, the lover needs to hope to be loved back, demanding a response in order to confirm that her love is real love (Marion, *The Erotic Phenomenon* [Chicago: University of Chicago Press, 2007], 221).

26. Jackson, *Priority of Love*, 68–69.
27. Jackson, *Political Agape*, 42.
28. Jackson, *Priority of Love*, 1–27, 68–69.
29. Jackson, *Priority of Love*, 10.
30. Jackson, *Priority of Love*, 10.
31. This is not to argue that, at the philosophical and theological level, Jackson's case for "the priority of love" is misled. My contribution hints at the fact that, even if that is the case—that is, the ontological priority of agape—the examples we use to ground such priority are riddled with erotic undertones.

flicted relationship between agape and eros. Such contribution explores concepts, notions, and experiences that bridge the gap between both kinds of love. I offer here a queer reading of agapic love as expressed in Matt 25:31–46 by reading Christian *caritas* through the lenses of Roman *caritas* and its pictorial representation by Peter Paul Rubens. I explore in contextual fashion what insights contemporary experiences of bondage and S&M, as examples of queer experience, may offer to the theological reflection on agapic/erotic love. If one could accuse theology of not giving eros its due credit, one could also chastise queer theory for having undertheorized agape. While love plays a surprisingly small role in the conceptual debates on queer desire, theology recently has started to think about eros—and its cognates, such as desire, lust, and passion—in productive ways. What are the implications of situating eros at the center of a paradigmatic text of Christian charitable love (Matt 25:31–46)?

My goal is twofold. First, in intertextual fashion, I show how the agapic ethical demands in Matt 25:31–46 can be fulfilled by a queer act, specifically that of a woman breast-feeding a starving man, as depicted in the motif of *Caritas Romana*. Second, in contextual fashion, I suggest ways in which contemporary queer bondage practices fulfill Christian charity. Such a theoretical and hermeneutical exercise is queer in three different ways. First, from a methodological standpoint, I use queer criticism not only as an optic that, as now traditionally understood, pushes back against "regimes of the normal"[32] but more specifically as a hermeneutical approach that estranges textual meaning from traditional understandings and offers unorthodox, bizarre, "against the grain" readings—in this case revealing how erotic practices can fulfill Matthew's ethical demands, thus unexpectedly situating eros at the center of agape.

Second, thematically I conceive of contemporary queer practices as ethically significant rather than as merely pleasurable experiences. Bondage redefines notions of the body and imagines new ways of relating to each other, which has important implications for how scholars think about love.[33] By reading the biblical text in contextual fashion from the experience of S&M, I show how specific sexual practices transform and disrupt

---

32. Michael Warner, "Introduction," in *Fear of a Queer Planet: Queer Politics and Social Theory*, ed. Michael Warner (Minneapolis: University of Minnesota Press, 1993), xxvi.

33. As I shall show, going back to Michel Foucault, sexuality can be used "to arrive at a multiplicity of relationships" (Foucault, "Friendship as a Way of Life," trans.

traditional considerations of agapic love. S&M, notes Mark Jordan, poses a challenge for the most "liberal" Christian ethics.³⁴ My contribution suggests a way out of this dilemma by demonstrating how the gospel precepts are, in fact, fulfilled by those practices.

Third, from a historiographical perspective, a queer optic offers an intercontextual reading that explores virtual connections across periods, frustrating the grasp that historical-critical, literary, and sociological studies hold on the biblical text. Queer historicism here seeks to transcend authorial intention and intended audience as the exclusive criteria to understand, explain, or expand textual meaning, and it does so through the lens of artistic representation.³⁵ I use queer practices of bondage as portals to historical thinking.³⁶ Consequently, I read Matthew, Valerius Maximus's texts, and Peter Paul Rubens's pictorial representation intertextually as building blocks of an erotohistoriography that traces and brings together pleasurable and loving experiences to imagine eros and agape as mutually complementary in the present.³⁷

In sum, my exegetical argument and hermeneutical moves constitute an exercise in queer imagination, a contextual interpretation that summons bondage as a practice that allows the contemporary reader to move from text to representation and vice versa, back and forth from the biblical past to the queer present. Although my argument refrains from making historical claims about first-century notions of erotic and agapic love, since Christian ideas of agape travel across time and space, I argue that they are susceptible to reappropriation in the present to envision new ways of loving, relating, and pleasuring each other.

Matthew 25:31–46 and Its Ethical Underpinnings

Matthew 25:31–46 and its equation of love for Jesus with love for the disenfranchised occupies a central role in Christianity's elaboration of

---

John Johnston, in *Foucault Live: Collected Interviews, 1961–1984*, ed. Sylvère Lotringer [New York: Semiotext(e), 1996], 308).

34. Mark Jordan, *The Ethics of Sex* (Malden, MA: Blackwell, 2002), 167.

35. Martin, *Sex and the Single Savior*, 149–85.

36. Elizabeth Freeman, "Time Binds, or, Erotohistoriography," *Social Text* 23.3–4 (2005): 59.

37. Elizabeth Freeman, *Time Binds: Queer Temporalities, Queer Histories* (Durham, NC: Duke University Press, 2010), 95–136.

caritas as a form of love that comes from God and pours into the Other.³⁸ The pericope supported the theological elaboration known as "the seven works of mercy," including Tobit's "burying the dead."³⁹ Still today, the text provides theological grounding for Christianity-inspired activism and charity. Especially within the Catholic tradition, one can find myriads of communities, groups, journals and magazines, awards, and charity projects named "Matthew 25." Given its implied link between judgment, salvation, and care for impoverished people,⁴⁰ it is hardly surprising that the pericope plays a central role in liberationist theologies that focus on "political love."⁴¹ The material emphasis placed on hunger, thirst, impris-

---

38. Gary A. Anderson, *Charity: The Place of the Poor in the Biblical Tradition* (New Haven: Yale University Press, 2013), 149–61.

39. Suzanne Roberts, "Contexts of Charity in the Middle Ages: Religious, Social, and Civic," in *Contexts of Charity in the Middle Ages: Religious, Social, and Civic*, ed. Jerome B. Schneewind (Bloomington: Indiana University Press, 1996), 24–53. The seven corporeal works of mercy slowly consolidated in the Catholic tradition: feed the hungry, give drink to the thirsty, shelter the homeless, clothe the naked, visit the sick, visit the imprisoned, and bury the dead. They became paired with the spiritual works: give good counsel, teach the ignorant, admonish sinners, console the afflicted, pardon offenses and injuries, bear offenses with patience, and pray for the living and the dead. In parallel we encounter seven sacraments (baptism, confirmation, Eucharist, penance and reconciliation, anointing of the sick, holy orders, and matrimony) and seven deadly sins (lust, gluttony, greed, sloth, wrath, envy, and pride), which in turn are in opposition to the seven virtues (chastity, temperance, charity, diligence, kindness, patience, and humility). See James Keenan, *The Works of Mercy: The Heart of Catholicism* (Plymouth, UK: Rowman & Littlefield, 2008). See an analysis of the influence of Matt 25 in Jon Sobrino's theology in Todd Walatka, "Principle of Mercy: Jon Sobrino and the Catholic Theological Tradition," *TS* 77 (2016): 96–117.

40. See Gutiérrez, *Theology of Liberation*, 194; Leonardo Boff, *Jesus Christ Liberator: A Critical Christology for Our Time* (Maryknoll, NY: Orbis Books, 1978), 71–72; and Esther D. Reed, "Refugee Rights and State Sovereignty: Theological Perspectives on the Ethics of Territorial Borders," *Journal for the Society of Christian Ethics* 30 (2010): 59–78.

41. Given that liberation theology has thoroughly theorized the political, economic, and religious power imbalances between the North and the South, a text built upon the separation between nations according to their righteousness offers the perfect biblical support to understand sin in its political consequences. See Enrique D. Dussel, *Historia de la filosofía latinoamericana y filosofía de la liberación* (Bogatá: Editorial Nueva América, 1994), 120; Pedro Casaldáliga and José M. Vigil, *Espiritualidad de la liberación* (Managua: Editorial Envio, 1992), 53; and Sobrino, *Jesus in Latin America*.

onment, exile, sickness, and nakedness hinders spiritual renderings of virtue,[42] while the identification of the "Son of Man" with the "least of these" biblically grounds a Christology from and for the disenfranchised. Such prophetic reading, in the words of liberation theologians themselves, is also granted because, as many commentators have noted, Matt 25:35–36 is a paraphrase of Isa 58:7 where, in the context of a call to fasting, the prophet explains how proper worship includes "divid[ing] your bread with the hungry, bring[ing] the homeless poor into the house, [and] cover[ing] the naked when you see him," thus providing the evangelist with a scriptural basis to weave together discipleship, worship, and care for the poor.[43] The list is probably more illustrative than comprehensive, thus strengthening the agapic nature of its injunctions.[44]

Scholars have traditionally focused on the identity of the beneficiaries. To whom is Matthew referring by "the least of these"? Ulrich Luz charts a threefold approach in the tradition. First, the *universal interpretation* considers that the criterion for judgment is the works of charity done to the impoverished, as liberationist theologies agree. Second, the *classic interpretation* identifies "my lowliest brothers" with the Christian community and consequently locates the criterion for salvation in how Christians relate to less-favored Christians. Third, *exclusive interpretations* envision a final judgment in which the pagans are judged according to how they have treated Christians.[45] The most common interpretation identifies the beneficiaries with the Christian community itself. For instance, Joong Suk Suh locates the text's binarism of sheep and goats within a broader Matthean concern for those missionaries (identified as sheep) within the community not sufficiently supported by their fellow

---

42. For a sociohistorical analysis of food politics in the Gospel of Matthew that grants a materialist reading of the pericope, see Carol Bakker Wilson, *For I Was Hungry and You Gave Me Food: Pragmatics of Food Access in the Gospel of Matthew* (Eugene, OR: Pickwick, 2014).

43. For a literary analysis of the relationship between Matthew and Isaiah, see Robert H. Gundry, *Matthew: A Commentary on His Handbook for a Mixed Church under Persecution* (Grand Rapids: Eerdmans, 1994), 513–16.

44. Rudolf Schnackenburg, *The Gospel of Matthew* (Grand Rapids: Eerdmans, 2002), 257–58.

45. See Ulrich Luz, *Matthew 21–28: A Commentary*, Hermeneia (Minneapolis: Fortress, 2005), 268–75; Sherman W. Gray, *The Least of My Brothers: Matthew 25, 31–46; A History of Interpretation*, SBLDS 114 (Atlanta: Scholars Press, 1989).

Christians (goats).⁴⁶ The pericope strengthens the identification of Jesus with the underdogs (or rather sheep) while encouraging the goats to support them materially.⁴⁷ In sum, the Matthean emphasis on righteousness and salvation has sent scholars on a quest to identify the "least of my brothers," which, in turn, hinges on identifying who is meant by the sheep and the goats.⁴⁸

Beyond the debate around the "benefactors" and "beneficiaries," Matt 25:31–46 condenses the pedagogical purpose of the gospel. It encourages its readers "to recognize the rigor of the divine demand, with its imperative to observe all that has been commanded (28:20), lest any believer be caught in the position of the goats at the judgment, shockingly unaware of God's requirements."⁴⁹ The ideal disciple is to shape her behavior after the "boundary-breaking acts of mercy that Jesus has modeled,"⁵⁰ situating the injunction to care for the disenfranchised within the exclusive realm of agapic love.

Scholarly interpretations of the biblical pericope take for granted that the pericope works with an exclusively agapic concept of love. Contextual theologies that focus on the body as a source of pleasure obviate the Matthean text as a source to theorize the erotic nature of love.⁵¹ Matthew 25:31–46 is consequently papered over in the debates around agape/eros

---

46. Joong Suk Suh, "Das Weltgericht und di Matthäische Gemeinde," *NovT* 48 (2006): 217–33.

47. See Alicia Vargas, "Who Ministers to Whom: Matthew 25:31–46 and Prison Ministry," *Dialog* 52 (2013): 128–37; Sigurd Grindheim, "Ignorance Is Bliss: Attitudinal Aspects of Judgment according to Works in Matthew 25:31–46," *NovT* 50 (2008): 313–31. "The lowliest" have traditionally been identified with the Christian community (Frederick Dale Bruner, *Matthew: A Commentary*, rev. ed., 2 vols. [Grand Rapids: Eerdmans, 2004], 2:564, 575).

48. See George Strecker, *Der Weg der Gerechtigkeit: Untersuchung zur Theologie des Matthäus* (Göttingen: Vanderhoeck & Ruprecht, 1971), 226–32; Benno Przybylski, *Righteousness in Matthew and His World of Thought* (Cambridge: Cambridge University Press, 1980); and Frank J. Matera, *New Testament Ethics: The Legacies of Jesus and Paul* (Louisville: Westminster John Knox, 1996), 36–65.

49. Kathleen Weber, "The Image of Sheep and Goats in Matthew 25:31–46," *CBQ* 59 (1997): 674.

50. Grindheim, "Ignorance Is Bliss," 331.

51. A comprehensive survey of the history of reception confirms that the pericope has never been studied from an erotic perspective. See Gray, *Least of My Brothers*, 331–64.

because it reads as purely agapic. There is no room for eros, it seems, in the selfless actions of *caritas*.

In the following two sections, I offer a queer supplement to this understanding of gospel ethics as exclusively agapic. First, I introduce the myth of Pero and Cimon as a parallel tradition that represents *Caritas Romana*, and I expand its meaning by dwelling on its pictorial representation by Rubens in the seventeenth century. I demonstrate how the action, first narrated by Valerius Maximus and then re-presented by Rubens, fulfills Matthew's agapic demands. Such an intertextual approach is an erotohistoriographical exercise understood as a search across time and space for configurations of bodily pleasures that may or may not inhabit our present. The task of queering the gospel here takes the shape of an intertextual approach that conceives of *caritas* as an umbrella that brings together different thematic renderings of it to illuminate the contemporary debate on agape/eros. Second, I offer a queer reading of those sources to advance a contextual queer/kinky reading of the text that takes the practice of bondage as its point of departure. An intertextual reading of *caritas* creates a plethora of different meanings that are, in turn, read from the contextual experience of bondage. S&M is here a theological locus that filters through the surplus of historically produced significations and suggests a supplementary reading that renders the Matthean pericope as an injunction to love erotically.

Queering *Caritas Christiana* through *Caritas Romana*

Valerius Maximus, a first-century Roman writer, inaugurates the tradition of Roman charity by narrating how the young Pero visits her father, Myco (later known as Cimon), who has been condemned to starve to death in prison. She secretly breast-feeds him and thus saves his life. The guards discover her and, impressed by her altruism, forgive and release her father.[52] The episode, known as *Caritas Romana*, was famous in Roman art; even-

---

52. Valerius Maximus actually narrates two stories of women breast-feeding a parent. In the first episode the daughter breast-feeds her mother; in the second she breast-feeds her father. Only the last one became known as *Caritas Romana* and was widely reproduced in the visual arts. Such development is not without certain irony because the author terms it an "external" or "foreign" example (Valerius Maximus, *Fact.* 5.4 and ext. 1).

tually, the Renaissance and the Baroque would rescue it for aesthetic and theological reasons.[53]

Peter Paul Rubens (1577–1640) created a version of *Caritas Romana* salient for its erotic undertones. The erotohistoriographical task of tracing pleasurable experiences across time and space finds in Rubens's representation a paradigmatic building block to explore the connections of *caritas* and *eros*. Rubens, a proponent of an extravagant and voluptuous Baroque style, is known for emphasizing movement and color and most notably for his sensual representation of the human body, especially his ample women.[54] *Cimon and Pero* (fig. 3.1) portrays Pero as richly clothed, sitting on a socle, absent in ecstasy as she breast-feeds her father. Pero is a fleshy woman with an elaborate hairdo and a distinctive pale skin tone. Cimon, for his part, appears half-naked (notably muscular, given the fact that he is starving), with bound hands and feet, and visibly focused on obtaining the nourishing milk from his daughter's breast. Two guards observe the scene through the cell's window.

Rubens's representation shares many features with other depictions of the Roman theme. A pyramid-like arrangement of the characters enhances the narrative because Cimon necessarily ought to be placed at the level of Pero's breasts, with his hands fettered at the back. There is usually an accentuated contrast between the light coming out of the characters, especially Pero, and the darkness typical of the prison setting. *Caritas Romana*, after all, is a story about life on the verge of death, light amid darkness, hope amid despair. Pero's garments are rich in detail and color, signaling, materially, a wealthy woman but also, symbolically, an exuberant womanhood, whereas Cimon's tunic is simple and torn, depicting his powerlessness. Despite these similarities, Rubens's take on the myth is also unique for several reasons. Besides the stylistic features so typically Rubenesque, three peculiarities render this representation unique. First, the soldiers in the background, acting as witnesses, signal the voyeuristic nature of the main act. Compositionally, they add depth and perspective

---

53. Robert Rosenblum, "Caritas Romana after 1760: Some Romantic Lactations," in *Woman as Sex Object: Studies in Erotic Art*, ed. Thomas B. Hess and Linda Nochlin (New York: Newsweek, 1972), 46–63.

54. Tine Meganck, Sabine van Sprang, Inga Rossi-Schrimpf, and Marie-Andrée Lambert, "Rubens on the Human Figure: Theory, Practice and Metaphysics," in *Rubens on the Human Figure: Theory, Practice and Metaphysics*, ed. Joost vander Auwera (Tielt: Lannoo, 2007), 52–64.

Peter Paul Rubens, *Cimon and Pero (Roman Charity)*, 1630–1640, oil on canvas, 155 cm x 190 cm. Courtesy of Rijksmuseum, Amsterdam.

to the scene, whereas thematically they mark a contrast between the intimate setting of the main act and their role as representatives of the public domain. Second, Pero's gaze is expressive and ambiguous and her sexuality overemphasized.[55] Third, Cimon's deportment is inexpressive, impassive, almost inscrutable.[56] How does Pero and Cimon's depiction fit the broader

---

55. Pero is always depicted as focusing on her breast or clearly concerned about not being watched. See, for instance, the theme of *Caritas Romana* authored by Jan Janssens (1620–1625, Real Academia de San Fernando, Madrid), Dirck Van Baburen (ca. 1623, York Art Gallery, York,), Charles Mellin (ca. 1628, Musee du Louvre, Paris), Giovanni Andrea Sirani (ca. 1660, private collection), Giovanni Domenico Cerrini (ca. 1670, Fondazione Cassa di Risparmio di Perugia, Perugia), Jean-Baptiste Greuze (ca. 1767, the J. Paul Getty Museum, Los Angeles), Johan Zoffany (ca. 1769, National Gallery of Victoria, Melbourne), and Rembrandt Peale (1811, Smithsonian American Art Museum, Washington, D.C.).

56. These features are even more salient if compared to other representations of *Caritas Romana* by Rubens, for example, a version hanging in the Hermitage dated to approximately 1612. Although both pictures share many artistic features, including color palette, composition, and light distribution, a swift comparison throws into relief the erotic emphasis of the copy displayed at the Rijksmuseum. The Hermitage piece, like most representations, features a Pero specially concerned with squeezing

Rubenesque gender ideology, and what representational features contribute to our debate?

Pero's overtly sexualized features and Cimon's stoic portrayal are part of a wider artistic style in which gender representation follows a scripted pattern, as Lisa Rosenthal shows. Inspired by Lipsius's neo-Stoicism, Rubens reflects coeval gender ideologies while rendering them unstable.[57] He defines family by the absent figure of the father who belongs to a different realm of activity, the state.[58] Family takes shape around the figure of the mother, the absent father being the condition of possibility of the familial bond.[59]

The troubled relationship between mother and fatherhood evinces a deeper problem in Rubens's representation of the relationship between masculinity and femininity. Rosenthal demonstrates how Rubens understands masculinity as the ability to master one's appetites, "as the need to either subjugate or pull away from the dangers of feminine seduction,"[60] and as the demand to defeat other men in agonistic fashion.[61] Mastery of the self is the moral basis for the masculine figure that claims to rule the ideal state. The traditionally observed link between femininity and sexuality/domesticity and between masculinity and statehood/public does not entail an impervious construction of masculinity.[62] For instance, when analyzing Rubens's diptych of Hercules (*Hercules Crowned by Victory*; *Drunken Hercules*), Rosenthal notices how the drunken Hercules "is not simply a negative and devalued opposite to the crowned Hero but also exposes to us the fragility of the heroic construction of masculinity."[63] The phallic symbol in *Hercules Crowned by Victory* is taken away by the child in *Drunken Hercules*, throwing into relief the crisis in the representation of *virtus* typified

---

milk out of her breast and a Cimon defeated, moribund, slowly coming back to life as he gets the nourishment needed.

57. Lisa Rosenthal, *Gender, Politics, and Allegory in the Art of Rubens* (New York: Cambridge University Press, 2005), 81–86.

58. Rosenthal, *Gender, Politics, and Allegory*, 30.

59. Rosenthal, *Gender, Politics, and Allegory*, 31. Rosenthal further argues that Rubens defines family as a sentimental unit based on the mother-child bond. Fatherhood only contributes to that definition as the outsider (Rosenthal, *Gender, Politics, and Allegory*, 46).

60. Rosenthal, *Gender, Politics, and Allegory*, 79.

61. Rosenthal, *Gender, Politics, and Allegory*, 78.

62. Rosenthal, *Gender, Politics, and Allegory*, 85.

63. Rosenthal, *Gender, Politics, and Allegory*, 104.

"as a choice between domination over others or infantilizing dependence on them."[64] Hercules, it seems, can enter the feminine realm only at the expense of appearing emasculated and infantilized.[65] If masculinity is then exclusively achieved and maintained by dominating women or by fleeing from them into war, one wonders how we should interpret Cimon's total state of emasculation.

On the one hand, Rubens's piece of art cannot overcome the constraining limits of the plot. In *Caritas Romana*, his stereotypical notions of gender difference are toned down, for masculinity, as the myth goes, requires femininity for its vital survival: it is impossible to picture an aging and starving father as a paradigm of masculinity. On the other hand, Rubens accentuates the imperiling power of femininity and sexuality, building on the topos of the *Weibermacht*.[66] Pero's exultant sexuality manifests in the disclosure of her breasts and her look of rapture, her superior position, and her command of the scene, epitomizing an idea of femininity not only overtly sexual but exceedingly threatening.[67] Rubens here seems to be reworking the Petrarchan notion that the male lover needs to "step down" as a condition of entering the marital institution.[68] Although such an institution is missing here, Cimon's impassive attitude transpires a bodily resistance to the demeaning, emasculating action of being submitted to a woman's breast. Pero's pleasure, loose body, and elated demeanor oppose Cimon's *virtus,* understood as his stoic resistance to giving himself over to the feminine charm.[69] Cimon's (surprisingly) muscular tone is an antidote to the supposedly complete emasculation occurring by Pero's actions in the role of "the phallic woman/mother."[70]

---

64. Rosenthal, *Gender, Politics, and Allegory*, 105.

65. Rosenthal, *Gender, Politics, and Allegory*, 110.

66. Rosenthal, *Gender, Politics, and Allegory*, 126.

67. Ian Maclean, *The Renaissance Notion of Woman: A Study in the Fortunes of Scholasticism and Medical Science in European Intellectual Life* (Cambridge: Cambridge University Press, 1980), vii.

68. Rosenthal, *Gender, Politics, and Allegory*, 123.

69. None of these features appear in the Hermitage version (Metropolitan Museum of Art, *Dutch and Flemish Paintings from the Hermitage* [New York: Metropolitan Museum of Art, 1988], 102–3).

70. See Sabine Sielke, "Phallic Mother," in *Encyclopedia of Feminist Literary Theory*, ed. Elizabeth Kowalewski-Wallace (New York: Garland, 1997), 432; Sylvie Gambaudo, "We Need to Talk About Eva: The Demise of the Phallic Mother," *Janus Head* 12 (2011): 155–68.

The interpretation of Pero as an overly sexual "top" woman is not the only possible one. Rubens's Cimon and Pero closely resemble many other Christian-themed artistic representations in which Mary breastfeeds Jesus or a Madonna nurtures several infants. The function of the breast as a life-giving, nurturing organ definitely renders *Caritas Romana*, thematically and representationally, close to *Caritas Christiana*. Breasts symbolize the nurturing nature of motherhood, from its biological function to the most sublime religious meaning. Consequently, as they epitomize motherly love, they are the ideal embodiment of agape.[71] Jackson, for instance, sees in Guido Reni's *Charity*, painted around the same period as Rubens's piece, a classic example of agapic love. In Jackson's view, the mother's relation to the middle child symbolizes agapic unconditionality, whereas the second infant—supported by the Madonna's left hand—stands for "love's passionate disposition to serve, its willingness to give of the self's very substance to nurture another in need."[72] One could reasonably argue that Pero's breasts fall under this economy of love, for she carefully holds Cimon with her left hand while lovingly directing him to her nurturing fluid with her right one.[73] Since the Christian theme inspires, both thematically and compositionally, most representations of the Roman myth during and after the Renaissance, we can conclude that *Caritas Romana* complies with the demands of *Caritas Christiana*.[74]

The nurturing breast is an essential part of the Roman myth and of Rubens's painting mainly because Cimon's survival depends on it.[75]

---

71. Marilyn Yalom, *A History of the Breast* (New York: Knopf, 1997), 9–48.

72. Jackson, *Love Disconsoled*, 17.

73. Pero's might be thought to resemble Mary's milk, which was thought to have miraculous healing powers (Dyan Elliott, *Fallen Bodies: Pollution, Sexuality, and Demonology in the Middle Ages* [Philadelphia: University of Pennsylvania Press, 1999], 115; Miri Rubin, *Mother of God: A History of the Virgin Mary* [New Haven: Yale University Press, 2009], 211–16).

74. In fact, most representations of the *Caritas Romana* scene hinder erotic undertones. In some cases the Christian inspiration is literal, as when the artist features a baby (e.g., Carlo Cignani, *Cimon and Pero*, ca. 1690–1700, Kunsthistorisches Museum Vienna). In other instances, the artist plays subtly with erotic motifs, as in *Caritas Romana* by Jean-Jacques Bachelier, where, as Robert Rosenblum ("Caritas Romana after 1760," 44) argues, the daughter-father composition is invested with an eroticism bordering on incest.

75. Yalom, *A History of the Breast*, 6.

However, Rubens's exclusive artistic and thematic features grant and even call for a supplementary reading: Pero's rapturous gaze into the distance, Rubens's luxurious portrayal of her femininity, and the gender dynamics whereby two adults (as opposed to a woman and infant) are interacting calls for an understanding of the act of love beyond its agapic and nurturing function. To be sure, Pero resembles a *décolleté* Renaissance-style Madonna, but in her posture, gaze, and demeanor she looks like typical Baroque ecstasy-filled representations. In other words, the nurturing breast does not account for Rubens's conception of sexual difference in general and Pero's sexualized undertones in particular.[76]

Yet oversexualization does not equate with eroticization. The hypersexualized representation of the female body does not necessarily imply *jouissance*. Rubens's mystification of sexual violence cautions against drawing unambiguous interpretations of Pero's demeanor.[77] What I interpret as erotic ecstasy could also possibly be absentmindedness, shame or, given Cimon's objectifying gaze, resistance. These alternative readings, on the one hand, complicate univocal interpretations of the artistic scene and, on the other, suggest ways in which S&M synthesizes conflicting conceptualizations of the body and desire.

First, Pero could be a wet nurse. No interpretation or commentary considers the fact that Pero may not be a mother and consequently is not ready to breast-feed naturally. Only women who are actively breast-feeding (typically a baby) produce milk that typically "lets down" when they think of the child. Pero's "absentmindedness" could actually depict her thinking of her child so that milk comes out. The agapic action of feeding her moribund father is enabled by the mental disposition of fabricating milk by thinking of the nonexistent/absent infant.

Second, Pero could be a daughter, which would give the picture incestuous overtones. In this reading, the fulfillment of her filial duties does not hinder the shame that comes from experiencing the sexual pleasure sometimes associated with breast-feeding. Pero's agapic action throws into

---

76. As Klaske Muizelaar and Derek L. Phillips put it, "the viewer's attention is drawn to a part of the body associated with sex and sensuality" (*Picturing Men and Women in the Dutch Golden Age: Paintings and People in Historical Perspective* [New Haven: Yale University Press, 2003], 104).

77. Margaret D. Carroll, "The Erotics of Absolutism: Rubens and the Mystification of Sexual Violence," *Representations* 25 (1989): 3–30.

relief the inescapable grasp of eros in that eroticism surfaces even when sexual desire is not invoked.[78]

Third, Pero could be resisting Cimon's fixating gaze. Driven by her filial obligations, according to this reading, Pero is split between filial duties and aversion to giving herself up. Her resistance is a psychological mechanism to prevent blame or shame or to avoid a total surrender to the objectifying gaze of the male. Agape implies here, from Pero's perspective, no more than a mechanical act of providing the father with the material means for survival. In other words, resistance is a way to stress her duties as a daughter and disavow her objectification as a sexual woman.

Absentmindedness, shame, and resistance do not necessarily stand in opposition to each other or to an erotic reading of the scene.[79] Eroticism surpasses sexuality by bringing together different affects and dispositions, locating them across different genital and nongenital body parts, and making unthinkable "queer" connections that erotohistoriography retrieves in order to illuminate our past-inhabited present. As Amy Hollywood argues, the Baroque is characterized as representing a wide array of bodily affects that go beyond sexuality, thus hinting at a graphic representation of feminine *jouissance*.[80] Because of this surplus of meaning, Pero's expression and demeanor parallel that unspeakable ecstasy that Jacques Lacan theorized and exemplified with reference to Bernini's Saint Teresa.[81] Of course, the interpreter should not forget that Cimon and Pero, like Saint Teresa's ecstasy, are cultural representations authored by a male

---

78. Virginia Schmied and Deborah Lupton, "Blurring the Boundaries: Breastfeeding and Maternal Subjectivity," in *Abjectly Boundless: Boundaries, Bodies and Health Work*, ed. Trudy Rudge and Dave Holmes (Farnham: Ashgate, 2010), 27.

79. Affect theory shows how these emotions/affects assemble together with different consequences (Silvan Tomkins, *Shame and Its Sisters: A Silvan Tomkins Reader*, ed. Eve Kosofsky Sedgwick and Adam Frank [Durham, NC: Duke University Press, 1971], 133–77).

80. Amy M. Hollywood, *Sensible Ecstasy: Mysticism, Sexual Difference, and the Demands of History* (Chicago: University of Chicago Press, 2002), 162. *Caritas Romana* could be studied as an example of Lacanian female *jouissance* in line with the ecstasies of the saints (Luce Irigaray, *Speculum of the Other Woman* [Ithaca, NY: Cornell University Press, 1985], 191).

81. Jacques-Alain Miller, ed., *The Seminar of Jacques Lacan, Book XX: Encore, on Femininity Sexuality, the Limits of Love and Knowledge 1972–1973* (New York: Norton, 1998), 76; Tom Hayes, "A Jouissance beyond the Phallus: Juno, Saint Teresa, Bernini, Lacan," *American Imago* 56 (1999): 331–55.

artist, calling for a cautious reading.[82] However, Rubens's general tendency to play with ambiguity, going back and forth between pleasure and pain, refusal and acceptance, and desire and disavowal and the crystallization of that tendency in Pero's depiction, makes *Caritas Romana* a suitable piece of art for a queer reflection on love.[83]

At this point, the reader might suspect how the oversexualization of Pero, the varied suggested meanings about her disposition, and the troubling gender dynamics conveyed by *Caritas Romana* help in bridging the gap between the notions of eros and agape. At the level of the narrative, the Roman portrayal of *caritas* does fulfill the agapic demands of Matt 25:31–46. The notion of a woman visiting her father in prison and saving him from death by breast-feeding him can be read as a "queer" realization of the gospel ideals. "He was thirsty," and "she gave him to drink"; "he was naked," and "she clothed him"; "he was sick," and "she took care of him," all while "he was in prison" and "she came to him."

The ideal of *Caritas Romana* fulfilling the requirements of agapic love, although completely unexplored in contemporary scholarship on *caritas*, love, eros, or Matt 25:31–46, is hardly new. Caravaggio (1572–1610), for instance, likewise envisioned a complementarity of the pagan and the religious traditions in *The Seven Works of Mercy* (fig. 3.2). Two men in the background, carrying a corpse, illustrate the act of "burying the dead." A

---

82. Luce Irigaray, for instance, criticizes Lacan for deploying "the phallic gaze" (*Speculum of the Other Woman*, 47).

83. Carroll, "The Erotics of Absolutism," 3; *Caritas Romana* evokes many meanings. Here I am exploring only one aspect of the gendered dimension of Rubens's work. The myth of Pero and Cimon, however, as any other cultural representation, is appropriated in different historical periods to serve different ideological purposes. Robert Rosenblum considers that in its earlier depictions in the Pompeii frescos it represented filial virtue, but later in the seventeenth century the meanings multiplied to include "everything from the sacrificial heroism of the French Revolution to the exploratory sexuality of the Marquis de Sade" (Rosenblum, "Caritas Romana after 1760," 43). Caroline Winterer further argues that the artistic motif appropriately became a metaphor of empire, being a lactating woman a paradigmatic example of the role of the metropolis in relationship to the colonies (Caroline Winterer, *The Mirror of Antiquity: American Women and the Classical Tradition, 1750–1900* [Ithaca, NY: Cornell University Press, 2007], 79–80). Winterer mentions other meanings such as the relationship between the Old and the New World in Edmund Burke's speeches, a symbol for the role of African and Indian women in the Atlantic economy that erases the material labor they carry out by suggesting "that lactation was a physiological process that required no labor whatsoever" (Winterer, *The Mirror of Antiquity*, 80).

pilgrim, shell in hand and asking the innkeeper for a room, represents "sheltering the homeless." Saint Martin of Tours greets and comforts a beggar, while tearing his robe in half to illustrate the action of "clothing the naked" and "visiting the sick." Samson quenches his thirst by drinking from the jawbone of an ass, illustrating the "refreshing of the thirsty." Pero and Cimon's story, finally, fulfills the acts of "visiting the imprisoned" and "feeding the hungry."[84]

Caravaggio's take on *Caritas Romana*, if compared to Rubens's, stands out as exaggeratedly measured. His interpretation, in fact, incorporates most of the visual features common to other representations, rendering Rubens's approach even more unique. *The Seven Works of Mercy* features Pero modestly dressed, with her head covered, breasts hardly visible, more concerned with not being caught than focusing on the action, while Cimon desperately sneaks his head out of the window cell to grasp some nurturing fluid.[85] *Caritas*'s erotic surplus in Rubens turns here into a sneaky, almost guileful act of delivering milk. Erotohistoriography finds here no material to work with, and *jouissance* is missing altogether. Such contrast throws into relief even more the erotic and sexualized nature of Rubens's representation, a feature that, as I show in the next section, lends itself to a radical queering of *caritas* as agapic love.

Reading *Caritas* from a Queer Perspective

How does reading *Caritas Christiana* (Matt 25:31–46) through a representation of *Caritas Romana* (Rubens) in light of a contemporary contextual lens queer the Christian notion of *caritas*? In this section, I argue that Rubens's representation has the potential to be a catalyst that impels the viewer to imagine a queer version of agapic love, bridging the gap between eros and agape. Impelled by the erotohistoriographical impetus to track bodily performances and erotic practices across time and space dissociated from heteronormative reproductive imperatives, the queer reader

---

84. For a detailed artistic analysis, see Steven F. Ostrow, "Caravaggio's Angels," in *Caravaggio's Angels*, ed. Lorenzo Pericolo and David M. Stone (Farnham: Ashgate, 2014), 123–48. For a theological appraisal, see Michael A. Mullett, *The Catholic Reformation* (London: Routledge, 1999), 204–8.

85. This does not imply that there is no room for a queer interpretation of Caravaggio's paintings, such as that offered in Leo Bersani and Ulysse Dutoit, *Caravaggio's Secrets* (London: British Film Institute, 1999).

Michelangelo Merisi da Caravaggio, *The Seven Works of Mercy*, 1607, oil on canvas, 390 cm x 260 cm. Pio Monte della Misericordia, Naples.

interprets the image/text as a historical source to think about queerness in the present. A queer act of eroticism fulfills the gospel's ethical demands, illustrating how the agapic ideal finds its culmination in an erotic practice.

Rubens's Cimon and Pero is a reading of a text, an interpretation that triggers a response on the part of the viewer/reader, who, in turn, is transformed in the act of viewing. Such transformation equips the reader to reinterpret the text in a new light. The viewer of the work of art becomes, we could say, an informed interpreter. Rubens's artwork is an expansion of Valerius Maximus's text.[86] The painting does not merely replicate the text; it offers a unique understanding that reconfigures the way the reader and the text interact. To look at the painting is to look at the text in a new light.[87] Visual exegesis is a cognitive process that allows the text to reveal multiple meanings that exceed literality while unveiling the existential conditions of the reader. The work of art feeds on the excess of textual meaning to the point where a new hermeneutical access opens up a set of meanings that can no longer be articulated in words.[88] In this model, the painter is a reader who plays with the surplus of textual meaning to produce an existential response that is other than that of the text,[89] whereas the final interpreter becomes a conduit who receives, transforms, and creates connections between text, representation, and contexts.[90] The effect of the representation on the beholder is much more than a function of the authorial intention, for there are always countless gaps between intention and reception.[91] What the contemporary (queer) interpreter makes out of textual and artistic versions of *Caritas Romana* and *Caritas Christiana* cannot be foreclosed in advance.

---

86. The painting does not simply visualize the narrative but opens it up to a wide range of discursive strategies (Paolo Berdini, *The Religious Art of Jacopo Bassano: Painting as Visual Exegesis* [New York: Cambridge University Press, 1997], 35).

87. J. Cheryl Exum, "Lovis Corinth's Blinded Samson," *BibInt* 6 (1998): 410–25.

88. Martin O'Kane, *Painting the Text: The Artist as Biblical Interpreter* (Sheffield: Sheffield Phoenix, 2007), 31.

89. Berdini, *Religious Art of Jacopo Bassano*, 121.

90. The final interpreter creates meanings that create the text anew. Here the idea that visual exegesis unveils the existential conditions of the reader is especially relevant because it accounts for the ways in which queer readers interpret texts in light of their experience, which, in turn, is continually reinterpreted by the texts and the works of art.

91. Robin Jensen, *The Substance of Things Seen: Art, Faith, and the Christian Community* (Grand Rapids: Eerdmans, 2004), 32.

Let me turn now to delineate a possible visualization, that is, a contextual hermeneutical path that takes the experience of S&M as a starting point to explore commonalities and divergences in the sources so far considered. By considering the present existential conditions of the interpreter as a definitional feature, visual exegesis makes possible a queer understanding of *Caritas Romana* that, in turn, allows for a queering of *Caritas Christiana*. The contextual experience of queerness brings new light to the intercontextual meanings explored in the previous sections. Or, to put it erotohistoriographically, contemporary queer sex is a portal to theological thinking.

There is something sexually unsettling about a man in bondage (notice the handcuffs, the chains, the dungeon setting, and the guards' uniforms in Rubens's representation) drinking from a woman's nipples. There is something sexually unnerving about a muscular old man in total submission to a young woman's breasts as she carefully administers her fluids and looks away in an expression of ecstasy. There is something erotically significant in the action of obtaining pleasure from breast-feeding an elderly man. And there is something theologically meaningful when those actions fulfill the requirements of agapic love that the tradition has mapped onto Matt 25:31–46.

In their oft-cited article "Sex in Public," Lauren Berlant and Michael Warner narrate a scene they witnessed:

> A boy, twentyish, very skateboard, comes on the low stage at one end of the bar, wearing Lycra shorts and a dog collar. He sits loosely in a restraining chair. His partner comes out and tilts the bottom's head up to the ceiling, stretching out his throat. Behind them is an array of foods. The top begins pouring milk down the boy's throat, then food, then more milk. It spills over, down his chest and onto the floor. A dynamic is established between them in which they carefully keep at the threshold of gagging. The bottom struggles to keep taking in more than he really can. The top is careful to give him just enough to stretch his capacities. From time to time a baby bottle is offered as a respite, but soon the rhythm intensifies. The boy's stomach is beginning to rise and pulse, almost convulsively.[92]

Berlant and Warner consider that this kind of public spectacle calls into question what counts as sexual and nonsexual, what is public and private

---

92. Lauren Berlant and Michael Warner, "Sex in Public," *Critical Inquiry* 24 (1998): 565.

in sex, and what are the limits of sexuality understood as subjectivity and intimacy. The similarities between this scene and the one portrayed by Rubens are clear: the bondage elements, the dungeon scene, the sexual role of milk and breast-feeding, the power dynamics between the top and the bottom, the voyeurism involved, and, most important to my reading, the blurred lines that separate eroticism, nurturing, and pain. Both scenes offer good examples of what Foucault called the "desexualization/degenitalization" of pleasure. Foucault sees S&M as an example of creative ways in which certain subcultures are inventing new forms of relationality.[93] Bondage channels the queer desire to untangle pleasure from practices, body parts, and dispositions that "sexuality" has configured as normative.[94] It maps new ways of experiencing the erotic by deconstructing the pain/pleasure binarism that is informed by heteronormativity.[95]

There are a number of issues to consider here. First, *Caritas Romana* and queer *caritas*—to name the scene narrated by Warner and Berlant—disavow sex as orgasm, disentangle pleasure from the heteronormative injunction to penetrate,[96] from the dominant, mainstream notion of locat-

---

93. In New Testament studies we find a recent push to rethink sex, gender, and sexuality in similar creative ways. See Benjamin Dunning, *Christ without Adam: Subjectivity and Sexual Difference in the Philosophers' Paul* (New York: Columbia University Press, 2014); and Dunning, *Specters of Paul: Sexual Difference in Early Christian Thought* (Philadelphia: University of Pennsylvania Press, 2011); Joseph A. Marchal, *Appalling Bodies: Queer Figures before and after Paul's Letters* (Oxford: Oxford University Press, 2020); Jimmy Hoke, *Feminism, Queerness, Affect, and Romans: Under God?*, ECL 30 (Atlanta: SBL Press, 2021).

94. Foucault argues that S&M does not create aggression but rather invents new forms of pleasure. Bondage is a creative enterprise that desexualizes/degenitalizes pleasure by experimenting with practices, dispositions, body parts, and situations. See David M. Halperin, *Saint Foucault: Towards a Gay Hagiography* (New York: Oxford University Press, 1995), 85–91.

95. See Margot Danielle Weiss, *Techniques of Pleasure: BDSM and the Circuits of Sexuality* (Durham, NC: Duke University Press, 2011).

96. By heteronormativity I understand the cultural system that naturalizes a set of binary relations between sex (man/woman), gender (male/female), and desire. In this particular case, heteronormativity equates sex with the penetration of a woman's vagina by a man's penis. In other words, heteronormativity poses heterosexuality as prescriptive sex. Accordingly, one could possibly argue that S&M as a queer practice opposes heteronormativity and signals alternative and creative ways to heterosexual practices; however, as I show through the contemplation of various of potential readings of *Caritas Romana*, the ultimate ethical and political impact of bondage for the

ing the peak of pleasure in genital orgasm.[97] In both cases, *jouissance*, often associated with orgasmic pleasure, is disentangled from a teleology of gratification, from the notion that erotic practices follow a scripted path leading to sexual release in the form of ejaculation.[98] In a way, *jouissance* finds in Pero's ambiguous expression and in the top woman and the bottom boy's deportments, paradigmatic examples of its ineffability. We do not know what it is, but we do know they are having fun.

Second, the dismissal of a teleology of orgasmic economy partially explains the range of mental and bodily dispositions on (dis)play. Although we are not informed how the bondage practice affects the top woman and the bottom boy's expressions in queer *caritas*, we can imagine the top's fixated gaze, carefully administering the milky fluids, and the bottom boy in disgust/disavowal as he struggles with the gagging. The range of possibilities that we have considered when analyzing Pero's demeanor becomes, when understood as a bondage practice, surprisingly cohesive. Absentmindedness, shame, disavowal are ways to explore the limits of bodily pleasures, venues to defer immediate sexual gratification, mental dispositions to scrutinize what is possible beyond orgasmic het*ero*sexuality, experimental attitudes to contest sexual, gender, and kinship roles.[99] What happens between the top and the bottom is, as Pat Califia puts it, a process of building sensations, of going back and forth between pain and pleasure, endurance and overcoming limits.[100] Whereas in het*ero*sexual life rejection, pursuit, resistance, and compliance come before "sex," in S&M these strategic relations are inside "sex," redefining the limits of pleasure.

The range of dispositions attributed to Pero finds a perfect counterexample in a recent "picture-painting" authored by Max Sauco (fig. 3.3).[101] This example of *Caritas Romana*, like Rubens's, also draws on the blurred lines between the erotic and the agapic. The picture-painting represents

---

debate on different kinds of love depends on the "trajectory of visualization" that the interpreter takes.

97. Halperin, *Saint Foucault*, 85–90.

98. Karmen Mackendrick, *Counterpleasures* (Albany: State University of New York Press, 1999), 111.

99. Sexual/erotic acts, queer or not, intend to experiment with one's body in the context of a relational experience—real or imagined—established for the purpose of obtaining pleasure.

100. Pat Califia, *Public Sex: The Culture of Radical Sex* (San Francisco: Cleis, 2000), 174.

101. See *Romana Caritas*, photograph by Max Sauco, 2011.

Fig. 3.3. Max Sauco, *Caritas Romana*, 2011

Pero, a pregnant woman looking defiantly at the camera while spilling an abundant quantity of milk on Cimon and on the floor. However, what in Rubens's art could be interpreted as absentmindedness, disavowal, or shame is here clearly presence, affirmation, and even defiance. We do not know what it is, we know they are having fun, and they are having fun in queer multiple ways.

This sample of bodily and mental dispositions would be notably lacking if I did not mention the impact of the AIDS crisis on the configuration of desire. After all, breast milk is, along with semen, blood, and vaginal and rectal secretions, one of the fluids containing HIV, making breast-feeding a risky practice. The queer beholder, anachronistic as this interpretation is, sees in Pero's evasiveness a hint of concern or excitement. The agapic action of breast-feeding is tainted with the threat of death, the erotic disposition enhanced or hindered by the risk factor.[102]

---

102. In some queer communities, the risk of virus transmission is a source of enjoyment (Tim Dean, *Unlimited Intimacy: Reflection on the Subculture of Barebacking* [Chicago: University of Chicago Press, 2009]).

Third, I have alluded to the incestuous tones in *Caritas Romana*, noticing how the fact that the act of breast-feeding transpires between a daughter and a father might account for feelings of shame or disavowal. S&M practices draw on the taboo of incest, overcoming its literal meanings and saturating familial power relations with erotic meanings (that is, daddy/mommy, son/daughter).[103] Reading *Caritas Romana* as queer *caritas* shows how the power differentials inherent to family bonds are redeployed for the goal of obtaining pleasure. Pero's *jouissance* issues from her role as a top "daughter," her absentmindedness/shame/resistance as techniques of deferring gratification to gain pleasure through the fantasy of violating the incest taboo. We do not know what it is, we do know they are having fun, and we guess some ways in which they are having it.

Conclusion: The Erotic Fulfillment of the Gospel Ethics

Rubens pictures an oversexualized ecstatic Pero as a top and a muscular emasculated Cimon as a bottom. Yet a contemporary queer interpreter—maybe leaning toward a more traditional feminism—might interpret the scene in quite different, sometimes oppositional, ways. In fact, in art as in BDSM, the most difficult hermeneutical task is to make sense of facial expressions, not least because in bondage masks often cover the faces of the participants. One could possibly argue that Pero is experiencing pain rather than pleasure, her evasive gaze expressing her desire to be absent from a situation she experiences as violent or awkward. Please, let's get this over with! No erotic rapture but sexual rape, Pero being tortured under the fixated gaze of Cimon. Perhaps it is a case once again of a male author offering his chauvinistic rendering of female *jouissance*.

The kinky voyeur may read Rubens's painting as a story of pleasure that derives from an act of agapic love or as a cautionary tale of pain coming out of filial obligations. From a queer perspective it is no longer possible to pinpoint what counts as eros or agape in the described scene. Shame, resistance, disavowal, fear, to name a few, are dispositions not only compatible with eros but also required in the queer explorations of desire. As Stephen Moore and Virginia Burrus so accurately put it referring to an artistic representation of the Song of Songs, "how to distinguish ultimately

---

103. See some examples in Weiss, *Techniques of Pleasure*, 15.

between the pain-filled pleasure of a bottom and the pleasureless pain of a battered woman?"[104]

Interpreting Rubens's work of art through the lens of S&M rereads Matt 25:31–46 as a pericope demanding of the erotic. The action of a top woman fulfilling the agapic demands while in erotic rapture becomes a trope for a *caritas* that not only dismisses pleasure (or pain) but also requires it, a paradigmatic example of an erotic act that fulfills the gospel ethics.[105] This inter(con)textual interpretation reveals that the biblical ethical demands of feeding the hungry, quenching the thirsty, sheltering the homeless, clothing the naked, and visiting the imprisoned—traditionally providing substantive material for a theophilosophical reflection on agape and its distinction from eros—should not be easily or naively interpreted as falling under the umbrella of a *caritas* devoid of queerness. Of course, this is not to make a historical claim on first-century Christianity or seventeenth-century Flemish thought, for erotohistoriography is not equipped to grant historical affirmations on the biblical past or the Baroque.

Yet a historiography of eros scans historical sources for queer experiences that offer material for theological reflection: erotohistoriography contributes to erototheology. Despite the exegetical disagreements mentioned, all interpreters agree that what the gospel proposes as agape are boundary-breaking acts of love. Pero's action as an exemplary *caritas* equates boundary-breaking with queer and entangles agape with eros.

---

104. Burrus and Moore, "Unsafe Sex," 49.
105. One could equally pursue a mapping of the agapic onto the erotic to explore a Christian contribution to bondage.

4
THE GOSPEL OF TORTURE
(MARK 15:1–39)

Can so many Americans have come to accept torture as a matter of dull routine?[1]

A "World" Crisis

It is a truism to state that our world is in crisis. Less considered is the fact that the world of the victims of torture has been destroyed. Adnan Farhan Abdul Latif, a Guantanamo prisoner who suffered a severe car accident in 1994 that left him with serious sequels and who was sold in the wake of 9/11 by the Pakistani forces for a $5,000 bounty, writes in his "Hunger Strike Poem": "Where is the world to save us from torture? Where is the world to save us from the fire and sadness? Where is the world to save the hunger strikers?"[2]

Latif committed suicide in 2012 by overdosing on medications he had been hoarding for months. At thirty-two years old, he had been tortured with unimaginable cruelty: not only did he suffer from the consequences of extreme isolation (see ch. 5 for more details), but when he participated in hunger strikes, twice a day the medics strapped him and shoved liquid food through his nose and esophagus. The world ends at every second for those who experience torture. Although numbers are irrelevant, the United States has held 780 Guantanamo detainees. As of June 2023, thirty remained.

---

1. Stephen F. Eisenman, *The Abu Ghraib Effect* (London: Reaktion Books, 2007), 8.
2. Marc Falkoff, *Poems from Guantanamo: The Detainees Speak* (Iowa City: University of Iowa Press, 2007), 51–52.

To read the above lines barely grasps the uttermost destruction of Latif's world. Abu Zubaydah, still held prisoner in Guantanamo, offers a first-person graphic testimony of the experience of being tortured under extenuating circumstances. In December 2019, the *New York Times*, in partnership with the Pulitzer Center on Crisis Reporting, published an article that included Zubaydah's drawings of his experience being waterboarded, hit, shackled, and forced to be awake, among many other barbarities.[3] The release of the Abu Ghraib prison pictures, stamped in our memory as a "sign of the times," begins to conjure up in our imagination what those practices look like.

To contemplate Zubaydah's drawings generates a set of different emotions than reading Latif's poems. It elicits unique reactions, also somewhat different from those experienced by looking at Abu Ghraib's photographs. Zubaydah's drawings enter, perhaps against his intent, the realm of artistic representation, escaping the objectification of the tortured subject that one is likely to perceive in the photographs. The drawings evince the collapse of a subject in ways that no words or photograph can capture without attempting to exhaust the meaning of the tortured body: exasperation, destruction, apophatic suffering, desubjectification, dehumanization do not begin to capture the graphic content, but they constitute a meaningful bridge—fraught with gaps and on the verge of collapse—between the indescribable pain of the victim, held in isolation on US soil, and the interpreter's gaze, shocked at such cruelty in an allegedly democratic state but sitting on a comfy chair writing about it.

Brushing off the history of Western art against the reality of torture, Stephen F. Eisenman coined the term "the Abu Ghraib effect" to describe the moral blindness that contemporary citizens experience when confronted with the extreme violence of torture immortalized in the infamous pictures that leaked the abuses of the US army in Iraq in 2003. Eisenman, an art historian, maps the history of Western art, starting with classical Greece and reaching out into the seventeenth century, as conveying a pathos formula, "the motif of tortured people and tormented animals who appear to sanction their own abuse."[4] As I develop throughout the chapter, the notion that the pain inflicted on the victim is externalized and

---

3. Mark Denbeaux, Jess Ghannam, and Abu Zubaydah, *American Torturers: FBI and CIA Abuses at Dark Sites and Guantanamo* (Newark: Seton Hall University School of Law, Center for Policy and Research, 2023).

4. Eisenman, *The Abu Ghraib Effect*, 16.

presented as power constitutes one of the defining features of torture itself. Eisenman elaborates: "It is the mark of reification in extremis because it represents the body as something willingly alienated by the victim (even to the point of death) for the sake of the pleasure and aggrandizement of the oppressor."[5]

Goya, Picasso, Shann, Golub, and Bacon represent a shift in this transhistorical pattern of objectifying the victim. The Gemma Augustea, the frieze at the Pergamon altar, or the Trajan column in the Roman Forum reaffirms the notion that political power extracts the victim's suffering and displays it for public consumption: "the domination, destruction, enslavement or exile of a native people—even of its children—is represented as both moral and necessary."[6] In chapter 5, we will have an opportunity to come to terms with the reality of solitary confinement as a continuation of such suffering. For the time being, however, I would like to keep our focus on a pattern whereby the narrative of artistic representation serves the purposes of imperialism through a mystification of the victim of torture pain.[7]

Images from Abu Ghraib exemplify the lingering effects of Western imperialism, which transforms suffering into spectacle, dehumanizes the subject, and diverts attention away from the torturer's brutality: the glorification of pain is compounded by the erasure of the torture's work and the dismissal of the victim as human. Given this "effect," it is even more critical that we highlight those examples that go against the grain. Eisenman sees in Leon Golub's *Interrogation II* a description of "the emotional insensibility of the torturers, and the complete physical vulnerability of the victim."[8] The hermeneutical key here is that this type of art draws "on an ancient pathos formula in order to expose its [the pathos's] artifice and viciousness, turn it upside down, and render it useless as a weapon in the war of the powerful against the vulnerable."[9]

The history of the representation of Jesus's crucifixion in Western art truly represents the most vivid example of a retroactive "Abu Ghraib effect,"

---

5. Eisenman, *The Abu Ghraib Effect*, 16.
6. Eisenman, *The Abu Ghraib Effect*, 58.
7. Eisenman (*The Abu Ghraib Effect*, 60–72) compellingly shows how Renaissance art is imbued with the ideology of European Christianity superiority to Muslims from the East.
8. Eisenman, *The Abu Ghraib Effect*, 107.
9. Eisenman, *The Abu Ghraib Effect*, 107.

a theater of suffering oblivious to the victim's pain,[10] an eroticization of torture, and an instrumentalization of oppression for theological, cultural, or political purposes. Consider, for instance, two representational extremes of the cross painted in the same decade: Salvador Dalí's *Christ of Saint John at the Cross* (1951; fig. 4.1) and Francis Newton Souza's *Crucifixion* (1959; fig. 4.2) depart from the tradition in dramatically different ways. Dalí's rendition, one of the most celebrated religious paintings of the past century, is inspired by Saint John of the Cross's sketch of the crucifixion.[11]

> My aesthetic ambition ... was completely the opposite of all the Christs painted by most of the modern painters who have all interpreted him in the expressionistic and contortionistic sense, thus obtaining emotion through ugliness. My principal preoccupation was that my Christ would be beautiful as the God that he is.[12]

It is unclear whom Dalí has in mind when referring to modern painters. Still, his aesthetic argument reacts against a representational trend in contemporary art in which the crucifixion becomes a locus to evoke the disasters of the twentieth century. On this front, Souza's *Crucifixion* epitomizes visual representation as a political indictment. It remains uncertain what Souza's Christ's ultimate reference is.[13] In an insightful study of postcolonial art in Britain, Gregory Salter establishes close connections between Souza's biographical details and his artistic technique. Born in the Portuguese colony of Goa, Souza migrated to Britain in 1949, where he found himself uprooted and lost. The male body, Salter suggests, stands for a home that has been lost in the hybrid space of a colonial subject in the heart of the empire. The *Crucifixion* here, then, is a "tortured expression of long-term alienation or despair."[14] Blackness, migration, and emasculation are dimensions that connect the personal and the political. Regardless

---

10. Leo Steinberg, *The Sexuality of Christ in Renaissance Art and in Modern Oblivion* (New York: Pantheon, 1984).

11. Juan Carlos Oliver Torelló and Lino Cabezas Gelabert, "La imagen del crucificado en Salvador Dalí, José María Sert y Juan de la Cruz: Hipótesis de realización del dibujo del monasterio de la Encarnación de Ávila," *Locus Amoenus* 14 (2016): 215–32.

12. Quoted in Gabriele Finaldi, *The Image of Christ* (London: National Gallery London, 2000), 198.

13. Gregory Salter, *Art and Masculinity in Post-war Britain: Reconstructing Home* (London: Routledge, 2020), 125.

14. Salter, *Art and Masculinity in Post-war Britain*, 120.

4. THE GOSPEL OF TORTURE (MARK 15:1–39)

Fig. 4.1. Eugenio Salvador Dalí, *Christ of Saint John at the Cross*, 1951, oil on canvas, 205 cm x 116 cm. Credit: Art Gallery and Museum, Kelvingrove, Glasgow, Scotland. Photo © CSG CIC Glasgow Museums Collection/Bridgeman Images Kelvingrove Art Gallery and Museum, Glasgow.

Fig. 4.2. Francis Newton Souza, *Crucifixion*, 1959, oil paint on board, 183 cm x 122 cm. Tate Museum, London.

of how we understand Souza's art, it is not, as Dalí argues, a search for emotion through ugliness. For Dalí, the contortionist body, as he puts it, has the religious edification of the viewer in mind. What Souza, Bacon, and Golub create is a disruption of the aesthetic extraction of pain for the sake of reinforcing the viewer's pleasure: they enact a performative undoing of the viewer's subjectivity consistent, although by no means equal, with the destruction of the tortured body.

These artists expose how torture involves the amplification of bodily pain objectified and made visible outside of the body and "objectified pain [being] denied as pain and read as power."[15] The theatricality of the Abu Ghraib pictures and the aestheticization of Dalí's *Crucifixion*—two examples that could not possibly be more different in terms of their representational politics—result in a mystification of the torture's pain either through objectification or sublimation. The representation of the cross, of course, sits at the very center of the Christian message, opening the doors for theological renderings. Equally essential and substantially less explored is the fact that the cross is a means of torture and Jesus is a victim of torture. The question ensues: What is the relationship between the victim's pain and its representation, whether textual or visual? In this chapter, I argue that a thick theorization of torture allows us to establish a criterion to discern literary obfuscations of the victim.

A Definitional Crisis

"There is nothing left of me, only this hysteric eagerness in my breast to grasp for air."[16] So ends Hernan Valdés's detailed testimony of torture under the Chilean dictatorship, condensing in one sentence the discrepancies between the wholeness of the literary author and the destruction of the tortured body, between the urgency of giving voice to pain and language's inadequacy to express what happens during torture. These contradictions riddle many narratives about extreme pain under torture, including the gospels' accounts of the crucifixion. Curiously enough, although no one would question that the historical reality of crucifixion

---

15. Elaine Scarry, *The Body in Pain: The Making and Unmaking of the World* (Oxford: Oxford University Press, 1987), 28.

16. Hernán Valdés, *Tejas verdes: Diario de un campo de concentración en Chile* (Barcelona: Laia, 1974), 164: "No queda nada de mí, sino esta avidez histérica de mi pecho por tragar aire."

is a case of torture, there has been little sustained attention to crucifixion as torture, at least from the victim's perspective.[17] To be sure, historical and historical-critical studies have explored in detail the mechanics of the cross and the historical reliability of the available accounts.[18] Literary studies have also considered Mark's theology of the cross and its effects on the intended audience.[19] Material, textual, and literary evidence point to the crucifixion as Rome's most humiliating form of punishment.

---

17. Martin Hengel's contribution details the mechanics of the crucifixion and offers an extensive study of the religious, cultural, and political attitudes about this capital punishment. Many scholars mention the term *torture* but use it in confusing ways. For instance, Hengel seems to think that torture and crucifixion are two different things, the first leading to the latter (see Hengel, *Crucifixion in the Ancient World and the Folly of the Message of the Cross* [Philadelphia: Fortress, 1978], 5, 16, 141, 153, and 156; same in Granger Cook, *Crucifixion in the Mediterranean World*, WUNT 327 [Tübingen: Mohr Siebeck, 2019], 12, 428, and 452). Most explicitly when analyzing Dionysius of Halicarnassus's account of a slave's crucifixion, Hengel argues that "nothing in the text suggests that the slave was crucified after the torture" (Hengel, *Crucifixion in the Ancient World*, 94, 132). Other scholars do not even mention it (Simon J. Joseph, *Jesus and the Temple: The Crucifixion in Its Jewish Context* [Cambridge: Cambridge University Press, 2018]; David H. Wenkel, *Jesus' Crucifixion Beatings and the Book of Proverbs* [London: Springer, 2018]). In other cases, torture is identified with the "instrument of torture" defined as the cross. See David W. Chapman, *Ancient Jewish and Christian Perceptions of Crucifixion*, WUNT 244 (Tübingen: Mohr Siebeck, 2008), 9. Helen K. Bond seems to think that torture refers only to the gory elements and delinks torture from "mockery or the final abandonment" (Helen K. Bond, "A Fitting End? Self-Denial and a Slave's Death in Mark's Life of Jesus," NTS 65 [2019]: 424). A notable exception to this lack of theorization of torture as it relates to the crucifixion can be found in Jennifer A. Glancy, "Torture: Flesh, Truth, and the Fourth Gospel," BibInt 13 (2005): 107–36.

18. The sources here are extensive. Torture as an analytical category is mostly deployed in archaeological, textual, and historical scholarship that explores the vicissitudes of the practice with close attention to the misconceptions about the procedure itself and the literary evidence in Greco-Roman sources. See Chapman, *Ancient Jewish and Christian Perceptions*; David W. Chapman and Eckhard J. Schnabel, *The Trial and Crucifixion of Jesus: Texts and Commentary*, WUNT 344 (Tübingen: Mohr Siebeck, 2019); Cook, *Crucifixion in the Mediterranean World*; and Gunnar Samuelsson, *Crucifixion in Antiquity: An Inquiry into the Background of the New Testament Terminology of Crucifixion*, WUNT 310 (Tübingen: Mohr Siebeck, 2011). For a careful and sharp analysis of the *status quaestionis*, see Felicity Harley, "Crucifixion in Roman Antiquity: The State of the Field," JECS 27 (2019): 303–23.

19. See Stephen Simon Kimondo, *The Gospel of Mark and the Roman-Jewish War of 66–70 CE: Jesus' Story as a Contrast to the Events of the War* (Eugene, OR: Wipf & Stock, 2019), 214–18; David M. Rhoads, *Reading Mark: Engaging the Gospel* (Min-

Similarly, studies on Mark's Gospel paint a gruesome picture of such a punitive institution, analyzing how this deprecating punishment is rhetorically presented to intended audiences or how Mark edits preexisting sources.[20]

These attempts, however, skip over the raw experience of torture and its literary manifestations, in part because they do not theorize torture as such. Subsequently, this study defines the contours of the term and focuses on the ethics of torture and its narrative aftermath by seeking to understand how the Gospel of Mark bears the scars of torture and how the grammar of torture bleeds into some of the main gospel plot lines.[21]

---

neapolis: Fortress, 2004), 52–53; and Samuel Simon, *A Postcolonial Reading of Mark's Story of Jesus*, LNTS 340 (London: T&T Clark, 2007), 147.

20. Harley, for instance, after assessing the pros and cons of the minimalist and maximalist positions on the definition of "crucifixion," advocates for a use of the term closer to the broader category of suspension in order to "register the horrific nature of that specific category, and its significance within spectacle culture as such" (Harley, "Crucifixion in Roman Antiquity," 323).

Scholarly interest in the Markan account of the crucifixion continues to this day. The following studies have been important in the development of my own argument: Bond, "A Fitting End," 425–42; Geert Van Oyen and Patty Van Cappellen, "Mark 15:34 and the Sitz im Leben of the Real Reader," *ETL* 91 (2015): 569–99; Joel Marcus, "Crucifixion as Parodic Exaltation," *JBL* 125 (2006): 73–87; William S. Campbell, "Engagement, Disengagement and Obstruction: Jesus' Defense Strategies in Mark's Trial and Execution Scenes (14.53–64; 15.1–39)," *JSNT* 26 (2004): 283–300; Jeffrey W. Aernie, "Cruciform Discipleship: The Narrative Function of the Women in Mark 15–16," *JBL* 135 (2016): 779–97; José Enrique Aguilar Chiu, "A Theological Reading of Ἐξέπνευσεν in Mark 15:37, 39," *CBQ* 78 (2016): 682–705; Nathan Eubank, "Dying with Power: Mark 15:39 from Ancient to Modern Interpretation," *Bib* 95 (2014): 247–68; Allan Georgia, "Translating the Triumph: Reading Mark's Crucifixion Narrative against a Roman Ritual of Power," *JSNT* 36 (2013): 17–38; Chris Keith, "The Role of the Cross in the Composition of the Markan Crucifixion Narrative," *Stone-Campbell Journal* 9 (2006): 61–75; Sharyn E. Dowd and Elizabeth Struthers Malbon, "The Significance of Jesus' Death in Mark: Narrative Context and Authorial Audience," *JBL* 125 (2006): 271–97; and Gerard Stephen Sloyan, *The Crucifixion of Jesus: History, Myth, Faith* (Minneapolis: Fortress, 1995).

With regard to Mark's editing of preexisting sources, Nickelsburg, who identified the Markan passion narrative as a narrative of the persecution and vindication of the righteous one has proven most influential. See George W. E. Nickelsburg, "The Genre and Function of the Markan Passion Narrative," *HTR* 73 (1980): 153–84.

21. For a similar analysis applied to classical texts, see Jennifer R. Ballengee, *The Wound and the Witness: The Rhetoric of Torture* (Albany: SUNY Press, 2010).

Such a task demands sustained attention to the constitutive elements of torture, an exploration of how those elements crystalize in the narrative, and, finally, a reflection on the complex relationships between extreme pain, its expressions, and its witnessing.[22] Although my argument draws heavily from historical-critical and literary scholarship on Mark 14–15, it takes issue with the way these approaches neutralize the victim's pain, offering a disembodied notion of death by torture. To be sure, such sadistic capital punishment ought to be understood in its mechanics and in the way textual witnesses theologize the deceased, but we are missing crucial literary connections and, most importantly, fundamental ethical insights if we neglect the victim's pain in its radicality, ineffability, and inexpressibility.

Talking about torture—its structure and its painful effects—requires reconsidering Elaine Scarry's unprecedented reflections in *The Body in Pain*.[23] Long deemed the inaugurating contribution to comprehend the phenomenology of torture, Scarry's theoretical intervention, amply deployed across disciplinary boundaries, has had little purchase in biblical studies, an omission all the more surprising, given that crucifixion, arguably the most prominent narrative in the gospels, represents torture in one of its purest forms. Capture and interrogation, physical abuse, humiliation, and deliberately inflicting pain in intensifying ways are constitutive

---

22. David Tombs has been the most consistent and staunch proponent of tackling crucifixion as torture, particularly in its implications for sexual abuse. There are numerous similarities between Tombs's approach and mine: an intercontextual approach that considers contemporary geopolitical contexts as a template to study torture (e.g., Latin American dictatorial regimes) and a sustained attention to textual elements that qualify the crucifixion as torture. There are also numerous differences between Tombs's argument and mine: whereas Tombs focuses on the historical reality of the crucifixion and consequently uses a comparative and comprehensive approach to the gospels, I focus exclusively on the textual and literary elements in Mark. More important, similar to most historical arguments, Tombs misses the connections between pain and language, between torture and its literary manifestations. See Tombs, "Prisoner Abuse: From Abu Ghraib to *The Passion of the Christ*," in *Religion and the Politics of Peace and Conflict*, ed. Linda Hogan and Dylan Lee Lerhke [Eugene, OR: Pickwick, 2009], 175–201; Tombs, "Honor, Shame, and Conquest: Male Identity, Sexual Violence, and the Body Politic," *Journal of Hispanic/Latino Theology* 9 (2002): 21–40; and David Tombs and Jayme R. Reaves, "#MeToo Jesus: Naming Jesus as a Victim of Sexual Abuse," *International Journal of Public Theology* 13 (2019): 387–412.

23. Scarry, *Body in Pain*.

elements of torture. They are enacted in the events that center this study: a mob with swords and clubs (Mark 14:43) captures Jesus and takes him to the high priest, who in turn gathers the chief priests, scribes, and elders (14:53); Jesus is interrogated, accused, physically abused (14:65), tied and subjected to a second interrogation by Pilate (15:1); he is then further abused by soldiers (15:17–20), crucified and mocked (15:29) until he breathes his last (15:37). This chapter analyzes, from a literary perspective, what it means for the Markan narrative to account for pain in its crudest form.

It is interesting to notice that focus on pain, torture, injury, and agony in the gospels features most prominently within contextual theologies that draw thick connections between the predicaments of marginalized communities and the gospel narratives.[24] So, for instance, Latin American liberation theology has coined the term "pueblo crucificado" (crucified people) to describe the plight of the vast majority of the population in the subcontinent and to substantiate a reading of the cross as torture.[25] Within the black tradition, James Cone suggests compelling parallels between Jesus suffering at the cross and the suffering of thousands of African Americans who were lynched in the nineteenth and twentieth centuries.[26] Biblical scholarship produced in the Global North tends to look askance at these contributions for not meeting the criteria of objectivism and textual accuracy, for catering to the dangers of anachronism, or for being theological rather than historical. Such ideological considerations feed into a self-understanding of the discipline as bias-free, disembodied, and universal.[27] My argument shows how, contrary to these claims, sustained attention to the phenomenology of torture, to the literary analysis of its witnessing, and to the testimonies of those who have survived enhances literary analysis rather than obscures it.

---

24. For a philosophical analysis on the epistemology of lived experience, see José Medina, *The Epistemology of Resistance: Gender and Racial Oppression, Epistemic Injustice, and Resistant Imaginations* (New York: New York University Press, 2013).

25. Sobrino, *Jesus in Latin America*.

26. James H. Cone, *The Cross and the Lynching Tree* (Maryknoll, NY: Orbis Books, 2011).

27. For a recent critique in terms of whiteness, see David G. Horrell, "Paul, Inclusion and Whiteness: Particularizing Interpretation," *JSNT* 40 (2017): 123–47. For a comprehensive analysis of ethos of the discipline, see Segovia, *Decolonizing Biblical Studies*. More recently, see Moore and Sherwood, *Invention of the Biblical Scholar*, 69–75.

The Grammar of Torture

Let us start, then, with the phenomenology of torture. For Scarry, torture encompasses three phenomena: a deliberate inflicting of pain in "ever-intensifying ways," the amplification of bodily pain objectified and made visible outside of the body, and "objectified pain [being] denied as pain and read as power."[28] Not a chronological description but a theoretical map to grasp the phenomenology of torture, Scarry's notion of torture incorporates two elements: the physical act of pain infliction and the verbal act of interrogation: "the pain is traditionally accompanied by 'the question.'"[29] Both components work to achieve the ultimate effect of torture: the destruction of language and, ultimately, the erasure of a world. As she puts it, "to witness the moment when pain causes a reversion to the pre-language of cries and groans is to witness the destruction of language."[30]

The relationship between both components, the physical and the linguistic, is often misunderstood and misconstrued because theorists traditionally have understood the acquisition of information as the motive for torture. Although, for obvious reasons, most ethicists hold the ethics of torture in contempt, they tend to ascribe the potential obtaining of valued, hidden, treasured information as the motive of torture itself. Such decoupling of the linguistic and the physical dimensions of interrogation and pain infliction is relevant to New Testament studies because scholars tend to understand the crucifixion either in isolation from or a step removed from the acts of interrogation. Although it is tempting to explain the irrational, deliberate, and sustained infliction of pain on the victim by scrutinizing the motives in the interrogation process, such explanatory strategy, Scarry argues, situates interrogation outside the process, erasing the fact that the question and the action are two sides of the same coin. Instead of approaching capture, interrogation, and crucifixion as three narrative moments conducive to the climax of death, the grammar of torture requires an integrative analysis that understands them in sync.

Scarry's account of torture has become widely influential for its reflections on the relationships between pain and the destruction of the world and language. She theorizes torture as the ground where two worlds are at war. The torturer's world, both numb to the victim's agony and enflamed

---

28. Scarry, *Body in Pain*, 28.
29. Scarry, *Body in Pain*, 28.
30. Scarry, *Body in Pain*, 6.

4. THE GOSPEL OF TORTURE (MARK 15:1–39)

in its desire to maximize pain, is fueled by the feigned urgency of the question; meanwhile, the victim's world, submerged in crass pain, neutralizes the form and content of the question, which is always superficial, an obstacle to the stopping of pain.[31] Pain is world destroying. The moment the torturer drills the victim's nerves, her conscious world empties. The destruction of language accompanies world destruction because pain is quintessentially nonlinguistic. Pain is inexpressible, incommunicable, a quality that further contributes to the collapse of the victim's world: "physical pain always mimes death and the infliction of physical pain is always a mock execution."[32] There is no world or language in death. These apophatic and nihilistic dimensions of extreme pain throw into relief the paradoxical nature of accounting for pain. If torture destroys language, how might it be linguistically expressed? If extreme pain equates to the destruction of the victim's world, how does the literary world account for such destruction? It is precisely here where the hermeneutical task needs to proceed with utmost care. The contemporary interpreter is ultimately witnessing an account of torture that is entangled with the inexpressibility of pain and embedded in a process in which the victim's world wreaks havoc. To put it briefly, at this juncture biblical interpretation encounters the ethics of torture, the dilemma of how to explore the literary expression of the inexpressible. It is within this framework that my argument specifies narrative elements that reach beyond language to convey pain and world destruction (e.g., Mark 15:37).

Testimonials consistently show that the process of destroying the victim's world reduces the tortured psychic and bodily dispositions to absolute exhaustion and desperation: the self disentangles from itself, gasping for the last breath of agency with the exclusive purpose of making pain stop. The world becomes weightless, as if vanishing behind the thin veil of a consciousness so strained that it cannot hold anything beyond its bare survival. Such annihilation of one's world represents the triumph of betrayal, the disavowal of any remaining link keeping the victim—now on the verge of death—connected to the realm of the living, both at the personal (family, friends, disciples) and institutional (nation, religion, voluntary associations) levels. In the following, my argument will explore how these underlying components of torture—in the form of capture, inter-

---

31. Scarry, *Body in Pain*, 29.
32. Scarry, *Body in Pain*, 31.

rogation, mocking, beating, humiliation, and, finally, hanging—should inform our considerations of narrative elements, such as the "cry of dereliction" (Mark 15:34) or the tearing apart of the temple's veil (15:38). At the cusp of torture, one's worldly anchorage—relationships, institutions, beliefs, values—and one's language (15:37) become null (15:33).

Torture as World Destruction

Torture conceives of the world as a war zone. For the torturer, the existing world is pending destruction, and his actions aim at eliminating any threat to its orderliness. The victim's existence, on the other hand, endangers the torturer's world's stability. Torture condenses a process in which oppositional visions of future worlds collide, hence the torturer's ultimate goal of annihilating the victim's project for a new reality. The victim's body, his past actions, his alliances, and his institutions threaten the here and now, so his mere existence, an existence entangled with a utopian project, is invested with menacing authority. Here torture is a process that turns constitutive elements of the victim's world on its head. Josephus, for instance, portrays the fate of those Jews who were caught fleeing the city of Jerusalem during Titus's siege in 70 CE "as being scourged and subjected to all possible kinds of torture before being crucified opposite the wall" (μαστιγούμενοι δὴ καὶ προβασανιζόμενοι τοῦ θανάτου πᾶσαν αἰκίαν ἀνεσταυροῦντο τοῦ τείχους ἀντικρύ).[33] Here Josephus is not as specific as Mark. Both in terms of vocabulary and vividness, he spares the readers most details by subsuming them under the term "torture" (πᾶσαν αἰκίαν; B.J. 5.449). He goes on to specify that Titus used such a gruesome spectacle to induce the remaining Jews to surrender: "but he would rather not stop the crucifixions so that the spectacle would trigger them to surrender, because they would be afraid that similar actions would give them the same fate" (τό γε μὴν πλέον οὐκ ἐκώλυεν τάχ᾽ ἂν ἐνδοῦναι πρὸς τὴν ὄψιν ἐλπίσας αὐτοὺς <ὡς>, εἰ μὴ παραδοῖεν, ὅμοια πεισομένους).[34]

In this instance, torture refers to a literal war of the worlds. Josephus places the resistant Jews and the Roman armies as pawns in a battlefield where torture/crucifixion functions as the torturer's weapon to dissuade

---

33. Josephus, B.J. 5.449. Translations are my own.
34. Josephus, B.J. 5.451. Josephus provides many examples where crucifixion is deployed by the Romans to qualm insurrection: B.J. 2.75; 2.167; 2.241; 2.253; 2.305–308; Josephus, A.J. 17.354–355, 18.1–10, 26–27.

the other party from further resistance, a way of forcing the victims to capitulate, to give up their world. Torture functions as a spectacle where the wrecking of the victims' world is on full display. Although historical and genre differences between Josephus's and Mark's accounts of crucifixion leave little room for parallel analysis, in both cases torture channels the imposition of one world over the other. Let me further explore how Mark builds the victim's (i.e., Jesus's) world and its ensuing demise.

Soon after Jesus's violent capture (καὶ μετ' αὐτοῦ ὄχλος μετὰ μαχαιρῶν καὶ ξύλων παρὰ τῶν ἀρχιερέων καὶ τῶν γραμματέων καὶ τῶν πρεσβυτέρων; "and with him [Judas], came a crowd armed with swords and clubs, sent by the chief priests, the scribes, and the elders"; Mark 14:43), he is taken in front of the high priest and other officials (14:53), where several witnesses accuse him of trying to destroy the material temple and build a new one "not made with hands" (14:58). The high priest's interrogation starts precisely with questioning the victim's authoritative status: "Are you the Christ?" (14:61). Are you, in other words, one who claims to abolish the current order and establish a new one? The victim's last utterance before he is led to hang ratifies the torturer's fears (ἐγώ εἰμι; "I am"; 14:62) as it specifies how such new order comes from another world ("you will see the Son of Man seated at the right hand of Power and coming with the clouds of heaven"; 14:62). The ripping of the temple's veil (15:38) confirms the temple's symbolic destruction. Additionally, sandwiched between the capturer's/priest's interrogation and Jesus's detainment at Pilate's palace (15:1–15), Mark locates Peter's denial (14:54, 66–72), the last disciple to abandon Jesus after everyone else (14:50–52). Both Jesus's links to the temple and Jesus's relationships with his disciples are constitutive elements of the victim's world. If torture, as Scarry reminds us, expands the world of the torturer while constraining the world of the victim, then we should understand both elements as exemplary loci for world construction and world destruction. The narrative space between the victim's world's maximum expansion (in 14:62, his world comes from above) and its utter destruction (15:33, 37–38) unfolds a drama where a carefully constructed world of relationships, teachings, visions, and hopes comes to an end.

From a literary perspective, world creation relies, among other elements, on establishing affinity relationships among characters (usually sharing common projects), on ramping up conflict with antagonists, and on delineating all kinds of boundaries with other created worlds inhabited, in turn, by other characters.³⁵ Plot lines weave together, undo, and re-create complex relationships between actors who react to each other on shifting grounds. Such are the elements that shape the victim's world. The institutions a character inhabits, the relationships he builds, and the antagonisms he creates materialize the contours of his world as much as the limits of his body and the reach of his actions and visions. The goal of the torturer, understood here as a collective character, is to destroy such boundaries and reinstitute a world that he perceives under attack. Although such observations owe much to most recent developments in narrative theory, I should notice that such theorization is simply a way of grounding well-studied theological themes such as the kingdom of God in literary theory. The kingdom of God, a salient Markan topic,³⁶ encapsulates Jesus's world—a project of its own, a scenario populated by disciples, beneficiaries, teachings, actions, visions, and institutions. It is within such a view that we turn our attention to discipleship and the temple as paradigmatic examples of what constitutes the victim's world, even as it is eventually threatened and destroyed under the rule of torture.

Mark features the apostles as major characters and as models of discipleship.³⁷ Their narrative makeup presents them as flawed personae, invit-

---

35. Recent narrative studies demonstrate how character construction relies on intra and textual elements and on the construction that readers make of both. See Michal Beth Dinkler, "Building Character on the Road to Emmaus: Lukan Characterization in Contemporary Literary Perspective," *JBL* 136 (2017): 687–706. For a critique of such an approach that neglects the role of actual readers, see Luis Menéndez-Antuña, "Of Social Death and Solitary Confinement: The Political Life of a Gerasene (Luke 8:26–39)," *JBL* 138 (2019): 643–64. This critique is relevant to the present study because it shows that centering contemporary lived experiences of oppression illuminates the gospel's witnessing of torment (see figures below).

36. See R. T. France, *Divine Government: God's Kingship in the Gospel of Mark* (Vancouver: Regent College Publishers, 2003); Gabi Markusse and Paul Middleton, *Salvation in the Gospel of Mark: The Death of Jesus and the Path of Discipleship* (Eugene, OR: Pickwick, 2018); Thomas R. Hatina, "Who Will See 'The Kingdom of God Coming with Power' in Mark 9,1—Protagonists or Antagonists?," *Bib* 86 (2005): 20–34; Frank J. Matera, "Ethics for the Kingdom of God: The Gospel according to Mark," *LS* 20 (1995): 187–200; Mark Rowe, *God's Kingdom and God's Son: The Background to Mark's Christology from Concepts of Kingship in the Psalms* (Leiden: Brill, 2002), 115–61.

37. The literature on Markan characterization is extensive and, as one could expect, hardly consensual. Leif E. Vaage convincingly argues that we find instructions on how to enter the kingdom in the middle of the gospel (8:27–10:52) and where Jesus instructs the disciples on how to practice discipleship. Mark defines the entrance into

ing audiences to sympathize and engage with their misunderstandings.[38] Mark's creation of Jesus's world, his proposal as kingdom of God, heavily relies on the configuration of relational ties around discipleship. Discipleship involves leaving a world behind in order to step into a new one. Following Jesus means abandoning everything (Mark 10:28) and situating oneself differently in "this world." As Leif E. Vaage argues, "the brash breakage of ordinary kinship ties and the disregard of other social norms as the first step of discipleship soon involve revisiting the very region just forsaken or previously forsaken."[39] This "domestic asceticism," as Vaage terms it, interweaves discipleship with political utopianism by presenting the latter as a transformative way of inhabiting the world.

In this narrative, "the most fully characterized individual," Peter, epitomizes the flawed nature of Markan discipleship.[40] His actions and sayings operate as check points for the audience to rectify errors in Jesus's project. Take, for instance, Peter's misunderstanding of Jesus's messianism (Mark 8:27–9:1). Jesus proposes a model of messianism where discipleship

---

the kingdom in terms of "unorthodox social practices" (Vaage, "An Other Home: Discipleship in Mark as Domestic Asceticism," *CBQ* 71 [2009]: 741–61).

38. By narrative makeup I refer here to the consideration of characterization in light of source criticism (Dowd and Malbon, "Significance of Jesus' Death," esp. 278).

39. Vaage, "An Other Home," 753.

40. Scholarship has long debated Peter's role as a literary character, his influence in the gospel's composition, or his presumptive role in shaping the community of reception. Peter is mentioned first and last (Mark 1:16; 16:7), is the main character in numerous episodes (8:23; 10:28; 14:66–72), and is reiteratively mentioned by name as part of the close group of disciples (9:1; 10:33). Ernest Best calls him the "protopenitent for Mark's community" (Best, *Disciples and Discipleship: Studies in the Gospel according to Mark* [Edinburgh: T&T Clark, 1986], 175). Timothy Wiarda argues that Peter is the spokesperson for the group (Wiarda, "Peter as Peter in the Gospel of Mark," *NTS* 45 [1999]: 19). Robyn Whitaker suggests that the rebuke and recall of Peter single him out as a "distinguished figure above all others," "not despite his failure, but precisely because of his failure" (Whitaker, "Rebuke or Recall? Rethinking the Role of Peter in Mark's Gospel?" *CBQ* 75 [2013]: 667). Other scholars consider Peter as a negative character. See Terence V. Smith, *Petrine Controversies in Early Christianity: Attitudes toward Peter in Christian Writing of the First Two Centuries*, WUNT 15 (Tübingen: Mohr Siebeck, 1985), 190. My argument does not take a position on such distinct characterizations, but it draws on them to show that Peter is a constitutive part of Jesus's world. On the flawed nature of Markan discipleship, see Richard Bauckham, *Jesus and the Eyewitnesses: The Gospels as Eyewitness Testimony* (Grand Rapids: Eerdmans, 2006), 175.

equals rejection and forfeiture of one's life. Peter's rebuke triggers Jesus to spell out the ethical implications of a new model of discipleship (8:34–9:1). The narrative creates a world in which Jesus as a teacher and a messiah predicts his own demise and redefines how disciples have understood his role as miracle worker, preacher, and exorcist. It is a world in which disciples ought not rebuke their master, a world in which disciples are to follow their teacher to the cross. It is a world, if we contextualize the pericope, in which blind men see (8:22–26) and disciples are invited to see (9:2).

The intertwining of Peter's and Jesus's worlds peaks in the torture scene.[41] The juxtaposition of both plots—Peter's betrayal and Jesus's interrogation—creates a series of dramatic parallels: whereas the priest questions Jesus, a lowly slave girl questions Peter; although accusations against Jesus are false, those against Peter ring true; Jesus confesses three times "I am," while Peter denies him the same number of times.[42] At a moment when the victim's world is pending destruction, the supreme apostle is accused of belonging to such a world, both in terms of relationship ("you were with Jesus the Nazarene"; Mark 14:67; see 3:14) and location ("truly you are one of them, for you are also a Galilean;" 14:70; see also 1:16; 16:7). The drama, which had made it clear that the world Jesus had borne through relationship building started to collapse right at the moment when the mob captures him ("all of them deserted him and fled"; 14:50), climaxes when Peter breaks down and weeps (14:72). In other words, the peril posed by torture effects the abandonment of those who, up to this point, had populated the victim's world. Now, only Jesus's body stands as a threat to the world of the torturer.

The persecuted body of Jesus (Mark 3:19; 9:31; 10:32–33; 11:18; 14:18–21, 41), itself a converging point of discipleship (13:9–12), sits at the center of the processes of world making and world destroying.[43] Peter's denial confirms that the victim's world, built upon a network of relationships, collapses. The disappearance of the disciples signals both that the victim

---

41. A perfect example of a Markan sandwich. See Joel Marcus, *Mark 8–16: A New Translation with Introduction and Commentary*, AYB 27A (New Haven: Yale University Press, 2009), 1022.

42. Whitaker, "Rebuke or Recall," 675.

43. Michal Beth Dinkler argues that the disciples' misunderstandings of Jesus contribute to the suffering of Jesus himself (Dinkler, "Suffering, Misunderstanding, and Suffering Misunderstanding: The Markan Misunderstanding Motif as a Form of Jesus's Suffering," *JSNT* 38 [2016]: 316–38).

stands now by himself and that torture isolates the victim in order to destroy his world. The severance of the relational world peaks as torturers turn their focus on the victim's body. The destruction of the victim's body means the destruction of its most intimate relational links (15:34).

Whereas discipleship is an "institution of allegiance" inviting its members to abandon their world and bear the cross of a new reality, the temple is the physical and theological locus of dis-allegiance, a place that the religious elite misuse for their own benefit to the detriment of those in need. Subsequently, the temple functions as a war zone between two different worlds: Jesus advocating an ethical use and his opponents defending a religious status quo. The conflict starts early on when God, tearing the heavens apart to declare affiliation, places its divine presence in the body of Jesus (Mark 1:10–11).[44] Jesus's eruption into the "house of God" (11:15–18) seals the irreconcilable nature of the oppositional views on the temple's function. It is not surprising, then, that the temple features prominently in the midst of torture. Jesus's conflicting relationship with the institution first grounds the torturer's accusation (14:58; 15:29) and then metaphorizes the victim's demise (15:38). The war of the worlds, to put it differently, is about the victim's body as much as it is about its metonymic and symbolic links with other realities (discipleship and temple, in this case).

Jesus's body's close ties with the temple's body crop up frequently in Mark.[45] For instance, the apocalyptic discourse (Mark 13:1–37) takes place at the temple (13:1–2). Here Jesus forecasts its total destruction (οὐ μὴ ἀφεθῇ ὧδε λίθος ἐπὶ λίθον ὃς οὐ μὴ καταλυθῇ; "there will not be stone upon stone that will not be destroyed"; 13:2), creating a series of literary resonances between the fate of the temple and the fate of the victim: the cos-

---

44. In Mark, the temple functions in the narrative not primarily as a strictly religious/cultic institution but as part of a larger theopolitical conflict between Jesus and the leaders. The temple is implicated as the primary mechanism for the leaders' self-serving exploitation of the common people (represented by the poor widow), and it is targeted to the extent that it serves this exploitive function. In other words, Jesus condemns the temple to destruction because of its rebellious caretakers, not because of its cultic system, and he proves superior because he yields authority over the temple's caretakers, not by virtue of some anticult agenda. See Ira Brent Driggers, "The Politics of Divine Presence: Temple as Locus of Conflict in the Gospel of Mark," *BibInt* 15 (2007): 246.

45. J. Bradley Chance, "The Cursing of the Temple and the Tearing of the Veil in the Gospel of Mark," *BibInt* 15 (2007): 268–91.

mological signs in Mark 13:24–25 anticipate the darkening of the earth in 15:33, and the evocation of God's reign as coming from the clouds in 14:62 replicates the reference in 13:26. Furthermore, the obscure saying about "the abomination of desolation" (τὸ βδέλυγμα τῆς ἐρημώσεως; 13:14)[46] ties together Jesus's and the temple's destiny.[47] Such abomination, Kloppenborg argues, refers to the imperial siege practice of *evocation deorum*, whereby the conquest of the land also meant the "calling out" of the tutelary deity before its inhabitants were enslaved and the rest of the buildings razed.[48] This separation of the enemy from its protective deity is replaced, at least for the gospel's original audience, with the body of Jesus.[49] When Jesus overturns the money exchangers' tables (11:15–18), he is contesting the torturer's use of the temple while linking his persona to the institution. Both destinies are linked (11:18; see also 12:10–12). The prediction of the destruction of the temple (13:1–2; see also 11:12–21, 27–34; 12:1–12; 13:5–37; 15:33, 37–39) chains Jesus's death with the temple's demise. No longer viable, the victim's failed project for the institution, in conflict with his torturers' vision, results in God abandoning it. The darkening of the sky and the tearing of the temple's veil (15:33, 38) metaphorize its breakdown.[50] The centurion's confession, whether one understands it as serious or ironic, confirms that Jesus's now-dead body is the place for God, once the temple's demise has been confirmed (15:39).

---

46. In his seminal essay, S. G. F. Brandon argues that this cryptic saying refers to the desecration of the temple in August 70, when Titus erected legionary standards that had cultic functions also because it bore the emperor's images in the courtyard. The ungrammatical masculine would refer to Titus himself (Brandon, "The Date of the Markan Gospel," *NTS* 7 [1961]: 126–41).

47. John S. Kloppenborg, "*Evocatio Deorum* and the Date of Mark," *JBL* 124 (2005): 419–50.

48. Kloppenborg, "*Evocatio Deorum*," 434.

49. Kloppenborg, "*Evocatio Deorum*," 441.

50. Kloppenborg, "*Evocatio Deorum*," 449. John Paul Heil extends the identification of Jesus's body with the community: "The narrative invites its audience to become the community that supplants and surpasses the temple by implementing in their lives Jesus's teaching within the temple (Mark 11:1–12:44) and outside the temple (13:1–37), but they are able to do so only with the empowerment of Jesus's death and resurrection (14:1–16:8)" (Heil, "The Narrative Strategy and Pragmatics of the Temple Theme in Mark," *CBQ* 59 [1997]: 99). In the next section I will provide an interpretation of these metaphoric elements as examples of the destruction of language.

4. THE GOSPEL OF TORTURE (MARK 15:1–39)

In a world where one's relationships have been banished and one's project of a new world is on the verge of collapse, the victim is at the mercy of derision, precisely for the failure of such a project. Bystanders' mocking of the tortured that he would destroy the temple and rebuild it in three days (Mark 15:29) and the torturer's derision and physical torment (15:20) and sarcasm (15:31) represent the conquering of the torturer's world over the victim's world, which is now at a point of exhaustion. Uttering a loud cry and giving up his last breath (ὁ δὲ Ἰησοῦς ἀφεὶς φωνὴν μεγάλην ἐξέπνευσεν; 15:37), immediately followed by the ripping of the temple's veil from top to bottom (καὶ τὸ καταπέτασμα τοῦ ναοῦ ἐσχίσθη εἰς δύο ἀπ' ἄνωθεν ἕως κάτω; 15:38) bring the victim's fight for life to an end. Scarry writes, "for what the process of torture does is to split the human being into two, to make emphatic the ever present but … only the latent distinction between a self and a body, between a 'me' and 'my body.'"[51] Scholars' inattentiveness to pain's centrality leads them to paper over those literary connotations expressing the effects of torture. The *velum scissum* is a case in point. In 1989 Timothy Geddert listed thirty-five possible interpretations, and a connection between the victim's broken body and the tearing apart of the temple's veil is nowhere to be found.[52] More recent studies fare no better.[53] It may be the case, as Timothy Wardle and many others notice, that the "death of the Son of God in Mark brings an end to the continued efficacy of the Jerusalem temple," but such a parallel is predicated on the thematic connections between the body in pain and the traumatic events around the temple's destruction.[54]

One could name many more instances where the world of the victim revolves around the temple and discipleship. For the sake of the present argument, it is worth emphasizing that understanding torture in its world-

---

51. Scarry, *Body in Pain*, 48–49.
52. Timothy Geddert, *Watchwords: Mark 13 in Markan Eschatology*, JSNTSup 26 (Sheffield: JSOT Press, 1989), 141–43. See also Stephen Motyer, "The Rending of the Veil: A Markan Pentecost?," *NTS* 33 (1987): 155–57; and Howard M. Jackson, "The Death of Jesus in Mark and the Miracle from the Cross," *NTS* 33 (1987): 29.
53. See Daniel M. Gurtner, "The Rending of the Veil and Markan Christology: 'Unveiling' the ΥΙΟΣ ΘΕΟΥ (Mark 15:38–39)," *BibInt* 13 (2007): 292–306; Gregory McKinzie, "The Symbolism of Divine Presence in Mark 15:33–39," *ResQ* 60 (2018): 219–21; and Aguilar Chiu, "Theological Reading," 39.
54. Timothy Wardle, "Mark, the Jerusalem Temple and Jewish Sectarianism: Why Geographical Proximity Matters in Determining the Provenance of Mark," *NTS* 62 (2016): 73.

destroying facet requires examining in retrospect the constitutive elements of the victim's world. It is here where the narrative of torture draws close literary connections between the climax of pain, total abandonment, and the destruction of the temple. It is also here where the ethics of representing torture warns against conceiving Jesus's relationship with the temple or with his disciples as the triggers, as the judicial causes for torture. To do so is to justify the torturer's logic, to cater to a grammar of torture that upholds "rebellion" or "resistance"—the excuses here are countless—as legitimizing instances to instill the crudest pain on the victim.[55] The accusation that Jesus intended to destroy the temple should not be understood as the cause of torture but as a verdict that the victim's world has no place in the torturer's world,[56] particularly when accusations are patently false (Mark 14:55–56).[57] The question, as Scarry puts it, is always a wound, and the answer is already a scream.

Torture and the Destruction of Language

To claim that the victim's utterances are screams is to say that language is no longer available. Although my argument proceeds making an analytical distinction, language destruction equates world destruction and vice versa: as extreme pain undoes one's world it also erases language's ability to name it, express it, account for it. On the side of language, however, torture also demands expression and linguistic articulation. Accounting for torture, testimonials coincide (see figures below), hits on the paradoxical nature of a borderline experience: on the one hand, torture destroys propositional language; on the other, it conjures an urgency, at least in its aftermath, to make some type of sense, only expressible via words.

---

55. Michel Foucault's insights that torture has nothing to do with fairness and everything with the maintenance of political power represents here the genealogical underside of Scarry's argument. For Foucault this "'ceremony of punishment' is not an act of justice, is an 'exercise in terror'" (Foucault, *Discipline and Punish*, 49).

56. In the next section I will argue that considering the accusation as the origin of torture risks accepting the logics of torture itself.

57. Although at the historical level there are good reasons to believe that Jesus's action at the temple is the main reason for his assassination, my focus is on the narrative and literary representation of torture. For a discussion on the historical relationship between Jesus and the temple, see Jostein Ådna, "Jesus and the Temple," in *Handbook for the Study of the Historical Jesus*, ed. Tom Holmén and Stanley E. Porter (Leiden: Brill, 2019), 2635–75.

Nihilism—the destruction of values that comes with the destruction of the victim's world—demands, in its wake, values. Torture seeks to eliminate the subject of speech while simultaneously pretending that she can speak.[58] Torment demands utterances even as it enforces silence. Scarry further elaborates that "the moment language bodies forth the reality of pain, it makes all further statements and interpretations seem ludicrous and inappropriate, as hollow as the world content that disappears in the head of the person suffering."[59] Not only does torture eradicate the victim's capacity for language, but it also foregrounds the inability of language ever to account for such pain. Subsequently, when attempting to convey such experience, literature resorts to analogies, symbols, metaphors, gaps, breaks, and silences to pit language against itself.[60]

Torture, grounded on pain cycles (its anticipation, recovery, reenactment, etc.), inscribes the cusp of pain on the tortured body, forcing it desperately to reach out for experiences, memories, perceptions, and emotions that will alleviate its demise. The tortured mind dwells on spatial and temporal elements that precede and follow pain. Agony, a peak of the process of the worlds at war in which the tortured experiences his world in the process of being unmade, unhinges the body from itself even as it forces it to reach beyond itself. The narrativization of pain seems to look back at pain and see in the experience a moment when the total isolation and solipsism of pain reaches out, grasping to hold on to the familiar. Consider the following first-hand testimonies of survivors as they reflect back on their experience.[61]

---

58. Scarry, *Body in Pain*, 47.

59. Scarry, *Body in Pain*, 60.

60. Cathy Caruth, *Unclaimed Experience: Trauma, Narrative, and History* (Baltimore: Johns Hopkins University Press, 2016), 1–9.

61. I have chosen these three testimonies coming from women who were tortured in Chile under the Pinochet regime because they reflect compellingly on the relationship between body, subjectivity, and language. It is important not to conflate the experiences of those who have survived torture (especially because torture takes many forms), but it is also fundamental to trace common threads in the way these experiences issue forth in linguistic form. For similar testimonies, see James Dawes, *That the World May Know: Bearing Witness to Atrocity* (Cambridge: Harvard University Press, 2007): 164–230; Primo Levi, *The Drowned and the Saved*, trans. Raymond Rosenthal (New York: Random House, 1989); Levi, *Survival in Auschwitz and the Reawakening: Two Memories*, trans. Marion Wiesel (New York: Hill & Wang, 2006); and Stevan M. Weine, *Testimony after Catastrophe: Narrating the Traumas of Political Violence* (Evanston, IL: Northwestern University Press, 2006).

I was just a set of "basic functions"—as you call them—not working at all. Or were they? The basic functions of my heart thumping in my chest or that of breathing bloody air in and out of my lungs, for example, continued to work despite my wish to die there and then.... Can I live with the dying of my body?[62]

Maybe the experiencing of pain has no language—as you assert—in the conventional way of understanding language, i.e., words producing meaning. However, I strongly believe that pain does find a voice in the yelling, in the screaming, even in the loss of those "basic functions" we were talking about before when, in my case, electrodes inside my vagina threatened with the disintegrating of my/self. You yell, you piss yourself and you are saying "it is hurting so much I cannot put it into f**** words!," because the pain is deeper than flesh and bones; it travels beyond your physical body, into some space within yourself which cannot make meaning of what is happening outside. You say to yourself: "I am losing the only way I have known until now to describe what is going on inside me, I am losing my tongue, I am losing meaning." I insist, though, that pain does have a voice, if not in words, then in its performance.... The other thing in relation to your assertion that pain has no voice is that there are some of us (lots, indeed) who shout our pain in public by writing, painting, dancing, singing, talking pain. And we, sometimes, do this by disrupting the boundaries of discipline and polite behavior.[63]

But, as I've said before, I felt as if I had no voice because I had no way of expressing my pain in words, which did not mean I was totally silent. My written text is full of ellipses, of gaps. They are my resistance to say more then and now, my refuge from the spoken language, my feminist/feminine imaginary. Remember the conversations I had with myself, the singing in my head, the tricks I used to keep my/self company and not to go insane."[64]

These testimonies throw into relief the multilayered relationship between torture and language. Although these witnesses have different views on how proper articulation remains possible in the aftermath of torture, they all convey the notion that the narrative expression of pain cannot

---

62. Consuelo Rivera-Fuentes and Lynda Birke, "Talking with/in Pain: Reflections on Bodies under Torture," *Women's Studies International Forum* 24 (2001): 660–61.
63. Rivera-Fuentes and Birke, "Talking with/in Pain," 661.
64. Rivera-Fuentes and Birke, "Talking with/in Pain," 663. There are quite similar testimonies in Olga Behar, *Las guerras de la paz* (Bogotá: Planeta, 1990), 167.

be linear, propositional, or formulaic. The incommunicability of pain is pain's most salient feature. Its inexpressibility is language's most striking barrier and, as a consequence, literature's ultimate frontier. Writing about torture seems to be writing about the apophatic experience, trying to capture an unrepresentable catastrophe. In such a titanic task, literature seeks to humbly fill in the gaps between language and experience.[65]

In the previous section, I explored how torture, with its world-destroying power, retrospectively maps onto the Markan apocalypse. Jesus warns his disciples that they "will be delivered over to councils, be beaten in synagogues," and will stand in front of governors and kings (Mark 13:9). Apocalypticism, after all, is a genre invested in staging worlds at war (brother versus brother, father versus child, children versus parents, false versus true prophets).[66] Mark uses several literary elements to convey the idea that torture destroys language. The most obvious one is that, under the extenuating circumstances of the crucifixion, the victim no longer can come up with words (λόγος). When the body gives up, language is no longer possible (ὁ δὲ Ἰησοῦς ἀφεὶς φωνὴν μεγάλην ἐξέπνευσεν; "And as Jesus cried out loud, he expired"; 15:37).[67] The victim's final grunt, unarticulated and opaque, stands in clear contrast with previous verses, in which everyone participating in the torturous process gets to speak.[68] If the cry of dereliction signals the destruction of the world, the "loud cry" literalizes the death of language.[69] Indeed, the world as we know it breaks down, and the "Son of Man comes in clouds with great power and glory" (13:26). When the victim's world is destroyed, only language remains (ὁ οὐρανὸς καὶ ἡ γῆ παρελεύσονται, οἱ δὲ λόγοι μου οὐ μὴ παρελεύσονται; "the heaven and the earth will pass away, but my words will not pass away"; 13:31), but its presence is nowhere to be found once torture finds its way deep into the body. The victim's promise that his words will not pass away—even after

---

65. Michael Richardson, *Gestures of Testimony: Torture, Trauma, and Affect in Literature* (New York: Bloomsbury, 2016).

66. See, e.g., Dereck Dashke, "Apocalypse and Trauma," in *The Oxford Handbook of Apocalyptic Literature*, ed. John Joseph Collins (Oxford: Oxford University Press, 2014), 457–73.

67. This expression is used in the case of the Gerasene to express social death. See Menéndez-Antuña, "Of Social Death."

68. Pilate (Mark 15:2, 4, 7, 9, 12, 14), observers (15:29), chief priests and scribes (15:31), bystanders (15:35), the sour-wine provider (15:36), and the centurion (15:39).

69. For an exploration of the multivalence of the yell/cry (Spanish: *grito*), see Ana Lidia M. Domínguez, *Una historia cultural del grito* (Madrid: Taurus, 2022).

torture has destroyed language—relies on the performative function of the written testimony, on the conditions of possibility enabling the speech act. If we consider the short Markan version as the original ending, the cry of dereliction (15:34) constitutes the victim's last words but ones that are meant to be written (9:12).

In two different moments, Jesus breathes his last (ὁ δὲ Ἰησοῦς ἀφεὶς φωνὴν μεγάλην ἐξέπνευσεν; 15:37, 39). Both moments sandwich the tearing of the veil (15:38). While in the previous section I suggested the *velum scissum* as a symbol referring to the world's collapse in terms of Jesus's relationship with the temple, I further propose that it is a metaphor for the destruction of the victim's body right at the moment of language's annihilation. To be sure, the interpretation of this theophany has shifted from historical considerations to literary and theological ones.[70] No longer understood as a "real event," the veil metonymically stands for the temple's new status in the wake of Jesus's death. It is surprising, however, that no argument mentions the possibility of the veil as a literary motif to convey what language can no longer express: the pain involved in the torturous death of the Son of God.[71] Flesh and veil are torn apart, their ripping evoking a similar sound, in a play of literary connections that finds echoes in Heb 10:20 (ἣν ἐνεκαίνισεν ἡμῖν ὁδὸν πρόσφατον καὶ ζῶσαν διὰ τοῦ καταπετάσματος, τοῦτ' ἔστιν τῆς σαρκὸς αὐτοῦ; "opening for us a new and living path through the veil, that is, his flesh").[72]

It might be the case that the veil's ripping inaugurates a new world,[73] but such inauguration is predicated on the victim's torn flesh that can no longer speak yet still it speaks (see testimonies above): the collapse of language encounters its way out, a way of speaking out through the ripping apart of the veil (and the darkening of the earth). It is actually pretty common to find among victim's testimonies an expression of their inex-

---

70. David Ulansey, "The Heavenly Veil Torn: Mark's Cosmic *Inclusio*," *JBL* 110 (1991): 123–25.

71. See Chance, "The Cursing of the Temple," 286.

72. Although it is outside of the scope of the present chapter to go into the details of this obscure verse, it is enough to say that there is a close thematic reference between Jesus's flesh and the ripping apart of the temple. See David M. Moffitt, "Unveiling Jesus' Flesh: A Fresh Assessment of the Relationship between the Veil and Jesus' Flesh in Hebrews 10:20," *PRSt* 37 (2010): 71–84; Mark A. Jennings, "The Veil and the High Priestly Robes of the Incarnation: Understanding the Context of Heb 10:20," *PRSt* 37 (2010): 85–97; and Gurtner, "Rending of the Veil."

73. Chance, "Cursing of the Temple," 284–85.

pressible pain through metaphors of darkness and textiles being ripped apart. Juan Cassassus, a survivor himself, writes: "The victim feels that the structures that secured his identity burst out. He is thrown into darkness, with no sense of time or space. In such darkness, there is no longer any parameter to relate to any kind of experience."[74] Donatella Di Cesare adds: "whoever survives torture, she is not only different from before, she is completely other, to the point that one cannot recognize those threads, nexus that could mend and fix that shred."[75] The survivor here considers the contemporary self as totally Other, as a textile that has been torn apart and can no longer be stitched together. Such destruction of the self through pain should caution against adhering to thick conceptions of agency. If the self vanishes at the cusp of torture, then we should understand the victim's ipsissima verba not so much as an expression of his agency (Mark 15:34) but as a literary device geared toward conveying the inexpressible. To understand the victim as an agent in full command of his actions is to not take seriously the victim's plight and to paper over the narrative's struggles to express such torment. Furthermore, to understand Jesus as a character in full command of what he says, right when speech is no longer possible, is to follow torture's logic, because it "systematically prevents the prisoner from being the agent of anything and simultaneously pretends he is the agent of some things."[76]

To be clear, my argument does not discard theological or narrative connections between the metaphors around darkness (Mark 15:33) and the tearing apart of the temple's veil (15:38). To be sure, Mark here, as in many other instances, draws on a wide variety of intra and extratextual references that create a network of meanings to theologize the event of torture. My argument makes no pronouncement on historical-critical or theological interpretations (see below) as hermeneutical keys to understand the passion narratives. My contribution does, however, emphasize that such renderings skip too quickly over the grueling details of pain and torture, even as they obscure the power dynamics between the worlds of the torturer and that of the victim. Simply put, this is a narrative about torture, extenuating pain, and utmost humiliation, so literary motifs, even in their metaphoricity, are intertwined with these grounding realities. The narra-

---

74. Juan Casassus, *Camino en la oscuridad* (Santiago de Chile: Editorial Debate, 2013), 48.

75. Donatella Di Cesare, *Tortura* (Barcelona: Gedisa, 2018), 65.

76. Scarry, *Body in Pain*, 47.

tive, to recap, explains that the torturers flog (15:15), humiliate (15:17–19), wound his head (15:17), strike him and spit upon him (15:19), mock him (15:20), and offer wine with myrrh, to add insult to injury (15:23).[77] The extent to which the victim is subjected to pain allows forensic evidence to term it sadistic.[78] Consequently, to center the victim's pain, as Mark does, means to explore how language struggles with injury.

Analgesic Literary Strategies

If the Gospel of Mark should be understood as the "book of torture" in the sense that it stays closer (literarily) to the experiences of those who experience the destruction of the world and language that accompanies extreme forms of punishment, what are we to say of other crucifixion accounts? I suggest that Matthew and Luke receive and adapt many of these elements but sprinkle the reality of torture with literary elements that assuage the trauma ensuing from torture. I tentatively call these elements *analgesic literary strategies* because they work to blunt the edge of pain as portrayed in Mark. For instance, when Luke incorporates two evildoers (Luke 23:32) who initiate a dialogue with the victim at the peak of crucifixion, not only is the evangelist erasing the isolation that we encounter in Mark; the writer also opens the door for "language" to make an appearance in the camera of torture. Luke 23:43 says, "And he said to him, 'Truly I say to you, today you will be with me in paradise.'" Luke 23:46 adds, "Father, into your hands I give my spirit.' When he had said this, he gave up his spirit."[79] Matthew's approach is more subtle: the writer here respects some of the literary strat-

---

77. Very much like scholars who paper over the event of the crucifixion as a case of extreme pain, they interpret the myrrh as an analgesic. An empirical experiment shows that, when myrrh is added to wine so that the liquid is saturated, the taste of the wine becomes too bitter to drink. It was an effective form of torture for a man suffering from the thirst caused by hypovolemic shock and dehydration. See Erkki Koskenniemi, Kirsi Nisula, and Jorma Toppari, "Wine Mixed with Myrrh (Mark 15.23) and Crurifragium (John 19.31–32): Two Details of the Passion Narratives," *JSNT* 27 (2005): 379–91.

78. Hengel, *Crucifixion in the Ancient World*, 25–87; Koskenniemi, Nisula, and Toppari, "Wine Mixed with Myrrh," 4; Samuelsson, *Crucifixion in Antiquity*, 292.

79. See Mark Jeong, "The Collapse of Society in Luke 23: A Thucydidean Take on Jesus' Passion," *NTS* 67 (2021): 317–35; Robyn Whitaker, "A Failed Spectacle: The Role of the Crowd in Luke 23," *BibInt* 25 (2017): 399–416; Peter Rice, "The Rhetoric of Luke's Passion: Luke's Use of Common-Place to Amplify the Guilt of Jerusalem's Lead-

egies that characterize Mark ("Why, God, have you abandoned me?"; Matt 27:46), but as soon as Jesus dies there is a theological coda that redeems torture: "And the resting-places of the dead came open; and the bodies of a number of sleeping saints came to life (Matt 27:52).[80] These are just examples that lead to the highest level of mystification of torture that we find in the gospels, with John at one extreme of such mystification ("it is finished;" John 19:30).

By restituting agency to the victim, a grammar of torture erases the inexpressible void that befalls on the victim's subjectivity. This is a moment when Matthew and John make use of the gaps between pain and language to create a series of literary elements that restore agency to the victim, converting the torture into a mirage. Matthew here sticks closer to the reality of torture destroying language, respecting the Markan account's emphasis on Jesus's abandonment as world destruction: Luke (23:45), in turn, has Jesus crying in a loud voice: "Father, in your hands I commend my spirit," inserting a theological comment that both diminishes the dramatism of the metaphor and restitutes articulated language to the victim. John's analgesic literary strategies, in turn, are off the charts: Jesus's last words are "It has been completed," referring to a plan that was set up from the beginning (John 19:30) and over which he has full command (19:11): You would have no authority over me at all unless it had been given you from above.[81]

---

ers in Jesus' Death," *BibInt* 21 (2013): 355–76; Gregory E. Sterling, "*Mors philosophi*: The Death of Jesus in Luke," *HTR* 94 (2001): 383–402.

80. Dale C. Allison Jr., "Anticipating the Passion: The Literary Reach of Matthew 26:47–27:56," *CBQ* 56 (1994): 701–14; Raj Nadella, "The Ambivalent Pilate: Reverse Mimicry in Matthew's Gospel," *Bangalore Theological Forum* 45 (2013): 56–65; Alida Euler, "Drinking Gall and Vinegar: Psalm 69:22; An Underestimated Intertext in Matt 27:34, 48," *ZNW* 112 (2021): 130–40.

81. Carola Diebold-Scheuermann, *Jesus vor Pilatus: Eine exegetische Untersuchung zum Verhör durch Pilatus (Joh 18,28–19,16a)*, SBB 32 (Stuttgart: Verlag Katholisches Bibelwerk, 1996); Michael Theobald, "Gattungswandel in der johanneischen Passionserzählung: Die Verhöre Jesu durch Pilatus (Johannes 18,33–38; 19,8–12) im Licht der *Acta Isidori* und anderer Prozessdialoge," in *Studies in the Gospel of John and Its Christology*, ed. Joseph Verheyden, Geert Van Oyen, Michael Labahn, and Reimund Bieringer, BETL 265 (Leuven: Peeters 2014), 447–83; Winfried Verburg, *Passion als Tragödie? Die literarische Gattung der antiken Tragödie als Gestaltungsprinzip der Johannespassion*, SBS 182 (Stuttgart: Verlag Katholisches Bibelwerk 1999), 91–100; Uta Poplutz, "Das Drama der Passion: Eine Analyse der Prozesserzählung Joh 18,28–19,16a unter Berücksichtigung dramentheoretischer Gesichtspunkte," in *The Death of Jesus in the Fourth Gospel*, ed. Gilbert van Belle, BETL 200 (Leuven: Leuven

The Ethics of Accounting for Torture

Scarry's take on torture staunchly dismisses any attempt to theorize torture outside or beyond the victim's pain. To speak about torture is to unapologetically center the experience of the tortured. In other words, the body in pain (not its cause, telos, or circumstance) is the focal point of interpretation. This ethical stance tasks biblical hermeneutics with the assignment of probing the gospels as literature of pain. To be sure, the Markan account might be understood as an instance of noble death, resistance, vindication, or even as an antiblasphemy manifesto, to name a few, but to do so without carefully unpacking how the narrative conveys (struggles to convey, as most writings about torture do) the raw nature of pain, how the grammar of torture bleeds into the narrative plots, risks neutralizing torment, sanitizing torture, and objectifying the victim. Shelly Rambo reminds us of trauma language that "is compelling language not insofar as it contains truths but insofar as it testifies to truths that cannot be contained."[82] Aware of the paradoxical nature of pain, impossible to pour into language while demanding to be poured, this chapter's goal has been to testify to the centrality of torture in the passion narrative even as it spills over the rest of the gospel.

Torture itself, one could argue, is not the representation of torture. The experience of pain and its narrativization belong to separate domains. It

---

University Press 2007), 769–82; Thomas Söding, "Die Macht der Wahrheit und das Reich der Freiheit: Zur johanneischen Deutung des Pilatus-Prozesses (Joh 18,28–19,16)," *ZTK* 93 (1996): 35–58; Jean Zumstein, *Kreative Erinnerung: Relecture und Auslegung im Johannesevangelium*, 2nd ed., ATANT 84 (Zürich: Theologischer Verlag 2004), 241–52; Steven A. Hunt, "The Roman Soldiers at Jesus' Arrest: 'You are Dust, and to Dust You Shall Return,'" in *Character Studies in the Fourth Gospel: Narrative Approaches to Seventy Figures*, ed. John Steven A. Hunt and Donald Francois Tolmie, WUNT 314 (Tübingen: Mohr Siebeck 2013), 554–67; Beate Kowalski, "'Was ist Wahrheit?' (Joh 18,38a): Zur literarischen und theologischen Funktion der Pilatusfrage in der Johannespassion," in *Im Geist und in der Wahrheit: Studien zum Johannesevangelium und zur Offenbarung des Johannes sowie andere Beiträge*, ed. Konrad Huber, NTA 52 (Münster: Aschendorff Verlag 2008), 201–27; Detlev Dormeyer, "Joh 18:1–14 Par Mk 14.43–53: Methodologische Überlegungen zur Rekonstruktion einer Vorsynoptischen Passionsgeschichte," *NTS* 41 (1995): 218–39; Manuel Benéitez Rodríguez, "Un extraño interrogatorio: Jn 18,29–32," *EstEcl* 68 (1993): 459–96.

82. Shelly Rambo, *Spirit and Trauma: A Theology of Remaining* (Louisville: Westminster John Knox, 2010), 165.

is precisely this gap between the victim's subjective experience and the objective literary account that should, I am arguing, be at the center of an ethics of biblical interpretation invested "in the pain of others."[83] Let me conclude, to bring the ethical point home, by hinting at how scholarship on Mark talks about pain in ways that contemporary trauma and torture studies find deficient. It is both relevant and urgent for scholarship to tend to the geopolitical context of testimonies of torture. Focusing on the political backgrounds of certain regimes under which torture takes place helps us to connect regimes of terror with terrorized bodies. These accounts make little sense if divorced from the terrorism that facilitated their widespread deployment in the first place. David Tombs and others remind us that crucifixion as torture ties closely with the Roman Empire and its expansive forces. It is also pertinent that scholars pay attention to material circumstances, such as the mechanics of inflicting pain and the strategies that systems of torture generate to maximize harm. Martin Hengel's contribution helps us understand the vicissitudes of Roman execution, its forensic elements, and its punitive tactics. Equally important is to explore the literary forms and genres that autobiographies and other testimonial literature inhabit and how the adoption of those forms theorize trauma and death. Helen Bond's case for "passion as noble death" compellingly argues that Mark theologizes the crucifixion to make it fit broader Greco-Roman patterns of honor. These approaches, however, skip a bit too fast over the irreducible reality of pain, its inexpressibility, and the dilemma that it poses to language. In other words, they decenter the victim's pain and leave questions about the literary representation of pain unaddressed. And they do so, despite the text's heavy emphasis on a victim experiencing torture and torment.

---

83. Susan Sontag, *Regarding the Pain of Others* (London: Penguin, 2019).

5
THE GOSPEL OF SOCIAL DEATH
(LUKE 8:26–39)

> I heard someone screaming far way and it was me. I fell against the wall, and as if it were a catapult, was hurled across the cell to the opposite wall. Back and forth I reeled, from the door to the walls, screaming. Insane.[1]

Mass Incarceration and Solitary Confinement

In the previous chapter, I suggested that one of the features of contemporary representations of the crucifixion is their demystification of pain. Souza's work pulls the viewer into the destruction of body, language, and world enacted in the crucifixion as torture-like testimonies of victims and an ensuing theorization of such world-destroying pain pulls the reader away from the position of a disinterested reader and into the narrative trauma of Jesus's crucifixion. In this chapter, I seek to deal further with the phenomenology of torture by addressing mass incarceration and its cruelest version of punishment in the form of solitary confinement.

The United States has the highest incarceration rate in the world, with around two million people behind bars. Mass incarceration, mass imprisonment, or the carceral state refer to the fact that the US has privileged prison as the medium to create a safe society. Extremely high rates of incarceration result in the tearing apart of families and the social fabric, with a considerably higher impact in poorer communities and populations of color. Although scholars disagree on the ultimate root of this phenomenon, the "war on drugs" initiated in the 1970s, the increasing crimi-

---

1. Jack Henry Abbott, *In the Belly of the Beast: Letters from Prison* (New York: Vintage Books, 1991), 27, quoted in Lisa Guenther, *Solitary Confinement: Social Death and Its Afterlives* (Minnesota: University of Minnesota Press, 2013), 183.

nalization of poverty, and the rise of the privatized prison continue to play a role in the perpetuation of the carceral state.[2]

To take seriously this social, political, and cultural crisis involves reflecting on the ethical issues involved. Theological studies have paid attention to restorative justice, the task of activism and ministry in the midst of such desolation, the racialization of the lockdown system, while also reflecting on the role of forgiveness, reparations, and abolition.[3] Christopher Ringe, for instance, argues that, in a phenomenological sense, mass incarceration is "hell on earth."[4]

---

2. Megan Comfort, "Punishment beyond the Legal Offender," *Annual Review of Law and Social Science* 3 (2007): 271–96; John Hagan and Ronit Dinovitzer, "Collateral Consequences of Imprisonment for Children, Communities, and Prisoners," *Crime and Justice* 26 (1999): 121–62; James P. Lynch and William J. Sabol, "Prison Use and Social Control," in *Policies, Processes, and Decisions of the Criminal Justice System: Criminal Justice 2000*, ed. Julie Horney (Washington, DC: National Institute of Justice, 2000): 7–44; Mary Pattillo, David Weiman, and Bruce Western, eds., *Imprisoning America: The Social Effects of Mass Incarceration* (New York: Russell Sage, 2004); Steven Raphael and Michael A. Stoll, eds., *Do Prisons Make Us Safer? The Benefits and Costs of the Prison Boom* (New York: Russell Sage, 2009); Sara Wakefield and Christopher Uggen, "Incarceration and Stratification," *Annual Review of Sociology* 36 (2010): 387–406; Bruce Western, *Punishment and Inequality in America* (New York: Russell Sage, 2006); Christopher Wildeman and Bruce Western, "Incarceration in Fragile Families," *Future of Children* 20 (2010): 157–77; James William Kilgore, *Understanding Mass Incarceration: A People's Guide to the Key Civil Rights Struggle of Our Time* (New York: New Press, 2015); Heather Schoenfeld, *Building the Prison State: Race and the Politics of Mass Incarceration*, Chicago Series in Law and Society (Chicago: University of Chicago Press, 2018); Todd R. Clear and Natasha Frost, *The Punishment Imperative: The Rise and Failure of Mass Incarceration in America* (New York: New York University Press, 2014); Sean Joe, "Analyzing Mass Incarceration," *Science* 374.65 (2021): 237.

3. On activism and ministry, see Tanya Erzen, *God in Captivity: The Rise of Faith-Based Prison Ministries in the Age of Mass Incarceration* (Boston: Beacon, 2017); David K. Beedon, *Pastoral Care for the Incarcerated: Hope Deferred, Humanity Diminished?* (Newcastle: Palgrave, 2022). On the racialization of the lockdown system, see Antonios Kireopoulos, Mitzi Budde, and Matthew D. Lundberg, eds., *Thinking Theologically about Mass Incarceration: Biblical Foundations and Justice Imperatives* (Mahwah, NJ: Paulist, 2017). On forgiveness, reparations, and abolition, see Joshua Dubler and Vincent W. Lloyd, *Break Every Yoke: Religion, Justice, and the Abolition of Prisons* (New York: Oxford University Press, 2020).

4. Christophe Ringe, *Necropolitics: The Religious Crisis of Mass Incarceration in America* (Lanham, MD: Lexington Books, 2020), 115–32.

Exploring the reality of incarceration conjures up a set of questions about subjectivity and community. Who are we, as a society, when millions of people are imprisoned in our backyard, and we decide to look elsewhere? What do we learn about subjectivity when we pay attention to the consequences of incarceration as it falls like a hammer on the shoulders of marginalized individuals?

Solitary confinement, also known as "administrative segregation" or "the hole," is a practice used in the US correctional system in which prisoners are confined to a small cell for twenty-two to twenty-four hours a day, with minimal human contact or environmental stimulation. The use of solitary confinement in the US has raised significant concerns due to its severe psychological and physical effects on inmates. According to a study by the Bureau of Justice Statistics, in 2016, approximately 61,000 prisoners were held in some form of restrictive housing, with about 12,000 of them being in long-term solitary confinement. Moreover, it is estimated that over 2,000 prisoners have spent six or more consecutive years in solitary confinement.[5]

The statistics regarding the impact of solitary confinement are alarming. According to a report by the American Civil Liberties Union (ACLU), individuals in solitary confinement are more likely to experience mental health issues such as depression, anxiety, and hallucinations.[6] The risk of self-harm and suicide is also significantly higher among those subjected to long periods of isolation. In fact, a study published in the *Journal of the American Academy of Psychiatry and the Law* found that over half of all prison suicides in the US occur in solitary confinement.[7] Additionally, prolonged periods of isolation can exacerbate preexisting mental health conditions and even lead to the development of new psychiatric disorders. The lack of social interaction and sensory stimulation can cause severe psychological distress, leading to symptoms akin to posttraumatic stress disorder (PTSD).

---

5. Association of State Correctional Administrators and Arthur Liman Public Interest Program at Yale Law School, *Reforming Restrictive Housing: The 2018 ASCA-Liman Nationwide Survey of Time-in-Cell* (October 2018), https://tinyurl.com/SBLPress06108a1.

6. See American Civil Liberties Union, *The Dangerous Overuse of Solitary Confinement in the United States* (New York: ACLU Foundation, 2014).

7. Jeffrey L. Metzner and Jamie Fellner, "Solitary Confinement and Mental Illness in U.S. Prisons: A Challenge for Medical Ethics," *Journal of the American Academy of Psychiatry and the Law* 38 (2011): 104–8.

Furthermore, the use of solitary confinement has disproportionate effects on certain demographics within the prison population. African American prisoners are more likely to be placed in solitary confinement, compared to their white counterparts.[8] Moreover, individuals with mental health issues are often placed in isolation due to the lack of adequate mental health treatment facilities within the prison system. This further exacerbates their conditions and perpetuates a cycle of suffering. Not by coincidence, judicial scholars have started to consider solitary confinement under the umbrella of torture.[9]

The experience of those suffering under the extreme conditions of solitary confinement epitomizes the "other side of the abyssal line" in our midst. Referring to contemporary postcolonial societies, Santos reminds us that the abyssal line does not match the North/South or West/East cartographical borders but rather serves as an ultimate marker of humanity. If "the crucial difference between abyssal and nonabyssal exclusion is that only the former is premised upon the idea that the victim or target suffers from an ontological *capitis diminiutio* for not being fully human, rather a fatally degraded sort of human being,"[10] the physical cell literalizes the abstract idea of the abyssal line because it strips the prisoner of the basic conditions of livability in the midst of an overabundance culture. In the steps of an altogether philosophical tradition—Foucault in hand—Achille Mbembe coins the term *necropolitics* to refer to a type of population management that entails the subjugation of life to the power of death:

> sovereignty consists in the power to manufacture an entire crowd of people who specifically live at the edge of life, or even on its outer

---

8. Association of State Correctional Administrators and Arthur Liman Public Interest Program at Yale Law School, *Aiming to Reduce Time-In-Cell: Reports from Correctional Systems on the Numbers of Prisoners in Restricted Housing and on the Potential of Policy Changes to Bring About Reforms* (November 2016), https://tinyurl.com/SBLPress06108b2.

9. Samuel Fuller, "Torture as a Management Practice: The Convention against Torture and Non-disciplinary Solitary Confinement," *Chicago Journal of International Law* 19 (2018): 102–44; Terry Allen Kupers, *Solitary: The Insider Story of Supermax Isolation and How We Can Abolish It* (Berkeley: University of California Press, 2017); Konrad Franco, Caitlin Patler, and Keramet Reiter, "Punishing Status and the Punishment Status Quo: Solitary Confinement in U.S. Immigration Prisons, 2013–2017," *Punishment and Society* 24 (2022): 170–95.

10. Santos, *End of the Cognitive Empire*, 23.

edge—people for whom living means continually standing up to death, and doing so under conditions in which death itself increasingly tends to become spectral, thanks both to the way in which it is lived and to the manner in which it is given. This life is a superfluous one, therefore, whose price is so meager that it has no equivalence, whether market or— even less human; this is a species of life whose value is extra-economic, the only equivalent of which is the sort of death able to be inflicted upon it.[11]

The interpretative challenge, as in the case of torture *stricto sensu*, involves approaching an experience in which the subject has been desubjectified, in which the prison system has rendered the victim speechless. On this front, the notion of the human is deployed *as in brackets* because it is already charged with exclusions.[12] How do we, then, get closer to an experience that, as we will see, is alien to the victim herself?

A Gerasene in Political Death

Luke introduces a man from the region of the Gerasenes (Luke 8:26) and portrays him with no clothes, no home, and dwelling among the tombs (8:27). Anonymous, naked, homeless, out of the city, this persona not only lives with the dead but also experiences social death;[13] that is, the Gerasene, having been severed from the domain of the political, is virtually dead to his community. Briefly put, the human has been expelled from the realm of humanity. My argument suggests that an exploration of those socially dead in the present, more specifically of those prisoners subjected to the extreme conditions of solitary confinement, refines traditional understandings of the Gerasene *as character*.

An intercontextual approach takes thick descriptions of contemporary experiences of solitary confinement as a starting point to explore this char-

---

11. Achille Mbembe, *Necropolitics* (Durham, NC: Duke University Press, 2019), 37–38.

12. Alexander Weheliye considers that the most significant contribution of black studies "is the transformation of the human into a heuristic model and not an ontological *fait accompli.*" See Alexander G. Weheliye, *Habeas Viscus: Racializing Assemblages, Biopolitics, and Black Feminist Theories of the Human* (Durham, NC: Duke University Press, 2014), 8.

13. Orlando Patterson, *Slavery and Social Death: A Comparative Study* (Cambridge: Harvard University Press, 1982).

acter. By presenting the phenomenological descriptions of prisoners' experiences under the extreme conditions of solitary confinement, a trajectory of interpretation exposes, on the one hand, which elements of subject formation are relevant for a thick construction of the Gerasene as a character and, on the other, how such a meaning-making process depends on experiences readily available to professional and flesh-and-blood interpreters.[14]

In the present chapter, prisoners are not real readers; reading with those under solitary confinement, if the study were to pursue an ethnographical account, would require a socialization conducive to eliminating prisoners' solitude, the sine qua non of their status as socially dead. Instead, this trajectory of interpretation takes their published self-reports and the subsequent phenomenological analysis as a frame for a character analysis that bridges both the historical gap between the phenomenon of social death in the past and in the present and the existential split between the living conditions of the Gerasene and the professional critic.

Tending to the experiences of victims, as in the previous chapter, tests the limits of language and, consequently, the interpreter's ability to convey what remains inexpressible. The question raises the stakes for the interpreter who wishes to go beyond a mere exposition of the effects of torture on the victim but rather wants to peek into a grammar of suffering that leaves the interpreter herself defenseless. To witness the destruction of the self inevitably initiates the destruction of the witness, undoing the gaze that seeks to comprehend the event. Concerning the task of biblical interpretation, the goal is to unbind the Gerasene from textual confinement and to bring him into the realm of the living. Regarding the task of reaching the other side of the abyssal line, the goal is to unbind the prisoner from the reader's obliviousness.

The suggested trajectory of interpretation proceeds in two steps: after a detailed phenomenological analysis of solitary confinement as social

---

14. For a thoughtful discussion of the problem of flesh-and-blood readers as it pertains to the interpretation of Luke from a reader-response perspective, see James A. Metzger, *Consumption and Wealth in Luke's Travel Narrative*, BibInt 88 (Leiden: Brill, 2007), 36–61. Metzger grounds his ideological approach "on two features of his own social and historical context at the beginning of the twenty-first century: rampant overconsumption and unprecedented personal wealth" (Metzger, *Consumption and Wealth*, 56). Similarly, my approach takes the reality of mass incarceration in the United States and its dehumanizing consequences as the springboard for an analysis of the Gerasene as a socially dead character.

death in the contemporary US prison system, an approach that analyzes the Gerasene as socially dead follows. The Gerasene is, undoubtedly, what narrative criticism typically terms a minor character, a persona textually circumscribed at the service of the major character. He is also an exceptional character: a character exploration through the lens of social death distilled from the experiences of those under solitary confinement reveals that the Gerasene is the only character in the gospels with an apolitical status. The Gerasene's exemption from the political is predicated both on his living among the dead and, more importantly, on the lack of basic structures that support the political (language, home, clothes, city).[15] As the story implicitly suggests, his relationship with other characters in the polis (8:27: ἐκ τῆς πόλεως) has been dramatically severed; his dwelling among the dead substitutes his location among the living. Accordingly, the plight of the Gerasene resembles the prisoner's in that both have been removed from the political realm understood in its most literal sense. In the second part, the Gerasene comes forth as a character with a subjectivity marked by his (a)relationality, a figure whose apolitical predicament manifests his political singularity.

When studying the crucifixion as torture, I argued that it is a hermeneutical overreach to ascribe agency to the victim's words in the narrative. Extreme pain destroys the narrative insofar as the narrative conveys meaning. Here, the role of the literary author veils the raw experience of the victim, whether a real person or a literary character, whether a victim herself or the biblical critic. In this chapter, I resort to the work of Francis Bacon to explore how the desubjectification of extreme pain under solitary confinement relinquishes a narrative and how the Gerasene's words themselves represent a resistance, failed as it might be, to represent the character's wholeness. At the same time, I will show how the visual representation of torture under solitary confinement underlines elements that

---

15. The Gerasene is, to use a term coined by Giorgio Agamben, an example of bare life, of an individual who, although within the realm of the political, has no political rights, "a legally unnamable and unclassifiable being" (Agamben, *State of Exception* [Chicago: University of Chicago Press, 2005], 5). Social death, the concept privileged in this analysis, is not synonymous with bare life, since both terms presume different notions of the political sphere. For the sake of terminological clarity, I use "apolitical" to describe the most extreme cases of social death such as the prisoners in solitary confinement or this "certain man" (Luke 8:27) so as to signal that, unlike in other paradigmatic instances such as slavery, colonization, or concentration camps, the subject is deprived of the sociality attached to living with other fellow human beings and, as a result, her subjectivity dissipates.

the narrative is unable to convey because of, in the case of the gospel, the plot's redemptive nature and, in the case of the victim's testimonies, their propositional nature.

Right during the exposition about the prisoner's/Gerasene's plight, I suggest we take a visual detour through the work of Francis Bacon. Bacon was known for his exploration of the human condition and often depicted the darker aspects of existence, including violence, suffering, and anguish. In his *Crucifixion* series, he delves into the theme of torture. Bacon's artwork serves multiple purposes: a fascination with the human body and its vulnerability to pain and violence, a metaphor for the universal experience of suffering, an existential reflection on the condition of the postmodern subject in the wake of the horrors of World War II, a commentary on the capacity for cruelty and inhumanity, a highly symbolic exploration of the human condition. Without negating any of these readings, here I will focus on Bacon's paintings as critique of institutionalized violence and the effect it has on the victim and, perhaps more relevantly for our purposes, on the viewer herself.

Social Death, Solitary Confinement, and the Phenomenological Interpreter

Social Death and Solitary Confinement

Both Mark (5:1–20) and Luke (8:26–39), with notable redactional differences, unequivocally characterize the demon-possessed as delinked from the social world, dwelling among the dead, homeless, naked, and chained.[16] My argument shows how thick phenomenological descriptions of experiences of present-day isolated prisoners expose certain unexplored features in the figure of the Gerasene. Cut off from the social and political realms, phenomenology suggests, the humans—both the prisoner and the Gerasene—become unhinged; untied from sociality, individuality collapses; radically isolated, subjectivity comes undone and bodily perceptions become deranged.

Orlando Patterson's *Slavery and Social Death: A Comparative Study* coined the expression "social death" to describe the effect of slavery on

---

16. Matthew describes two demon-possessed men (8:28–34), partially mitigating the solitary status of the Markan and Lukan Gerasene.

5. THE GOSPEL OF SOCIAL DEATH (LUKE 8:26–39) 137

sociality, shifting the study of slavery from a historically abstracted, factual approach to one attentive to personal relations. Patterson offered an operational definition of slavery as social death as "the permanent, violent domination of natally alienated and generally dishonored persons."[17] Recent scholarship has built on this analysis of the conditions of subject formation under slavery[18] and expanded the notion of social death to describe how extreme conditions of livability—Nazi camps, migratory movements, sexual exploitation, total confinement, and the like—distort, undo, unhinge, and unglue subjectivity through the deprivation of intersubjectivity. Subjectivity, in other words, reaches a vanishing point when it is consistently and permanently severed from the relationship with other subjectivities. The "social non-person,"[19] "the socially dead," deprived of meaningful interpersonal connections, starts to lose a proper understanding of their relationship to temporality (to a proper sense of their past, present, and future) and spatiality (to a proper sense of belonging to a land, family, and nation).[20]

US supermax prisons' perpetuation of slavery's social dynamics and its effects on subject formation are nowhere more evident than in the reality of solitary confinement, the enforced penitentiary regime whereby inmates experience extreme isolation, deprivation of interpersonal contact, confinement within the walls of minuscule cells, ban from the social, political, cultural, and biological world. In the wake of Trans-Atlantic slavery, the supermax industrial system, with its rooted racialized history and its capitalist embeddedness,[21] deprives the subject of the basic conditions of interrelationality, endangers the stability of the structures holding the subject together, and throws into relief the annihilation of a subjectivity

---

17. Patterson, *Slavery and Social Death,* 13. For a critique of Patterson's somewhat abstracted notion of social death, see Vincent Brown, "Social Death and Political Life in the Study of Slavery," *American Historical Review* 114 (2007): 1231–49.

18. For a theological account, see Willie James Jennings, *The Christian Imagination: Theology and the Origins of Race* (New Haven: Yale University Press, 2010), 22.

19. Patterson, *Slavery and Social Death,* 5.

20. See a brief exploration of the theory of social death applied to other Lukan narratives in Luis Menéndez-Antuña, "Black Lives Matter and Gospel Hermeneutics: Political Life and Social Death in the Gospel of Luke," *CurTM* 45.4 (2018): 29–34.

21. See Michelle Alexander, *The New Jim Crow: Mass Incarceration in the Age of Colorblindness* (New York: New Press, 2012), esp. 26–35; Kupers, *Solitary*; and Dan Berger and Toussaint Losier, *Rethinking the American Prison Movement* (London: Routledge, 2017), esp. 143–74.

deprived of the condition of its possibility (relationality) and of a body stripped of its political status. What are the consequences of social death, of the subject's removal from her political world, on her subjectivity? What are the effects of living in a tomb, to use an expression that both qualifies the contemporary prisoner and the Gerasene, on the living person? In the following, a phenomenological analysis suggests that chaining the subject (8:29: ἐδεσμεύετο ἁλύσεσιν καὶ πέδαις φυλασσόμενος; "he was shackled and chained while under vigilance"), removing the prisoner from the polis, unhinges the subject from herself.

The Phenomenology of Solitary Confinement

The modern prison, Foucault famously argued, produced the modern prisoner, a new character, a persona under strict surveillance forced to come to terms with its own wickedness.[22] Whereas formerly the sovereign exerted power on the transgressor as an act of public dissuasion, the new institutionalized regime created the modern persona of the prisoner, the delinquent, the monster, the rapist, the murderer, characters in need of isolation, required to learn how to think properly through prolonged managed seclusion. This apparatus of enforced habits, rules, and orders aimed at interiorization is the precursor of the contemporary system of solitary confinement.

These regimental shifts gave way to anthropological changes in which, under the banner of humanization, the subject became radically redefined as a monadic entity, as a self-contained individuality and, consequently, amenable to total isolation. A system designed to bring people to terms with themselves, "to convert them into 'republican machines,'" ends up destroying the very matrix of personhood.[23] Lisa Guenther's phenomenological analysis of the consequences of solitary confinement on subjectivity under the duress of social death offers a template to tease out, in the next section, the implications of understanding the Gerasene as socially dead. The purpose here is twofold. First, I present a phenomenological account of the unhingement of selfhood caused by social death. Solitary confinement, as an extreme version of social death, deprives the subject of a relationship to the world, of the ultimate horizon of any meaningful

---

22. Foucault, *Discipline and Punish*, 3–69.
23. Guenther, *Solitary Confinement*, 22.

experience. Second, I also introduce the notions of intercorporeality, the perception of one's body as dependent on other bodies, and of interanimality, the assumption that humans share with other animals an intersubjective way of being in the world. Both concepts underscore the basic conditions of livability, demonstrate that subjectivity collapses when one is isolated,[24] and permit a thick description of the Gerasene's social death.

Guenther situates the detainee within institutional developments of the state-induced penitentiary punishment system, offering a phenomenological account of its effects on subjectivity. She, in short, demonstrates that there is no subjectivity without relationality: total isolation, lack of the experience of a shared world with other bodies, and dispossession of common participation in a horizon of meaning with other subjects lead to a wavering of perceptual reality and, ultimately, to the ego's collapse. On the basic premise that subjectivity, that ego coherence, requires intersubjectivity for its survival, phenomenology attributes the unhingement of the self not to depression, psychosis, or paranoia but to a phenomenological space where the subject no longer can sustain subjectivity. Phenomenology then depsychologizes and demedicalizes the traumatic experiences of prisoners subjected to social death. The intersubjective basis for a sense of concrete personhood and for a grounding in the objective world irreducible to one's personal impressions is structurally undermined.[25] Consider the following testimonies:

> After twenty-three days of darkness, Abbott came unhinged, no longer able to identify with his own body and voice: "I heard someone screaming far way and it was me. I fell against the wall, and as if it were a catapult, was hurled across the cell to the opposite wall. Back and forth I reeled, from the door to the walls, screaming. Insane."[26]

---

24. A cell is usually six feet by twelve, painted white or pale gray. It includes a bed, a table and a seat, a toilet, and a sink. The door, made of perforated stainless steel, resembles a wire mesh that obstructs the prisoner's view and allows natural light to filter through or pepper spray used on prisoners during cell extractions. There is a slot in the door (cuff port) through which food trays are exchanged and hands cuffed for removal from the cell. There are no windows or simply a very small window, and fluorescent lights are lit twenty-four hours a day with surveillance cameras on.

25. Guenther, *Solitary Confinement*, 35.

26. Abbott, *In the Belly of the Beast*, 27, quoted in Guenther, *Solitary Confinement*, 36–37.

> Melting, everything in the cell starts moving; everything gets darker, you feel you are losing your vision.[27]

> I went to a standstill psychologically once—lapse of memory. I didn't talk for 15 days. I couldn't hear clearly. You can't see—you're blind—block everything out—disoriented, awareness is very bad. Did someone say he is coming out of it? I think what I'm saying is true—not sure. I think I was drooling—a complete standstill.[28]

These testimonies evince the undoing of the boundaries between subject and object, individuality and surroundings, the self and itself, the body and the mind, the consciousness and the dream, the vision and the touch. Not unlike the Gerasene in Mark, who "day and night cries out" and "cuts himself with stones" (5:5), or in Luke with his brusque, abrupt reactions (8:28), they illustrate how, under solitary confinement, the self is unable to attribute one's actions to oneself, incapable of perceiving one's sensations as one's own. The unhingement of the body, of consciousness and perception, through disciplinary punitive processes demonstrates the radical relationality of the body itself. Confinement ultimately produces in humans (and animals) an unhingement of the basic structures of relationality, destroying the elementary fabric of our relationality and collapsing individuality. This bracketing of the structures that shape humanity in its primary sense is also a bracketing of humanity's animality, in that both, human animals and nonhuman animals, share a primary existential structure dependent on a network of relations with other living and nonliving beings.

Prisoners describe their experience as a form of living death. Their bodies live, breathe, eat, defecate, speak, wake, and sleep (with difficulty), but any meaningful sense of embodiment is missing.[29] Sensory deprivation, ontological derangement, disembodied sensitivity, metaphysical unhingement, and boundary-less identity express the phenomenological experience of continued isolation. Take, for instance, sensory perception. Not only do inmates lose vision, perspectival dimension, and the sense of

---

27. Stuart Grassian, "Psychopathological Effects of Solitary Confinement," *American Journal of Psychiatry* 140 (1983): 1452, quoted in Guenther, *Solitary Confinement*, 145.

28. Grassian, "Psychopathological Effects," 1453, quoted in Guenther, *Solitary Confinement*, 215–16.

29. Kay R. Jamison, *An Unquiet Mind* (New York: Knopf, 1995), 165.

inner balance, but, most notably, solitary confinement leads to a loss of the clarity of one's psychological and bodily boundaries: one's flesh as if melting away with the walls, one's consciousness skipping away as if belonging somewhere else. This undoing of the basic structures of subjectivity, phenomenology explains, is due to the systematic deprivation of the necessary conditions to sustain the basic structures of consciousness.

The perspectival nature of our sensory perception is limitless—we perceive objects and bodies from virtually infinite viewpoints—establishing a differentiation, a gap, between subject and object that is, in turn, reinforced by the experience of sharing a world of objects with other subjective perspectives. Touching, for instance, involves a crossing over of touching and being touched as a not-synchronized moment of experience. The chiasm of touching and being touched is the site of differentiation through mutual overlapping and divergence, a sensory structure that expresses the structure of being itself: I can only see myself as visible among others. Due to the lack of any reciprocity caused by isolation, one's notion of the limits between body and the surrounding world blurs, the flesh starts to melt with the concrete, the walls waver, voices are not one's own. Isolation cuts off any proper relationship of the self to itself by annihilating the interrelational dimension of subjectivity. The pressure on the self is so heavy that it deprives consciousness of its reference points, ultimately rendering a subject faceless and matterless. This alienation of the self from oneself frames what in the next section, taking Cicero's understanding of *oikeiosis* as being at home and *allotriosis* as living in alienation, will characterize the Gerasene's unhinged status.

Prisoners are unable to retreat to a space of anonymity, a location to group the self together, an inner place for subjectivity to construct itself in relationship with the Other. The "night" is foisted on the subject so that consciousness no longer can decide what it is and what it is not.[30] Similarly to prisoners who crash their heads into the walls or lacerate themselves as desperate attempts to feel their own body when no one else sees it, the isolation of the Markan Gerasene (5:5a) precedes his crying out and auto-mutilation (5:5b), while the Lukan Gerasene dwelling among the dead

---

30. Maurice Merleau-Ponty explains that "what brings about both hallucinations and myth is a shrinkage in the space directly experienced, a rooting of things in our body [rather than in a shared world], the overwhelming proximity of the object, the oneness of man and the world" (Merleau-Ponty, *Phenomenology of Perception* [London: Routledge, 2005], 339).

(8:27) has lost the ability to converse with the living (8:28). Such lack of relationality and distortion of bodily boundaries creates a dissolution of the structures of language itself. Guards and prisoners themselves use the term *monster* to convey the loss of verbalization and the loss of the subject of speech as prisoners experience inner voices but are unable to locate their origin.[31] This exclusive confinement to oneself, this deprivation of intimacy explains the dissolution of the matrix of the ego (see the prisoners' testimonies above). The violent outbursts and self-damaging actions are an attempt to reestablish boundaries between one's bodily limits and the material surroundings. Cut off from any meaningful relationship to others, to the world, and to oneself, deprived of language as the means of communicating with others about a world that is possessed in common,[32] the detainee's humanity disintegrates.

Bacon's Subject

To be a monster is to be unrecognizable as a human. In the case of solitary confinement, to be considered a monster dislodges any ethical responsibility from the victim and places it on the institutional structures that ban the subject from humanity. Desubjectification, annihilation, and unhinging transpire as the conditions of livability are exhausted, rendering the body unable to recognize itself and the consciousness unable to narrate its own circumstances. We are focusing here on the same moment of acute exacerbation of the basic structures of subjectivity, prior to a possible recomposing of the subject that opens space for the narrative itself.

Francis Bacon's uniqueness, Ernst van Alphen argues, lies in its ability to perform on the viewer what it portrays on the canvas: pain as loss of self.[33] Bacon seeks to undo the artistic Western tradition by calling into

---

31. Lorna A. Rhodes, *Total Confinement: Madness and Reason in the Maximum Security Prison* (Berkeley: University of California Press, 2004), 175.

32. Emmanuel Levinas, *Totality and Infinity: An Essay on Exteriority*, trans. Alphonso Lingis (Pittsburgh: Duquesne University Press, 1969), 76.

33. Ernst van Alphen, *Francis Bacon and the Loss of Self* (Cambridge: Harvard University Press, 1993). Van Alphen staunchly dismisses any historical or biographical reading of Bacon as a way to impose a narrative of meaning on what he considers a visual exploration of meaninglessness. For an account of Francis Bacon linking biographical information with artistic choices, see Mark Stevens and Annalyn Swan, *Francis Bacon: Revelations* (New York: Knopf, 2020); and Michael Peppiat, *Francis Bacon in Your Blood: A Memoir* (London: Bloomsbury, 2015); Joerg Bose, "Images of

5. THE GOSPEL OF SOCIAL DEATH (LUKE 8:26–39)

question the very act of representation: "expectations of narrative, reflection, chiaroscuro, life-likeness, discovery of truth, beauty and the body."[34] Here I am particularly interested in the question of narrative in the sense that expressing a sequential account of a series of events already betrays the nature of what torture does. In fact, Bacon's artwork undermines "the most basic assumptions we hold, consciously or unconsciously, about the reassuring effect of representation as a stronghold against inevitable death."[35] Consider the following examples that Bacon has: *Three Studies for a Crucifixion* (fig. 5.1) and *Crucifixion* (fig. 5.2).

First, although the titles of these works reference the well-known event of the crucifixion, no element in them alludes to the conspicuous motifs of the crucifixion: there is no cross and no recognizable victim. The viewer, at least at first sight, struggles to find referential materials that allow her to interpret the scene. The titles seem to be the only clear point of reference, an anchor to establish some type of criteria in a sea of signs that confuse: Who are the human-like characters arranged as a couple that populate panels 1 and 3 of figure 5.1? Do the wrecked body-like blots (panels 2 and 3 in figure 5.1 and all three panels in figure 5.2) reference the victim? What is the relationship between the characters in every panel? Are we supposed to interpret each tryptic sequentially? Do they convey a story? What about the drilling colors that shape the background in the first scenario or are combined with a dull tone, seemingly representing the floor, in the second one?

Van Alphen convincingly argues that Bacon's artwork relies on conventions of narrativity just to show the extent of their inefficiency. First, characters or figures in the panels share a common space, suggesting some type of interaction between them. For instance, in the first panel of figure 5.1, two characters seem to be walking past what might be the lower part of the legs of a third character. Similarly, in the third panel of figure 5.2, two figures seem headed (or maybe they are sitting down) in the opposite direction of the flesh-like presence of a victim. Second, the fact that Bacon resorts to a tryptic composition suggests that he is conveying a story. In Western art, it is common for a crucifixion tryptic to portray a sequential

---

Trauma: Pain, Recognition, and Disavowal in the Works of Frida Kahlo and Francis Bacon," *Journal of the American Academy of Psychoanalysis and Dynamic Psychiatry* 33 (2005): 51–70.

    34. Van Alphen, *Francis Bacon and the Loss of Self*, 11.
    35. Van Alphen, *Francis Bacon and the Loss of Self*, 14.

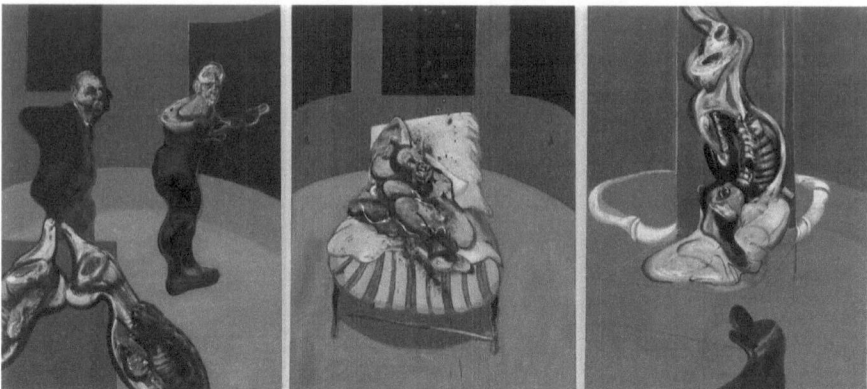

Fig. 5.1. Francis Bacon, *Three Studies for a Crucifixion*, 1962, oil on canvas, triptych, 198.1 x 144.8 cm each. Guggenheim Museum, New York.

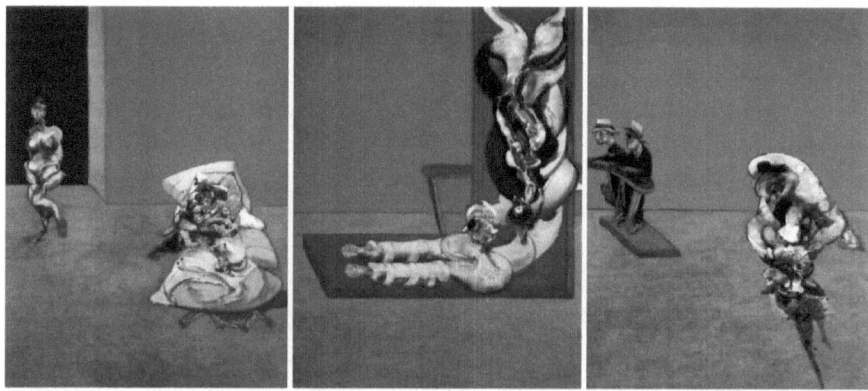

Fig. 5.2. Francis Bacon, *Crucifixion*, 1965, oil on canvas, triptych, 197.5 x 147 cm each. Bayerische Staatsgemäldesammlungen, Munich.

set of events or to situate characters and events that are closely related in the gospel narratives in the same space. For instance, Goswijn van der Weiden, the famous sixteenth-century Flemish painter, arranged crucifixion triptychs following the threefold sequence of bearing the cross, crucifixion, and descending of the cross.[36] Third, characters simulate movement, which creates a sense of development in time.[37]

---

36. Goswijn van der Weyden, *Triptych with the Crucifixion*, ca. 1517, triptych, 19 x 16 inches. D'Amour Museum of Fine Arts. See https://tinyurl.com/SBLPress06108g2.
37. Van Alphen, *Francis Bacon and the Loss of Self*, 23–24.

The appearance of narrative—grounded in the relationality of the characters, the arrangement of the tryptic, and the perceived movement—is effectively deconstructed because figures are blocked from each other by inner frames (see, for instance, the geometrical encasing of the body in panel 3 in figure 5.1 or in panel 2 in figure 5.2). Furthermore, there is a disruption of relationality because the panels show no continuity: In figure 5.2, what would be the logical relation between the fleshly body in the second panel or between the passer-by in the first panel and the two figures in the third one? Finally, there is no relational force between the characters in the scene. The viewer squints, trying to make a connection between the figures, without realizing that such effort is predicated on the notion that narrativity should guide interpretation.

Gilles Deleuze proposes to distinguish between the figurative and the figural. Figurative refers to a mode of representation that employs recognizable images or forms to convey meaning. It involves the use of symbols, metaphors, and other forms of representation that are based on resemblance or analogy. Figurative representation operates within established structures of meaning and relies on shared cultural codes and conventions. On the other hand, figural refers to a specific mode of expression that goes beyond representation. It is a way of thinking and creating that breaks free from the constraints of traditional forms and structures. The figural is an aesthetic concept that disrupts the dominant modes of signification and representation. It challenges the fixed meanings and interpretations of symbols, deforming the figurative into submission and sensation.[38] For Deleuze, Bacon is a master of the figural in the sense that the figures are never characters because their representation curtails any possible relationship with a subject outside of the painting. Figures are references to themselves.[39]

This lack of referentiality, an absence of anchoring interpretive points for the viewer, leads to what Van Alphen calls the loss of self. The novelty in Bacon's artwork resides in the fact that the figural performs on the viewer what the figures themselves experience. The witness, confronted with the figures independent from discursive perceptions of the self, sees

---

38. Gilles Deleuze, *Francis Bacon: The Logic of Sensation*, trans. D. W. Smith (Minneapolis: University of Minnesota Press, 2002), 8.

39. Jennifer Rivera Zambrano, "Pintar las fuerzas: Deleuze y Nietzsche en la pintura de Francis Bacon," *Cuestiones de Filosofía* 16 (2014): 28–40.

herself divested of her subjectivity, detached from the contexts that would situate her in reality.

In the previous section, I explored how isolation leads to the disintegration of one's sense of self because the boundaries of one's body dissolve into the surrounding environment. Solitary confinement bans the possibility of touching others, seeing others, and sharing with them a world: touching, smelling, moving, seeing, hearing, talking, and tasting are essentially shared experiences. The sensory world is a social world. Van Alphen suggests that Bacon triggers a viewing experience that temporarily brackets the witness from such basic structures of subjectivity. The loss of self happens through a rather sophisticated dynamic in which artwork exploits the conditions of subject formation: we rely upon the gaze of the Other to experience our body, because we have only fragmented views of our body. We have access to our body as a whole through the Others' addresses. Being looked at as an object is a condition for becoming a subject. Here lies the meaning of the shocking experience: Bacon pictures figures unreliant on the gaze of the Other. Bacon's figures should be interpreted "first, figuratively, as the confinement of the subject within his inner sensations, and second, more literally, as the demarcation of the subject's position, always alone on the border of the world."[40] Bacon provides the viewer—of course momentarily, fragmentally, sweeping—with a taste of what the prisoner in extreme isolation experiences durably. The subjectivity of the viewer, Van Alphen continues,

> is forced to engage in a confrontation with figures that block the very possibility of subject construction. But these works are not committed to this negative view for the sake of negativity. Their target is a specific element of subject formation in the Western world. They aim, that is, to respond through their specifically visual discourse to cultural discourses that are central to our culture.[41]

The silence that Bacon's artwork inflicts on the viewer should give us pause to reflect on the conditions of subject formation amid total isolation. It is such silence that creates an experience that allows the viewer to touch on the experience of the Other precisely because there are no external points of reference and, more importantly, no resort to narrativity. Accordingly,

---

40. Van Alphen, *Francis Bacon and the Loss of Self*, 119.
41. Van Alphen, *Francis Bacon and the Loss of Self*, 163.

visual art provides a comparative point of reference to study the construction of the Gerasene as socially dead because, on the one hand, it brings us closer to the unhingement of subjectivity under extreme conditions of isolation but, on the other, distances us from him insofar as his experience is subsumed in a redemptive plot.

The Lukan Gerasene as Socially Dead

Whereas my argument has presented social death in the form of solitary confinement as a lens to thicken character descriptions of the Gerasene, New Testament interpretation has known him mostly to be a colonized, demon-possessed persona. These identity markers are not equal, nor are they incompatible.[42] The brutal effects of solitary confinement on prisoners' subjectivity resemble the consequences of empire on the colonized. Certainly, Frantz Fanon's description of demon possession as a result of self-displacement and annihilation under colonial rule parallels what phenomenology has discovered in the experiences of prisoners. With its systematized subjugation of the Others and their humanity, Fanon argues, "colonialism forces the colonized to constantly ask the question: 'Who am I in reality?'"[43] The colonized "cannot ascertain the existence of an object," experiences "blurred mental and sensory perception"; the patient cannot "demobilize his nerves," is constantly tense, on hold, "between life and death," "stiff as a corpse."[44] Socialized into nonbeing, the colonized experiences a social death marked by mental illness, demon possession, and animality: "When the colonist speaks of the colonized he uses zoological terms," Fanon further elaborates, "allusion is made to the slithery movements of the yellow race, the odors from the 'native' quarter, to the hordes, the stink, the swarming, the seething, the gesticulations."[45] Beaten up, alienated from his time, place, and people, the colonized, like the confined inmate, becomes an

---

42. See, e.g., a compelling interpretation that incorporates insights from cultural anthropology, literary patterns, and political insights in Giovanni B. Bazzana, *Having the Spirit of Christ: Spirit Possession and Exorcism in the Early Christ Groups* (New Haven: Yale University Press, 2020), 60–101. Bazzana focuses on the Markan account, with no reference to Luke, but his insights into the exorcism as a "means to reshape imaginatively the local structure of ethnic identities in Gerasa" easily map onto the Lukan account (Bazzana, *Having the Spirit of Christ*, 101).

43. Frantz Fanon, *The Wretched of the Earth* (New York: Grove, 2004), 182.
44. Fanon, *The Wretched of the Earth*, 212.
45. Fanon, *The Wretched of the Earth*, 7.

animal who overreacts at the mere touch of the Other.⁴⁶ Patterson's conception of the slave as marked by dishonor, powerlessness, and natal alienation, Fanon's description of the colonized in terms of corpse, and Guenther's account of the inmate as unhinged, despite obvious differences, advance a shared understanding of social death as the status of a subject who, deprived of her political world, turns, precisely because of such deprivation, into a nonperson. Social death describes the political status of the "political animal" when such animal has been deprived of living in the polis.

Trajectory of Interpretation: The Gerasene under Solitary Confinement

Luke is particularly attentive to locating its characters in the public domain, and although the author uses the term πόλις in a nontechnical sense, the narrative consistently places Jesus and other characters in the political realm.⁴⁷ Right before the Gerasene's episode, Jesus and the twelve

---

46. New Testament scholarship—most notably Paul Hollenbach, Richard Horsley, and Gregory Wiebe—has taken up Fanon's influential account of the malaise of the colonized (the Decapolis is, after all, colonized territory). Whereas Hollenbach understands demon possession as a psychological disease, Horsley interprets the encounter between Jesus and the Gerasene as a fight with the Roman Empire. Wiebe criticizes both authors for neglecting first-century notions of demon possession: "where Horsley argues that the struggle is really against oppressive empire, presuming spiritual agents do not exist, ancient Christ-believers argued the inverse." See Hollenbach, "Jesus, Demoniacs, and Public Authorities: A Socio-historical Study," *JAAR* 49 (1981): 567–88; Richard A. Horsley, *Hearing the Whole Story: The Politics of Plot in Mark's Gospel* (Louisville: Westminster John Knox, 2001), 121–48; and Gregory David Wiebe, "The Demonic Phenomena of Mark's 'Legion': Evaluating Postcolonial Understanding of Demon Possession," in *Exegesis in the Making: Postcolonialism and New Testament Studies*, by Anna Runesson, BibInt 103 (Leiden: Brill, 2011), 211. More recently, Warren Carter, focusing on the Markan account, explores the gendered and militarized nature of the exorcism and portrays Jesus as a paradigm of military victory and the demon-possessed as a representation of all colonized people. See Warren Carter, "Cross-Gendered Romans and Mark's Jesus: Legion Enters the Pigs (Mark 5:1–20)," *JBL* 133 (2014): 147. See also Matthias Klinghardt, "Legionsschweine in Gerasa: Lokalkolorit und historischer Hintergrund von Mk 5,1–20," *ZNW* 98 (2007): 28–48, and Markus Lau, "Die Legio X Fretensis und der Besessene von Gerasa: Anmerkungen zur Zahlenangabe 'ungefähr Zweitausend' (Mark 5,13)," *Bib* 88 (2007): 351–64.

47. Luke uses *polis* in a nontechnical manner. The gospel describes villages such as Nazareth, Capernaum, Gadara, and Nain as cities. See Halvor Moxnes, *The Economy of the Kingdom: Social Conflict and Economic Relations in Luke's Gospel* (Eugene, OR: Wipf & Stock, 1997), 50. Luke contains almost forty instances of the word πόλις

travel through towns and villages (Luke 8:1: αὐτὸς διώδευεν κατὰ πόλιν καὶ κώμην) proclaiming the news to people who came to listen to the protagonist from different cities (8:4: κατὰ πόλιν). Similarly, Luke 8:26–39 introduces both Jesus and the Gerasene through their geopolitical location.[48] Whereas Jesus and his disciples are sailing to the country of the Gerasenes (opposite Galilee) and step on the Decapolis,[49] thus signaling a mission among gentile territory, the Gerasene is introduced as a man "from the city" (8:27) possessed by demons (8:27, 35; also 8:29, 33, 36, 38),[50] naked, homeless, and dwelling in the tombs (8:27). Regarding his actions, he falls down, cries, yells, and asks not to be tormented (8:28). His chained and shackled status emphasizes his communal standing (8:28)[51]:

(city) and twelve of the word κώμη (village). See also Richard L. Rohrbaugh, "The Preindustrial City in Luke-Acts," in *The Social World of Luke-Acts: Models for Interpretation*, ed. Jerome H. Neyrey (Peabody, MA: Hendrickson,1991), 129–43.

48. Although there are numerous differences between the Markan and Lukan versions, several elements of character analysis on the latter apply to the former. For a presentation of narrative variations, see Luke Timothy Johnson, *The Gospel of Luke* (Collegeville, MN: Liturgical Press, 1991), 138–40; Joel B. Green, *The Gospel of Luke*, NICNT (Grand Rapids: Eerdmans, 1997), 337–39; and Slawomir Szkredka, *Sinners and Sinfulness in Luke: A Study of Direct and Indirect References in the Initial Episodes of Jesus/Activity*, WUNT 434 (Tübingen: Mohr Siebeck, 2017), 153. In Luke, for instance, it is Jesus's first (and last) incursion into gentile territory. Redaction criticism, pointing at the Lukan heavy editing, underscores numerous differences in terms of characterization: the demon-possessed does not adjure but begs (Mark 5:8//Luke 8:28). Unlike in Mark, where the Gerasene hurts himself with stones and also dwells in the mountains (Mark 5:5), the Lukan Gerasene is a man from the city, has no home, and no clothes (Luke 8:27). From a theological viewpoint, Jean-Philippe Fabre argues that in Mark, unlike Luke, the pericope is a "plot of revelation" whereby Jesus announces his power to the gentiles. The Gerasene, in this view, becomes a foil for the universality of the gospel diffusion (its obstructions, its necessity, its legitimacy, its time limits, its actors). See Jean-Philippe Fabre, "Le possédé de Gérasa (Marc 5, 1–20)," *Bib* 98 (2017): 55–71.

49. The encounter takes place in the Decapolis, a group of ten cities situated on the other side of the Galilean Sea, administratively dependent on the province of Syria with organizational networks homologous to the Greek *polis*.

50. The following hermeneutical observations do not imply a causal explanation between the Gerasene's status as (a)political character and demon-possessed: social death is no etiology. The study seeks to thicken characterization features to explore the political status of a character as character from the perspective of those who might have similar experiences in the present.

51. Wolter notices that the verb συναρπάζω means "violent snatching away" in reference to people dragged away against their will and who cannot be contained through

while Jesus lives with the living (he is traveling with his disciples [8:26] and he returns to a welcoming crowd [8:40]), the Gerasene dwells among the dead and lives in complete isolation.[52]

The Gerasene, at the narrative level, is undoubtedly a minor character, his minority status predicated on his short interaction with Jesus, the main character. From the perspective of social death, however, the Gerasene's minority status relies on his characterization as being removed from any collective ties and experiencing alienation from the political sphere (Luke 8:27–39). While Luke situates other demon-possessed people in communal spaces (a synagogue in 4:33, a household in 9:38–39), the Gerasene is characterized, quite ironically, by the name of a city (Gerasa) with which he currently has no political ties. More specifically, the narrative portrays this minor character outside of the house—the basic political unit (8:27: ἐν οἰκίᾳ οὐκ ἔμενεν)—living in the tombs (8:27: ἐν τοῖς μνήμασιν) and in deserted places (8:29: εἰς τὰς ἐρήμους).

As characterization studies are quick to point out, minor characters like the Gerasene not only delineate the contours of the protagonist, but also embody major narrative themes. In this case, the interaction shapes Jesus as a successful if controversial exorcist (Luke 8:37) and, following postcolonial readings, as an anticolonial activist under God's command.[53] By portraying the Gerasene as "a captive outside Israel," the pericope is a peculiar fulfillment of the programmatic statement in which Jesus presents himself as preaching the gospel to the poor and delivering the captives (4:18) outside of the land of Israel (4:27).[54] Luke suggests a connec-

---

the use of extreme coercive measures. See Michael Wolter, *The Gospel according to Luke: Volume I (Luke 1–9)* (Waco, TX: Baylor University Press, 2016). See also Acts 6:12; 19:29; 27:15; and Philo, *Flacc.* 95; and Josephus, *A.J.* 19.157. Regarding ἁλύσεις (v. 29) implying massive coercive force, see Polybius, *Hist.* 3.82.8; and Dionysius of Halicarnassus, *Ant. rom.* 6.26.2; 27.3; 79.2.

52. The homeless Gerasene is not the homeless Jesus (Luke 9:58), for Jesus appears from the start in the midst of a community. See Robert J. Myles, *The Homeless Jesus in the Gospel of Matthew* (Sheffield: Sheffield Phoenix, 2014). Furthermore, Jesus uses other people's houses for a wide variety of purposes, such as sleep and banquets (Luke 4:38; 5:17, 27–29; 8:20; 9:52; 10:38; 11:37–52; 14:1; 19:5; 24:29–30).

53. Robert Beckford, *Documentary as Exorcism: Resisting the Bewitchment of Colonial Christianity* (London: Bloomsbury, 2014), 65–70.

54. Regardless of how we interpret Jesus as Elijah; see John C. Poirier, "Jesus as an Elijianic Figure in Luke 4:16–30," *CBQ* 69 (2007): 349–63. The connection between the programmatic statement and the liberation of the Gerasene is thematic rather

tion between the objects of such promise (the poor and the captives) and the demon-possessed by placing the pericope of the demon-possessed at the Capernaum synagogue immediately afterward (4:31–36). Although Jesus does not explicitly release the Gerasene from the chains, the hero's actions are essential to the transformation of the Gerasene from prisoner status to free person.

The Gerasene is anonymous (Luke 8:27: ἀνήρ τις; "a certain man"; see also Acts 3:2), deprived of the features that characterize the human as political (no city, no home, no clothes).[55] The demon-possessed man's apolitical status is most salient in a gospel known for the importance placed on a renovated household as the "economy of the kingdom" and urban spaces as a place of socialization.[56] This economic dislocation from the institution of the household situates the Gerasene as devoid of human ties: with no immediate family and deprived of a relationship with his ascendancy, progeny, or extended bonds,[57] unable to be part of a household (as the head or as a member), no participation in the workforce, the Gerasene contrasts with the typical Lukan disciple, who is assumed to be married with children, has parents and siblings (Luke 14:26), and is a member of voluntary associations.[58]

Displacement from his political community raises the following question: Is this anonymous man, this demon-possessed person, a political character?[59] Severed from any meaningful tie with the com-

---

than lexical. For similar semantic connections, see Samuel O. Abogunrin, "Jesus' Sevenfold Programmatic Declaration at Nazareth: An Exegesis of Luke 4.15–30 from an African Perspective," *Black Theology* 1 (2003): 225–49.

55. See Rohun Park, "Revisiting the Parable of the Prodigal Son for Decolonization: Luke's Reconfiguration of Oikos in 15:11–32," *BibInt* 17 (2009): 507–20.

56. Moxnes, *Economy of the Kingdom*, 23.

57. Luke conceives the family in extensive manner in Luke 12:52–53.

58. Adriana Destro and Mauro Pesce, "Fathers and Householders in the Jesus Movement: The Perspective of the Gospel of Luke," *BibInt* 11 (2003): 211–38.

59. The relationship between the οἶκος and the πόλις goes back to Plato, who equates them as having similar constitutions and closely tied to σωφροσύνη and δικαιοσύνη (*Amat.* 138c); in Aristotle, see *Pol.* 1.1.2, 125a; for Arius Didymus (in Stobaeus, *Flor.* 2:148.5–7 [Wachsmuth and Hense]), the οἶκος is the source of the πόλις; see Brendan Nagle, "Aristotle and Arius Didymus on Household and πόλις," *Rheinisches Museum für Philologie* 145 (2002): 198–223. Roman literature's examples of naming domestic rule as a prerequisite for political virtues abound; see Kate Cooper, "Closely Watched Households: Visibility, Exposure and Private Power in the Roman Domus," *Past and Present* 197 (2007): 3–33. Philo, echoing Aristotle, argues that "the future statesman

munal, the Gerasene's status as human dissipates. The demon-possessed man is socially dead: on the one hand, the tombs are the site of literal death, where dead bodies lie; on the other, they are the place of political death.⁶⁰ The Gerasene's homelessness, outside the οἰκωνονομία, implies a lack of economic, political, gender, and familial status, especially in a narrative that defines the domestic space as a site of salvation, solidarity, and patronage.⁶¹ The Gerasene, with a Legion inside, lives in solitude as a nonperson and consequently as an apolitical character. The hero's action, the exorcism, functions, then, as a hinge between two political statuses, for although initially this man lives at the outskirts of the polis and has no *oikia* (Luke 8:27), he ends up returning to his home, to his city, regaining his long-lost political standing.

Furthermore, the Gerasene's nakedness (Luke 8:27: οὐκ ἐνεδύσατο ἱμάτιον; "he was wearing no clothes") and prisoner status (8:29: ἐδεσμεύετο ἁλύσεσιν καὶ πέδαις φυλασσόμενος; "bound in chains and guarded in shackles") qualify the precarity of this apolitical life. His dwelling among the tombs is ontologically definitional, a condition defining his subjectivity, not merely a location with metaphorical meaning. Subjectivity's unhingement through the severance of relationality with "a world" (see the prisoners' testimonies above) marks the Gerasene's interaction with his interlocutor as notably abrupt, the Gerasene yelling, falling to the ground, and querying with strident voice (8:28: ἀνακράξας, προσέπεσεν,⁶²

---

needed first to be trained and practiced in household management [οἰκωνονομία]; for a household [οἰκία] is a city [πόλις] compressed into small dimensions and household management may be called a kind of state management [πολιτεία]; just as a city too is a great household [οἶκος μέγας] and the government of a city [πολιτεία] a general household management. All of this shows clearly that the manager of a household is identical with the statesman, even though what is under the purview of the two may differ in number and size" (*Ios.* 8.38–39 [Colson]). Dio Chrysostom (*4 Regn.* 69–70) argues that it is better for the ruler to be in chains (πέδαις) before acquiring the ability to rule himself through wisdom (φρονῆσαι).

60. Isa 65:4 condemns the practice of dwelling among the tombs for the sake of dream oracles, a Hellenic custom; see Julian, *Gal.* 340a; James F. Strange, "Tombs, the New Testament and the Archaeology of Religion," *RevExp* 106 (2009): 399–419.

61. John H. Elliott, "Temple versus Household in Luke-Acts: A Contrast in Social Institutions," *HvTSt* 47 (1991): 88–120.

62. The verb ἀνακράζω in the gospels refers to a sound proffered by those who are possessed or react to an extraordinary event (Mark 1:23; 6:49; Luke 4:33; 23:18). The same abruptness is related to the verb προσπίπτω (Mark 3:11; 5:33; 7:25; Luke 8:47; 16:29).

φωνῇ μεγάλῃ). Commentaries explain the Gerasene's character as violent, etiologically triggered by the demons, as acknowledging Jesus's superiority, or as a narrative device that anticipates the resolution.[63] From the perspective of social death, however, the character's subjectivity is deranged, raising the question of who is the ultimate subject of speech.[64] The Gerasene has no λόγος, a word that usually implies articulated communication by or about Jesus,[65] only φωνή, a term that, since Aristotle, was understood as distinct from the properly human voice:

> Of all the animals, only humans have speech [λόγος]. On the other hand, the voice [φωνῇ] falls to the other animals and is a sign of the painful and the pleasant. (Their nature has developed to this point: they perceive pain and pleasure and can indicate these to each other.) On the other hand, speech [λόγος] makes visible the useful and the harmful, so as to make clear the just and the unjust. This, in relation to the other animals, is peculiar to humanity. The human animal alone has a perception of good and bad, just and unjust, and so on. And the communion of these makes a household and a city.[66]

Aristotle's incalculably influential definition of the political realm in terms of *logos*, *politeia*, and *oikia* conceives of the human as an animal with *logos*, speech constituting the political realm. Cicero culturally translates the Aristotelian definition into Roman parlance,[67] foregrounding the human

---

63. Violent: Leon Morris, *Luke: An Introduction and Commentary*, TNTC (Nottingham: Inter-Varsity Press, 2008), 175; triggered by demons: John T. Carroll, *Luke: A Commentary*, NTL (Louisville: Westminster John Knox, 2012), 192–93; acknowledging Jesus's superiority: Green, *Gospel of Luke*, 338–39; Pyung Soo Seo, *Luke's Jesus in the Roman Empire and the Emperor in the Gospel of Luke* (Eugene, OR: Pickwick, 2015), 136; narrative devices: Johnson, *Gospel of Luke*, 138–39.

64. Michal Beth Dinkler argues that in Luke's Gospel the demons are gatekeepers of speech, determining when they can or cannot speak (Dinkler, *Silent Statements: Narrative Representations of Speech and Silence in the Gospel of Luke*, BZNW 191 [Berlin: De Gruyter, 2013]: 112–13).

65. Luke 1:2, 4, 20, 29; 3:4; 4:22, 32; 5:1, 15; 6:47; 7:7, 17; 8:11, 15, 21; 9:26, 28, 44; 10:39; 11:28; 12:10; 16:2; 20:3, 20, 33; 23:9; 24:17, 19, 44.

66. Translation from Samuel A. Chambers, *The Lessons of Rancière* (New York: Oxford University Press, 2013), 93.

67. Cicero translates *logos* as "ratio et oratio" (Pierre Manent, *Metamorphoses of the City: On the Western Dynamic*, trans. Marc LePain [Cambridge: Harvard University Press, 2013], 133–36).

on the abilities of *ratio* and *oratio* as the foundations of *naturalis societas*, a prerogative of the human species that distances humans from other animals, who have no share in reason and language (Cicero, *Off.* 1.50). Both elements, prerequisites of the moral life, Cicero argues, constitute humanity's suitability for *societas* (Cicero, *Leg.* 1.32). Speech and reason (*ratio et oratio*), human prerogatives, ground *societas* (Cicero, *Leg.* 1.22). Cicero's *appetitus societatis* translates the Stoic notion of *oikeiosis*, a concept that expresses the human self-recognition of the body belonging to oneself and of one's belonging to humanity (Cicero, *Fin.* 3.63), an extension attributable to *ratio*.[68] *Oikeiosis*, put simply, refers to the ability to feel at home with one's humanity and to recognize it in others. Derived from *oikos* and opposed to *allotriosis* (alienation), *oikeiosis* condenses the political status of the Gerasene once he returns to the *oikos* and recuperates his rationality.

If *oikeiosis* is a fitting term to name the recuperation of the Gerasene's humanity, one might argue that *allotriosis* encapsulates his initial status of alienation. As already suggested, two of the main features that define the estrangement of contemporary prisoners is their removal from human contact—hence their loss of ability to relate with others—and their subjection to 24/7 vigilance—hence their incapacity to relate to themselves. If isolation from others results in a subjectivity that collapses because it has no point of relationality, subjection to continuous vigilance removes any sense of privacy, incapacitating the subject to create a space of interiority, a locus for the self to reconstitute itself. Although Luke does not specify further details of the Gerasene's captivity, it does mention that the Gerasene was being watched, kept under guard (8:29: φυλασσόμενος) at the very moment of his total derangement (8:29: διαρρήσσων τὰ δεσμὰ ἠλαύνετο ὑπὸ τοῦ δαιμονίου εἰς τὰς ἐρήμους; "and breaking the chains he was sent by the demon into desert areas"). Sustained isolation paired with unrelenting surveillance explain the loss of rationality and speech.

The Gerasene has no *logos*, only voice (φωνή),[69] an obstacle eventually resolved when he recovers the ability of speech, of narration (Luke 8:39: διηγοῦ), a process paralleling the gradual status change from an apolitical

---

68. See Benajamin Straumann, "*Oikeiosis* and *Appetitus Societatis*: Hugo Grotius' Ciceronian Argument for Natural Law and Just War," *Grotiana* 24–25 (2003–2004): 41–66.

69. The Lukan voice (φωνή), one could possibly argue, is a term applied primarily to those characters whose subjectivity is problematic in terms of their relationality (Luke 4:33; 11:27; 17:13, 15; 23:23), those whose subjectivity demands no relationality

character to a political one (8:39: "return to your home").[70] The transition from the apolitical to the political, from voice to speech, from social death to social life occurs through the reacquisition of *ratio*; the Gerasene recovers "his right mind" (8:35: σωφρονοῦντα). Such characterization is hardly surprising: under solitary confinement, the hollowing of subjectivity leaves the subject with no speech, only voice(s) (see the prisoners' testimonies above).

The narrative transition from crying out and falling on the ground (Luke 8:28; also 4:33) to getting his mind back (8:35), from merely having a voice (8:28: φωνή) to being capable of telling a story (8:39; see also διήγησιν in 1:1) parallels the transition from isolation to socialization, from the apolitical realm to the political sphere. The pericope initially portrays the Gerasene as unhinged and out of control but also as desubjectified. Although from a narrative perspective the shift between singular and plural (singular in 8:27, 28, 29, 35 and plural in 8:31, 32) corresponds to the division between the Gerasene and Legion (inconsistently when the narrator refers to the spirit in the singular in 8:29), from the perspective of characterization these changes picture the Gerasene as divided within himself, complicating any attempt to identify who is/are ultimately the subject(s) of speech. The act of speech, nonetheless, occurs immediately when the Gerasene recognizes Jesus "as the son of highest God"[71] and articulates a question that suggests a certain coherence in the subject: "What is there between you and me?" (8:28: Τί ἐμοὶ καὶ σοί). The Synoptic Gospels attribute this sentence only to the demon-possessed when they beg not to be destroyed (Matt 8:29; Mark 1:24; 5:7; Luke 4:34),[72] but in this case these words also signal the opening of a relationship between the self and the Other, a precedent for the future restoration of the Gerasene as a relational, and thus political, being. The relational dimension is further emphasized by the Gerasene's christological confession (Luke 8:28) that

---

(voice from heaven in 3:22 and 9:35) or whose subjectivity is in trouble (the crowd in 23:23; Jesus in 23:46).

70. For an insightful exploration of normal and abnormal language and the relationship between agency, silence, and embodiment, see Choi, *Postcolonial Discipleship of Embodiment*, 109–32.

71. Green, *Gospel of Luke*, 339–40.

72. Ritva H. Williams, "The Mother of Jesus at Cana: A Social-Science Interpretation of John 2:1–2," *CBQ* 59 (1997): 685–86. For a historical mapping of this saying in the Synoptics and John, see Luis Chacón, "Principales líneas de interpretación de Jn 2,3c–4 en la historia de la exegesis," *EstEcl* 77 (2002): 385–460.

both fulfills Luke 1:76 and assigns a relational status (son/father) to Jesus that the Gerasene lacks himself. The return of this anonymous man to the polis not only follows the recuperation of his own mind, of his clothes (8:35: ἱματισμένον), and of his home (8:39) but more crucially parallels the rehabilitation of his own speech (8:39: διηγοῦ and κηρύσσων).

Transitions

The innovation of Bacon's work in the Western intellectual tradition lies in portraying the very act of desubjectification. Art historians have contextualized this achievement within existentialism in the sense that Bacon exposes the void of the human experience in the wake of the collapse of metaphysical foundations.[73] Bacon's obsession with the human body as the center of our perception and subjectivity—versus the Cartesian legacy of the body as an instrument—creates a crisis in Western dualisms such as reason and emotion, body and mind, feeling and intellect. The body, divested of any ontological framework, dangerously resembles a carcass: blurring a distinction between the social and the psychological world, Bacon also undoes the bodily borders that separate our inner and outer experiences. As John Russell puts it:

> What painting had never shown before is the disintegration of the social being which takes place when one is alone in a room which has no looking-glass. We may well feel at such times that the accepted hierarchy of our features is collapsing, and that we are by turns all teeth, all eye, all nose.[74]

Russell, along with most of Bacon's exegetes, refers here to the existential threat that a lack of relationality poses to the structures of subjectivity, highly exacerbated by "the violence, dehumanization, and disintegration

---

73. Rina Arya, "The Existential Dimensions of Bacon's Art," in *Bacon: Critical and Theoretical Perspectives*, ed. Rina Arya (Bern: Lang, 2012), 81–102; Franziska Nori and Barbara Dawson, eds., *Francis Bacon and the Existential Condition in Contemporary Art* (Ostfildern: Hatje Catz, 2013).

74. John Russell, *Francis Bacon* (London: Thames & Hudson, 1993), 38. See also Michael Peppiatt, *Francis Bacon: Anatomy of an Enigma* (New York: Farrar, Straus & Giroux 1997); and Nicholas Chare, *After Francis Bacon: Synaesthesia and Sex in Paint* (Ashgate: Routledge, 2017).

of Western civilization that was revealed in a post-Holocaust world."[75] These readings do not exhaust the wealth of meaning that Bacon's artwork distills. From a phenomenological perspective,[76] the series of the *Crucifixion* visualize the experience of those victims of institutionalized isolation. Consider the following testimony:

> to be frightened of the world; to be walled off from it and harangued by voices; to see life as distorted faces and shapes and colors; to lose constancy and trust in one's brain: for most the pain is beyond conveying.[77]

The victim verbalizes the destruction of perception ensuing from total isolation. It is compelling that he resorts to an imaginary of shapes and colors as they spiral into chaos. The victim also refers to the inexpressibility of pain in such situations, even as he deploys language to convey such extreme experience. We have explored to what extent Bacon's withholding of a narrative framework underlines the experience of desubjectification. On this front, artwork touches on the experiences of the victims in ways that the testimonies, always verbal and inevitable in a narrative form, cannot.[78]

The reader witnesses the unhingement of a Gerasene through a description of his political circumstances (homelessness and isolation) destroying his basic structures of subjectivity (language and perception). The shift from the apolitical to the political realm, I have argued, relies on the interaction between the victim and the healer. The insertion back into

---

75. Rina Arya, *Francis Bacon: Painting in a Godless World* (Farnham: Lund Humphries, 2012), 83.

76. From a phenomenological analysis of Bacon, see Federico Rodríguez Gómez, "Francis Bacon: Notas sobre la carnalidad," *Investigaciones Fenomenológicas* 2 (2010): 399–410.

77. Jamison, *Unquiet Mind*, 119.

78. My argument here is that the visual impacts the interpreter in ways that the literary cannot. While authors such as Samuel Beckett have made the body the canvas for decay, vulnerability, and frailty, literary and visual representations differ on their effects; see Jane Hale, "Framing the Unframable: Samuel Beckett and Francis Bacon," *Samuel Beckett Today/Aujourd'hui* 2 (1993): 95–102; Peter Fifield, "Gaping Mouths and Bulging Bodies: Beckett and Francis Bacon," *Journal of Beckett Studies* 18 (2009): 57–71. In a way, Bacon's portraits hit our nervous system in ways that the literary, even when conveying the victim's first-person accounts, cannot; see Semir Zeki and Tomohiro Ishizu, "The 'Visual Shock' of Francis Bacon: An Essay in Neuroesthetics," *Frontiers in Human Neuroscience* 7 (2013): art. 850, https://doi.org/10.3389/fnhum.2013.00850.

the world of the living occurs through a redemptive narrative that restores voice, sociality, and reason back to the victim. The hermeneutical task sits at a crossroads. On the one hand, in light of the proposed trajectory of interpretation, the similarities between the plight of the Gerasene and the situation of the victim of solitary confinement come to the front. The narrative features elements that perform what they portray (e.g., the inconsistency in the use of pronouns in Luke 8:29) may be an unintentional authorial slip, but it also creates a grammatical gap that resembles the subjectivity rift. On the other hand, the redemptive final punch, inextricable from the uplifting of the story's hero—Jesus as a powerful and authoritative exorcist—betrays a mystification of the victim's circumstances. It is on this front that art expresses what the narrative could never have done.

Victims of solitary confinement, like those who survive torture, do not just live on. The self does not revert to what it was. Torture, as an epitome of trauma, breaks and reconfigures subjectivity into a self that never was. In her memoir on disability, Christina Crosby concludes, "I may be perverse, but I'm terrified of what I'll lose in making my peace with what I've lost."[79] She can live on only through grief: her healing is in her pain. In the case of life after prison, or when prisoners are released from solitary confinement, witnesses share a similar experience: confusion and disorientation upon entering a world that has become foreign. For most, living "normally" in the "normal world" becomes an unattainable goal.[80] Unlike the Gerasene, the prisoner has not been "healed" (8:36: ἐσώθη).[81]

Concluding Comments

Many detainees under solitary confinement refer to their experience as "living in tombs."[82] The prison cells, architecturally designed to cut off any

---

79. Christina Crosby, *A Body Undone: Living On after Great Pain* (New York: New York University Press, 2016), 197.

80. Marieke Liem and Robert J. Sampson, *After Life Imprisonment: Reentry in the Era of Mass Incarceration* (New York: New York University Press, 2016); Bruce Western, *Homeward: Life in the Year after Prison* (New York: Russell Sage Foundation, 2018).

81. See also the impact on communities bearing the burden of higher rates of incarceration in Bruce Western, Anthony A. Braga, Jaclyn Davis, and Catherine Sirois, "Stress and Hardship after Prison," *American Journal of Sociology* 120 (2015): 1512–47.

82. See Jean Casella, James Ridgeway, and Sarah Shourd, eds., *Hell Is a Very Small Place: Voices from Solitary Confinement* (New York: New Press, 2016); and Taylor Pen-

sign of outside life, sever the living being from the world of the living, corrupting, as presented in the previous section, worldly experience, unhinging subjectivity, undoing consciousness, distorting body boundaries, maddening reason. The prisoner's anonymity equals the Gerasene's, a marker of social death, characterizing those on the verge of the political. The Gerasene, a living being among the dead, represents the extreme hardship of a life situated at the limits of the human, making him an exception rather than a representation.[83] The *animal (a)politicus* lives in the tombs, the place for death, and in the wilderness, the place of the beasts. The Gerasene is homeless in at least three dimensions: literally, he is homeless; philosophically, he is *oikeiosis*-less; and phenomenologically, he lacks language, the house of being.

The Gerasene's body—explained as schizophrenia, colonization, as a literary device covering a historical character, as a locus of indigenous spatial worldviews, a stigmatized body, or a sick or disabled body[84]—is an apolitical body at the extreme of human life. Notice the following testimony: "Self-inflicted cutting … is sometimes in order to see the evidence of why I am hurting. I see that I have a reason for all the pain, because I see my blood. The man is doing these things to hurt himself, to have evi-

---

dergrass and Mateo Hoke, eds., *Six by Ten: Stories from Solitary* (Chicago: Haymarket, 2018).

83. Versus Warren Carter, who considers the demon-possessed as a representation of all occupied peoples (Carter, "Cross-Gendered Romans," 144–45).

84. Schizophrenia: T. Hawthorn, "The Gerasene Demoniac: A Diagnosis," *ExpTim* 66 (1954–1955): 79–80; literary device: John F. Craghan unburies the historical persona of the demon-possessed by analyzing the original textual setting, the community's milieu, and the author's redaction (Craghan, "The Gerasene Demoniac," *CBQ* 30 [1968]: 522–36); locus of indigenous spatial worldviews: Helen C. John, "Legion in a 'Living Landscape': Contextual Bible Study as Disruptive Tool (Luke 8:26–39 Interpreted in Owamboland, Namibia)," *ExpTim* 128 (2017): 315; stigmatized body: Aimé Mpevo Mpolo, "Sexualité et résistance aux envoyés en Mc 5,1–6,29: Analyse structurelle et transtextualité," *Science et Sprit* 66 (2014): 243–67; sick or disabled body: Graham Twelftree, "Deliverance and Exorcism in the New Testament," in *Exorcism and Deliverance: Multi-disciplinary Studies*, ed. William K. Kay and Robin A. Parry (Milton Keynes: Paternoster, 2011), 45–68, (61–62); Holly Joan Toensing, "Living among the Tombs: Society, Mental Illness, and Self-Destruction in Mark 5:1–20," in *This Abled Body: Rethinking Disabilities in Biblical Studies*, ed. Hector Avalos, Sarah J. Melcher, and Jeremy Schipper, SemeiaSt 55 (Atlanta: Society of Biblical Literature, 2007), 131–43.

dence of his pain."[85] This body in pain, this highly emotional body,[86] violently snatched away, pitted against itself, the body under the dominion of evil violence, is also a body deprived of intercorporeality (his communion is only with corpses). As a flat character, the Gerasene has no interiority, but as a socially dead persona he has an unhinged subjectivity, the literary coinciding with the phenomenological. The Gerasene, living in the tombs, dwells in "total night," embodying a life situated at the margins of the political. The Gerasene, like prisoners subjected to solitary confinement, starts to recover his own identity at the moment he is allowed to enter into the political, that is, at the moment when his space becomes populated by other political animals. At this point, the political animal is no longer human because that would entail subsuming the recovery under a universalized notion of humanity, one predicated on the exclusion of the slave, the colonized, or the imprisoned.[87] The prisoner, unlike the Gerasene, does not revert to the fruitful life experienced before confinement.

---

85. Christine Guth, "An Insider's Look at the Gerasene Disciple (Mark 5:1–20)," *Journal of Religion, Disability, and Health* 11.4 (2008): 68.

86. Torsten Löfstedt, "Jesus the Angry Exorcist: On the Connection between Healing and Strong Emotions in the Gospels," *SEÅ* 81 (2016): 113–26.

87. Rather than seeing violence as a force inflicted upon the "subject," violence constitutes the "subject." Hortense Spillers invokes this ontological dimension in her reference to the enslaved as "being for the captor." See also the category of "onticide" in Calvin Warren, *Ontological Terror: Blackness, Nihilism, and Emancipation* (Durham, NC: Duke University Press, 2018), the notion of "ontological plasticization" in Zakiyyah Imam Jackson, *Becoming Human: Matter and Meaning in an Antiblack World* (New York: New York University Press, 2021), and "ontological captivity" in Andrés Fabián Henao Castro, "Ontological Captivity: Toward a Black Radical Deconstruction of Being," *Differences* 32 (2021): 85–113.

6
THE GOSPEL OF LOVE IN TIMES OF COLONIALITY (JOHN 13:1-20)

Truly I tell you that the slave is no better than his master. (John 13:16)

Remember what I have taught you that the slave is no better than his master. (John 15:20)

His Excellency the Count de Casa Bayona decided in an act of deep Christian fervor to humble himself before the slaves. One Holy Thursday he washed twelve Negroes' feet, sat them at his table, and served them food in imitation of Christ. But their theology was somewhat shallow and, instead of behaving like the Apostles, they took advantage of the prestige they thus acquired in their fellow-slaves' eyes to organize a mutiny and burn down the mill. The Christian performance ended with *rancheadores* [trans.: "men whose job it was to pursue and capture fugitive slaves"] hunting down the fugitives and sticking on twelve pikes the heads of the slaves before whom His Excellency had prostrated himself.[1]

Theological Abstraction and Coloniality

Gospel passages known as the Last Supper (Mark 14:12-26; Matt 26:17-30; Luke 22:7-39), despite their diverse thematic emphases and textual differences,[2] epitomize convivial love: Jesus delivers himself symbolically in the form of bread and wine and requests that his disciples follow suit in

---

1. Manuel Moreno Fraginals, *The Sugarmill: The Socioeconomic Complex of Sugar in Cuba, 1760-1860.* trans. Cedric Belfrage (New York: Monthly Review Press, 1976), 53.
2. Judas's betrayal, for instance, in Mark 14:17-20 and Matt 26:22 and omitted in Luke 22:1-6, appears next to visual references to the Beloved Disciple, only present in John 13:23.

his remembrance. In theology and art, this tradition has been shaped to represent the essence of Christian agape. Footwashing in John (13:1–20) takes up this theme and exemplifies it via a ritual of role reversal: love in the form of footwashing, love to the end (13:1), and a command to love one another "as I have loved you" (13:34). The pericope, so it seems, encapsulates the notion that the master lowers himself to the slave's status, and so honor is bestowed via submission.[3] Love and obeying Jesus's law go hand in hand (13:34; 14:15, 21, 23, 24; 15:12, 17). Footwashing in John and conviviality in the Synoptics differ significantly in their theological emphases, character dynamics, and literary influences, but they equally point toward a vision of Christian agape as communitarian and egalitarian.

Biblical scholars, with notable exceptions, have tended to isolate both episodes for sensible exegetical reasons: the footwashing and Last Supper scenes evince differing literary and historical contexts. Exegetical arguments have gravitated toward a set of narrowly defined topics: incongruencies between the two accounts' dates, historical *Sitze im Leben*, theological meanings, or anthropological accounts.[4] From a theological perspective,

---

3. The study of enslavement in the New Testament and early Christianity has experienced a revival in the wake of Jennifer A. Glancy's groundbreaking contribution: *Slavery in Early Christianity* (Minneapolis: Fortress, 2006]; see also Glancy, "Boasting of Beatings (2 Corinthians 11:23–25)," *JBL* 123 (2004): 107–13; Glancy, "Obstacles to Slaves' Participation in the Corinthian Church," *JBL* 117 (1998): 481–501; and Glancy, "Hagar as/against Bare Life," *JFSR* 37 (2021): 103–21. See also Candida Moss, "The Secretary: Enslaved Workers, Stenography, and the Production of Early Christian Literature," *JTS* 71 (2023): 20–56; and Moss, *God's Ghostwriters: Enslaved Christians and the Making of the Bible* (London: Harper Collins, 2024); Katherine A. Shaner, *Enslaved Leadership in Early Christianity* (New York: Oxford University Press, 2018); Ronald Charles, *Silencing of Slaves in Early Jewish and Christian Texts* (London: Routledge, 2019); Mary Ann Beavis, *The First Christian Slave: Onesimus in Context* (Eugene, OR: Cascade, 2021); Laura S. Nasrallah, *Archaeology and the Letters of Paul* (Oxford: Oxford University Press, 2019), 40–75.

4. For the differing dates, see Kenneth L. Waters, "Jesus and the Passover in Mark 14:1–12: A Chronological Confusion?," *Studia Biblica Slovaca* 12 (2022): 180–210. For the historical *Sitz im Leben*, see Santiago Guijarro Oporto, "El Evangelio de Marcos como 'relato progresivo': El trauma de la guerra y la propuesta de un nuevo comienzo," *RevistB* 81 (2019): 315–344; Colin J. Humphreys, *The Mystery of the Last Supper: Reconstructing the Final Days of Jesus* (Cambridge: Cambridge University Press, 2011). For a theological account of the different narrative, see Brant Pitre, *Jesus and the Last Supper* (Grand Rapids: Eerdmans, 2015); see also James Arcadi, *An Incarnational Model of the Eucharist* (Cambridge: Cambridge University Press, 2018); Humphreys, *Mystery of the*

however, they share similar motifs. Francis Moloney has famously argued that John 13 (along with 6:51c–58 and 19:34) makes a clear reference to the sacrament of the Eucharist via the term τρώγω (13:18: Ὁ τρώγων μετ' ἐμοῦ τὸν ἄρτον ἐπῆρεν ἐπ' ἐμὲ τὴν πτέρναν αὐτοῦ; "the one eating bread with me raised his heel against me") and the use of λαμβάνει in 13:30 (similar to bread miracles in Matt 14:19; 15:36; Mark 6:41; 8:6; Luke 9:16; John 6:11; and the Last Supper narratives in Matt 26:26; Mark 14:22; Luke 22:19).[5]

Similarly, from an artistic perspective, there is a long tradition in Western art that weaves together the convivial and the footwashing scenes. From a cultural studies perspective, resemblances between the gospels' scenes become magnified. Allegedly the most famous footwashing scene in art history closely weaves together both scenes by situating the footwashing in the foreground and the Last Supper in the background, connected through a perspectival play that leads the viewer's gaze from Jesus washing Peter's feet to Jesus presiding over the meal.[6] Although it is true that, from a historical perspective, John 13 does not have a Passover meal as its immediate background (13:1: Πρὸ δὲ τῆς ἑορτῆς τοῦ πάσχα; "Before the meal of the Passover"), the sign of footwashing takes place in the context of a dinner (13:2: δείπνου). Historically, literarily, and theologically, the differences between both biblical motifs have centralized a good portion of the exegetical accounts,[7] but from a cultural studies perspective

---

Last Supper. For an anthropological account, see Andrew McGowan, *Ascetic Eucharists: Food and Drink in Early Christian Ritual Meals* (Oxford: Clarendon, 1999).

5. Francis J. Moloney argues that substitution of ἐσθίω for τρώγω in the citation of the LXX version of Ps 40:10b in John 13:18 links this pericope with the eucharistic passage in John 6:51–58 (Francis J. Moloney, "The Structure and Message of John 13:1–38," *ABR* 34 [1986]: 6–7). See also Moloney, *A Body Broken for a Broken People: Eucharist in the New Testament* (Melbourne: Collins Dove, 1990); Moloney, "John 21 and the Johannine Story," in *Anatomies of Narrative Criticism: The Past, Present, and Futures of the Fourth Gospel as Literature*, ed. Tom Thatcher and Stephen D. Moore, RBS 55 (Atlanta: Society of Biblical Literature, 2008), 237–51; Moloney *Love in the Gospel of John: An Exegetical, Theological, and Literary Study* (Grand Rapids: Baker, 2013). See also Ben Witherington III, *Making a Meal of It: Rethinking the Theology of the Lord's Supper* (Waco, TX: Baylor University Press, 2007), 63–86.

6. Jacopo Tintoretto, *The Washing of the Feet*, 1548–1549, oil on canvas. Museo del Prado, Madrid; Juan de Juanes, *The Last Supper*, 1562, oil on panel. Museo del Prado, Madrid.

7. John's Last Supper follows a chronology different from the Synoptics. In John 12:1–3, six days before the Passover, Mary "then took an expensive pound of pure nard ointment and anointed Jesus's feet, and with her hair she wiped his feet" (12:3).

a clear-cut distinction between footwashing and meal sharing becomes blurred.

In the Christian imagination, the Lord's Supper is equated with egalitarian and universal accounts of love: to sit at the table entails participating in the all-encompassing agapic love.[8] Historically, not all Christian meals were eucharistic, and early Christians performed several types of convivial practices, but they all shared a reference to love between equals (agape) and a reference to love from above.[9] This interpretive tendency to overestimate the universalizing reach of love intensifies in theological readings of footwashing (John 13) because they paper over some difficult aspects of the pericope, flattening thorny dynamics and aggrandizing moral values. The politics of heuristic research tend to occlude the politics of inequality that populate the pericope (i.e., the relationship between enslaver and enslaved) in the sense that scholarship's search for a gospel of love obfuscates first-century conditions of enslavement.[10]

This would be Nisan 10, the day when the lamb, according to Jewish customs, would be purchased. The supper would take place on Nisan 13, and Jesus would have been crucified on Nisan 14, when the Passover meal would take place. Given the differences with the Synoptic account, much work has been devoted to the historicity of the event (Jamie Clark-Soles, "Of Footwashing and History," in *John, Jesus, and History, Volume 2: Aspects of Historicity in the Fourth Gospel*, ed. Paul N. Anderson, Felix Just, S.J., and Tom Thatcher, ECL 2 [Atlanta: Society of Biblical Literature, 2009], 255–70). There is also growing evidence demonstrating that the Lord's Supper and the eucharistic meal refer to different early Christian practices; see Andrew McGowan, "The Myth of the 'Lord's Supper': Paul's Eucharistic Meal Terminology and Its Ancient Reception," *CBQ* (2015): 503–21.

8. Gerald A. Klingbeil, "When Action Collides with Meaning: Ritual, Biblical Theology, and the New Testament Lord's Supper," *Neot* 50 (2016): 423–39.

9. Alistair C. Stewart, *Breaking Bread: The Emergence of Eucharist and Agape in Early Christian Communities* (Grand Rapids: Eerdmans, 2023). For a discussion of the Pauline agape meal, see Robert Jewett, *Romans: A Commentary*, Hermeneia (Minneapolis: Fortress, 2007), 804–16; Jewett, "The Agape Meal: A Sacramental Model for Ministry Drawn from Romans 13:8," *AJBI* 33 (2007): 73–92.

10. Comparatively speaking, the figure of the enslaved is scarce in the gospel. The captive makes a first appearance in John 4:51, where a royal man (βασιλικός) encounters his slaves as they find him on his way home to share the news that the miracles has happened: the son was healed as Jesus said his words (4:50); John 8:34–35 equates enslavement to sin and following the son with freedom. Notice here that John 8:35 acknowledges the social death of the slave: the slave does not remain in the family forever, but the son remains forever. In John 15:15, Jesus contraposes the topos of the slave with the topos of the friend: he will not call his disciples "slaves" because slaves

For instance, scholars have offered theological readings of footwashing as an exemplary act (ὑπόδειγμα) alongside ethical lines (example of humility), sacramental (Eucharist, baptism, or sin forgiveness), soteriological, and even polemical (against excessive use of footwashing).[11] These interpretations, heterogenous as they may be, share in their understanding of the ritual as linked to Jesus's death on the cross. John C. Thomas argues that there is no parallel in antiquity about a superior washing his subordinates' feet and concludes that the pericope retains a symbolic punch: footwashing would be a sacramental practice to forgive postbaptismal sins.[12] Theological explanations prominently equate footwashing with Jesus's death, establishing a parallel between Jesus's action of servitude and Jesus's salvific death and resurrection. Jesus's love, whose ultimate sign is his willingness to be crucified, finds a metaphorical and proleptical sign in footwashing.[13] This Johannine *semeion* "of Jesus' departure and glorification," "placed directly within the context of Jesus' relationship with the Twelve," constitutes "an act of love and example of humble service on Jesus' part which is to be reproduced by their disciples in their dealings with one another."[14] Fernando Segovia, for instance, advocates for a redactional approach that locates 13:1–3 and 12–20 as an addition in sync with 1 John's *Sitz im Leben*.[15] This highly influential exegetical approach has equally important theological ramifications because scholars have debated on where to place the emphasis: the soteriological interpretation (13:6–

---

do not understand what their master is doing. However, in 15:20, "a slave is no greater than his master; if they persecuted the master, they will persecute you." The last three instances are not metaphorical: they refer to the high priest's slave (Malchus), a victim of Peter's sword (18:10), and include two references to slaves in the courtyard while Jesus is being tortured (18:16, 18:26): here we encounter the girl slave who opens the door to Peter and questions him about his knowledge of Jesus (18:17), a group of slaves around the fire (18:18), and, finally, one of the high priest's slaves who asks the final question for the third denial of Peter's allegiance to Jesus (18:26).

11. Francis J. Moloney, "A Sacramental Reading of John 13:1–38," *CBQ* 53 (1991): 237–56; Luise Abramowski, "Die Geschichte von der Fußwaschung (John 13)," *ZKT* 102 (2005): 176–203.

12. John C. Thomas, *Footwashing in John 13 and the Johannine Community*, JSNTSup 61 (Sheffield: JSOT Press, 1991), 126–72.

13. Alan R. Culpepper, "The Johannine 'Hypodeigma': A Reading of John 13," *Semeia* 53 (1991): 133–52.

14. Fernando F. Segovia, "John 13:1–20, The Footwashing in the Johannine Tradition," *ZNW* 73 (2009): 48.

15. Segovia, "John 13:1–20," 37.

11) proleptically announces Jesus's saving power at the cross, whereas the ethical rendering emphasizes the exemplary nature of Jesus's humbling service (13:12–18).[16]

Thomas notices how most accounts of footwashing take place in convivial settings, performed by an enslaved person.[17] No wonder Mark Matson reads John 13 as an epitome of role reversal whereby the master/enslaver becomes the enslaved and exemplifies how honor is acquired within the community.[18] From this perspective, one can easily read Peter's protest as a resistance to overthrowing cultural norms, an aversion to placing the master in the position of the slave. Comparative exegetical exercises grounding John 13 in the context of ancient Jewish, Greek, and Roman sources tend to signal the unique character of the Johannine chapter.[19] In one of the most thorough and extensive studies on the topic, Bincy Matthew concludes:

> the footwashing is the ὑπόδειγμα of that loving act through which the Son enacts the transforming power of love, through which the disciples— the slaves—receive the life of their Lord, a life that holds them together as

---

16. The soteriological interpretation appears entangled with a christological one, whether accounting for the vicarious meaning of the crucifixion (David Gibson, "The Johannine Footwashing and the Death of Jesus: A Dialogue with Scholarship," *Scottish Bulletin of Evangelical Theology* 25 [2007]: 50–60), its cleansing effect (Otfried Hofius, "Die Erzählung von der Fußwaschung Jesu: Joh 13,1–11 als narratives Christuszeugnis," *ZKT* 106 [2009]: 156–76), or atoning death (Mark A. Matson, "To Serve as Slave: Footwashing as Paradigmatic Status Reversal," in *One in Christ Jesus: Essays on Early Christianity and "All That Jazz," in Honor of S. Scott Bartchy*, ed. David L. Matson and K. C. Richardson [Eugene, OR: Wipf & Stock, 2014], 113–31). For the ethical rendering, see Marianne M. Thompson, "'His Own Received Him Not': Jesus Washes the Feet of His Disciples," in *The Art of Reading the Scripture*, ed. Ellen F. Davis and Richard B. Hays (Grand Rapids: Eerdmans, 2003), 258–73.

17. Thomas, *Footwashing in John 13*, 46.

18. Mark A. Matson, "To Serve as Slave."

19. The first comparative studies emphasizing parallels between Greco-Roman and Jewish practices come from the German world (Wolfram Lohse, "Die Fußwaschung [Joh 13, 1–20]: Eine Geschichte ihrer Deutung" [diss., Erlangen, 1967]; Bernhard Kötting, "Fußwaschung," *RAC* 8:743–77), influencing Kötting's thesis of the ritual as a sign of eschatological hospitality (Arland J. Hultgren, "The Johannine Footwashing as a Symbol of Eschatological Hospitality," *NTS* 28 [1982]: 541). In a similar vein, see Richard Bauckham, "Did Jesus Wash His Disciples' Feet?," in *The Testimony of the Beloved Disciple: Narrative, History, and Theology in the Gospel of John* (Grand Rapids: Baker, 2007), 191–206.

members of the same household of the Father and the Son. It is through the disciples' faithful enactment of the ultimate signs of friendship and love that the dream of Jesus comes true, namely that the world may have abundant life (cf. 10:10). The love revealed in the footwashing is the law of the personal and communitarian dimension of being a disciple of Jesus (cf. 13:34–35). The perfect love of Jesus is multi-dimensional; Christological, soteriological, eschatological, ecclesial and, in its application, it can be even called the ethical imperative of the Gospel. The meaning of the footwashing is impregnated with an application for the future in view of the unknown "other."[20]

This rather aspirational and inspirational theological rendering merges together typical Johannine motifs—love and life, Father and Son, signs and examples, world and life, community, and discipleship —with an action, a symbol (σημεῖον) that turns out to be the epitome of love in all of its dimensions.[21] Theological distillations remain hegemonic, even when exegetical methods draw from historical, literary, or socioscientific approaches. The problem, in my view, lies not so much in the theological meaning making from exegetical insights but on how these productions disingenuously paper over the thorniest questions of power and inequality. One can hardly skip the view that exegetical conclusions have been drawn in advance, as if the idea of a universalistic and inclusive vision of love was there all along.

Consider, for instance, those scholarly accounts that zero in on the master-slave dynamics. Christoph Niemand makes a distinction between footwashing as duty and as intimacy/love. The first one features socially inferior subjects (slaves mostly), while the second is performed within the family structure (son, wife, father). Ultimately, footwashing condenses the christological Johannine vision of unconditional love unlike that of the

---

20. Bincy Mathew, *The Johannine Footwashing as the Sign of Perfect Love*, WUNT 464 (Tübingen: Mohr Siebeck, 2018), 428. Given the role-reversal game performed, studies in cultural anthropology have pointed at the significance within the Greco-Roman matrix (Eduardo Emilio Aguero, "Discipulado, amor y amistad en Juan 13:21–30: Una aproximación desde la antropología cultural," *RevistB* 80 [2018]: 79–103). Clark-Soles argues that, although we find no examples in the Roman milieu, given Jesus's embeddedness in Jewish scriptures (LXX, Joseph and Aseneth, 1 Samuel), the scene likely borrows from these antecedents: "an act of sacrificial love" rather than a rite of status reversal (Clark-Soles, "Of Footwashing and History," 264).

21. "This symbol is a real anamnesis of the splendor of Jesus' power and love, which points to Jesus' sign of perfect loving" (Mathew, *The Johannine Footwashing*, 428).

slave who performs out of duty: "It is not because Jesus wanted to express the humiliating, painful, and shameful passion that he washes the feet of his people, but because he wishes to demonstrate the Savior's visible love and tangibility."[22] To put oneself in the place of a slave implies, on the part of Jesus, a rejection of all hierarchical relationships with the telos of configuring new social relationships.[23] In this reading, Jesus's action constitutes a reversal of the transfiguration because, as he changes his clothes, he presents himself in another form (Mark 16:12).[24] Footwashing turns out to be the ultimate epitome of the most intense love possible,[25] destined to "offer a holistic perspective on ethical decision-making, including aspects of the concrete situation."[26] It is not uncommon to encounter the reality of enslavement glamorized for the sake of theological accounts:

> The Gospel of John, in substance, proposes the function of master-slave as necessary for religious experience, but this function is altered. Once

---

22. Christoph Niemand, "Was bedeutet die Fusswaschung: Sklavenarbeit oder Liebesdienst? Kulturkundliches als Auslegungshilfe für Joh 13,6 –8," *PzB* 3 (1994): 126: "Nicht weil Jesus die demütigende, schmerzliche und schmachvolle Passion hier ausdrücken wollte, wäscht er den Seinen die Füße, sondern weil er die Liebe des Erlösers sichtbar und sinnenfällig machte" (my trans.). See also Jerome H. Neyrey, "The Footwashing in John 13:6–11: Transformation Ritual or Ceremony?," in *The Social World of the First Christians: Essays in Honor of Wayne A. Meeks*, ed. L. Michael White and O. Larry Yarbrough (Minneapolis: Fortress, 1995), 198–213; Mary Coloe, "Welcome into the Household of God: The Footwashing in John 13," *CBQ* 66 (2004): 400–415.

23. Bauckham, "Did Jesus Wash," 192. See also Peter Carlos Okantey, "Jesus, the Originator of Servant Leadership: A Narrational Texture Analysis of John 13:1–17," *Journal of Biblical Theology* 5 (2022): 250–59. Such transgression of domination relationships extends to gender dynamics in Nina Müller van Velden, "When Gender Performance Is Not Straightforward: Feet, Masculinity and Power in John 13:1–11," *Neot* 53 (2019): 291–309; Agüero, "Discipulado, amor y amistad," 79–103. See also Ingrid Rosa Kitzberger, "Love and Footwashing: John 13:1–20 and Luke 7:36–50 Read Intertextually," *BibInt* 2 (1994): 190–205.

24. Juraj Feník and Róbert Lapko, "Jesus's Inverse Transfiguration in John 13," *Neot* 55 (2021): 347–64.

25. Jan G. van der Watt, "The Meaning of Jesus Washing the Feet of His Disciples (John 13)," *Neot* 51 (2017): 25–39; Francis J. Moloney, "Εἰς Τέλος (v. 1) as the Hermeneutical Key to John 13:1–38," *Salesianum* 76 (2014): 27–46.

26. Olivia Rahmsdorf, "'You Shall Not Wash My Feet εἰς τὸν αἰῶνα' (John 13.8): Time and Ethics in Peter's Interactions with Jesus in the Johannine Narrative," *JSNT* 41 (June 2019): 458–77.

the master transforms himself, the typical functions of the slaves should be taken by all members of the group in their mutual relations.[27]

This chapter takes issue with the ideological and cultural effects prevalent in this type of reading. I pursue an expository countertheological reading that illustrates how the ethics of the Last Supper/footwashing take up new meanings when contextualized in specific political contexts. Rather than transcending and transforming "the only ontologically based inequality among human beings, between him and us,"[28] I suggest that such egalitarian accounts—visually immortalized and symbolically reinforced in the history of Western art—require a thicker understanding of how meanings shift amid volatile political contexts. Abstract theological and exegetical versions of conviviality and service benefit from attending to the entanglements of biblical love (the exemplary message of Jesus giving up his life and washing his disciples' feet), with its ostensible colonial and postcolonial legacies. To this end, I introduce the meaning of the convivial scene/footwashing within three different artistic contexts with their own thematic emphases: enslavement, paternalism, and coloniality. Tomás Gutiérrez Alea (*La última cena*), Luis Buñuel (*Viridiana*), and Yinka Shonibare (*Last Supper Exploded*) take up different elements of the convivial scene/footwashing and expose the contradictions ensuing from any Christian ethics inattentive to contextual frameworks.

A Love Action in Three Acts

La última cena (Tomás Gutiérrez Alea)

Manuel Moreno Fraginals's work *The Sugarmill* analyzes the world sugar trade and its reliance on the slave trade, particularly in Cuba. Cuban planters designed one of the world's most sophisticated slave societies of the eighteenth century, one that would collapse, according to Moreno Fraginals, because new technology opened the way for slave rebellions. This monumental work offers a periodization of five stages in the production of sugar, with its ensuing effects on enslavement, as the ruling and man-

---

27. Adriana Destro and Mauro Pesce, *Encounters with Jesus: The Man in His Place and Time* (Minneapolis: Fortress, 2011), 43.

28. Sandra M. Schneiders, "The Foot Washing (John 13:1–20): An Experiment in Hermeneutics," *CBQ* 43 (1981): 87.

agerial classes navigated international affairs such as the shifting from Spain toward the United States as one of the main trading partners or the effects of the Haitian revolution on the world supply of slaves. A brief anecdote, quoted at the beginning of this chapter, inspired the famous movie *La última cena* by the Cuban director Tomás Gutiérrez Alea. The movie zooms in on this event and makes it the central piece of the plot, also drawing on the seemingly irreconciled contradictions between the religious authorities, the managerial class, and the ruling elite. Gutiérrez Alea delights in exposing the conspicuous contradictions of Catholic faith and practice lived out amid an enslavement enclave. These contradictions come into sharp contrast when the Count of Casa Bayona, a slave-holding plantation, decides on the occasion of Holy Week to host a dinner, inviting a preselected group of twelve slaves to instruct them in the doctrines of Christianity.

Following a dislocated and quite syncretic biblical sequence, the previous day the Count had washed the slaves' feet during the worship service. Gutiérrez Alea's rendition of this sign, like the one eucharistic one following during the dinner, evinces the absurdity ensuing from literalizing the subject position of enslaver/enslaved: the scene opens with a pensive Count, solemn liturgical music in the background, washing his hands and preparing to perform an act of the humblest nature. The moment the Count bends over to wash and kiss the first slave's feet, the captive bursts out laughing because he is being tickled. In a close-up shot, the camera captures the incredulity of the captive, who has no clue what is happening. Immediately afterward, the Count attempts to wash Sebastián's feet. Sebastián, one of the few captives who remain named, centers the first movie scene: here, Manuel (Mayoral) drags Sebastián back to the plantation after Sebastián's failed escape attempt. In front of the whole crew, the Mayoral beats the captive up and cuts his ear off as an exemplary punishment to anyone who dares to seek freedom. Now, at the footwashing, wound up and in a state of lethargy due to torture, Sebastián starts convulsing at the moment when the Count pours water onto his feet to wash them.

The footwashing scene throws into sharp relief the contradictions of status reversals within oppressive political structures. The captives' reactions—laughter first, spasms second—visualize the likely viewer's response to a ridiculous situation that exploits the contradictions between faith and politics. Moreno Fraginals, commenting on the role of theological missions, states:

6. THE GOSPEL OF LOVE IN TIMES OF COLONIALITY (JOHN 13:1-20)

> When the mills had patron saints and the producers believed in God, there was time to spare and the hours dedicated to mass, catechism, or rosary were not stolen from production and did not affect costs. And in the long run this produced an atmosphere of greater tranquillity and better guarantees of the slaves' submissiveness.[29]

This religious function crops up discursively during the movie's centerpiece. On the dinner day (fig. 6.1), sitting at the center of the table, Count Bayona takes up the place of Jesus, treats the slaves to a copious meal, and instructs them in a theology of redemption through suffering and acceptance:

> Everything here is for you. Today Christ gathered with his friends, the saints, the disciples, to say goodbye to them.... Someone must make sacrifices for the suffering humanity. Someone must bear the burden of God's punishment without complaining, in silence for everything evil that people do.[30]

The Count seeks to educate the slaves at the table about happiness and heaven[31] and argues for their submission, resorting to a series of traditional narratives. For instance, the story of Francis of Assisi teaches that the ultimate happiness comes from accepting that any suffering inflicted on us comes from God. The camera frames the Count circling the table as he catechizes, leaving the slaves out of the field. The melodramatic music situates the viewer at the level of the attendants, making her assume that the slaves are as engaged with the Count's words as the viewer is. After a brief silence, the slaves burst out laughing because they grasp the teaching's punchline: they are being instructed to enjoy their beatings.

The demystification of the Christian narrative climaxes in Olofi's myth. Sebastián, the initial runaway, takes center stage just as the Count falls asleep:

---

29. Moreno Fraginals, *The Sugarmill*, 53.
30. "Todo esto es para ustedes. Hoy Cristo se reunió con sus amigos, con los santos, sus discípulos, para despedirse de ellos.... Alguien tiene que sacrificarse por toda la humanidad que sufre, alguien cargará con el castigo de Dios sin protestar, en silencio por todo lo malo que el hombre hace" (Tomás Gutiérrez Alea, director, *La última cena*, 1978, my trans.).
31. Dennis West, "Esclavitud y cine en Cuba: El caso de La última cena," in *Tomás Gutiérrez Alea: Poesía y revolución*, ed. Tomás Gutiérrez Alea (Gran Canaria: Filmoteca Canaria, 1994), 161.

Fig. 6.1. Still from *La última cena*, directed by Tomás Gutiérrez Alea, 1978.

> When Olofi made the world, he made it complete with day and night, good and bad. Truth and Lie. One day Truth and Lie met and had a fight. Lie cut off Truth's head. Headless, Truth took Lie's head. Now Truth goes around with the body of Truth and the head of Lie.

Sebastián picks up the pig's head and places it in lieu of his own. The scene openly conveys the idea that the Count's instruction on Christian suffering is predicated on a lie and presents Sebastián as the head of a revolutionary movement—references to the Cuban revolution are hard to miss—invested in burning down a religious and political system built on enslavement.[32] After promising freedom to one of the attendants who has been enslaved for years and assuring the rest that they will not have to work the following day (Good Friday), the Count drunk-sleeps. The next morning, he leaves for a nearby property; as he returns later in the day, he finds out that the Mayoral, a managerial landlord overseeing the enslaved, did not honor his promise of granting rest to the slaves. Consequently, the slaves revolt, kill the supervisor, and burn down the mill.

Despite its historical tone, *La última cena* purposely distances itself from a neutral account of history, invested in bringing up the dialectical

---

32. John C. Havard, "Typological Rhetoric of Tomás Gutiérrez Alea's *La última cena*," *Hipertexto* 7 (2008): 58–67.

contradictions between theology and history.³³ In his *Dialéctica del espectador*, Gutiérrez Alea acknowledges Bertolt Brecht and Sergei Eisenstein as determinative influences in his approach to filming.³⁴ Gutiérrez Alea disavows a Hollywood cinematography that seeks to immerse the viewer rather than inviting her to reflect critically on filmed events. At peak moments, the camera calls upon the viewer to identify with a character's discourse or action (camera movements, dramatic music, etc.) just to shut down the identification process by inserting a scene that throws into relief its absurdity. Gutiérrez Alea continuously incorporates bathetic moments that laugh at "history," "religion," or "solidarity," throwing into relief the double-faced nature of civilized discourse. Master narratives, Gutiérrez Alea poses, are infected with the absurdity of their obliviousness to the material conditions of enslavement.

Stimulated by Marxist reflections on colonialism and coloniality through the lens of Italian neo-realists,³⁵ Gutiérrez Alea portrays the Caribbean world wrecked though empire and enslavement, political and economic systems legitimized by a religion complicit with the trappings of torture. Fanon's *The Wretched of the Earth*, published fifteen years earlier, frames theoretically a plot that transcends history via metaphoricity: historical events are not anecdotal but parabolic.³⁶ Paul Schroeder suggests that the scene fulfills two purposes: on the one hand, it dramatizes "how material interests can deform and eventually turn against noble and legitimate human aspirations such as humility and brotherly love"; on the other, it "dramatize[s] the transculturation between Europe and Africa as it played out in Cuba," particularly by expanding on the representation of slaves' multiple voices beyond the stereotypes of brutes

---

33. Carolina Rueda argues that Gutiérrez Alea uses the technique of *mise en abyme* as a way to insert himself as an anticolonial commentator. See Carolina Rueda, "Mise en abyme, parodia y violencia en La ultima cena de Tomás Gutiérrez Alea," *Apuntes Hispánicos* 9 (2008): 17–26.

34. Tomás Gutiérrez Alea, *Dialéctica del espectador* (Havana: Unión de Escritores y Artistas de Cuba, 1982).

35. For the concept of coloniality, see Nelson Maldonado-Torres, "On the Coloniality of Being: Contributions to the Development of a Concept," *Cultural Studies* 21 (2007): 240–70.

36. Jose Antonio Evora, *Tomás Gutiérrez Alea* (Madrid: Cátedra/Filmoteca Española, 1996), 45. See also Nancy Berthier, "Cine y revolucion: Memorias del subdesarrollo de Tomás Gutierrez Alea," in *The Cinema of Latin America*, ed. Alberto Elena and Marina Diaz (London: Wallflower Press, 2003), 99–108.

or superheroes.[37] *La última cena*, a visual essay in dialectical historiography, exposes how the founding texts of the New Testament and their subsequent theologies are entangled with the colonial project; it also warns against interpretations oblivious to broader ethical and political frameworks and voices and visualizes those outside the historical record. Gutiérrez Alea ultimately offers an exercise in historical imagination in which the subalterns, lacking any representation in the archive, populate the screen with their views on colonialism, enslavement, European enlightenment, and Catholic doctrine.

Sebastián, the beaten-up slave, assumes the position of Judas when the Count requires him to sit by his side. During the conversation the Count asks him, "Who am I? I ask you in the name of Jesus Christ!"[38] Sebastián responds by spitting in his face. Such action evinces how ridiculous it is to claim love and equality in the midst of enslavement. Similar to how John plays with ambiguity and misunderstanding, Gutiérrez Alea plays with the misunderstandings between sound doctrine and its reception among the slaves. When Count Bayona refers to the body of Christ as being eaten, one of the slaves shows horror at the cannibalistic hint. When the Count says, "A day like today, Christ gathered with his friends, the saints … who were like his slaves.… Christ was going to die," the slave responds, "No, no, no, my master cannot die. My master is too good."[39] The movie then becomes a sort of guerrilla exegesis that makes Christian discourse implode.

Viridiana (Luis Buñuel)

Flavio Fiorani argues that *La última cena* performs a double denunciation: Catholic paternalism and a verdict of universalist discourses (Christian salvation or Marxism's version).[40] Whereas I have focused on the second element, here I shall broach paternalism as it shows up in Luis Buñuel's

---

37. Paul A. Schroeder, *Tomás Gutiérrez Alea: The Dialectics of a Filmmaker* (New York: Routledge, 2016), 81–82.

38. "Quien soy? Te lo pido en nombre de Jesucristo!" (Gutiérrez Alea, *La última cena,* my trans.).

39. "Un dia como hoy, Cristo se reunió con sus amigos, los santos … sus discípulos que eran como… sus esclavos… Cristo iba a morir." "Non, no, mi amo no se puede morir. my amo es muy bueno" (Gutiérrez Alea, *La última cena,* my trans.).

40. Flavio Fiorani, "Sentarse a la Mesa del Señor. Metaforizaciones y conflictos in La ultima cena de Tomás Gutiérrez Alea," *Saggi Altre Modernitá* 6 (2011): 85–96. Juan Antonio Hernández argues, in "Multitud, devenires y éxodo: La última cena de Tomás

6. THE GOSPEL OF LOVE IN TIMES OF COLONIALITY (JOHN 13:1–20)   175

Viridiana (1961), a film featuring another celebrated version of the Last Supper. Buñuel's *Viridiana*, a cinematographic free version of the novel *Halma*, by Benito Pérez Galdós, represents the Spanish-Mexican director's return to Spain after years of exile due to his political views. Since Francisco Franco's regime, which had triggered the director's ousting, would still hold power for almost another fifteen years, Buñuel's return was not uncontroversial. *Viridiana* testifies to that conflictual relationship. Buñuel's idiosyncratic take on national Catholicism irritated both the national political and religious status quo and the Vatican.

The narrative first presents Viridiana inside the confines of her convent, where she is a novice about to take her sacred vows. The monastery symbolizes a secluded and confined environment distinct from the secular realm, serving as a sanctuary of discipline and chastity, providing respite from a tumultuous and indulgent world. The tranquil and enduringly planned sanctuary is disrupted when the Mother Superior informs Viridiana that her uncle, Don Jaime, who had financially supported her study, wishes her to visit before her formal commitment to religious life. "I don't want to leave the convent, Mother.... I have no desire to see the world again, but if you order me to...." Upon departing from her secluded existence, Viridiana is confronted with an initial encounter with a world in disorder. A once-glorious real estate deteriorates at the same pace as its owner. Don Jaime's reclusive behavior and aversion to modern conveniences such as electricity may be attributed to the profound impact of his wife Elvira's untimely death on their wedding night. He remains deeply immersed in recollections of their shared history, exhibiting a strong desire to preserve and maintain the essence of that bygone era. This internal disposition serves as a symbolic representation of the cultural and political barrenness experienced in Spain during the rule of Franco.[41]

Don Jaime's libidinal passions skyrocket once Viridiana arrives at his property. She rejects his sexual initiation with even more religious zeal and confidence, her gloomy countenance betraying her disgust for the society in which she has been compelled to live. The movie borrows from several biblical motifs without taking them at face value. Rita, Don Jaime's niece, provides a naïve, vibrant counterpoint to Viridiana's

---

Gutiérrez Alea," *Revista Iberoamericana* 69.205 (2003): 839–48, that the critique of paternalism possibly extends to Castro's policies.

41. Amparo Martínez Herranz, *La España de Viridiana* (Zaragoza: Prensas de la Universidad de Zaragoza, 2013).

gloom with her playful antics. Viridiana is introduced to Rita, a symbol of temptation who represents the alluring and hedonistic aspects of life that she so steadfastly rejects, in a scene when Rita offers her an apple. The maid Ramona looks through a keyhole and sees Viridiana praying while surrounded by symbols of Christ's crucifixion: a hammer, nails, a sponge, and a crown of thorns. In response to Viridiana's first reluctance, Don Jaime asks her to wear his late wife's clothing, drugs her, and seemingly rapes her. When Viridiana is all set to depart back to the convent, Don Jaime's suicide leaves her stuck in the property. Viridiana ends up turning the property into a sort of charity foundation, much to the chagrin of Jorge, Don Jaime's illegitimate but rightful successor, who wishes to develop a fruitful farm.

Buñuel's depiction of the Last Supper stands out among the film's many allusions to religious and biblical themes (fig. 6.2). Placed at the movie's final strip, this dramatic finale visualizes a liberation of all the character's desire restrictions. Viridiana, inspired by her religious fervor, hosts a luncheon for a group of homeless people. Beggars take over a lavish mansion and have a riot, complete with Handel's *Messiah* playing in the background (one of the beggars apparently picked this record randomly from a stack). Buñuel replicates Da Vinci's iconic mise-en-scène, ridiculing it with a series of camp motifs.[42] Coplera, for instance, one of the female beggars, raises her skirt and takes a shot with her vagina at the climax of the feast.[43] Right at this moment, everyone in the scene freezes, and a rooster crows.

Don Amalio, a blind man who, given his ethical failures, stands for Judas, occupies the center spot in the place of Christ. The debacle ends with a rape attempt on Viridiana, interrupted by Jorge's intervention. In the last coda, Viridiana finally gives up her religious vocation, gets sexually involved with Jorge, and ends up playing cards with Jorge and the maid, the plot suggesting a ménage à trois.[44]

---

42. Vicente Sánchez-Biosca suggests that the scene references the Da Vinci painting but, perhaps more subtly, draws on how that scene presided over many of Spanish dining rooms. See Vicente Sánchez-Biosca, "El intertexto religioso en Viridiana (Luis Buñuel)," *Intertextualitat i recepció* 11 (1998): 138.

43. Catherine Sundt, "Religion and Power: The Appropriation of Da Vinci's *The Last Supper* in *Viridiana* and *L'última cena*," *Romance Notes* 49 (2009): 71–79.

44. For a psychoanalytic reading, see Julián Daniel Gutiérrez-Albilla, "Picturing the Beggars in Luis Buñuel's 'Viridiana': A Perverse Appropriation of Leonardo Da Vinci's 'Last Supper,'" *Journal of Romance Studies* 5 (2005): 59–73.

6. THE GOSPEL OF LOVE IN TIMES OF COLONIALITY (JOHN 13:1-20)   177

Fig. 6.2. Still from *Viridiana*, directed by Luis Buñuel, 1962.

The Last Supper scene, chastised by the religious establishment for being a liturgic parody, functions both as an illustration of Viridiana's Christian ideals around charity and as a cultural and political commentary on their nefarious consequences. José L. Rodríguez argues that Buñuel signals the destructive consequences of totalizing thought and "how the ideals of purity, unity and wholeness" are inevitably accompanied by "chaos, fragmentation, and destruction."[45] Without dismissing this approach, I want to suggest that Buñuel's iconoclastic take on the biblical and artistic scene of the Last Supper points at the inner contradictions of any ethical instance that does not critically consider its wider political infrastructures. In this case, Buñuel stabs at a bourgeois mindset and a patronizing Catholicism entangled with a dictatorial regime.[46] Such critique, however, is not external but from within the mechanics of the Chris-

---

45. José L. Rodríguez, "Contamination and Transformation: A Kristevan Reading of Luis Buñuel's *Viridiana*," *Studies in Hispanic Cinema* 1 (2005): 175.

46. Emilio Riera critiques the officialist condemnation of the film by making a clear distinction between original sources and their reception. Accordingly, he argues, Buñuel "does not group the beggars in an arrangement similar to the figures in Da Vinci's Last Supper in order to belittle Christ and his apostles by comparing them to some drunkards. Hence, Buñuel is not mocking Christ himself, but the manner in which Christ's image is worshipped" (Riera, "Viridiana," in *The World of Luis Buñuel*, ed. Julio Mellen [New York: Oxford University Press, 1986], 222).

tian grammar itself. Vicente Sánchez-Biosca goes so far as to suggest that, for Buñuel, religion constitutes a source of happiness; consequently, it is of the utmost importance to live it out from within. Rather than approaching religion as an enemy, Buñuel, like the fetishist, delights "in its crevices, extending the climax, and underlining unnoticed connections, exploring them with delectation."[47]

As in Gutiérrez Alea's movie, wherein the captives are invited to share "peacefully" the table with the captor with ultimate destructive consequences, in *Viridiana* the beggars take over the property violently. We may read both events as the political medium to subvert the bourgeois order in an act of conscientization. Such a Marxist reading gives short shrift to the complexity of Gutiérrez Alea and Buñuel's position. In the case of *La última cena*, numerous captives remain complicit with the mechanics of enslavement, and here the beggars lack any will to undo the system; they would rather momentarily enjoy the goods at their disposal for the sake of it. In *Viridiana*, perhaps, the ultimate act of rebellion is to be found not so much in the beggars' positionality but in the director's identification with one of the characters. Right when everyone sets up the *tableau vivant*—Don Amalio, the blind man, in the central position resembling Christ—Enedina steps out of the frame to take a picture, replacing Da Vinci's position as a painter and Buñuel's location as a director. In such a gendered replacement, Enedina does not use a brush or a camera but her own sexual organ to "click" the picture. Marsha Kinder poignantly observes that Enedina performs "a sex change," conflating both sides of the gaze—voyeurism and exhibitionism—"which are traditionally gendered male and female, respectively. Hence, Enedina's obscene gesture marks the moment in the film that is more subversive on several registers: religion, class, gender, and cinematic enunciation."[48]

Viridiana is not alien to the coloniality's trappings. Buñuel's critique of a dated Catholic has a feud-like real estate as its environment. Whereas *La última cena* assumes a straightforward relationship between metropo-

---

47. Vicente Sánchez-Biosca, "Escenas de liturgia y perversión en la obra de Buñuel," *Archivos de la Filmoteca: Valencia: Filmoteca de la Generalitat Valenciana* 35 (2000): 10; Alicia García Ruiz claims a similar dialectical relation of Buñuel with patriarchal structures in "'Quo tendas anagogia:' Viridiana o la historia de un inconsciente," *Asparkía: Investigació Feminista* (2005): 71–93.

48. Marsha Kinder, *Blood Cinema: The Reconstruction of National Identity in Spain* (Berkeley: University of California Press, 1993), 316.

lis and colony correspondent with the unidirectional impulse of the slave trade, *Viridiana*'s setup is more subtle but not less significant, especially in its gendered manifestations. After Don Jaime's suicide, his estranged son Jorge arrives with his Argentinian wife. He, jointly with Viridiana, has inherited the property and is getting ready to renovate it. In one scene, frequently papered over by critics, Jorge examines a dagger left by his father and claims "ay, pampa mia," an expression that locates him as an Argentinian migrant, an *indiano* returning home.

The figure of the *indiano* has enormous cultural purchase in Spain: it represents those Spanish migrants who became wealthy in the Americas and returned to their homeland usually with pompous wealth. This new rich class was known for being snotty and showy. Jorge complicates this picture because as an architect he "represents the enlightenment ethos of progress."[49] Martin-Marquez views Jorge as a character embodying coloniality:

> As an enlightened colonizer, Jorge apparently seeks to institute a more secular regime of wage labor on the property.... Jorge disparages Viridiana's traditional notion of Christian charity, which has led her to take in a group of beggars whom she provides with food and shelter in exchange for token tasks that would have little or no value in the free market.... In feudal fashion, Jorge continues to exercise a broadly defined droit du seigneur over the sexual labor of the housemaid Ramona.... Jorge is depicted as lord and master over the domestic space of the house, where he is tended to by faithfully Ramona.[50]

Martin-Marquez concludes that *Viridiana* reverses back the expected linearity of the metropolis-colony by representing Spain as a premodern estate waiting to be civilized. In her opinion, the movie reinforces, however, gendered roles—what we have called the coloniality of gender—because it constructs "woman" as a virgin soil.[51]

Buñuel's visual critique of the agapic meal could be analyzed as a case of reception history, as an example among many other renditions on the biblical theme. Cultural studies, however, takes iterations of the biblical texts not simply as interpretations of an original meaning but as proper

---

49. Susan Martin-Márquez, "Coloniality and the Trappings of Modernity in 'Viridiana' and 'The Hand in the Trap,'" *Cinema Journal* (2011): 103.

50. Martin-Márquez, "Coloniality and the Trappings," 105.

51. Martin-Márquez, "Coloniality and the Trappings," 114.

interpretations themselves, as "thinking pieces." Buñuel's rendition of this biblical motif lays bare the asymmetrical power dynamics in the Christian meal whereby a bourgeoisie and religious elite, plagued with good intentions, clean their consciousness through charitable actions: the benefactor centers her personal salvation by claiming a moral high ground. The agapic component implodes as the scene visualizes the hypocrisy of a theology advocating for purification at the expense of the marginalized Other. Buñuel further resists, however, any romanticization of the impoverished, portraying them as flawed characters in their own right, with as many moral pitfalls as the bourgeoisie he so adamantly criticizes.[52] Buñuel's indictment on Christian love, ultimately, conveys his critique of an ethics of personal moral improvement grounded on bourgeois values and libidinal repression:

> On another level, however, the political unconscious of the work acts as a background against which to make another reading of it. A proposal is then detected in patriarchal letters, to the extent that the construction of the problem can be read in terms of possession and control of the female body, it is a question of property, expropriation, and appropriation. Come and eat all of it because this is my body, the saint would say. Blood of the old and eternal alliance. Blood of the grail who serves the ideology of the form in Viridiana. Foundation Blood.[53]

Biblical discourses around love based on the Last Supper/footwashing conspicuously abstract relationality from its political circumstances. Pedro García Olivo coins the expression "síndrome Viridiana":

> Well-intentioned bourgeois and petty bourgeois wanted to "help" the working class. They wanted to "emancipate it," "liberate it," and "redeem it." They were not used to physical work, but they put themselves at

---

52. Gabriel Sánchez Rodríguez, "Viridiana: La perversión de la miseria," *Comunicación y Hombre* (2016): 191–207.

53. García Ruiz, "Quo tendas anagogia," 91: "En otro nivel, en cambio, el inconsciente político de la obra actúa como trasfondo contra el cual hacer una lectura más de la misma. Se detecta entonces una propuesta declinada en letras patriarcales, en la medida en que la construcción del problema se deja leer en términos de posesión y control del cuerpo femenino, es una cuestión de propiedad, expropiación, y apropiación. Venid y comed todos de el porque este mi cuerpo, diría la santa. Sangre de la alianza vieja y eterna. Sangre del grial a quien sirve la ideología de la forma en Viridiana. Sangre de la Fundación" (my trans.).

the forefront thinking of themselves as a "vanguard," illuminating and directing the movement.⁵⁴

The Viridiana syndrome encapsulates an ethical disposition whereby charity becomes a means for self-improvement and virtue-signaling. Unlike in the gospel narratives, in Viridiana, as well as in *La última cena*, we witness a clapback from the beneficiaries of agapic efforts, a snappy reaction to well-intentioned attempts to know the needs of the impoverished better than themselves.

Last Supper Exploded (Yinka Shonibare)

Yinka Shonibare becomes the last invitee at the table to explore the connections between convivial love, service, and coloniality. A British Nigerian distinguished artist, Shonibare has become famous for his captivating studies on cultural identity, colonialism, and globalization. He often marries fabric and fashion in his art, employing Dutch wax fabric to communicate potent messages about identity and the passage of history. Shonibare artistically reconstructs historical scenarios, critiquing colonial history from unconventional, non-European viewpoints. He further navigates the waters of power, dichotomy, and gender, challenging stereotypes and inspecting feminine and masculine intricacy. His art exhales commentary on societal issues such as inequality, consumer culture, and the depiction of underrepresented communities. Versatile in his choice of mediums, Shonibare's mixed media, sculpture, and installation art pieces are infused with the narrative depth that found objects lend. Shonibare's artworks reinterpret historical accounts, critique colonial narratives, and underscore the urgency to question Eurocentric viewpoints. Shonibare integrates various mediums in his creations, including mixed media, sculptures, installations, and found objects, establishing immersive, visually striking experiences. He scrutinizes colonialism's impact on globalization and Western dominance.

---

54. Pedro García Olivo, "El síndrome de Viridiana en la política y la búsqueda de sustitutos funcionales del proletariado," *Centro Cultural Universidad del Tolima* 9.18 (2010): 74: "Burgueses y pequeño-burgueses bienintencionados quisieron 'ayudar' a la clase trabajadora; quisieron 'emanciparla,' 'liberarla,' y 'redimirla'. No procedían del trabajo físico, pero se pusieron al frente, tal una 'vanguarda', iluminando y encauzando" (my trans.).

Shonibare's exploration transcends the surface-level examination of African identity and digs deeper into broader themes such as power dynamics, globalization, and hybridity. With African textiles and fashion woven into his work as symbolic representations, he lays bare the rich cultural heritage of Africa while subtly highlighting the Western world's perspectives juxtaposed against Africa's. His art turns out to be more than just a display; it is a conversation about identity in the modern world.

Shonibare's art's most recognizable feature is his use of Dutch wax. The cloth is a signifier of an entangled postcolonial world, a metaphor for the inextricable link between Europe and its African colonies, their mutual invention, and how such configuration remains a buried subtext in the official histories that are told. For starters, the fabric, whose official name is Dutch wax, is perceived by the Western eye as essentializing Africanness. Everything about it screams Africa, not least because it is widely deployed by people of African descent in the main metropolises in the West to claim African pride. The material history of such an idiosyncratic pattern, however, is illustrative of some of Shonibare's concerns: the printed fabric was based on Indonesian batik, manufactured in the Netherlands, Britain, and other countries and exported to West Africa, where it became popular, if foreign. When the Dutch colonized Indonesia in the seventeenth century, they imported the pattern into Europe, where they started manufacturing it with machines instead of hand-dyeing it. Africa began as the primary target market, which in turn started to provide feedback regarding patterns and color, modeling what the main companies in Holland would manufacture to cater to "African taste."[55] A cloth pervasively associated with Africanness is foreign to Africa. Furthermore, the cognitive dissociation of using a supposedly African cloth to dress essentially Victorian-era figures creates a cognitive dissonance in the viewer, who is confronted with the question: Is this African? Is this European? What era does it "represent"?

If batik clothing signals the postcolonial entanglements of nation building, trading routes, and capitalism's drives, the Victorian era, poignantly represented in the body posture and the clothing cut, represents a historical period known for driving imperialism, corruption, and puritanism. Tending to Shonibare's own testimony, one could argue that his aesthet-

---

55. Robert Hobbs, "Yinka Shonibare Mbe: The Politics of Representation," in *Yinka Shonibare Mbe*, ed. Rachel Kent (Munich: Prestel, 2008), 29.

ics spring from his desire to question the blackness others have imposed on him.[56] However, his work further complicates the dichotomies at play. Scholars have pointed out some obvious ones: European/African, British/Nigerian, white/black, modern/primitive, male/female; however, the work under consideration here brings new ones to the fore precisely because of its use of biblical sources and its play with other contemporary motifs. At first sight, two dichotomies stand out: animal/human and agape/eros.

In a way, Shonibare's clear referential points send interpretation in all kinds of oppositional directions and make any interpretive practice paradoxical: How are we to discern if the headless torsos refer to a critique of Enlightenment rationale, to the practice of beheading people during the French Revolution, an emphasis on the headless action of performing sex, a signifier that pushes the ambiguity about the race, class, gender, and status of the participants even further or that even equivocates the human nature of the protagonists or erases the primary feature of personal identity.

Most of Shonibare's artistic features apply to the Last Supper: problematized anthropology, sartorial incongruence, ethnic ambiguity, national discontinuity, anachronism, oversexualization. His landmark artistic features are in plain view: the characteristic use of batik with Victorian silhouettes, the beheaded mannequins, the explicit sexual material, the reference to sodomy, a clear reference to another classic work of art, a sense of excess.

To the untrained Western eye, batik essentializes Africanness. Before realizing that we are in front of an iteration of the Last Supper, the beholder's first impression is taken by a vivid, almost eye-straining palette of colors and patterns to the point it is hard, at least from the pictures, to separate out the different bodies in the composition. The cloth then does not only disavow the tracing of an origin that the modern stereotype imposed; it also evinces the history of coloniality itself. This consideration about

---

56. "When I was at college in London, my work was very political.... my tutor upon seeing this work, said to me: 'You are African, aren't you; why don't you make authentic African art? I was quite taken aback by this, but it was through the process of thinking about authenticity that I started to wonder about what signifiers of such 'authentic' Africanness would look like.... I realized that I didn't have to accept my designation as some sort of doomed other, I could challenge my relationship to authority with humor and parody in mimicking and mirroring" (Hobbs, "Yinka Shonibare Mbe," 30).

the garment simply represents a chain of meanings consciously overdetermined by layers of meanings hard to exhaust. Endless readability traversed by paradoxes: Africanness without Africa, theology without Christ, Enlightenment without reason, conviviality informed by exploitation, sexuality unmarked by embodiment, and referentiality with multitudinous references.

Madhavi Menon, in one of her fascinating readings, takes Shonibare's art as an exemplum of an anti-identitarian queer universalism. Based on her previous work on the antiontology of desire, Menon approaches the artist's work in its refusal to anchor meaning in fixed references. "Desire is that which in every instance hollows out ontology,"[57] because it lives in us but always travels beyond us. Desire is anti-identitarian in that it questions the coagulation of affects into identities. This superfluidity of desire troubles any attempt at caging it within specific nomenclatures. Such is the equation that links queerness and universalism and what allows Menon to advocate for the similitude between the universal with its dismissal of differences and the queer with its advocacy for a desire that transcends fixed bodies.

One can easily appreciate how the overreferentiality of Shonibare's art invites the interpreter to dwell in the infinity of desire. Menon adds, "Shonibare's minoritarian discourse is an obstacle to the status quo because it removes ontology as the basis for how we live and does not offer to replace it with anything else."[58] Shonibare's compositions, with their disruption of the expected (animal heads on kids' bodies, sartorial incongruence, ethnic discontinuity, etc.), redress and readdress the tenets of multiculturalism: to name a culture as different is to situate it versus a norm.

Shonibare's art starts with stereotypical cultural representations and turns them upside down but declines to offer a viable fixed alternative. Instead, we are left dumbfounded, questioned about our complicity in such iteration, and hollowed out in our own identity. Hylton argues that his art "reveals a world in which African and European history can be distilled into a 'beginners guide', where the Victorian era is typified by class division, suppressed libido and missionary zeal, and Africa is characterized as the land of exotic and the primitive."[59]

---

57. Menon, *Indifference to Difference*, 16.
58. Menon, *Indifference to Difference*, 37.
59. Richard Hylton, "Yinka Shonibare: Dressing Down," *Third Text* 12.46 (2008): 101.

6. THE GOSPEL OF LOVE IN TIMES OF COLONIALITY (JOHN 13:1–20) 185

The *Last Supper Exploded* (figs. 6.3 and 6.4) is a tableaux-vivant condensing all of Shonibare's artistic preoccupations. His most monumental and complex tableau presents Baccus—or something similar—replacing the central figure of Christ, transformed into a headless satyr, half-man and half-goat. Twelve headless disciples pose in sexual and animalistic abandonment, both an homage to the biblical scene and Da Vinci's rendition. Shonibare weaves together religion and politics, empire and colonies through a play that builds on Victorian-inherited notions of identity. Could the headless torsos reference the executions of the French Revolution? the neutral skin color, the hybridity of the postcolonial encounter? the two silver vases of tulips the financial capital crisis of the seventeenth century? Does the batik reference indigeneity and Africanness or the global market exploitation of trade? The list goes on. The "beheading of identity" signals the blurring between colonizing and colonized, not because they are morally and politically equal, but because the aristocracy and the colonized wealthy class participate in the same system.

Menon asks why it is that Shonibare's oeuvre becomes the content of African art catalogs. Indeed, Shonibare's pluri-semiotic messages address issues of disability, gender, desire, coloniality, capitalism, religion, and sexuality:

> The visual register anchored in the body is the basis for the generation of identitarian ontology. In a culture of such overwhelming visuality, the brilliance of Shonibare's art lies not only in challenging the regime of visual meaning-production, but also in asking us to interrupt the process by which a particular image gets encoded and decoded in automatic ways. This is why, for Shonibare, ethnicity and desire are bound up together—not because the two are identical, but because both race and sexuality are forms of identity that base themselves firmly in and on the body.[60]

These three vignettes share numerous similitudes and not less important differences. Their common focus on the agapic underpinnings of the Last Supper/footwashing offers three diverse thematic emphases: Gutiérrez Alea laughs at the absurdity of role reversal in the context of a slave society; Buñuel mocks the dated morals of Christian charity by adding gendered and sexual metaphors that eroticize the event; and Shonibare

---

60. Menon, *Indifference to Difference*, 28.

Figs. 6.3 and 6.4. Yinka Shonibare, Last Supper Exploded, 2013, mixed media, 2013, 5' 1/5" x 24' 1/3" x 8' 1/2". © Yinka Shonibare CBE. All Rights Reserved, DACS/Artimage 2024. Image courtesy Stephen Friedman Gallery. Photo: Stephen White & Co 2024.

enacts a gender and colonial role reversal without referents. These three approaches are iterations of a postcolonial critique in three modalities: empire/postcolonial, feminist/postcolonial, and queer/postcolonial.

Epilogue

Gutiérrez Alea, Buñuel, and Shonibare's scenes visualize the theological and philosophical contradictions of practicing agape under cultural conditions of steeped structural asymmetry, and they do so by resorting to historical, literary, and artistic sources, infusing them with irony and sarcasm. In the realm of theory, these renditions exemplify a way of thinking biblically about the present, the past, and the future amid their respective coetaneous cultural and political crises.

Gutiérrez Alea, a child of the Cuban revolution himself, put a magnifying lens on the allyships of the religious and political status quo with the material plundering of Cuba first through Trans-Atlantic enslavement and later through Fulgencio Batista's dictatorship. Buñuel, exiled to Mexico due to the triumph of Franco's regime in Spain, unveils the connivance of the religious establishment with the upper class, the Catholic bourgeois's removed sensibility from the material hardships of the impoverished, and the deleterious effects of agape as paternalism. Shonibare, a British Nigerian artist residing in the United Kingdom, reflects on the ties between the colonial enterprise and Africanness.

At the hermeneutical level, their contributions suggest exegetical concerns akin to contemporary scholarly questions—the entanglement of the critic's bio with one's ideological commitments, the ethical valence of emancipation in the interpretive task, or the determinative role of a present context when interpreting the past—and epitomize a way of approaching the historiographical task committed to the ideological exposure of past and present systems of domination. *La última cena*, *Viridiana*, and *Last Supper Exploded* as visual thinking pieces evince the role of a hermeneutic that, to put it in Fernando Segovia's wording of Pablo Neruda's poem, has made a pact of blood with the task of interpretation itself.[61]

Gutiérrez Alea zooms in on the contradictions between religion as ideology and history as the ground for colonization and capitalism. Buñuel targets a type of bourgeois ethics that claims the moral ground,

---

61. Segovia, "Criticism in Critical Times," 28–29.

ignorant of material circumstances and out of touch with the ethical leanings of a secular world. Shonibare charges our perceptions of traditional cultural references with a semiotic overload that leaves us in crisis. In all cases, the visualization of the convivial scene exploits the contradictions, the irony, and even the campiness of a theological message built on top of damaging social conditions. They demystify any sacramental elements as they have been distilled in the theological tradition by laying bare the contradictions of any agape version, oblivious to the geopolitical undergirding it. Their respective interpretations of the Last Supper/footwashing are not particularly helpful in gaining historical knowledge of convivial practices in the early Christian communities. Consequently, they provide little insight into the gospels' instructions on meal and ritual practices. By the same token, they are not historical representations of their respective circumstances. Buñuel's highly stylized representation of religious practices touches on irony and sarcasm rather than history, and Gutiérrez Alea's alleged historical tone works precisely because the film's numerous conventions and plots speak against its historicity. Shonibare's piece does away with historicity altogether, not because his work lacks historical referent, but because it meshes inconspicuously past, present, and future.

Gutiérrez Alea and Buñuel's sardonic representations are cautious tales against representations of the have-nots as innocent, morally superior, or fair. They warn against the bourgeois romanticizing of class divisions. They suggest that as beneficiaries of the haves, the have-nots, are as morally corrupt as their patrons and as likely to fall into immoral behavior. In other words, diagnosing structural economic inequality, both artists suggest, is not a matter of granting moral superiority to the oppressed but rather of exposing—ironically, sarcastically, caustically—the systems guilty of displacing entire populations to conditions of scarcity, precarity, and dispossession. Both films ascribe to a compelling narrative in which the portrayal of the subaltern resists equating her position with any superior moral ground. Buñuel and Gutiérrez Alea ultimately argue that the identification of the have-nots with good works is a product of bourgeois ideology.[62] Shonibare's route embodies an entirely different trajectory: its anti-identitarian aesthetics creates a labyrinth with no exits.

---

62. Kobena Mercer, *Travel and See Black Diaspora Art Practices since the 1980s* (Durham, NC: Duke University Press, 2016), 16.

Viridiana and *La última cena* provide little historical insight into first-century meal practices. Accordingly, both cultural productions have an oblique relation to mainstream disciplinary questions such as the literary relations between the sources (among the Synoptics themselves, with John's Gospel, and with the Pauline canon), the historicity of the event, its Jewish roots, its relationship with the Greco-Roman meals,[63] its eschatological implications, its functionality within specific liturgical or catechetical settings,[64] or the material dynamics animating the practice.[65] They visualize, however, the messiness of meal politics, and, in this regard, they remain an ideological warning post against any convivial imagery oblivious to the macro-political framework in which sharing food takes place.

As these cultural products speak from and to the urgent realities of their conception—political dictatorship and Christian nationalism in one case, legacies of enslavement and colonialism in the other—they throw into stark relief the constructed nature of their respective authors. It is here, at the intersection of subjectivity (Buñuel and Gutiérrez Alea as individual critics), political crises (authoritarianism and coloniality), and interpretation of a shared past with enormous cultural capital (Last Supper motifs and New Testament iconic topoi), that both directors acquire significance as critics. In other words, their authorship, production, and cultural import evince the intercontextual nature of the critical task.

---

63. Petra Dijkhuizen, "The Lord's Supper and Ritual Theory: Interpreting 1 Corinthians 11:30 in Terms of Risk, Failure, and Efficacy," *Neot* 50 (2016): 441–76.

64. Jason T. Lamoreaux, "Ritual Negotiation in 1 Corinthians: Pauline Authority and the Corinthian Community," *Neot* 50 (2016): 397–422; Rachel M. McRae, "Eating with Honor: The Corinthian Lord's Supper in Light of Voluntary Association Meal Practices," *JBL* 130 (2011): 165–81.

65. Suzanne Watts Henderson, "'If Anyone Hungers...': An Integrated Reading of 1 Cor 11.17–34," *NTS* 48 (2002): 195–208.

7
THE GOSPEL OF HIV (ACTS 9:1-8)

The Abyssal Line on This End

I remember growing up thinking that I was going to die of AIDS. This fear shaped my late childhood before I knew I was gay, even before I knew what sex was. When Rock Hudson died of AIDS in 1985, I was nine years old. When Freddy Mercury passed away in 1991, I was fifteen. For gay men in my generation, HIV stamped our infancy and early adolescence. Not even reaching the two-digit age, oblivious to the contours of homoeroticism but aware of some inner inclinations toward "same-looking humans," I was entangled in a series of cultural, political, and religious discourses that equated gay sex with death. Growing up and maturing sexually when millions of gay men around you are dying of AIDS represents both a biographical trauma and a generational crisis. The "psychological epidemic" compounds the medical one; the cultural crisis would leave indelible intimate wounds on those who were lucky enough to survive:[1] to live in the times of AIDS meant, as in many other traumas, to make sense amid the uttermost destruction. As Steven Schwartzberg puts it, "We have wearily attempted to juggle mammoth, seemingly incompatible tasks: mourning the dead, tending the ill, protecting the healthy."[2]

---

1. Walt Odets, *In the Shadow of the Epidemic: Being HIV-Negative in the Age of AIDS* (Durham, NC: Duke University Press, 1995), 23–39. HIV began as a pandemic in 1981 and has since become endemic. Although scholars frequently refer to it as an epidemic, properly speaking HIV is a pandemic because of the number of people affected globally. In the present chapter I use both terms interchangeably to respect different scholars' preferred terminology.

2. Steven Schwartzberg, *A Crisis of Meaning How Gay Men Are Making Sense of AIDS* (New York: Oxford University Press, 1996), 4.

The death toll of the AIDS global pandemic can hardly be overstated, as studies continue to deepen our understanding of its consequences on all the spheres of human life: the reshaping of family structures, the effect on migratory movements, the politics of international aid, the capillary transformation of old anthropological and political ideas of health, not to mention the impact on religious and theological vocabularies.[3] For gay

---

3. On family structures, see J. P. Ntozi and Samuel Zirimenya, "Changes in Household Composition and Family Structure during the AIDS Epidemic in Uganda," *The Continuing African HIV/AIDS Epidemic* (1999): 193–209; T. Apata et al., "Effects of HIV/AIDS Epidemic and Related Sicknesses on Family and Community Structures in Nigeria: Evidence of Emergence of Older Care-Givers and Orphan Hoods," *Journal of Science and Technology Education Research* 1.4 (2010): 73–84; M. J. Rotheram-Borus et al., "Families Living with HIV," *AIDS Care* 17.8 (2005): 978–87; E. Maxine Ankrah, "The Impact of HIV/AIDS on the Family and Other Significant Relationships: The African Clan Revisited," *AIDS Care* 5.1 (1993): 5–22; Robert Bor, Riva Miller, and Eleanor Goldman, "HIV/AIDS and the Family: A Review of Research in the First Decade," *Journal of Family Therapy* 15.2 (1993): 187–204.

On migratory movements, see Kevin D. Deane, Justin O. Parkhurst, and Deborah Johnston, "Linking Migration, Mobility and HIV," *Tropical Medicine & International Health* 15.12 (2010): 1458–63; Kathleen N. Deering et al., "The Impact of Out-Migrants and Out-Migration on the HIV/AIDS Epidemic: A Case Study from South-West India," *AIDS* 22 (2008): S165–81; Georgios Nikolopoulos et al., "Migration and HIV Epidemic in Greece," *The European Journal of Public Health* 15.3 (2005): 296–99; Yan Hong et al., "Rural-to-Urban Migrants and the HIV Epidemic in China," *AIDS and Behavior* 10 (2006): 421–30; Victoria Hernando et al., "HIV Infection in Migrant Populations in the European Union and European Economic Area in 2007–2012: An Epidemic on the Move," *Journal of Acquired Immune Deficiency Syndromes* 70.2 (2015): 204–11; Shao-hua Liu, *Passage to Manhood: Youth Migration, Heroin, and AIDS in Southwest China* (Stanford, CA: Stanford University Press, 2011).

On international aid, see Julia H. Smith and Alan Whiteside, "The History of AIDS Exceptionalism," *Journal of the International AIDS Society* 13.1 (2010): 1–8; Kevin J. Kelly and Karen Birdsall, "The Effects of National and International HIV/AIDS Funding and Governance Mechanisms on the Development of Civil-Society Responses to HIV/AIDS in East and Southern Africa," *AIDS Care* 22.2 (2010): 1580–87; Ida Susser, *AIDS, Sex, and Culture: Global Politics and Survival in Southern Africa* (Chichester: Wiley, 2011).

On the transformation of ideas on health, see Andrea M. Whittaker, "Living with HIV: Resistance by Positive People," *Medical Anthropology Quarterly* 6 (1992): 385–90; Paul Farmer, *Aids and Accusation: Haiti and the Geography of Blame* (Berkeley: University of California Press, 2006).

On religious and theological vocabularies, see Sima Barmania and Michael J. Reiss, *Islam and Health Policies Related to HIV Prevention in Malaysia* (Cham:

men, the HIV crisis has meant, among other things, a crisis of subjectivity: How do we relate to each other when relationality has been mediated through mortality? The impact of HIV on gay men's subjectivity—decades after the end of the pandemic in the Global North, thanks to the widespread use of ART for those infected and PREP for those who are not—endures: gay men, up to this day on gay hookup apps, still use the adjective *clean* to refer to a seronegative status.[4]

The AIDS pandemic shifted the ways gay men practiced sex, but it also changed cultural discourses about sexuality. The pandemic left nothing untouched: religion, politics, economics, and culture. Anthony Petro chronicles the braiding of Christian religious attitudes with the development of the AIDS epidemic, as the former came up with a series of discourses around sex, nation, and health—more implicit than explicit—that doubled down on a vision that awarded marriage and monogamy a renowned primacy status.[5] Anthony Petro's sophisticated argument about the moral epidemic of AIDS has several turns, but I wish to focus here on his insight that God's wrath—metaphorical for some, quite literal for others—will only stop as a result of a national adoption of a long-life, monogamous, heterosexual marriage, a notion that would later be adopted, conveniently repurposed by the gay movement. Petro concludes:

> There are many good reasons to support gay marriage. But we might ask why it is that the gay marriage movement has become so attached to the narrative of romantic sexual monogamy as the normative model for queer life and how this vision has become the salvific hope for ending HIV/AIDS. To criticize this narrative is not necessarily to criticize gay marriage. But I want to resist the conservative plot that would have AIDS

Springer, 2017); Stacey A. Shaw and Nabila El-Bassel, "The Influence of Religion on Sexual HIV Risk," *AIDS and Behavior* 18 (2014): 1569–94.

4. Brandon Andrew Robinson, "Doing Sexual Responsibility: HIV, Risk Discourses, Trust, and Gay Men Interacting Online," *Sociological Perspectives* 61 (2018): 383–98.

5. Amy S. Patterson, Marian Burchardt, and Louise Mubanda Rasmussen, *The Politics and Anti-politics of Social Movements: Religion and AIDS in Africa* (London: Routledge, 2016); Rijk van Dijk, Hansjörg Dilger, Marian Burchardt, and Thera Rasing, *Religion and AIDS-Treatment in Africa: Saving Souls, Prolonging Lives* (Farnham: Ashgate, 2014); Marian Burchardt, "A Moral Science of Sex," in *Faith in the Time of AIDS*, ed. Marian Burchardt (London: Palgrave Macmillan, 2015), 74–97; Anthony M. Petro, *After the Wrath of God: AIDS, Sexuality, and American Religion* (Oxford: Oxford University Press, 2015).

prompt gay men to grow into sexual adulthood defined by monogamy and marriage.[6]

This narrative, originating in the 1980s, would eventually convince generations of gay men that they could escape a biological pandemic if only they would not fall into a moral one. Conveniently, biblical studies had inaugurated in the mid-twentieth century the "homosexualized" Bible: liberal interpreters, informed by scientificism, turned the "confused category of 'sodomitical sin' and assigned to it a singular same-sex meaning."[7] In other words, the category of the homosexual invented in nineteenth-century medical discourses filtered through a core of biblical scholarship—supposedly scientific, objective, and historicist—that would serve as legitimization for the moralization of gay sex so endemic to the HIV pandemic. Homosexuality continued to make it into historicist accounts of the biblical past to the extent that the moralization of (gay) sex remained on the agenda.

From a global perspective, the eruption of homosexuality has informed notions of colonialism and statehood to this day, framing the terms of sexual rights in Latin America and Africa.[8] The ravaging effects of AIDS in Africa have inspired theologians and biblical interpreters alike to broaden the scope of emancipatory hermeneutics in a sort of African HIV theology. On this front, Musa Dube's work remains exemplary.[9] Although

---

6. Petro, *After the Wrath of God*, 196.

7. Heather R. White, *Reforming Sodom: Protestants and the Rise of Gay Rights* (Chapel Hill: University of North Carolina Press, 2015), 4. In fact, "heterosexuality" was also invented and equally deployed in biblical interpretation; see Daniel Boyarin, *Unheroic Conduct: The Rise of Heterosexuality and the Invention of the Jewish Man*, Contraversions 8 (Oakland: University of California Press, 1997); Jonathan Katz, *The Invention of Heterosexuality* (Chicago: University of Chicago Press, 2014); Louis-Georges Tin, *The Invention of Heterosexual Culture* (Cambridge: MIT Press, 2012). In biblical criticism, Dale B. Martin's critique of the import of "heterosexuality" in New Testament studies remains convincing (Martin, "Heterosexism and the Interpretation of Romans 1:18–32," *BibInt* 3 [1995]: 332–55).

8. Neville Wallace Hoad, *African Intimacies: Race, Homosexuality, and Globalization* (Minneapolis: University of Minnesota Press, 2007).

9. The ethical drives remains clear: "The graves of the 35.4 million people who died in our lifetime from this disease still call us all to reflect on what we teach, why we teach, and how we teach" (Musa W. Dube, "Remembering the Teacherly Moments of the HIV and AIDS Texts," *International Bulletin of Mission Research* 43 [2019]: 329); Dube, *The HIV and AIDS Bible: Selected Essays* (Scranton, PA: University of Scranton Press, 2008); Dube, "*Talitha Cum* Hermeneutics of Liberation: Some African Wom-

understandable given the recent backlash against sexual minorities, it is dispiriting to witness how gay sex continues to be trapped between cultural and theological discourses of approval and condemnation.[10] The problem is compounded in the Global South because "cross-cultural variations of the expression and representation of same-sex desire" fade into the background when they are studied "through the imperialist gaze of Euro-American queer identity politics or are appropriated through the economies of the West."[11] While liberation theology has been effective in understanding geopolitical contexts, it has been slow to address sex outside of heteronormative frameworks. On the other hand, queer theory has focused on the discontinuities between premodern and contemporary sexual knowledge, but its influence on biblical studies in the Global North remains limited. Although queer historiography has helped to denaturalize European sexuality, it does not offer much insight into queer global sexual cultures and subcultures.[12]

---

en's Ways of Reading the Bible," in *The Bible and the Hermeneutics of Liberation*, ed. Alejandro F. Botta and Pablo R. Andiñach, SemeiaSt 59 (Atlanta: Society of Biblical Literature, 2009), 133–46; Dube, *HIV/AIDS and the Curriculum: Methods of Integrating HIV/AIDS in Theological Programmes* (Geneva: WCC Publications, 2003); Dube, "Go tla Siama. O tla Fola: Doing Biblical Studies in an HIV and AIDS Context," *Black Theology: An International Journal* 8 (2010): 212–41.

10. See Adriaan S. van Klinken and Masiiwa Ragies Gunda, "Taking Up the Cudgels against Gay Rights? Trends and Trajectories in African Christian Theologies on Homosexuality," *Journal of Homosexuality* 59 (2012): 114–38; Masiiwa Ragies Gunda, *The Bible and Homosexuality in Zimbabwe: A Socio-historical Analysis of the Political, Cultural, and Christian Arguments in the Homosexual Public Debate, with Special Reference to the Use of the Bible* (Bamberg: University of Bamberg Press, 2010).

11. William J. Spurlin, *Imperialism within the Margins: Queer Representation and the Politics of Culture in Southern Africa* (New York: Palgrave Macmillan, 2006), 17.

12. Chantal Zabus, *Out in Africa: Same-Sex Desire in Sub-Saharan Literatures and Cultures* (Suffolk: Currey, 2013), 5. Queer historiography is a complex disciplinary field informed by a wide range of theoretical and methodological trajectories (phenomenology, psychoanalysis, feminism of varied sorts, deconstructionism, etc.). In biblical studies, the influence of David Halperin, arguably the most sophisticated queer historiographer in the wake of Michel Foucault's groundbreaking influence, looms large. He is one of Brooten's main interlocutors, an important reference to Dale Martin, and a prominent partner in "Sex and the Single Apostle" (Stephen D. Moore, *God's Beauty Parlor: And Other Queer Spaces in and around the Bible* [Stanford, CA: Stanford University Press, 2001], 133–72) and in Joseph A. Marchal's contribution ("'Making History' Queerly: Touches across Time through a Biblical Behind," *BibInt* 19 [2011]: 376–81). For a critical analysis of the trajectory of queer historiography

It is hard to overestimate the impact of Foucault on queer historiography. After his magnum opus *History of Sexuality*, sexuality became, rather than a transtemporal arrangement of the human experience, the product of modernizing forces of disciplinary power.[13] With its origin in France and dominance in US-based literary studies departments, Foucault's influence has become an intellectual staple in the Global North, especially because it created a historiographical gap between antiquity and modernity's regimes of truth concerning the relationship between sex and subjectivity. On this front, Foucault's heuristic power remains relevant for any transhistorical account of sexuality because, among other things, it exposes how putatively abstract notions such as nature, body, or essence are ensconced in contemporary systems of power/knowledge. Briefly put, sexuality represents a realm of the contemporary human experience encompassing orientations, affects, familial arrangements, or specific actions with no parallel in either premodern times or non-Western cultures.

In the Latin American context, Marcella Althaus-Reid appositely argues that the subjects of liberation theology were portrayed "as any old-fashioned moralizing tale," as "the deserving and asexual poor."[14] This trend is exacerbated when we factor the stigma of HIV into the equation. Theological and religious traditions in Latin America, including liberation theology, evangelical and neo-conservative Christian movements, and Catholicism, share a common view of sexuality as negative. While they

---

in New Testament studies, see Luis Menéndez-Antuña, "Is There a Room for Queer Desires in the House of Biblical Scholarship? A Methodological Reflection on Queer Desires in the Context of Contemporary New Testament Studies," *BibInt* 23 (2015): 399–427. For a survey of the applicability of queer historiography in Latin America and a constructive proposal to create a new genealogy of sexuality that draws from precolonial cultures, see Menéndez-Antuña, "Bible and Sexuality Studies," in *Oxford Handbook of the Bible in Latin and Latinx America*, ed. Fernando F. Segovia and Ahida Pilarski (Oxford: Oxford University Press, forthcoming).

13. Michel Foucault, *An Introduction*, vol. 1 of *The History of Sexuality* (New York: Vintage, 1990). Foucault posited different points of origin for "homosexuality" in different works; see Didier Eribon, "Michel Foucault's Histories of Sexuality," *GLQ: A Journal of Lesbian and Gay Studies* 7 (2001): 31–86. Furthermore, the now classical distinction between acts and identities, as Foucauldian scholarship has shown, has been affixed to that first volume of *The History of Sexuality* by later debate; see Lynne Huffer, *Mad for Foucault: Rethinking the Foundations of Queer Theory* [New York: Columbia University Press, 2010], 67–82).

14. Althaus-Reid, *Indecent Theology*, 30.

may disagree on the specifics of sexual ethics, they all view sexuality within a heteronormative and patriarchal framework. As a result, biblical critics must explore alternative ways to analyze sex and sexuality critically within the context of the Bible and theology. This requires mapping, designing, and investing in sex-positive hermeneutics in religious and cultural contexts that have been hastily formulated.

In chapter 3, I argued for the need to bring back the erotic to the center of the agapic: a vision of hermeneutics attentive to queer sexual practices beyond identitarian definitions. This choice does not discard other possible approaches: there is value in exploring how interpreters—in Latin America, Africa, and the Global North—draw arguments around sexuality from scripture and produce biblical arguments. Equally important remains the task of examining how biblical interpreters address issues such as sexual freedom, marital ethics, rights, sexual abuse, and the like. Both approaches have limitations for our purposes because they remain encased in a view of hermeneutics that takes its research agenda directly from a supposedly neutral reconstruction of important biblical themes. The predicament becomes, once again, manifest: the Bible leverages its support for stigmatizing cultural understandings of sex and HIV, but biblical scholarship remains unequipped to address those same issues.

In this chapter, I situate the task of biblical scholarship at the crossroads of theology and queer studies. Although such an intersection is not exceptional per se, my approach is rather unique because it weaves together a theology of fucking with recent political readings of sex in queer studies. As theorized in the introductory chapter, in contrast to Euro-American exegesis, the Global South does not wedge a gap between biblical interpretation, political theology, and ecclesiology. Similarly, both hemispheres shy away from tackling sex as such, not just as it refers to sexuality or gender. As I argue in the concluding section, it is not only theology and biblical interpretation that dread their approach to sex, but queer theory has also had its share of sex avoidance. Consequently, the ensuing reflections gravitate around three disciplinary questions. First, concerning biblical and theological studies, what does a biblical interpretation that centers sex look like, and what are the implications for our understanding of subjectivity? Second, concerning queer studies, how can we expand our understanding of sexual subcultures into available but insufficient theological vocabularies? Finally, regarding emancipatory hermeneutics, are there political gains at these theoretical intersections?

It may seem tendentious to start addressing these questions by focusing on gay male subcultures in the Global North: tending to the experience of gay urban men in the United States when women (cis or trans) and children globally have also been ravaged by the pandemic requires some explanation. Unpacking the intimate experiences of gay men who defy gender expectations—as they occupy the culturally assigned female position in the act of fucking—and sexual norms—as they transgress sanitized versions of safe sex—has the potential to place a wedge in the well-oiled machine of contemporary identitarian ascriptions. As I hope to demonstrate, some aspects of bareback subcultures amplify the self-shattering, ego-divesting, unbinding components of sex. Tim Dean and Oliver Davis sharply diagnose our current cultural and political moment:

> A rhetoric of identity—along with an array of largely covert identitarian assumptions—has colonized subjective, social, and political intelligibility: identities have become the lens through which too many people, progressive as well as conservative, view the world. We have, in the words of Walter Benn Michaels, "learned to love identity and ignore inequality."[15]

It is this strand of queer theory, one deeply invested in undoing identity, that I wish to milk in this chapter. Michel Foucault, Leo Bersani, and Tim Dean's contributions target the self-sufficient subject at the core of postmodern capitalism. Others, in a similar vein, acknowledging the racialized traps of identity, at least when thinking about sex, continue to draw from the most abject elements of sex to chip away at racial hierarchies.[16]

Theology and Queer Experience

Theology has reflected on the parallels between lovemaking—as intimacy among people—and divine love—as intimacy with the divine—but

---

15. Oliver Davis and Tim Dean, *Hatred of Sex* (Lincoln: Nebraska University Press, 2022), 33.

16. Kathryn Bond Stockton, *Beautiful Bottom, Beautiful Shame: Where "Black" Meets "Queer"* (Durham, NC: Duke University Press, 2006); Darieck Scott, *Extravagant Abjection: Blackness, Power, and Sexuality in the African American Literary Imagination* (New York: New York University Press, 2010); Tan Hoang Nguyen, *A View from the Bottom: Asian American Masculinity and Sexual Representation* (Durham, NC: Duke University Press, 2014); Mary C. Foltz, *Contemporary American Literature and Excremental Culture: American Sh*t* (London: Palgrave Macmillan, 2020).

making love is hardly the only manifestation of sex between people. Queers, especially queer gay men, belong to a subculture where fucking becomes an almost daily practice that happens everywhere. Anonymous sex in an office bathroom, for instance, speaks to a specific way of being in the world. My contribution explores the theological "meat" in the practices of subcultures that simply fuck, that have sex while skipping the heteronormative protocols of intimacy. I argue that certain queer practices of fucking (cruising and barebacking) provide the raw material for a queer theology of sex and for a queer approach to its biblical and artistic underpinnings. Experience as a source for theology has been the ground for fertile scholarly debate since the 1970s,[17] a debate fired by the rise (and decline) of all sorts of contextual theologies and theologies of the body/flesh.[18] In this chapter, the exploration of barebacking in the midst of the AIDS crisis and its aftermath is intended to counter heteronormative assumptions about relationality, subjectivity, and identity formation.[19] Furthermore, tending to how gay men work out new relationalities in the midst of death—how queers reframe cultural codes about masculinity and femininity, dominance and submission—will help us read the conversion of Paul in Acts 9, and Caravaggio's subsequent rendering, outside of hackneyed approaches to conversion.[20]

---

17. Ellen Leonard, "Experience as a Source for Theology," in *Proceedings of the Annual Convention*, ed. Catholic Theological Society of America (Washington, DC: Catholic Theological Society of America, 1988), 44–61. Contemporary theologies theologize experience differently; see D. L. Gelpi, *The Turn to Experience in Contemporary Theology* (New York: Paulist, 1994); Thomas M. Kelly, *Theology at the Void: The Retrieval of Experience* (Notre Dame, IN: University of Notre Dame Press, 2002).

18. Althaus-Reid, *Indecent Theology*; Mayra Rivera, *Poetics of the Flesh* (Durham, NC: Duke University Press, 2015).

19. Monika Hellwig, *Whose Experience Counts in Theological Reflection?*, The 1982 Père Marquette Theology Lecture (Milwaukee: Marquette University Press, 1982).

20. Maia Kotrosits approaches the subculture of barebacking with similar assumptions but with a different goal: whereas I focus on subjectivity formation, Kotrosits uses the AIDS crisis as a template to consider how the contiguity of time between the past and the present is disrupted via the anxiety of waiting. "Temporal suspense" and "the difficulty of living with a foreseeable future" link together cultures of barebacking and the anxiety in Mark's Gospel about when the end is; see Maia Kotrosits, "Queer Persistence: On Death, History, and Longing for Endings," in *Sexual Disorientations: Queer Temporalities, Affects, Theologies*, ed. Kent L. Brintnall, Joseph A. Marchal, and Stephen D. Moore (New York: Fordham University Press, 2018), 134–35.

This intercontextual understanding will address some theoretical challenges that have traditionally plagued the hermeneutics of experience.[21] Drawing from an ethnography of queer practices, unpacking the intimate experiences of gay men as they embody their erotic desires and inclinations, grounds our theological exploration of fucking in thick cultural descriptions. A "theology from this side" prioritizes experience, reflecting on "how we can accurately and critically use it."[22] On this front, my use of *experience* resembles the one embedded in contextual readings with flesh-and-blood readers at their center.[23] My argument pays sustained attention to the queer practices of barebacking and cruising to explore certain theological concepts—relationality and otherness—as a way to open up a thematic field in theology where queer sex, not simply the musings of queer theory, substantiates theological reflection. Accordingly, I place queer theology within contextual theology, as an instantiation of the call to tackle the religious subject as relational in the flesh, "formed and enacted through sustained affiliations and intense encounters."[24] As such, theology reflects on the practices of cruisers and barebackers and speaks to those who may find their experimenting with new modes of relatedness thought-provoking. Queer practices are, ultimately, a theological locus insofar as they instantiate new modes of relationality and subject formation.[25]

---

21. Owen C. Thomas, "Theology and Experience," *HTR* 78 (1985): 179–201.

22. Bernard Cooke, "The Experiential 'Word of God,'" in *Consensus in Theology? A Dialogue with Hans Küng and Edward Schillebeeckx*, ed. Leonard Swidler (Philadelphia: Westminster, 1980), 72.

23. In biblical studies, the experience of flesh-and-blood readers has been most notably theorized by Segovia, "Criticism in Critical Times"; and Karl Rahner, *Foundations of Christian Faith: An Introduction to the Idea of Christianity* (New York: Crossroad, 1982), 20. The notion of experience tends to refer to the quotidian, transcendental, psychological, phenomenological, or personal side of the relationship with the Divine Other, always with a subjective emphasis (Bernard Cooke, *Power and the Spirit of God: Toward an Experience-Based Pneumatology* [Oxford: Oxford University Press, 2008], 179–84), whereas descriptions of practice usually signal an outer and public manifestation (ethical, ritual, political, etc.). In this chapter, *experience* works to locate queer theology within the theoretical framework of contextual theologies and to explore how specific practices might inform the religious experience. The notion of practice refers to the ways certain queer communities practice sex (fuck).

24. Constance M. Furey, "Body, Society, and Subjectivity in Religious Studies," *JAAR* 80 (2012): 9.

25. Kathleen T. Talvacchia, "Disrupting the Theory-Practice Binary," in *Queer Christianities: Lived Religion in Transgressive Forms*, ed. Michael F. Pettinger, Kath-

Caravaggio, *The Conversion on the Way to Damascus*, 1601, oil on canvas. Santa Maria del Popolo, Rome.

The varied practices of men fucking each other adds a surplus of meaning to traditional theological sources (scripture, art, history, experience).

---

leen Talvacchia, and Mark Larrimore (New York: New York University Press, 2015), 184–94.

More pointedly, my contribution explores how reading a biblical text (Acts 9:1–19) through its artistic interpretation (Caravaggio, *The Conversion on the Way to Damascus*, fig. 7.1), read, in turn, in light of the queer practices of cruising and barebacking, offers a queer theology of relationality. Tim Dean's account of queer relationality in *Unlimited Intimacy* allows an intercontextual theological exploration of the relationship between the self and the immanent or transcendental Other that my argument brings to bear on the biblical text and its artistic rendition.[26]

Erotohistoriography—as an inquiry connecting bodily pleasures across times and spaces, as a method that conceives of the present (and the past) as a hybrid experience—traces bodily dispositions and pleasurable connections in the lives and afterlives of cultural artifacts.[27] Specifically, Paul's encounter with the Lord in Acts, a shocking encounter that transforms his body, finds echoes in Caravaggio's unique arrangement of the event, in the emotions it elicits for the viewers, reverberating up to this present in the experiences of queer men experiencing their own shocking encounters. Here I imagine how the contemporary interpreter travels back and forth between biblical art and texts, between past and contemporary dispositions, envisioning modes of queer relationality with the other/Other, between the called (Saul) and the caller (the Lord), the human and the divine, the bottom and the top.[28] In this iteration, the history of reception is traversed by queer temporality. Instead of analyzing historical events or literary topics (namely, Paul's conversion) or extricating how the pictorial materializes the text (how Luke and Caravaggio's versions of Paul differ), we focus on the shape of (queer) intimate relationships across time and space and the power they yield in interpreting biblical texts and ourselves.

The following interpretative exercise starts with an introduction to practices of barebacking and cruising (*Unlimited Intimacy*) and how they

---

26. Dean, *Unlimited Intimacy*; Mieke Bal, *Reading "Rembrandt": Beyond the Word-Image Opposition* (Cambridge: Cambridge University Press, 1991), 76.

27. Freeman, *Time Binds*, 95–136. Notions such as reception history and *Wirkungsgeschichte* have been severely criticized for essentializing texts as original entities that trigger "copies" across times and places. The term *cultural history* conveys more accurately the notion that the artistic representation is a performance of a cultural text that is, in turn, a performance itself (Beal, "Reception History and Beyond." See also Lyons, "Hope for a Troubled Discipline?"; James G. Crossley, *Jesus and the Chaos of History: Redirecting the Life of the Historical Jesus* (Oxford: Oxford University Press, 2015).

28. Furey, "Body, Society, and Subjectivity."

illuminate notions of relationality and hospitality. Second, I interpret Caravaggio's artwork precisely through those ideas: relationality as shattering, hospitality as openness to the Other, and so on. Third, I suggest how such an intercontextual hermeneutics offers a queer trajectory of visualization to read Paul's conversion in Acts 9:1–19. Finally, I advance how a theological understanding of relationality benefits from a queer notion of subjectivity.

By *queer* I mean first a hermeneutical approach. Queer criticism, in Warner's now-classic formulation,[29] defies regimes of the normal. Such defiance, a reading against the grain, yields bizarre yet plausible meanings, a plausibility predicated on the suggestive relationship between different parts of the argumentative moves. This version of queer critique introduces theology to a vocabulary both neglected and rejected, rendering the conceptual field of raw sex open to scholarly examination. Briefly put, *fuck* acquires theological currency. Second, queer, at the experiential level, refers to ethically significant practices insofar as they redefine the theological notions of relationality, subjectivity, otherness, hospitality, immanence, and transcendence. Such redefinitions have recently come under scrutiny for their normalizing effects,[30] their depoliticizing consequences,[31] and their failure to incorporate critical race theory and disability studies.[32] An intercontextual approach pitting the queer, the artistic, and the textual sources against each other throws into relief thematic connections that undo the normalizing effects of such sources considered independently. In the wake of this interpretive practice, the disciple-Lord relationship acquires a new taste, mirroring present queer practices in their awkwardness[33] and advocating for a type of discipleship unhinged from autonomous subjectivity. Ultimately, the queer optic offers an intercontextual reading that explores virtual connections across periods of time (eroto-

---

29. Michael Warner, *The Trouble with Normal: Sex, Politics, and the Ethics of Queer Life* (New York: Free Press, 1999).

30. Linn Marie Tonstad, "The Limits of Inclusion: Queer Theology and its Others," *Theology & Sexuality* 21 (2015): 1–19.

31. James Penney, *After Queer Theory: The Limits of Sexual Politics* (London: Pluto, 2014).

32. See Scott, *Extravagant Abjection*; Amber Jamilla Musser, *Sensational Flesh: Race, Power, and Masochism* (New York: New York University Press, 2014); and Nguyen, *A View from the Bottom*.

33. Kathryn Lofton, "Everything Queer?," in Talvacchia, Larrimore, and Pettinger, *Queer Christianities*, 195–204.

historiography), frustrating the grasp that historical, literary, sociological, and theological models hold on the biblical text (cultural hermeneutics).

Unlimited Intimacy and (De)subjectivity

For all queer theory's—and queer theology's—discourse about sex, both disciplines have paid little attention to actual sexual practices, acts, or subcultures, let alone the raw material of sex itself. Tim Dean's ethnographic study of barebacking and cruising as queer practices within specific subcultures remedies this void by documenting how queers engage in stigmatized practices and how in doing so they create a relationality that, under certain conditions, embraces a radical ethics of risk, of unlimited hospitality through impersonal intimacy. *Unlimited Intimacy* is a starting point for a *trajectory of visualization* that leads the interpreter through Caravaggio's work and the biblical texts that he brings alive.[34] Erotohistoriography takes the raw material of sex provided by Dean's ethnography to connect historical dots that delineate an erotheology.

In *Unlimited Intimacy: Reflections on the Subculture of Barebacking*, Tim Dean explores the practices of gay men belonging to a subculture that values barebacking (anal intercourse without condoms in the midst of the HIV health crisis) and cruising (random sexual encounters in public and semipublic spaces) as defining features. Many gay men, as it happens, value "unlimited" sexual intimacy despite the health risks it poses and, paradoxically in some cases, precisely because of its threats. Dean ultimately discusses the ethical valence behind actions such as bug chasing, the seemingly irrational action of pursuing contact with strangers to become HIV-positive. His study is remarkable, first, for skipping any a priori moralization of irrational sexual practices and, second, for offering unique, insightful ethical conclusions on queer relationality, community, transcendence, and spirituality.

Barebacking and cruising, as practices involving "intimacy with strangers without predicating that intimacy on knowledge or understanding of the other,"[35] lay the foundations of a subculture with distinctive and valuable insights on the ethics of risk, hospitality, subjectivity, and relationality. Dean's ethnography contributes to an exploration of the virtual

---

34. Berdini, *The Religious Art of Jacopo Bassano*, 35.
35. Dean, *Unlimited Intimacy*, 211.

connections that erotohistoriography draws between the present queer experience and its artistic and biblical echoes in the past. Queer practices channel, explore, and surface modes of sociality that reconceptualize subject formation (the relationship of the self to itself and the Other), the relation between the native and the stranger, and those between the ego and the symbolic. Ultimately, he suggests, these "exemplify a distinctive ethic of openness to alterity ... focused on the primacy of the other."[36]

Cruising, at least when it is not degraded through online hookup sites protocols or minute regulations of party attendance,[37] represents a metaphor for contact with otherness, epitomizing the touch of alterity. The intimacy involved in cruising skips the classical epistemological subject/object divide in that "it constitutes a philosophy of living whose ethics depends on whether the openness to strangeness is cultivated or, conversely, curtailed."[38] Cruising, especially when barebacking is involved, insofar as it represents a disposition of total openness to otherness, is "ethically exemplary."[39]

Queers build community through a type of intimacy that transcends sexuality precisely because it relies on the virus. Who in their right mind pursues anonymous barebacking aware of the medical and social consequences of becoming infected? *Unlimited Intimacy* considers it unethical to decide the morality of a practice without exploring the rationale behind it and advocates a type of promiscuity exemplary for its unlimited hospitality.[40] Barebacking, then, offers a notion of sex defined beyond the pursuit of pleasure, as a mediation through which the self explores the confusion of boundaries—"distinguishability of bodies" being undone through the shattering of identities. Thus, a queer ethic of sex points to the unstable relationship of the self to itself, presents the problematic dimension of self-identification, and undermines the boundaries that define identity. This is, as the early Bersani put it, the essence of sex, the self-shattering of identity, the sudden removal

---

36. Dean, *Unlimited Intimacy*, 176–77.
37. Dean, *Unlimited Intimacy*, 192–96.
38. Dean, *Unlimited Intimacy*, xii.
39. Dean, *Unlimited Intimacy*, xii. Also, adding some nuance, Dean argues that, insofar as it involves an instrumentalized practice of filtering sexual companions, barebacking needs critique.
40. Dean, *Unlimited Intimacy*, 3.

of the rational bricks that build the self's identity walls.[41] Barebacking and cruising exemplify sexuality's inherent queerness, its essential nonrationality, and its pervasive phantasmatic nature.

Barebacking, Dean justifies, is more than a good fuck; it crystalizes a transcendent intimacy, a touch of skin to skin that disavows the threat of being killed by crafting an impersonal closeness that barebackers experience as sacred. Barebacking and cruising blur physical, social, and psychological boundaries by disavowing autonomy, delinking intimacy from the epistemological imperative to "know" the Other. Anonymous intimacy evokes a transcendent touch precisely because it does not match carnal intercourse. It encompasses the set of feelings, experiences, and practices that involve contact with an anonymous and, under certain circumstances, total otherness.

The receptive partner—the bottom guy—is placed within an economy of intimacy where his rectum is made to do the theoretical work that the vagina/womb does in feminist theory.[42] One of gay male culture's riddles is, to put it simply, how to disentangle being fucked from femininity. For instance, Dean reports, the bottom lying down there (notice that I am starting to hint at Caravaggio's sexualized and eroticized presentation of Paul), addressed as "bitch" or "pussy," is the one who can "take it like a man." In the case of barebacking, this masculinization of the receptive position keeps the "homo" in place and creates a psychological disposition of practicality and heroism. On the one hand, bareback HIV culture "comes with the territory of being gay and sexually alive"; on the other, the subculture advances a male prototype able to look death in the face because "HIV infection is imagined as the ultimate sign of strength."[43]

This ethos of hypermasculinity and erotic transgresiveness, akin to working-class, blue-collar, militaristic sexuality, disavows any connection between male homosexuality and gender-inversion. When a symbolic system only accepts different degrees of masculinity, a resignification of the submissive position materializes: it takes "a man" to surrender completely to a man; it takes a man to "take it" like a man. The submissive position then embodies an ethics of extreme risk that

---

41. See Leo Bersani, *Is the Rectum a Grave? And Other Essays* (Chicago: University of Chicago Press, 2010).
42. Dean, *Unlimited Intimacy*, 78.
43. Dean, *Unlimited Intimacy*, 55.

brackets the normalizing aspects of health.[44] Skipping the indoctrinations of a risk-averse culture, the "bottom guy" advocates a "human finitude that modern life, especially modern medicine, has become expert in disavowing,"[45] bringing death close to life, offering an ethics of the future that is no longer grounded in an immanent utopianism but in a literal "carpe diem."

The desire of barebacking, of submitting oneself to being penetrated as an act of total openness, necessitates the notion of the top as a gift giver or gifter. The gifter, religiously put, is the one who does the conversion, the subject who inaugurates a new identity in whoever desires to convert. The gift, as donation and as poison alike,[46] establishes social bonds, cohesion, and redefines community through participating in the "bug brotherhood," a community formation that dispels the stigma of the infected as a pariah. Breeding, the act of a top man ejaculating without protection inside a bottom's ass, parallels at the unconscious level what in straight sex is reproductive insemination. This symbolic crafting of reproduction promotes a redefinition of kinship roles, friendships, and intergenerational relations. For instance, the stigma of HIV—especially during the epidemic crisis—made queer strangers into relatives "without the usual intermediary stages of friendship or cohabitation."[47] Stigma associated with the virus and with the idea of maleness giving up its active role creates a life-giving community shaped after an economy of the gift. Cruising alters the status of the stranger, similar to how breeding reformulates notions of kinship. If breeding alters the image of the rectum from a grave into a womb where sexual positions skip over the restraints of sexual difference, cruising advances the notion of a stranger as the perfect lover. Cruising is ultimately about how a self-shattering subject welcomes otherness precisely at the point when one is losing the boundaries of identity.

The intimate contact with a stranger who remains as such and whose strangeness is the sine qua non of cruising estranges one from oneself,

---

44. Michel Foucault, "The Politics of Health in the Eighteenth Century," in *The Essential Works of Foucault, 1954–1984*, ed. Paul Rabinow and James D. Faubion, 3 vols. (New York: New Press, 2000), 3:94.

45. Dean, *Unlimited Intimacy*, 66.

46. Jacques Derrida, "On the Gift: A Discussion between Jacques Derrida and Jean-Luc Marion," in *God, the Gift, and Postmodernism*, ed. John D. Caputo and Michael J. Scanlon (Bloomington: Indiana University Press, 1999), 54–78.

47. Dean, *Unlimited Intimacy*, 91.

posing a relationship with the otherness of the unconscious distinct from domination or self-sacrifice. Neither master nor slave, the self experiences total openness to the unknown impact of the Other, which, in turn, results in a dissolution of one's identity. If the primacy of subject formation is on otherness, cruising as *an ethos of opening to the world* is incompatible with identities. The pleasure of risking the self by opening it to alterity undoes the pleasures deduced from securing the self in the familiar. Without a specific goal or a particular object, proceeding aimlessly, cruising embodies a "centrifugal openness to the other,"[48] "a form of relationality uncontaminated by desire,"[49] a communality not aimed at having a relationship. In its ideal forms, the cruising subject leaves oneself behind in order for intimacy with an anonymous body to take place, a body without definition, a body defined by unlocatable differences that reflects back on my own body disposed of attributes. Identity-free contact equals unlimited intimacy; in that moment, "we relate to that which transcends all relations."[50] Ultimately, cruising and barebacking embrace, especially when considered from the bottom position, an ethics of openness grounded on the divestment of the self and the priority of the Other, a hospitality to the Other not unlike the one Caravaggio attributes to Paul.

Paul's Submission

Queer desires configured through and within networks of queer communities, and queer intimacies shaped by and proponents of an ideal hospitality and relationality, offer a privileged opportunity to explore theological bodies, the bodies emerging from a certain relationship with the Other. In what follows, Dean's explorations of these modes of relationality frame my views on Caravaggio's notion of relatedness. This hermeneutical move constitutes the second step in the trajectory of visualization described above insofar as Caravaggio's *Conversion on the Way to Damascus* visualizes queer relationality.

Leo Bersani, exploring Caravaggio's oeuvre, theorizes gay art as a homo-aesthetic "to which homosexual desire is essential, but which, precisely and paradoxically because of this, can dispense with homosexual

---

48. Dean, *Unlimited Intimacy*, 210.
49. Bersani, *Is the Rectum a Grave*, 45.
50. Bersani, *Is the Rectum a Grave*, 61.

identity."[51] Queer art is a mode of representation where queer disowns identitarian claims to offer a "nonspecific resistance to the dominant culture."[52] Such aesthetics feature eroticism as resistance to heteronormative relationality, and queerness promoting eroticism/sex as antisociality,[53] as ways of relating to the self and others that risk the normalizing strictures of socially sanctioned ego-formation. In Caravaggio's case, queerness disciplines the spectator's gaze in a desire not rooted in lack but in the fullness of material existence.[54]

Bersani and Ulysse Dutoit's Caravaggio is a painter of relationality that transgresses "straight" relatedness through compositional and thematic techniques such as blurring boundaries, decentering the gaze while exploring its relationship with desire. Caravaggio's bodies, they suggest, participate in a playfulness of decentering, disavowal, and disclosure that defines queer eroticism as a relationality not domesticated by sexual or gendered identities.[55] Caravaggio's theological innovation lies in his turn toward a new relatedness where transcendence is dispensed with, or, as Hammill suggests, Caravaggio "resuscitates the flesh that Paul relinquishes."[56] With Paul's prostrate disposition lies a humanity, a "being" with fleshly, material, earthly, *this-worldly* life. Caravaggio performs such materiality, Bersani and Dutoit argue, through the lack of a clear direction in the character's gaze, which in turn results in a decentering of the spectator's gaze. The viewer cannot figure the direction in the characters' gaze: their eyes inscrutable, sometimes veiled, others obscured.

In *The Conversion of Saint Paul,* Paul's physicality is detemporalized and dehistoricized; it is thrown physically so that he may be reoriented spiritually.[57] With no sign of the supernatural and Paul's arms raised as part of the jumble of human and animal arms and legs that occupy the center of the work, "nothing actually touches anything else, no form impinges on any other form, and yet the curious effect of this juxtaposi-

---

51. Bersani, *Is the Rectum a Grave,* 31.
52. Bersani, *Is the Rectum a Grave,* 32.
53. Robert L. Caserio et al., "The Antisocial Thesis in Queer Theory," *PMLA* 12.3 (2006): 819–28.
54. Bersani and Dutoit, *Caravaggio's Secrets,* 15–23.
55. Bersani and Dutoit, *Caravaggio's Secrets,* 13.
56. Graham L. Hammill, *Sexuality and Form: Caravaggio, Marlowe, and Bacon* (Chicago: University of Chicago Press, 2000), 66.
57. Bersani and Dutoit, *Caravaggio's Secrets,* 60.

tion of discrete but related forms is to put into question the very possibility of an empty space."⁵⁸ *The Conversion* suggests an uncongested connectedness where touch requires no contact and absence of the Other does not forfeit relationality. Paul's metaphysical receptiveness is an "ecstatic passivity,"⁵⁹ a unique disposition unparalleled in the history of art. Paul's foreshortened position, face upward, "looking" in the opposite direction from the spectator, legs open, arms reaching out, undecipherable countenance, relaxed and firm limbs, next to the phallic signifier of the sword, with disheveled hair resembles Bersani's rectum-as-a-grave bottom and Dean's ecstatic barebacker.

Caravaggio's Intimacy

Cloaked in red, lying flat on his back, a jockey in shock after being thrown on the floor, semitense muscles, arms yearning upward, half-open fingers, Paul's body is exceptional. Is it an open body receiving the Other, or is it closing itself before or after an (un)expected interaction? Is Paul dissolving into thin air, or is he holding his body's boundaries? What is Paul greeting or resisting? Might the sword lying next to him—a phallic symbol—be a signifier for Paul's defensiveness toward aggression? Or should we consider the subtle orifice formed by his skirt strategically situated instead of his groin to be a signifier for Paul's receptivity?

In the following trajectory of visualization, I explore, in intercontextual fashion, what elements in Paul's ecstasy visualize the ethics of hospitality distilled from bareback and cruising subcultures. In other words, I read Caravaggio's aesthetics through *Unlimited Intimacy*'s ethics or, more specifically, Paul's blade interpreted through the bottom's total submission. For starters, Paul is the receptive partner in relationship with the Other—masculine or feminine, human or divine. Paul's closed eyes hint at the anonymity of the event, for he cannot, and neither can the spectator, know who is "penetrating him." Paul's submissiveness is, however, ambiguous: agony and pleasure, discomfort and consolation, disconnection and closeness, unsafety and uncertainty, fear and anxiety, aversion and yearning.

Paul's gaze, eyes shut, addresses no one, human (spectator/companion), animal (horse), or divine (Lord). Bersani and Dutoit describe

---

58. Bersani and Dutoit, *Caravaggio's Secrets*, 61.
59. Bersani and Dutoit, *Caravaggio's Secrets*, 62.

Caravaggio's eroticism as a function of the noninterpretable address. The *enigmatic body* is the condition of the possibility of erotics, a bodily disposition that hints at a secret to which no one has access.[60] Paul's enigmatic nongaze poses dilemmas such as: Do we read his closed eyes as a sign of receptiveness, forgetfulness, denial, or presence? Do we interpret his open arms as reaching out or as waving in desperation or obliviousness? Whether we read Paul, along with the biblical text, as struck by the Other or, through the queer experience, in sexual submission, queer theology encounters here a fleshly body that experiences ecstatic submission. If the biblical narrative of Acts (9:1–19) foregrounds Saul's submission to the Lord, the queer practices of unlimited intimacy suggest the sexual act of Paul being penetrated. The lack of any supernatural signifier in Caravaggio's work points to the mystical experience. No compositional feature explicitly hints at the supernatural. Yet Paul's disposition refers to its biblical origin, which, in turn, disambiguates, if temporarily, what we are seeing. Only the artwork's title signals the Lord's conversion of Paul, whose bodily position resembles extraordinarily close the sexual Act of being bred.

Caravaggio's depiction of Paul's ecstatic queer and spiritual passivity is not, of course, the most prominent instance where sexual and religious desire coalesce. The carnal dimensions of the religious experience are a well-known trope in Christian mysticism: Santa Teresa de Ávila's report on her religious experience as much as Bernini's sculptural version epitomize such a confluence (see fig. 7.2). The quintessentially baroque *Santa Teresa in Ecstasy*, which is both an exaltation of the sensuous body and an ode to the mystical rapture, visualizes, like Caravaggio's Paul, the irruption of the Other in the forms of seduction and assault, blurring the limits of consent and molestation. Whereas Caravaggio visualizes the falling down of Paul (Acts 9:4) as losing himself, Bernini sculpts Teresa of Ávila's strong will at the peak of its weakness, at the rarest moment of losing autonomy, at her "*desmembramiento*" (dismemberment?).[61]

Thematic differences notwithstanding, several common representational and compositional features are salient. The elaborate folding in Teresa's clothing hiding her flesh resemble, similar to Paul's orifice,

---

60. Bersani and Dutoit, *Caravaggio's Secrets*, 9.

61. Julie B. Miller, "Rapt by God: The Rhetoric of Rape in Medieval Mystical Literature," in *The Subjective Eye: Essays in Culture, Religion, and Gender in Honor of Margaret R. Miles*, ed. Margaret R. Miles et al. (Eugene, OR: Pickwick, 2006), 251.

Fig. 7.2. Gian Lorenzo Bernini, *Ecstasy of Saint Teresa*, 1647–1652, marble. Santa Maria della Vitoria, Rome.

the most intimate surfaces of the body; by fully covering it, Bernini is displaying it.[62] Bernini sculpts an ambiguous movement: it is unclear whether the arrow is entering or withdrawing. It is equally uncertain, as in Paul's case, what we are to make of Teresa's eyes shut: pain, ecstasy, pleasure, absence, or, in S&M terms, all of these at the same time. Although her lips are partly open, like Paul's, she lacks the words to express her pleasure. Such enjoyment, Irigaray will suggest, a "pleasure without pleasure," is what allows Teresa to establish a relationship with the divine outside the phallic economy.[63] Lacan notes that Bernini's Teresa embodies "a transcendental experience of a-sexual jouissance beyond the phallus, from a perspective that is at least as phallic as the one adopted by the baroque sculptor."[64] The representational problem of visualizing the female orgasm comes to the fore: "if jouissance of the Other is effectively situated beyond the phallus, and therefore the symbolic, then God cannot have anything to do with it."[65]

---

62. Giovanni Careri, *Bernini: Flights of Love, the Art of Devotion* (Chicago: University of Chicago Press, 1995).

63. Hayes, "A Jouissance beyond the Phallus."

64. Dany Nobus, "The Sculptural Iconography of Feminine Jouissance: Lacan's Reading of Bernini's Saint Teresa in Ecstasy," *The Comparatist* 39 (2015): 35.

65. Nobus, "Sculptural Iconography," 34.

Whereas scholars have explained Teresa's (female) *jouissance*, Paul's semiecstatic disposition remains unexamined. Paul's legs open, which are inviting through the signifier of the hole, betray the receptive/female-like disposition that Bersani attributes to receptive anal sex. Caravaggio's Paul, in other words, is an artistic instantiation of Bersani's "seductive and intolerable image of a grown man, legs high in the air, unable to refuse the suicidal ecstasy of being a woman."[66] Paul's submission iconographically illustrates the eroticization of subordination, the indissociable nature of sexual pleasure and power.[67] Bernini positions the smiling cupid piercing Teresa as the phallus-bearer, while Caravaggio insinuates that the absent Lord/Other holds a phallus that is dispersed (the sword, the phallus on the back of the horse). Bernini's cherub's amused expression suggests a knowledge of what we ignore, whereas Paul's companion's undecipherable expression leaves us in deeper ignorance; his concealed countenance provides, unlike in Bernini, no hermeneutical frame. Whereas in Bernini the compositional elements unequivocally hint at Teresa's *jouissance*, in Caravaggio Paul's *jouissance* remains elusive.

The insights gained from the earlier exploration of queer practices allows us to supplement Caravaggio's Paul, beyond the comparison with Bernini's ecstatic representation, with queer notions of submission. Foucault, who first theorized submission in S&M as an ascetic practice destined to undo the gender equation male/dominant-female/dominated,[68] predates Bersani's conceptualization of submissiveness as "metaphysical sociability"[69] and of subjectivity predicated on the dissolution of the epistemological relationship of subject/object. Dean shall take up this notion of submission as the golden opportunity to explore unlimited hospitality, boundless openness to the Other.

The submissive male position that Foucault introduced, Bersani theorized, and Dean documented—the image of a man on his back prostrated

---

66. Bersani, *Is the Rectum a Grave*, 18.

67. Bersani and Dutoit's Caravaggio, it must be noted, depicts a different relational affectivity than the one implied in Bersani's *Rectum*, moving from one conception of sex as self-shattering to one of self-extension (Kent L. Brintnall, "Erotic Ruination: Embracing the 'Savage Spirituality' of Barebacking," in *Negative Ecstasies: Georges Bataille and the Study of Religion*, ed. Jeremy Biles and Kent L. Brintnall [New York: Fordham University Press, 2015], 51–67).

68. Michel Foucault, "Sexual Choice, Sexual Act," in Lotringer, *Foucault Live*, 322–34.

69. Bersani and Dutoit, *Caravaggio's Secrets*, 61.

on the ground, legs and arms raised in ambiguous ecstasy—is the centerpiece of Caravaggio's "theology of sex." First, the desexualization/degenitalization of pleasure relocates *jouissance* away from specific body parts. It is virtually impossible to decipher Paul's experience as he, defenseless on the ground, partially conceals his countenance from the interpreter: eyes closed, semiopened mouth, relaxed facial features, disheveled hair, maybe unconscious, maybe sleeping, possibly dreaming, perhaps absorbed in the pleasure/pain of the intense semiorgasm, the extended moment before or after the climax. There are no literal indications of sexual arousal, but Paul's unreadable disposition together with the subtle references to the phallus (sword) and the orifice (the folding of the strips in his skirt forms a gap between his legs) gesture toward male *jouissance*.

Second, Paul's ecstasy, notably toned down if compared to Teresa's, is located at the border of (un)consciousness, confusing the threshold between pleasure and pain. What is the enigma behind Paul's closed eyes? Ecstasy is here the aftermath of a rapture, having been struck by the divinity, Paul's receptivity in the instant of openness to the Other positions him as the bottom who is "taking it like a man." O'Hara, a gay activist, shares, in what might be a queer *ekphrasis* of *The Conversion*: "feeling a man's dick inside me, condomless—that's when the sex becomes spiritual in its intensity. Communion, in the true sense. Integral to that closeness is the knowledge that he intends to leave a piece of himself inside me."

The most glaring absence in Caravaggio's composition, unlike in Bernini's, is the absence of the Other, the tranquility of the companion and the horse accentuating such absence. The biblical interpreter knows this absence points to a presence, one that no other painter has missed. Such representational crisis signals anonymity; the interpreter is left wondering who, how, why, and where. This absence suggests anonymity; if you cannot represent it, you might as well "hide it." The unknowing Paul is the cruising subject involved in an anonymous scene, his eyes semiclosed as he experiences being penetrated.

Fourth, psychoanalytically, Paul in ecstatic receptiveness visualizes the idea of sex as a self-shattering experience, following Bersani, the essence of sex itself: a nondescribable impulse to pursue the not-necessarily pleasurable, an intensity that is averse to the stabilization of the ego coherence. Sex defined as the pleasure obtained from the deterioration of the ego's stability, a losing of the self resulting in the loss of identity. Paul's lack of direction, in this reading, his erratic grasping for something is the letting go of the self not knowing when it will be received back again—that letting go of the self that is proper to cruising practices.

Fifth, whereas Bernini literalizes the phallus in the arrow, Caravaggio's phallus is dispersed. With no point of contact between the sword, carefully disposed of, and Paul's body, this distance signifies that Paul, in submission to the Other, loses the phallic power that constitutes him as man. The phallus's proximity could be the source of a *jouissance* that, in light of our queer explorations, bestows Paul's masculinity back through the notion that "he is taking it like a man." The sword has a double-edge: abandonment of masculinity or empowerment of its reception, the pleasure of receiving it or the discomfort of letting it go. The helmet, however, a metonymy of the military armor, a symbol of Paul's warrior-like status, lying on the ground separated from Paul's head, hints at his emasculation, at the loss of his masculinity as he lies prostrate.

Sixth, the sword's phallic valence is complemented by the horse's hoof, pointed sideways, oddly contorted, so it points at Paul's groin. The colossal horse looms over the supine body of Paul, dominating him, suggesting a point of origin for Paul's *jouissance*: after all, the hairy white pattern on the stallion's shoulder and right leg, upon closer attention, is the profile of a man and his sexual organ ready to insert itself between Paul's open legs. Such receptivity takes us back to Paul's open arms and legs. What, if anything, is Paul receiving?

The undecidability of what counts as erotic, the blurring of the boundaries between pleasure and pain, the anonymity granted by the absence of the Other, the self-shattering experience accompanying intercourse, the anxious and rewarding processes of (de)masculinization, and the demanding openness of the religious and sexual experience throw into relief the similarities between the subjectivity of the barebacker and the mystic. As Bersani aptly puts it, in both experiences "the subject allows himself to be penetrated, even replaced, by an unknowable otherness"; the barebacker's openness to anonymity evokes the mystic's submission "to a divine will without any comfortably recognizable attributes whatsoever."[70] Bersani has nuanced the notion of the rectum as the burial of subjectivity, of anal sex as the repudiation of the ego-coherence and as the grave of phallic power, and suggested a notion of subjectiv-

---

70. Leo Bersani, "Shame on You," in *After Sex? On Writing since Queer Theory*, ed. Janet Hally and Andrew Parker (Durham, NC: Duke University Press, 2011), 105.

ity where the ego is sacrificed not for the sake of biological and psychic death but for the pleasure of finding itself scattered and replicated everywhere in the world.[71]

This shift from an ethics of self-shattering—that point in the erotic experience where the ego collapses—to one of imperfect self-replication, besides being inadequate to fully account for the submission/bottom position, according to Kent Brintnall, has serious political consequences for an ethics of hospitality grounded on an ontology of subjectivity.[72] Investment on the stability of the self, a defense of its cohesiveness plays in the hand, he further suggests, of dominant theoretical frameworks invested in the defense of the individual.[73] The alternative, Brintnall concludes, is embracing dispositions that risk self-dismissal, that promote the habit of "losing sight of the self,"[74] which is precisely, I suggest, the position that Caravaggio's Paul embodies as he lies prostrated in mystic ecstasy.

Saul's Conversion

It does not take queer theory musings to portray the apostle—the Saul of Acts, the Paul of the letters, or the Paul of the *Wirkungsgeschichte*—along the psychosocial lines of submission.[75] Brittany Wilson has recently argued that the blinding of Paul in Acts 9 destabilizes his masculinity. Wilson views Acts 9 as striking a blow against Paul's manhood: being "blinded" in the ancient world meant being emasculated, losing self-control implied dropping manliness, and being subjected to God was understood as losing the Greco-Roman status of heroic masculinity. Wilson concludes that the blinding is an emasculating process required to present the apostle as the ideal disciple, that is, a man in subordination to the supremely male man, Jesus Christ the Lord.[76]

---

71. Mikko Tuhkanen, *Leo Bersani: Queer Theory and Beyond* (Albany: SUNY Press, 2014), 108.
72. Brintnall, "Erotic Ruination."
73. Brintnall, "Erotic Ruination," 66.
74. Brintnall, "Erotic Ruination," 67.
75. For a debate over the genre of Acts 9 as conversion or call, see Charles W. Hedrick, "Paul's Conversion/Call: A Comparative Analysis of the Three Reports in Acts," *JBL* 100 (1981): 415–32; and Larry W. Hurtado, "Convert, Apostate or Apostle to the Nations: The 'Conversion' of Paul in Recent Scholarship," *SR* 22 (1993): 273–84.
76. Brittany E. Wilson, "The Blinding of Paul and the Power of God: Masculinity, Sight, and Self-Control," *JBL* 133 (2014): 386.

Acts, traditional Lukan scholarship argues, presents Paul as an exemplary man insofar as he excels at public speaking and at controlling his body.[77] According to Greco-Roman ideals, the argument goes, Paul's control over his own actions warrants his manly status: he no longer commits acts of violence against Jesus's followers (Acts 8:3; 9:1-2, 13-14; 22:4-5; 26:9-11), remains calm when crisis strikes (27:17-36), discusses self-control with Felix (24:25), and counters the accusation of being out of his mind by claiming his use of reason (26:24-25). Against these manly traits, Wilson suggests, the blinding emasculates the apostle by portraying him as a loser in the contest of power with the divinity and by stripping him of sight, one of the main features of masculinity. Masculinity's reliance on vision in Greco-Roman literature, Wilson concludes, equates Paul's loss of sight with loss of manhood,[78] positioning Paul along with other disciples closer to the status of the slave (Luke 1:38; Acts 2:18; 4:29; 16:17; 20:19). By losing sight, Paul gains revelation.

If masculinity, as Wilson argues, requires self-control, power over, and the ability to stay on top, Luke can only *remasculinize* Paul by presenting him as a superior example, as the one capable of mastering submission. Here Acts' rhetorical moves resemble Dean's study of bareback subcultures, where submission equates exemplary masculinity through the "commitment to no-excuses submission and no-limits endurance."[79] The paradox that Paul can only "see" when he loses his ability to see[80] parallels the queer notion that a bottom can only be masculine by overcoming his emasculation. But the Paul who "sees" and "becomes masculine" constitutes the aftermath of Caravaggio's snapshot of absolute ego-abandonment.

Paul's blinding serves as a turning point where the prosecutor (penetrator) Saul sees his masculinity reconfigured through an act of submission: "in this one-on-one contest of power, Jesus clearly comes out on top, for the light (and presumably voice) comes from heaven (v. 3) and Saul falls to the earth (v. 4). Saul, the single most persistent persecutor of Jesus, is literally brought down."[81] Paul's eventual recovery and subsequent

---

77. For literary analysis of these motifs, see Luke Timothy Johnson and Daniel J. Harrington, *The Acts of the Apostles* (Collegeville, MN: Liturgical Press, 1992), 169-75.
78. Wilson, "Blinding of Paul," 383.
79. Dean, *Unlimited Intimacy*, 56.
80. Wilson, "Blinding of Paul," 383.
81. Wilson, "Blinding of Paul," 372.

missional performance suggests a temporary recovery of his lost status,[82] undermined by being subjected to his persecutor and to the Holy Spirit (e.g., Acts 16:6–10; 20:22). A "slave of God" (16:17; 20:19) Paul is, in terms of the teratogenic grid, a bottom.[83]

Wilson's argument is, in the end, a historical-critical rehash of the original and more radical view put forth by Stephen Moore in "Sex and the Single Apostle," where *l'enfant terrible* of biblical studies bases Paul's identity on his absolute gender and sexual submission to another man. Moore wryly notes, "it is Paul's own abjectly submissive role within this all-male threesome as slave of Christ that now defines his radical identity as a Christian."[84] Paul's letters are a *summa hypermasculinitas*, a christological treatise where the Lord tops every other bottom,[85] a queer reformulation of the Augustinian suggestion that Paul's conversion was a transformation from being an aggressive top into a submissive bottom, "from a marvelous persecutor of the Gospel" to "a more marvelous preacher."[86] A submission, however, that, at least in the epistolary corpus, is put to good rhetorical effect, making plain the difference between Caravaggio's Paul and the Paul from the letters.[87]

---

82. From a theological perspective, Aaron J. Kuecker conceives Acts 9 as a *theosis* where the Most High establishes a communion with Paul. Kuecker reaches an opposing view to Wilson and, as I show here, Stephen Moore, because for Kuecker the blinding is a *theosis* that "emphasizes nonviolence and self-giving" (Kuecker, "'You Will Be Children of the Most High': An Inquiry into Luke's Narrative Account of Theosis," *Journal of Theological Interpretation* 8 [2014]: 228).

83. On the teratogenic grid, see Holt N. Parker, "The Teratogenic Grid," in *Roman Sexualities*, ed. Judith P. Hallett and Marilyn B. Skinner (Princeton: Princeton University Press, 1997), 47–65; David Fredrick, "Mapping Penetrability in Late Republican and Early Imperial Rome," in *The Roman Gaze: Vision, Power, and the Body*, ed. David Fredrick (Baltimore: Johns Hopkins University Press, 2002), 236–64. See also Martin, *Slavery as Salvation*, 84. For a critique of Martin's influential view, see John Byron, "Slave of Christ or Willing Servant? Paul's Self-Description in 1 Corinthians 4:1–2 and 9:16–18," *Neot* 37 (2003): 179–98. For the now-classic Foucauldian argument about self-domination as a condition to dominate others, see Michel Foucault, *The Use of Pleasure*, vol. 2 of *The History of Sexuality* (New York: Vintage Books, 1990), 63–77.

84. Moore, *God's Beauty Parlor*, 165.

85. Moore, *God's Beauty Parlor*, 169.

86. Paula Fredriksen Landes, *Augustine on Romans: Propositions from the Epistle to the Romans and Unfinished Commentary on the Epistle to the Romans*, SBLTT 23 (Chico, CA: Scholars Press, 1982): 9–16.

87. As in cruising, where mastery follows self-divestment, Paul's submission is

The Touch of Immanence

The transpiring emasculation of Paul in Acts is the required step, biblical scholarship suggests, for a closer relationship between Paul and Jesus, between the apostle and the Lord, between the top and the bottom. Paul's submission, Caravaggio *theologizes*, is the condition of a relationship to otherness, a total rendition to the absolute Other, not unlike the radical hospitality that Dean's ethnography reports in the practices of queer subcultures. Caravaggio's Paul, in light of these biblical and theoretical reflections on submission, embodies queer eros, an openness to the Other expressed through a carnal hospitality to strangeness that is both ethical in its openness to the interpersonal unknown and theological in its receptiveness to the nonrepresentable Other.

What are the contours, we ought to ask, of Paul's hospitality? How does his submission inform any attempt to theologize queer relationality? What are Paul's contributions to a queer theology of raw sex? How does immanent submission to the other aid in theologizing Paul's submission to the Other? Emmanuel Levinas's conception of otherness as a condition of relationality in *Totality and Infinity* is a fitting starting point because it explores, through the notion of love/eroticism, the process whereby the self returns and transcends itself, "an event situated at the limit of immanence and transcendence."[88]

Plato's elaboration of eros in the *Symposium* as the quest for the soulmate and the return of the fragmented self toward home informs Levinas's account of love and hospitality. The problem with platonic eros, Levinas contends, is that it remains "fundamental immanence"—the Other understood as a resort to complete oneself.[89] Love is the way of self to come to itself, "the satisfaction of a sublime hunger,"[90] where Otherness can never

---

followed by Paul's "coercive universalism," the apostle using his downgraded status as a rhetorical topos to master others (Elizabeth A. Castelli, *Imitating Paul: A Discourse of Power* [Louisville: Westminster John Knox, 1991]; Joseph A. Marchal, *Hierarchy, Unity, and Imitation: A Feminist Rhetorical Analysis of Power Dynamics in Paul's Letter to the Philippians*, AcBib 24 [Atlanta: Society of Biblical Literature, 2006], Marchal, *Philippians: Historical Problems, Hierarchical Visions, Hysterical Anxieties* [Sheffield: Sheffield Phoenix, 2014]; Deborah Thompson Prince, "Picturing Saul's Vision on the Road to Damascus: A Question of Authority," *BibInt* 25 [2017]: 364–98).

88. Levinas, *Totality and Infinity*, 254.
89. Levinas, *Totality and Infinity*, 254.
90. Levinas, *Totality and Infinity*, 34.

be fully assimilated, the paradox being that the need for the Other is built on the transcendent exteriority of the beloved.[91] The Other posits itself as a mystery not fully graspable but possible, situating the erotic relationship between need (present) and desire (future). For Levinas, the simultaneity of "concupiscence and transcendence, tangency of the avowable and the unavowable, constitutes the originality of the erotic which, in this sense, is the equivocal per excellence."[92]

Levinas thinks about immanence in terms of solipsism and aversion to Otherness and conceives of transcendence as openness to alterity, as interrelationality. The Other's transcendence is the condition for an ethics grounded on the deprioritization of the self, resistant to objectifying the Other, and invested in undoing the dichotomy subject/object. Transcendence, as he famously puts it, "designates a relation with a reality infinitely distant from my own reality, yet without this distance destroying this relation and without the relation destroying this distance."[93] Transcendence as infinite Otherness manifests itself in the immanent face of the Other: "The dimension of the divine opens forth from the human face.... His very epiphany consists in soliciting us by his destitution in the face of the Stranger, the widow, the orphan."[94]

Mayra Rivera offers a critical supplement to Levinas's transcendence: "transcendence designates a relation with a reality irreducibly different from my own reality, without the difference destroying this relation and without the relation destroying the difference."[95] Rivera acknowledges Levinas's contribution regarding the primordial ontology of the Other that questions the identity of the self, but she is concerned that such a formulation obscures the irreducibility of the Other. Rivera emphasizes the communal dimension in the formation of the self and in the hospitality to the Other as she deconstructs the limiting constraints of Levinas's eros.[96] Following Irigaray, Anzaldúa, and Moraga, Rivera theorizes the self-Other relationship not only through the lover's face but in the whole body of the Other, in the web of relations that "constitutes each

---

91. Levinas, *Totality and Infinity*, 254–55.
92. Levinas, *Totality and Infinity*, 255.
93. Levinas, *Totality and Infinity*, 41.
94. Levinas, *Totality and Infinity*, 78.
95. Mayra Rivera, *The Touch of Transcendence: A Postcolonial Theology of God* (Louisville: Westminster John Knox, 2007), 82.
96. Rivera, *The Touch of Transcendence*, 78–82.

person's concrete and particular in-finity."[97] The caress, more than the face, seems to be a more suitable metaphor for transcendence because the touch does not diminish the distance nor does it prevent the relationship. The caress does not disambiguate the tension of immanence/transcendence because, as Perpich suggests, it includes "the possibility of the self's return to itself in sensuous enjoyment."[98] This philosophical drive to ground ontology in the materiality of the flesh and the body leaves unresolved Paul's openness to Otherness, for he, as Bernini's Teresa, is not being caressed or touched, yet he is still experiencing the erotic encounter with the Other.

Rivera, inspired by Irigaray, offers a theological framework that situates the Other—womb, planet, cosmos, God—as the origin of the human being and as the marker of subjectivity,[99] criticizing theologies that conceive of human participation in the divine as a movement away from creaturality, decoupling divine transcendence from ethics, and abstracting divinity from human history.[100] Divine touch, Rivera argues, "reveals the simultaneity of transcendence and intimacy, a divine enveloping through which God may caress creation and feel its joy and suffering."[101] The touch of the divine is an embrace, "a caressing of the cosmos," "never pure immanence but the site of transcendence in the flesh."[102] Through a relationship with the flesh of the other, we are in touch with the Other, a reminder that we are called to transform our bodies "so that they become capable of embracing without grasping."[103]

If transcendence takes place not only in the contemplation of the face of the Other (Levinas) but in the mutual touch, Caravaggio's elliptic portrayal of the Other could be interpreted as a fitting meditation of Rivera's reformulation of transcendence: the radical difference suggested by the Lord's absence and by Paul's body as it hints at the foundational relationship with the Other, embracing without grasping, almost touch-

---

97. Rivera, *The Touch of Transcendence*, 125.
98. Diane Perpich, "From the Caress to the Word: Transcendence and the Feminine in the Philosophy of Emmanuel Levinas," in *Feminist Interpretations of Emmanuel Levinas*, ed. Tina Chanter (University Park: Pennsylvania State University Press, 2001), 43.
99. Rivera, *The Touch of Transcendence*, 129.
100. Rivera, *The Touch of Transcendence*, 132.
101. Rivera, *The Touch of Transcendence*, 136.
102. Rivera, *The Touch of Transcendence*, 136.
103. Rivera, *The Touch of Transcendence*, 138.

ing without seizing. Paul's open arms visualize the vulnerability involved in the desire for the Other, who remains unknowable, cannot be integrated, reduced, or consumed, the Other who disrupts my identity, my sense of self. Paul's openness, his arms reaching out, is balanced by his carefulness (his limbs are somewhat tense). Paul's equivocal longing toward Otherness—the apostle's ambiguous desire—seems to embody a "metaphysical desire" as "it desires beyond everything that can simply complete it."[104]

In this trajectory of visualization, Levinas and Rivera's account of this transcendental relationship theologizes what Caravaggio visualizes: the ever conceptually elusive relationship between the subject and the Other. Despite their notable differences, both Rivera and Levinas share a notion of the subject as relational, porous, temporary, elusive, open, in-the-world, "intercarnational," but somewhat cohesive.[105] Queer theory throws here a wedge into the theological investment on the stability of subjectivity by emphasizing the very moment of total dissolution of the subject, by centering the moment where the self dissolves. If Brintnall is right to suggest that barebacking and cruising are ethically significant for the desubjectification they entail, it might be time (queer theory is here winking at Christian theology) "to bring sexy back" to Christian mysticism, that is, to put at the center of theology what Bersani dismisses precisely for its implausibility: "the awesome abjection of 'pure love,'" self-annihilation as the precondition for union with the Other, or, to put it in iconographic terms, time to read Caravaggio's dissolution of Paul along Bernini's Avila's "vivo sin vivir en mi" (I live without living in myself).[106] In this reading, the theological tradition of changing the apostle's name from Saul to Paul—rooted in the alleged conversion of Acts 9—attests to the annihilation of identitarian features.

Along with queer practices of utter submission, Caravaggio's prostrate, receptive, open, quietly ecstatic Paul portrays the apostle's disposition toward the gift (HIV) or the Gift (grace). Whereas in biblical scholarship, to say it with Moore or Wilson, the gift of faith (grace) given by the Lord is gained through the loss and recovery of manhood, in queer subcultures the gift materializes in sexual fluids shared within the community, almost as an internal bodily tattoo, as a mark of belonging,

---

104. Levinas, *Totality and Infinity*, 34.
105. Rivera, *Poetics of the Flesh*, 145–46.
106. Bersani, *Queer Theory and Beyond*, 52.

as a touch (literal) that spreads through the whole body. Consider the following report of a barebacker: "Seed is a gift, it's love, it's acceptance. Taking a man's cum—in your ass, down your throat, rubbed into your skin, whatever—even if you don't know his name, is closeness. It's an act of love and trust. Even if yawl just met."[107] This notion of intimacy throws into relief the links between bodily contact, love, the gift (of HIV), anonymity, and hospitality—the almost complete hospitable intimacy, the unlimited familiarity of the stranger, the moment of dissolution previous to reconfiguration, the precise moment of ego evanescence before the reintroduction of mastery. Caravaggio's Paul is evaporating instead of holding his body's boundaries, collapsing rather than reshaping himself: a literal barebacker (he is, after all, saddle-free, riding a horse) and a queer cruiser.

A Political Reading

An informed interpreter in the latest developments of queer sex will likely notice that many of the previous considerations have, as of late, become outdated. Many gay men in the Global North have access to PREP, considerably diminishing the type of risk that HIV infection poses to bareback practices. Tim Dean argues, in a revisiting take to his groundbreaking work on queer intimacy, that such development raises critical questions about the medicalization of sexuality and the role of "chemoprophylaxis" in the history of sex.[108] Here, however, I am more interested in thinking about the political effects ensuing from the type of subjectivities that we explored in the previous sections. Barebacking cultures may have gotten a hit since PREP has become widely available, but they continue to signal, in my view, a cautionary tale versus the tricks of identity politics in the Global North and a generative template to frame a theologically informed theory of subjectivity outside ego-formation, beyond the dominance of the enlightenment subject, and prior to the consolidation of the rational individual.

In *Hatred of Sex*, Tim Dean and Oliver Davis advance a theory of sex in the wake of *Hatred of Democracy*, Rancière's influential work on the

---

107. Dean, *Unlimited Intimacy*, 54.
108. Tim Dean, "Mediated Intimacies: Raw Sex, Truvada, and the Biopolitics of Chemoprophylaxis," *Sexualities* 18 (2015): 224–46.

complications of democratic practice.[109] Dean and Davis's main argument is both surprising—it chastises queer theory and liberal politics for their conniving complicity with conservative discourses on sex—and straightforward—it relies on Freud's notion of sex as essentially unbinding. It is also entirely predictable and sophisticated: first, anyone who has been paying attention to developments in queer theory knows that nonsexual reflections have eclipsed the sexual realm; and, second, its sophistication lies in a series of suggestive connections between the realm of the sexual and the political, without washing off the aporias contained in both.

Gayle Rubin had originally claimed that Paul's notion of sex as inherently sinful was taken up by Western cultures that termed it as a "dangerous, destructive, negative force."[110] In a secular or postsecular age, these ideas no longer rely on religion for their purchase. Dean and Davis suggest that contemporary liberal discourses on sex, with their emphasis on inclusivity and identity, have domesticated those aspects of sex that threaten the coherence of the ego, its masterful impulses, its centripetal drives, its prophylactic functions:

> The human ego, with its myriad defenses against disordering, is what hates sex once it reaches maximal intensity. Our culture's penchant for regarding sexual activity as an ego-enhancing pursuit, when it is treated as a conquest or as "notches on the belt," overlooks the extent to which sexual intensity also is capable of denuding the ego. Viewing sexual experience as a conquest of the other entails strenuous denials of how sex—its unbinding intensity—threatens to conquer me.[111]

Subcultures of barebacking, not necessarily as the epitome of transgression but as an exemplary invitation, throw into relief how community does not require identity. If "every identity is an imaginary formation, a province of the ego with its territorial borders,"[112] modes of relationality that circumvent identitarian reifications have the potential to be the Trojan horse on

---

109. Davis and Dean, *Hatred of Sex*; Jacques Rancière, *Hatred of Democracy* (London: Verso, 2014).

110. Gayle S. Rubin, "Thinking Sex: Notes for a Radical Theory of the Politics of Sexuality," in *Culture, Society and Sexuality*, ed. Richard Parker and Peter Aggleton (London: Routledge, 2006), 150.

111. Davis and Dean, *Hatred of Sex*, 28.

112. Davis and Dean, *Hatred of Sex*, 121.

this side of the abyssal line. It may not, after all, be coincidental that the Global South knows little about sexual identitarian categories.

In this chapter, I have sought to explore how the undoing of identity at the point of conversion—in Paul as much as in Caravaggio—has theological and sexual significance. The insight has purchase for its renovated reading of Paul's conversion. I also hope to invite critics to explore hermeneutical strategies that engage the complexities of Christian identity: its constructive forces as much as its eradicating drives.

CONCLUSION

I have recently started teaching a course on enslavement and early Christian literature. This is an academic project that lies ahead, but I would like to share here the contribution of a student as she reflected on what it means to center black knowledge in the study of enslavement in antiquity. For her, reflecting on the ways in which the practice of history veils the reality of the captive meant that, whereas before she would come to Scripture exclusively for inspiration and positivity, now reading and interpreting the New Testament meant visiting a cemetery. I do not wish to co-opt the voice of this brilliant young student when she expressed mourning and grief, relief and inspiration, encouragement and sadness, compassion and anger, as she encountered previously unseen biblical silences and unheard scriptural absences, but I find rich historiographical knowledge in this range of dispositions toward the past.

The voices of those who strive to live out queer love, who have experienced torture, who currently live in solitary confinement, who exist on the other side of the colonial line, or who carve out a generative subjectivity in the midst of the HIV pandemic speak in very different languages and dwell in diverse worlds. My purpose has not been to flatten out their differences in search of a cohesive ideological agenda but rather to dwell in their differences, inhabit their worlds, and sit next to their hopes and desperations. This is inevitably a fraught task—to account for other lives always is—but one worth pursuing not only for its ethical and political imperatives but for its epistemological ones. Hermeneutical practices cannot be circumscribed to extracting historical knowledge from the past; they should also extend an invitation to explore and embody the range of emotions, dispositions, and attitudes that make us human, rehearsing a reach beyond the abyssal line despite historical and philosophical limitations.

Consider the following case that centered a recent Supreme Court decision:

> For nearly three years, petitioner Michael Johnson whom the Illinois Department of Corrections has classified as "seriously mentally ill" based on his bipolar disorder, severe depression, and other diagnosed conditions—was held in solitary confinement at Pontiac Correctional Center, a prison two hours from Chicago. During that time, Johnson spent nearly every hour of his existence in a windowless, perpetually lit cell about the size of a parking space. His cell was poorly ventilated, resulting in unbearable heat and noxious odors. The space was also unsanitary, often caked with human waste. And because Pontiac officials would not provide cleaning supplies to Johnson unless he purchased them from the commissary, he was frequently forced to clean that filth with his bare hands. Johnson was allowed out of his cell to shower only once per week, for 10 brief minutes.[1]

This description of solitary confinement, penned by Justice Ketanji Brown Jackson (joined by Justices Sotomayor and Kagan), introduces a dissent decision to the Supreme Court for denial of certiorari. In a majority decision, the highest court in allegedly one of the pioneering world democracies considers that privation of fresh air, a basic routine exercise, and a daily shower does not constitute "unusual or cruel punishment."

There are multiple ethical reasons why any citizen in a democratic state should be concerned about our institutions' treatment of prisoners and alarmed at the sustained erosion of human rights. Supporting and contributing to a robust democratic ethos entails engaging, reflecting, and theorizing instances in which the humanity of others is under attack, carefully analyzing structures that keep humanity from flourishing. Such political and ethical drives have consequences for our study of history in the sense that tending to the Other decenters the experience of the abstracted scholar.

Implicitly contesting historical criticism's claims that contextualist studies focus only on "contemporary agendas" and explicitly protesting literary criticism's erasure of contemporary readership, this project shows how sustained theorization of contemporary contexts illuminates rather than obscures New Testament contexts. Cultural studies prove that, if we take recent developments in hermeneutics and literary theory seriously, theorizing the past and the present are not mutually exclusive: we can do both. Cultural studies balance an understanding of texts in their past

---

1. Supreme Court of the United States. Michael Johnson v. Susan Prentice et al. No. 22-693. Decided: 13 November 2023.

and present contexts, attentive to the political and cultural demands of our times. Incorporating cultural studies into New Testament criticism helps biblical scholarship out of certain isolation regarding other theological and philosophical disciplines, such as practical theology or theological ethics, and regarding other fields, such as art, ethnic studies, political philosophy, literature, or gender studies. Furthermore, at the pedagogical level, it reconnects biblical interpretation with the political and ethical concerns of many students, practitioners, and scholars who approach the New Testament in pursuit of its emancipatory potential.

Besides the mass incarceration crisis and the alienating effects of solitary confinement, here I have addressed queer sex, HIV, torture, and the legacies of enslavement. Many other crises call for further elaboration. On top of obvious ones such as rising wealth inequality, ecological collapse, new forms of colonialism, authoritarian upsurges, and migratory crises, we could also enlist surveillance capitalism, the sustained eradication of indigenous cultures, or the recurrence of pandemics. These are not simply abstract crises with their own theoretical challenges; they determine the lives of the majority world. Embodying active citizenship involves reckoning with our democracies' tainted colonial past, complicity in current coloniality, and refusal to imagine and build more equitable futures. On this front, the task of the cultural critic entails fleshing out an account of the myriad subjectivities and subcultures trapped but also flourishing in the midst of such crises. Equally, the duty of the biblical cultural critic involves traveling back and forth between past and present contexts, showing their entanglements, narrating their connections, and bringing forth their complicities.

My hope is that biblical criticism continues an epistemological path that equips the discipline to integrate present and past crises at the center of its research agendas. Of course, many biblical scholars consider this task alien to biblical criticism's methods, theories, and concerns. Many critics, willing to grant some scholarly status to these questions, patronizingly second-rate this type of scholarship. However, the dominance of historicism, I suggest, ill-equips biblical interpreters to address these concerns, creating an epistemological ethos that pushes these questions to the margins. Instead of embracing a healthy dose of intellectual humility and a salutary modicum of curiosity, historicism refuses to contextualize its roots and engage in interdisciplinary conversations on equal grounds. Just as unaware US citizens express their shock at how the rest of the world sees us—Why do they hate America [sic] so much?—historicist scholars react to minoritized critiques clutching their pearls: they possibly cannot understand what we stand for. I have experienced this type of interaction at every level of academic production: professional conferences, peer-review reports, personal conversations, and editors' comments. If communal experience has any value, minoritized scholars continue to suffer this epistemic dominance regularly.[2]

In the aftermath of the paradigm shifts in hermeneutical theory, one of the most enduring contributions of contextual knowledge sustains that meaning production occurs through the dialogical process between text and interpreter. To take seriously the notion that the interpreter, as part of broader interpretive communities and cultural, political, social, and historical contexts, plays a foundational role in hermeneutical processes raises first-order epistemological questions. My contribution seeks to rehearse the dialogical and dialectical interaction between text and interpreter, ancient and contemporary contexts, by going back and forth between the opposite ends of the historiographical continuum, traveling across time and space, establishing connections through art, texts, and experiences.

Biblical scholarship has addressed the hermeneutical and historiographical gaps in several creative ways. For instance, contextual hermeneutics rooted in identitarian features has tended to privilege minoritized experiences. Feminist, womanist, *mujerista*, queer, or disability studies have circumvented dominant research agendas by focusing on the concerns of underrepresented constituencies. Autobiographical critique grounds the interpreter's experience by deploying narrative methods, whereas theory-based criticism has abstracted individual and communal experiences into theoretical frameworks. An intercontextual approach like the one rehearsed in these chapters draws heavily from all these strategies, trying to toe the line between the risk of solipsism in identitarian approaches and the danger of abstracted disembodiment in theoretical traditions.

In these chapters, I have modeled the traditional figure of the abstracted critic after experiences on the other side of the abyssal line. Take, for instance, the example that focuses on the above-mentioned Supreme Court decision about Michael Johnson. It would be naïve, disingenuous even, to

---

2. Two recent contributions expose the lived implications of such dominance: Stephanie Buckhanon Crowder, *Are You For Real? Imposter Syndrome, the Bible and Society* (Eugene, OR: Wipf & Stock, 2023); and Parker, *If God Still Breathes*.

claim that we are all "Michael Johnson." This type of political platitude may have ethical import, but it is riddled with anthropological complexities and epistemological appropriations. The reality is that the cultural or literary critic—and most regular flesh-and-blood readers—could not be further removed from the victim's experience. Identitarian-based claims are of little help insofar as they are quick to chastise the critic for appropriating someone else's experience, whereas theory-based approaches tend to fly over the clouds, occupying themselves with abstracted subjectivities, spiraling temporalities, or rhizomatic assemblages.

Here, I have been suggesting a different ethos of interpretation, one that adopts cultural studies' faith in the ability of theories of meaning to illuminate specific realities. In this model, the critic may step out of her comfort zone by tending to thick descriptions of constituencies that traditionally fly under biblical scholarship's epistemological radars. Instead of taking the professional critic's experience and/or subject position as a starting point or her alleged unbiased disinterest, the critic may reach toward neglected subjectivities, displaced subcultures, and unacknowledged wisdom via methodological acuity, theoretical sophistication, and ethical and political concerns. Ultimately, unless academic prose steps out of its inertia-based historical inquiry, it will continue to favor whiteness as an epistemological ethos, a way of intellectual pursuit that refuses to locate itself even as it dismisses contextuality.

Historicism, scientificism, and objectivism—and their prodigal son, secularism—fence off contextual ecologies of knowledge, producing a type of scholarship alien to contemporary political crises and unequipped to think with progressive communities of interpretations that draw from theological wells. This development has kept church politics, at least superficially, outside of knowledge production, opening critical intellectual spaces removed from dogmatism and preconceived theological assumptions. However, this secularist drive—most apparent in the division between religious studies and theological programs—reinscribes a type of colonial epistemology that labels as anachronistic contemporary contextual concerns. A biblical scholarship aspiring to be global cannot do away with the religious experiences of the majority of the world.

On this side of the abyssal line, biblical scholarship straddles two paths. On one road, we have historicist obliviousness to contemporary readership; on the other, we have a contextualist obsession with identitarian claims. While the historicist route insists on keeping hermeneutics away from present concerns (preteritism), contextuality has forged a special brand of hermeneutics (presentism) grounded on readers' personal features. Undoubtedly, Epistemologies of the South contributes to the latter without excluding the former, but it also adds an important shift in its refusal to ground hermeneutics in the critics' identity. It loosens up the tight link between personal identity and scholarship by focusing on topics and problems rather than subjectivities.

Walking a tightrope between historicism and contextualism entails coming across other disciplinary quandaries. In this book, I have privileged critical theory and cultural studies—queer and postcolonial theory, feminist critique, trauma theory, media studies, and so on—but the product is far removed from the secular foundations that animate such studies. So, although I have little recourse to theological sources and thinkers, my hope is that, by reading religious texts via contemporary discourses, biblical scholarship moves into the realm of theological thinking without catering to the colonial epistemological inclinations of past theologies.

The historical-critical motto that only "more and better history" solves contemporary misconceptions about the Bible or has the capacity to illuminate present ethical concerns is epistemologically uninformed, politically irresponsible, and disciplinary-wise negligent. In this book, I have shown that stepping out of the historicist monopoly yields hermeneutical returns. Far from diminishing the scope of historicism, tending to cultural studies and its multifarious disciplinary manifestations helps us think of history otherwise and, in some cases, in a more sophisticated fashion. There is theology in nontheological sources, there is history in culture, there is politics in theology, and so on. An Yountae asks: What happens "when the theory that articulates new being and new order against colonial modernity, is intrinsically critical of the secular? And what if the re-envisioning of the new order entails a spiritual dimension?"[3]

Can we distill theology by using nontheological sources? One need not pledge confessional/doctrinal credos to engage with theological thinking. In this way, biblical critique transgresses historicism's monopoly and enters other disciplinary countries through political theology, ethics of interpretation, reception history, intercultural analysis, comparative ethics, or critical theories of religion. The task consists of distilling those trends, paths, and interpretive moves invested in emancipation, crediting

---

3. An Yountae, *The Coloniality of the Secular: Race, Religion, and Poetics of World-Making* (Durham, NC: Duke University Press, 2024), 4.

and incorporating subjugated knowledge, and discerning apposite strategies for global action.[4] The task of drawing the lines contouring a new type of biblical scholarship remains: experiential and theoretical, political and theological, contextual and historical, critical and artistic, global and local.

---

4. As Warren S. Goldstein, Roland Boer, Rebekka King, and Jonathan Boyarin put it ("How Can Mainstream Approaches Become More Critical?," *Critical Research on Religion* 3 [2015]: 8): "For the majority elsewhere—from the Caribbean through Africa and Asia to the Pacific—this was largely seen as elitist and perhaps even wasteful. Here the Bible has distinct cultural force, in a way that means its interpretation has strikingly immediate consequences. Critical discernment for the sake of human flourishing in these parts is not determined by a skeptical or engaged approach to religion; rather, it challenges either approach to exercise discernment."

BIBLIOGRAPHY

Abbott, Jack Henry. *In the Belly of the Beast: Letters from Prison*. New York: Vintage Books, 1991.

Abogunrin, Samuel O. "Jesus' Sevenfold Programmatic Declaration at Nazareth: An Exegesis of Luke 4.15–30 from an African Perspective." *Black Theology* 1 (2003): 225–49.

Abramowski, Luise. "Die Geschichte von der Fußwaschung (John 13)." *ZKT* 102 (2005): 176–203.

Ådna, Jostein. "Jesus and the Temple." Pages 2635–75 in *Handbook for the Study of the Historical Jesus*. Edited by Tom Holmén and Stanley E. Porter. Leiden: Brill, 2019.

Aernie, Jeffrey W. "Cruciform Discipleship: The Narrative Function of the Women in Mark 15–16." *JBL* 135 (2016): 779–97.

Agamben, Giorgio. *State of Exception*. Chicago: University of Chicago Press, 2005.

Aguero, Eduardo Emilio. "Discipulado, amor y amistad en Juan 13:21–30: Una aproximación desde la antropología cultural." *RevistB* 80 (2018): 79–103.

Aguilar Chiu, José Enrique. "A Theological Reading of Ἐξέπνευσεν in Mark 15:37, 39." *CBQ* 78 (2016): 682–705.

Aichele, George, Peter Miscall, and Richard Walsh. "An Elephant in the Room: Historical-Critical and Postmodern Interpretations of the Bible." *JBL* 128 (2009): 383–404.

Aichele, George, et al. *The Postmodern Bible*. New Haven: Yale University Press, 1995.

Alexander, Claire. "Stuart Hall and 'Race.'" *Cultural Studies* 23 (2009): 457–82.

Alexander, Michelle. *The New Jim Crow: Mass Incarceration in the Age of Colorblindness*. New York: New Press, 2012.

Allison, Dale C., Jr. "Anticipating the Passion: The Literary Reach of Matthew 26:47–27:56." *CBQ* 56 (1994): 701–14.

Alphen, Ernst van. *Francis Bacon and the Loss of Self.* Cambridge: Harvard University Press, 1993.
Althaus-Reid, Marcella. *Indecent Theology: Theological Perversions in Sex, Gender and Politics.* London: Routledge, 2000.
———, ed., *Liberation Theology and Sexuality.* Aldershot: Ashgate, 2006.
———. *The Queer God.* London: Routledge, 2003.
American Civil Liberties Union. *The Dangerous Overuse of Solitary Confinement in the United States.* New York: ACLU Foundation, 2014.
Anderson, Gary A. *Charity: The Place of the Poor in the Biblical Tradition.* New Haven: Yale University Press, 2013.
Anderson, Janice Capel, and Stephen D. Moore. *Mark and Method: New Approaches in Biblical Studies.* 2nd ed. Minneapolis: Fortress, 2008.
Anderson, Janice Capel, and Jeffrey L. Staley, eds. *Taking It Personally: Autobiographical Biblical Criticism. Semeia* 72. Atlanta: Scholars Press, 1995.
Ankrah, E. Maxine. "The Impact of HIV/AIDS on the Family and Other Significant Relationships: The African Clan Revisited." *AIDS Care* 5.1 (1993): 5–22.
Apata, Temidayo, M. A. Y. Rahji, O. M. Apata, J. O. Ogunrewo, and O. A. Igbalajobi. "Effects of HIV/AIDS Epidemic and Related Sicknesses on Family and Community Structures in Nigeria: Evidence of Emergence of Older Care-Givers and Orphan Hoods." *Journal of Science and Technology Education Research* 1.4 (2010): 73–84.
Arcadi, James. *An Incarnational Model of the Eucharist.* Cambridge: Cambridge University Press, 2018.
Arendt, Hannah. *Love and Saint Augustine.* Chicago: University of Chicago Press, 1996.
Arya, Rina. "The Existential Dimensions of Bacon's Art." Pages 81–102 in *Bacon: Critical and Theoretical Perspectives.* Edited by Rina Arya. Bern: Lang, 2012.
———. *Francis Bacon: Painting in a Godless World.* Farnham: Lund Humphries, 2012.
Association of State Correctional Administrators and Arthur Liman Public Interest Program at Yale Law School. *Aiming to Reduce Time-In-Cell: Reports from Correctional Systems on the Numbers of Prisoners in Restricted Housing and on the Potential of Policy Changes to Bring About Reforms* (November 2016). https://tinyurl.com/SBLPress06108b2.

———. *Reforming Restrictive Housing: The 2018 ASCA-Liman Nationwide Survey of Time-in-Cell* (October 2018). https://tinyurl.com/SBLPress06108a1.
Avalos, Hector. *The End of Biblical Studies*. Buffalo, NY: Prometheus, 2007.
Bahmann, Manfred K. *A Preference for the Poor: Latin American Liberation Theology from a Protestant Perspective*. Lanham, MD: University Press of America, 2005.
Bailey, Randall C., Tat-siong Benny Liew, and Fernando F. Segovia, eds. *They Were All Together in One Place? Toward Minority Biblical Criticism*. SemeiaSt 57. Atlanta: Society of Biblical Literature, 2009.
Bal, Mieke. *Quoting Caravaggio: Contemporary Art, Preposterous History*. Chicago: University of Chicago Press, 1999.
———. *Reading "Rembrandt": Beyond the Word-Image Opposition*. Cambridge: Cambridge University Press, 1991.
Ballengee, Jennifer R. *The Wound and the Witness: The Rhetoric of Torture*. Albany: SUNY Press, 2010.
Barclay, John M. G. "An Identity Received from God: The Theological Configuration of Paul's Kinship Discourse." *EC* (2017): 354–72.
Barmania, Sima, and Michael J. Reiss. *Islam and Health Policies Related to HIV Prevention in Malaysia*. Cham: Springer, 2017.
Barr, James. "Words for Love in Biblical Greek." Pages 3–18 in *The Glory of Christ in the New Testament: Studies in Christology in Memory of George Bradford Caird*. Edited by L. D. Hurst and N. T. Wright. Oxford: Oxford University Press, 1987.
Barreto, Eric D. "Introduction." Pages 1–6 in *Thinking Theologically: Foundations for Learning*. Edited by Eric D. Barreto. Minneapolis: Fortress, 2015.
Barthes, Roland. *The Pleasure of the Text*. Translated by Richard Miller. New York: Hill & Wang, 1975.
Bartholomew, Craig, C. Stephen Evans, Mary Healy, and Murray Rae. *"Behind" the Text: History and Biblical Interpretation*. Grand Rapids: Zondervan Academic, 2003.
Bauckham, Richard. *Jesus and the Eyewitnesses: The Gospels as Eyewitness Testimony*. Grand Rapids: Eerdmans, 2006.
———. *The Testimony of the Beloved Disciple: Narrative, History, and Theology in the Gospel of John*. Grand Rapids: Baker, 2007.
Bazzana, Giovanni B. *Having the Spirit of Christ: Spirit Possession and Exorcism in the Early Christ Groups*. New Haven: Yale University Press, 2020.

Beal, Timothy. "Reception History and Beyond: Toward the Cultural History of Scriptures." BibInt 19 (2011): 357–72.
Beavis, Mary Ann. *The First Christian Slave: Onesimus in Context*. Eugene, OR: Cascade, 2021.
Becker, Eve-Marie. *The Birth of Christian History: Memory and Time from Mark to Luke-Acts*. New Haven: Yale University Press, 2018.
Beckford, Robert. *Documentary as Exorcism: Resisting the Bewitchment of Colonial Christianity*. London: Bloomsbury, 2014.
Beedon, David K. *Pastoral Care for the Incarcerated: Hope Deferred, Humanity Diminished?* Newcastle: Palgrave, 2022.
Behar, Olga. *Las guerras de la paz*. Bogotá: Planeta, 1990.
Benéitez Rodríguez, Manuel. "Un extraño interrogatorio: Jn 18,29–32." EstEcl 68 (1993): 459–96.
Berdini, Paolo. *The Religious Art of Jacopo Bassano: Painting as Visual Exegesis*. New York: Cambridge University Press, 1997.
Berger, Dan, and Toussaint Losier. *Rethinking the American Prison Movement*. London: Routledge, 2017.
Berlant, Lauren, and Michael Warner. "Sex in Public." *Critical Inquiry* 24 (1998): 547–66.
Bersani, Leo. *Is the Rectum a Grave? And Other Essays*. Chicago: University of Chicago Press, 2010.
———. "Shame on You." Pages 91–109 in *After Sex? On Writing since Queer Theory*. Edited by Janet Hally and Andrew Parker. Durham, NC: Duke University Press, 2011.
Bersani, Leo, and Ulysse Dutoit. *Caravaggio's Secrets*. London: British Film Institute, 1999.
Berthier, Nancy. "Cine y revolucion: Memorias del subdesarrollo de Tomás Gutierrez Alea." Pages 99–108 in *The Cinema of Latin America*. Edited by Alberto Elena and Marina Diaz. London: Wallflower Press, 2003.
Bérubé, Michael. *The Aesthetics of Cultural Studies*. Hoboken, NJ: John Wiley & Sons, 2008.
Best, Ernest. *Disciples and Discipleship: Studies in the Gospel according to Mark*. Edinburgh: T&T Clark, 1986.
Black, Fiona C. ed. *The Recycled Bible: Autobiography, Culture, and the Space Between* SemeiaSt 51. Atlanta: Society of Biblical Literature, 2006.
Boehler, Genilma. "La visibilización de los sujetos invisibles: el método 'queer' para la Teología." *Pasos* 155 (2012): 2–9.

Boff, Leonardo. *Jesus Christ Liberator: A Critical Christology for Our Time.* Maryknoll, NY: Orbis Books, 1978.
Bonavía, Pablo. "Sinergia intergeneracional y teología de la liberación." Pages 9–12 in *La fuerza de los pequeños: Hacer teología de la liberación desde las nuevas resistencias y esperanzas.* Edited by Francisco Aquino Júnior, Geraldina Céspedes, and Alejandro Ortiz Cotte. Montevideo: Fundación Amerindia, 2020.
Bond, Helen K. "A Fitting End? Self-Denial and a Slave's Death in Mark's Life of Jesus." *NTS* 65 (2019): 425–42.
Bor, Robert, Riva Miller, and Eleanor Goldman. "HIV/AIDS and the Family: A Review of Research in the First Decade." *Journal of Family Therapy* 15.2 (1993): 187–204.
Bose, Joerg. "Images of Trauma: Pain, Recognition, and Disavowal in the Works of Frida Kahlo and Francis Bacon." *Journal of the American Academy of Psychoanalysis and Dynamic Psychiatry* 33 (2005): 51–70.
Boyarin, Daniel. *Unheroic Conduct: The Rise of Heterosexuality and the Invention of the Jewish Man.* Contraversions 8. Oakland: University of California Press, 1997.
Brandon, S. G. F. "The Date of the Markan Gospel." *NTS* 7 (1961): 126–41.
Brett, Mark G., ed. *Ethnicity and the Bible.* BibInt 19. Leiden: Brill, 1996.
Brintnall, Kent L. "Erotic Ruination: Embracing the 'Savage Spirituality' of Barebacking." Pages 51–67 in *Negative Ecstasies: Georges Bataille and the Study of Religion.* Edited by Jeremy Biles and Kent L. Brintnall. New York: Fordham University Press, 2015.
Brown, Vincent. "Social Death and Political Life in the Study of Slavery." *American Historical Review* 114 (2007): 1231–49.
Bruner, Frederick Dale. *Matthew: A Commentary.* Rev. ed. 2 vols. Grand Rapids: Eerdmans, 2004.
Buell, Denise Kimber. "Canons Unbound." Pages 293–306 in *Feminist Biblical Studies in the Twentieth Century: Scholarship and Movement.* Edited by Elisabeth Schüssler Fiorenza. BW 9.1. Atlanta: Society of Biblical Literature, 2014.
Burchardt, Marian. "A Moral Science of Sex." Pages 74–97 in *Faith in the Time of AIDS.* Edited by Marian Burchardt. London: Palgrave Macmillan, 2015.
Burkett, Delbert Royce. *An Introduction to the New Testament and the Origins of Christianity.* Cambridge: Cambridge University Press, 2002.
Burnaby, John. *Amor Dei: A Study of the Religion of St. Augustine; The Hulsean Lectures for 1938.* London: Hodder & Stoughton, 1938.

Burrus, Virginia, and Catherine Keller, eds. *Toward a Theology of Eros: Transfiguring Passion at the Limits of Discipline*. New York: Fordham University Press, 2006.

Burrus, Virginia, and Stephen D. Moore, "Unsafe Sex: Feminism, Pornography, and the Song of Songs." *BibInt* 11 (2003): 24–52.

Byron, John. "Slave of Christ or Willing Servant? Paul's Self-Description in 1 Corinthians 4:1–2 and 9:16–18." *Neot* 37 (2003): 179–98.

Califia, Pat. *Public Sex: The Culture of Radical Sex*. San Francisco: Cleis, 2000.

Campbell, William S. "Engagement, Disengagement and Obstruction: Jesus' Defense Strategies in Mark's Trial and Execution Scenes (14.53–64; 15.1–39)." *JSNT* 26 (2004): 283–300.

Capánaga, Victorino. "Interpretación Agustianiana del amor: Eros y agape." *Augustinus* 18 (1973): 211–22.

Careri, Giovanni. *Bernini: Flights of Love, the Art of Devotion*. Chicago: University of Chicago Press, 1995.

Carey, Greg. *Using Our Outside Voice: Public Biblical Interpretation*. Minneapolis: Fortress, 2020.

Carr, David McLain. *The Erotic Word: Sexuality, Spirituality, and the Bible*. Oxford: Oxford University Press, 2003.

Carroll, John T. *Luke: A Commentary*. NTL. Louisville: Westminster John Knox, 2012.

Carroll, Margaret D. "The Erotics of Absolutism: Rubens and the Mystification of Sexual Violence." *Representations* 25 (1989): 3–30.

Carter, Warren. "Cross-Gendered Romans and Mark's Jesus: Legion Enters the Pigs (Mark 5:1–20)." *JBL* 133 (2014): 139–55.

Caruth, Cathy. *Unclaimed Experience: Trauma, Narrative, and History*. Baltimore: Johns Hopkins University Press, 2016.

Casaldáliga, Pedro, and José M. Vigil. *Espiritualidad de la liberación*. Managua: Editorial Envio, 1992.

Casassus, Juan. *Camino en la oscuridad*. Santiago de Chile: Editorial Debate, 2013.

Casella, Jean, James Ridgeway, and Sarah Shourd, eds. *Hell Is a Very Small Place: Voices from Solitary Confinement*. New York: New Press, 2016.

Caserio, Robert L., Lee Edelman, Judith Halberstam, José Esteban Muñoz, and Tim Dean. "The Antisocial Thesis in Queer Theory." *PMLA* 12.3 (2006): 819–28.

Castelli, Elizabeth A. *Imitating Paul: A Discourse of Power*. Louisville: Westminster John Knox, 1991.

Castillo, José M. *Escuchar lo que dicen los pobres a la iglesia*. Barcelona: Cristianisme i Justícia, 1999.

———. *Los pobres y la teología: ¿Qué queda de la teología de la liberación?* Bilbao: Desclée de Brouwer, 1997.

Castro-Gómez, Santiago, and Ramón Grosfoguel. *El giro decolonial: Reflexiones para una diversidad epistémica más allá del capitalismo global*. Bogotá: Siglo del Hombre Editores, 2007.

Cavadini, John C. "Feeling Right: Augustine on the Passions and Sexual Desire." *AugStud* 36 (2005): 195–217.

Chacón, Luis. "Principales líneas de interpretación de Jn 2,3c–4 en la historia de la exegesis." *EstEcl* 77 (2002): 385–460.

Chambers, Samuel A. *The Lessons of Rancière*. New York: Oxford University Press, 2013.

Chance, J. Bradley. "The Cursing of the Temple and the Tearing of the Veil in the Gospel of Mark." *BibInt* 15 (2007): 268–91.

Chapman, David W. *Ancient Jewish and Christian Perceptions of Crucifixion*. WUNT 244. Tübingen: Mohr Siebeck.

Chapman, David W., and Eckhard J. Schnabel. *The Trial and Crucifixion of Jesus: Texts and Commentary*. WUNT 344. Tübingen: Mohr Siebeck, 2019.

Chare, Nicholas. *After Francis Bacon: Synaesthesia and Sex in Paint*. Ashgate: Routledge, 2017.

Charles, Ronald. *Silencing of Slaves in Early Jewish and Christian Texts*. London: Routledge, 2019.

Choi, Jin Young. *Postcolonial Discipleship of Embodiment: An Asian and Asian American Feminist Reading of the Gospel of Mark*. New York: Palgrave Macmillan, 2015.

Claassens, Juliana, and Klaas Spronk, eds. *Fragile Dignity: Intercontextual Conversations on Scriptures, Family, and Violence*. SemeiaSt 72. Atlanta: Society of Biblical Literature, 2013.

Clark-Soles, Jaime. "Of Footwashing and History." Pages 255–70 in *John, Jesus, and History, Volume 2: Aspects of Historicity in the Fourth Gospel*. Edited by Paul N. Anderson, Felix Just, S.J., and Tom Thatcher. ECL 2. Atlanta: Society of Biblical Literature, 2009.

Clear, Todd R., and Natasha Frost. *The Punishment Imperative: The Rise and Failure of Mass Incarceration in America*. New York: New York University Press, 2014.

Collins, John J. *The Bible after Babel: Historical Criticism in a Postmodern Age*. Grand Rapids: Eerdmans, 2005.

Coloe, Mary. "Welcome into the Household of God: The Footwashing in John 13." *CBQ* 66 (2004): 400–415.

Comaroff, Jean, and John L. Comaroff. *Theory from the South: Or, How Euro-America Is Evolving toward Africa*. London: Routledge, 2016.

Comfort, Megan. "Punishment beyond the Legal Offender." *Annual Review of Law and Social Science* 3 (2007): 271–96.

Cone, James H. *The Cross and the Lynching Tree*. Maryknoll, NY: Orbis Books, 2011.

Conway, Colleen M. *Sex and Slaughter in the Tent of Jael: A Cultural History of a Biblical Story*. New York: Oxford University Press, 2016.

Cook, Granger. *Crucifixion in the Mediterranean World*. WUNT 327. Tübingen: Mohr Siebeck, 2019.

Cooke, Bernard. "The Experiential 'Word of God.'" Pages 69–74 in *Consensus in Theology? A Dialogue with Hans Küng and Edward Schillebeeckx*. Edited by Leonard Swidler. Philadelphia: Westminster, 1980.

———. *Power and the Spirit of God: Toward an Experience-Based Pneumatology*. Oxford: Oxford University Press, 2008.

Cooper, Kate. "Closely Watched Households: Visibility, Exposure and Private Power in the Roman Domus." *Past and Present* 197 (2007): 3–33.

Córdova Quero, Hugo. "Queer Liberative Theologies." Pages 210–31 in *Introducing Liberative Theologies*. Edited by Miguel de la Torre. Maryknoll, NY: Orbis Books, 2015.

———. "Risky Affairs: Marcella Althaus-Reid Indecently Queering Juan Luis Segundo's Hermeneutical Circle Propositions." Pages 207–18 in *Dancing Theology in Fetish Boots: Essays in Honour of Marcella Althaus-Reid*. Edited by Lisa Isherwood and Mark D. Jordan. London: SCM, 2010.

Couldry, Nick. "The Project of Cultural Studies: Heretical Doubts, New Horizons." Pages 9–16 in *The Renewal of Cultural Studies*. Edited by Paul Smith. Philadelphia: Temple University Press, 2011.

Craghan, John F. "The Gerasene Demoniac." *CBQ* 30 (1968): 522–36.

Crook, Zeba A. "Render unto Caesar." *BAR* 49.2 (2023): 28.

Crosby, Christina. *A Body Undone: Living On after Great Pain*. New York: New York University Press, 2016.

Crossan, John Dominic. *Render unto Caesar: The Struggle over Christ and Culture in the New Testament*. New York: HarperOne, 2022.

Crossley, James G. *Jesus and the Chaos of History: Redirecting the Life of the Historical Jesus*. Oxford: Oxford University Press, 2015.

Crowder, Stephanie Buckhanon. *Are You For Real? Imposter Syndrome, the Bible and Society.* Eugene, OR: Wipf & Stock, 2023.

Cruz, Jon. *Culture on the Margins: The Black Spiritual and the Rise of American Cultural Interpretation.* Princeton: Princeton University Press, 1999.

Culpepper, Alan R. "The Johannine 'Hypodeigma': A Reading of John 13." *Semeia* 53 (1991): 133–52.

Cupples, Julie, and Ramón Grosfoguel. *Unsettling Eurocentrism in the Westernized University.* London: Routledge, 2019.

Dashke, Dereck. "Apocalypse and Trauma." Pages 457–73 in *The Oxford Handbook of Apocalyptic Literature.* Edited by John Joseph Collins. Oxford: Oxford University Press, 2014.

Davidson, Steed Vernyl. "Postcolonializing the Bible with a Little Help from Derek Walcott." Pages 156–81 in *Present and Future of Biblical Studies: Celebrating Twenty-Five Years of Brill's Biblical Interpretation.* Edited by Tat-siong Benny Liew. BibInt 161. Leiden: Brill, 2018.

Davies, Philip R., ed. *First Person: Essays in Biblical Autobiography.* New York: Sheffield Academic, 2002.

Davis, Oliver, and Tim Dean. *Hatred of Sex.* Lincoln: Nebraska University Press, 2022.

Dawes, James. *That the World May Know: Bearing Witness to Atrocity.* Cambridge: Harvard University Press, 2007.

Dean, Tim. "Mediated Intimacies: Raw Sex, Truvada, and the Biopolitics of Chemoprophylaxis." *Sexualities* 18 (2015): 224–46.

———. *Unlimited Intimacy: Reflection on the Subculture of Barebacking.* Chicago: University of Chicago Press, 2009.

Deane, Kevin D., Justin O. Parkhurst, and Deborah Johnston. "Linking Migration, Mobility and HIV." *Tropical Medicine & International Health* 15.12 (2010): 1458–63.

Decena, Carlos Ulises. *Circuits of the Sacred: A Faggotology.* Durham, NC: Duke University Press, 2023.

Deering, Kathleen N., Peter Vickerman, Stephen Moses, Banadakoppa M. Ramesh, James F. Blanchard, and Marie-Claude Boily. "The Impact of Out-Migrants and Out-Migration on the HIV/AIDS Epidemic: A Case Study from South-West India." *AIDS* 22 (2008): S165–81.

Deleuze, Gilles. *Francis Bacon: The Logic of Sensation.* Translated by D. W. Smith. Minneapolis: University of Minnesota Press, 2002.

Denbeaux, Mark, Jess Ghannam, and Abu Zubaydah. *American Torturers: FBI and CIA Abuses at Dark Sites and Guantanamo*. Newark: Seton Hall University School of Law, Center for Policy and Research, 2023.

Derrida, Jacques. *The Gift of Death*. Translated by David Wills. Chicago: University of Chicago Press, 1995.

———. "On the Gift: A Discussion between Jacques Derrida and Jean-Luc Marion." Pages 54–78 in *God, the Gift, and Postmodernism*. Edited by John D. Caputo and Michael J. Scanlon. Bloomington: Indiana University Press, 1999.

Destro, Adriana, and Mauro Pesce. *Encounters with Jesus: The Man in His Place and Time*. Minneapolis: Fortress, 2011.

———. "Fathers and Householders in the Jesus Movement: The Perspective of the Gospel of Luke." *BibInt* 11 (2003): 211–38.

Di Cesare, Donatella. *Tortura*. Barcelona: Gedisa, 2018.

Diebold-Scheuermann, Carola. *Jesus vor Pilatus: Eine exegetische Untersuchung zum Verhör durch Pilatus (Joh 18,28–19,16a)*. SBB 32. Stuttgart: Verlag Katholisches Bibelwerk, 1996.

Dijk, Rijk van, Hansjörg Dilger, Marian Burchardt, and Thera Rasing. *Religion and AIDS-Treatment in Africa: Saving Souls, Prolonging Lives*. Farnham: Ashgate, 2014.

Dijkhuizen, Petra. "The Lord's Supper and Ritual Theory: Interpreting 1 Corinthians 11:30 in Terms of Risk, Failure, and Efficacy." *Neot* 50 (2016): 441–76.

Dinkler, Michal Beth. "Building Character on the Road to Emmaus: Lukan Characterization in Contemporary Literary Perspective." *JBL* 136 (2017): 687–706.

———. *Literary Theory and the New Testament*. AYBRL. New Haven: Yale University Press, 2020.

———. *Silent Statements: Narrative Representations of Speech and Silence in the Gospel of Luke*. BZNW 191. Berlin: De Gruyter, 2013.

———. "Suffering, Misunderstanding, and Suffering Misunderstanding: The Markan Misunderstanding Motif as a Form of Jesus's Suffering." *JSNT* 38 (2016): 316–38.

Domínguez, Ana Lidia M. *Una historia cultural del grito*. Madrid: Taurus, 2022.

Dormeyer, Detlev. "Joh 18:1–14 Par Mk 14.43–53: Methodologische Überlegungen Zur Rekonstruktion einer Vorsynoptischen Passionsgeschichte." *NTS* 41 (1995): 218–39.

Dowd, Sharyn E., and Elizabeth Struthers Malbon. "The Significance of Jesus' Death in Mark: Narrative Context and Authorial Audience." *JBL* 125 (2006): 271–97.

Driggers, Ira Brent. "The Politics of Divine Presence: Temple as Locus of Conflict in the Gospel of Mark." *BibInt* 15 (2007): 227–47.

Dube, Musa W. "*Go tla Siama. O tla Fola*: Doing Biblical Studies in an HIV and AIDS Context." *Black Theology: An International Journal* 8 (2010): 212–41.

———. *The HIV and AIDS Bible: Selected Essays*. Scranton, PA: University of Scranton Press, 2008.

———. *HIV/AIDS and the Curriculum: Methods of Integrating HIV/AIDS in Theological Programmes*. Geneva: WCC Publications, 2003.

———. *Postcolonial Feminist Interpretation of the Bible*. St. Louis: Chalice, 2000.

———. "Remembering the Teacherly Moments of the HIV and AIDS Texts." *International Bulletin of Mission Research* 43 (2019): 320–33.

———. "*Talitha Cum* Hermeneutics of Liberation: Some African Women's Ways of Reading the Bible." Pages 133–46 in *The Bible and the Hermeneutics of Liberation*. Edited by Alejandro F. Botta and Pablo R. Andiñach. SemeiaSt 59. Atlanta: Society of Biblical Literature, 2009.

Dubler, Joshua, and Vincent W. Lloyd. *Break Every Yoke: Religion, Justice, and the Abolition of Prisons*. New York: Oxford University Press, 2020.

Dunning, Benjamin. *Christ without Adam: Subjectivity and Sexual Difference in the Philosophers' Paul*. New York: Columbia University Press, 2014

———. *Specters of Paul: Sexual Difference in Early Christian Thought*. Philadelphia: University of Pennsylvania Press, 2011.

Dussel, Enrique D. *Historia de la filosofía latinoamericana y filosofía de la liberación*. Bogatá: Editorial Nueva América, 1994.

———. *The Invention of the Americas: Eclipse of the "The Other" and the Myth of Modernity*. New York: Continuum, 1995.

Eisenman, Stephen F. *The Abu Ghraib Effect*. London: Reaktion Books, 2007.

Elliott, Dyan. *Fallen Bodies: Pollution, Sexuality, and Demonology in the Middle Ages*. Philadelphia: University of Pennsylvania Press, 1999.

Elliott, John H. "Temple versus Household in Luke-Acts: A Contrast in Social Institutions." *HvTSt* 47 (1991): 88–120.

Eribon, Didier. "Michel Foucault's Histories of Sexuality." *GLQ: A Journal of Lesbian and Gay Studies* 7 (2001): 31–86.

Erzen, Tanya. *God in Captivity: The Rise of Faith-Based Prison Ministries in the Age of Mass Incarceration*. Boston: Beacon, 2017.
Escobar, Arturo, and David L. Frye. *Pluriversal Politics: The Real and the Possible*. Durham, NC: Duke University Press, 2020.
Eubank, Nathan. "Dying with Power: Mark 15:39 from Ancient to Modern Interpretation." *Bib* 95 (2014): 247–68.
Euler, Alida. "Drinking Gall and Vinegar: Psalm 69:22; An Underestimated Intertext in Matt 27:34, 48." *ZNW* 112 (2021): 130–40.
Evora, Jose Antonio. *Tomás Gutiérrez Alea*. Madrid: Cátedra/Filmoteca Española, 1996.
Exum, J. Cheryl. "Lovis Corinth's Blinded Samson." *BibInt* 6 (1998): 410–25.
Exum, J. Cheryl, and Stephen D. Moore. "Biblical Studies/Cultural Studies." Pages 19–45 in *Biblical Studies/Cultural Studies: The Third Sheffield Colloquium*. Edited by J. Cheryl Exum and Stephen D. Moore. Sheffield: Sheffield Academic, 1998.
Fabre, Jean-Philippe. "Le possédé de Gérasa (Marc 5, 1–20)." *Bib* 98 (2017): 55–71.
Falkoff, Marc. *Poems from Guantanamo: The Detainees Speak*. Iowa City: University of Iowa Press, 2007.
Fanon, Frantz. *The Wretched of the Earth*. New York: Grove, 2004.
Farmer, Paul. *Aids and Accusation: Haiti and the Geography of Blame*. Berkeley: University of California Press, 2006.
Febus Perez, Beatriz. "El sujeto sexual en las teologías queer: ¿Implicaciones para una teologia queer latinoamericana de la liberación?" *Conexión QUEER: Revista Latinoamericana y Caribeña de Teologías Queer* 1 (2018): 145–74.
Felski, Rita. *Hooked: Art and Attachment*. Chicago: University of Chicago Press, 2020.
———. *The Limits of Critique*. Chicago: University of Chicago Press, 2015.
Feník, Juraj, and Róbert Lapko. "Jesus's Inverse Transfiguration in John 13." *Neot* 55 (2021): 347–64.
Ferrando, Miguel Ángel. "La interpretación de la Biblia en la teología de la liberación, 1971–1984." *Teología y Vida* 50 (2009): 75–92. http://dx.doi.org/10.4067/S0049-34492009000100007.
Fifield, Peter. "Gaping Mouths and Bulging Bodies: Beckett and Francis Bacon." *Journal of Beckett Studies* 18 (2009): 57–71.
Finaldi, Gabriele. *The Image of Christ*. London: National Gallery London, 2000.

Fiorani, Flavio. "Sentarse a la Mesa del Señor: Metaforizaciones y conflictos in La ultima cena de Tomás Gutiérrez Alea." *Saggi Altre Modernitá* 6 (2011): 85–96.

Foltz, Mary C. *Contemporary American Literature and Excremental Culture: American Sh*t*. London: Palgrave Macmillan, 2020.

Foucault, Michel. *Discipline and Punish: The Birth of the Prison*. Translated by Alan Sheridan. London: Peregrine, 1979.

———. "Friendship as a Way of Life." Translated by John Johnston. Pages 308–12 in *Foucault Live: Collected Interviews, 1961–1984*. Edited by Sylvère Lotringer. New York: Semiotext(e), 1996.

———. *An Introduction*. Vol. 1 of *The History of Sexuality*. New York: Vintage, 1990.

———. "The Politics of Health in the Eighteenth Century." Pages 90–105 in vol. 3 of *The Essential Works of Foucault, 1954–1984*. Edited by Paul Rabinow and James D. Faubion. 3 vols. New York: New Press, 2000.

———. "Sexual Choice, Sexual Act." Pages 322–34 in *Foucault Live: Collected Interviews, 1961–1984*. Edited by Sylvère Lotringer. New York: Semiotext(e), 1996.

———. "Truth and Power." Pages 109–33 in *Power/Knowledge: Selected Interviews and Other Writings*. Edited by Colin Gordon. Translated by Colin Gordon et al. New York: Vintage, 1980.

———. *The Use of Pleasure*. Vol. 2 of *The History of Sexuality*. New York: Vintage Books, 1990.

France, R. T. *Divine Government: God's Kingship in the Gospel of Mark*. Vancouver: Regent College Publishers, 2003.

Franco, Konrad, Caitlin Patler, and Keramet Reiter. "Punishing Status and the Punishment Status Quo: Solitary Confinement in U.S. Immigration Prisons, 2013–2017." *Punishment and Society* 24 (2022): 170–95.

Fredrick, David. "Mapping Penetrability in Late Republican and Early Imperial Rome." Pages 236–64 in *The Roman Gaze: Vision, Power, and the Body*. Edited by David Fredrick. Baltimore: Johns Hopkins University Press, 2002.

Freeman, Elizabeth. "Time Binds, or, Erotohistoriography." *Social Text* 23 (2005): 57–68.

———. *Time Binds: Queer Temporalities, Queer Histories*. Durham, NC: Duke University Press, 2010.

Fricker, Miranda. *Epistemic Injustice: Power and the Ethics of Knowing*. Oxford: Oxford University Press, 2009.

Fuller, Samuel. "Torture as a Management Practice: The Convention against Torture and Non-disciplinary Solitary Confinement." *Chicago Journal of International Law* 19 (2018): 102–44.

Furey, Constance M. "Body, Society, and Subjectivity in Religious Studies." *JAAR* 80 (2012): 7–33.

García Olivo, Pedro. "El síndrome de Viridiana en la política y la búsqueda de sustitutos funcionales del proletariado." *Centro Cultural Universidad del Tolima* 9.18(2010): 73–82.

García Ruiz, Alicia. "'Quo tendas anagogia:' Viridiana o la historia de un inconsciente." *Asparkía: Investigació Feminista* (2005): 71–93.

Gates, Henry Louis, Jr. *The Signifying Monkey: A Theory of Afro-American Literary Criticism*. Oxford: Oxford University Press, 1988.

Gambaudo, Sylvie. "We Need to Talk About Eva: The Demise of the Phallic Mother." *Janus Head* 12 (2011): 155–68.

Geddert, Timothy. *Watchwords: Mark 13 in Markan Eschatology*. JSNTSup 26. Sheffield: JSOT Press, 1989.

Gelpi, D. L. *The Turn to Experience in Contemporary Theology*. New York: Paulist, 1994.

Georgia, Allan. "Translating the Triumph: Reading Mark's Crucifixion Narrative against a Roman Ritual of Power." *JSNT* 36 (2013): 17–38.

Gibson, David. "The Johannine Footwashing and the Death of Jesus: A Dialogue with Scholarship." *Scottish Bulletin of Evangelical Theology* 25 (2007): 50–60.

Gillman, Laura. *Unassimilable Feminisms: Reappraising Feminist, Womanist, and Mestiza Identity Politics*. New York: Palgrave Macmillan, 2016.

Glancy, Jennifer A. "Boasting of Beatings (2 Corinthians 11:23–25)." *JBL* 123 (2004): 107–13.

———. "Hagar as/against Bare Life." *JFSR* 37 (2021): 103–21.

———. "Obstacles to Slaves' Participation in the Corinthian Church." *JBL* 117 (1998): 481–501.

———. *Slavery in Early Christianity*. Minneapolis: Fortress, 2006.

———. "Torture: Flesh, Truth, and the Fourth Gospel." *BibInt* 13 (2005): 107–36.

Goldstein, Warren S., Roland Boer, Rebekka King, and Jonathan Boyarin. "How Can Mainstream Approaches Become More Critical?" *Critical Research on Religion* 3 (2015): 3–12.

González Faus, José Ignacio. *Vicarios de Cristo: Los pobres en la teología y espiritualidad Cristianas; Antología comentada*. Barcelona: Cristianisme i Justícia, 2005.

Grant, Colin. "For the Love of God: Agapē." *JRE* 24 (1996): 3–21.
Grassian, Stuart. "Psychopathological Effects of Solitary Confinement." *American Journal of Psychiatry* 140 (1983): 1450–54.
Gray, Sherman W. *The Least of My Brothers: Matthew 25, 31–46; A History of Interpretation*. SBLDS 114. Atlanta: Scholars Press, 1989.
Green, Joel B. *The Gospel of Luke*. NICNT. Grand Rapids: Eerdmans, 1997.
Gregg, Melissa. *Cultural Studies' Affective Voices*. New York: Palgrave Macmillan, 2014.
Grindheim, Sigurd. "Ignorance Is Bliss: Attitudinal Aspects of Judgment according to Works in Matthew 25:31–46." *NovT* 50 (2008): 313–31.
Grosfoguel, Ramón. "The Structure of Knowledge in Westernized Universities: Epistemic Racism/Sexism and the Four Genocides/Epistemicides of the Long 16th Century." *Human Architecture: Journal of the Sociology of Self-Knowledge* 11 (2013): 73–79.
Grossberg, Lawrence. *Cultural Studies in the Future Tense*. Durham, NC: Duke University Press, 2010.
Guenther, Lisa. *Solitary Confinement: Social Death and Its Afterlives*. Minnesota: University of Minnesota Press, 2013.
Guijarro Oporto, Santiago. "El Evangelio de Marcos como 'relato progresivo': El trauma de la guerra y la propuesta de un nuevo comienzo." *RevistB* 81 (2019): 315–344.
Gunda, Masiiwa Ragies. *The Bible and Homosexuality in Zimbabwe: A Socio-historical Analysis of the Political, Cultural, and Christian Arguments in the Homosexual Public Debate, with Special Reference to the Use of the Bible*. Bamberg: University of Bamberg Press, 2010.
Gundry, Robert H. *Matthew: A Commentary on His Handbook for a Mixed Church under Persecution*. Grand Rapids: Eerdmans, 1994.
Gurtner, Daniel M. "The Rending of the Veil and Markan Christology: 'Unveiling' the ΥΙΟΣ ΘΕΟΥ (Mark 15:38–39)." *BibInt* 13 (2007): 292–306.
Guth, Christine. "An Insider's Look at the Gerasene Disciple (Mark 5:1–20)." *Journal of Religion, Disability, and Health* 11.4 (2008): 61–70.
Gutiérrez, Gustavo. "Expanding the View." Pages 3–38 in *Expanding the View: Gustavo Gutiérrez and the Future of Liberation Theology*. Edited by Marc H. Ellis and Otto Maduro. Maryknoll, NY: Orbis Books, 1990.
———. "The Irruption of the Poor in Latin America and the Christian Communities of the Common People." Pages 107–23 in *The Challenge of Basic Christian Communities*. Edited by Sergio Torres and John Eagleson. Maryknoll, NY: Orbis Books, 1981.

———. *The Power of the Poor in History: Selected Writings*. Maryknoll, NY: Orbis Books, 1983.

———. *A Theology of Liberation: History, Politics, and Salvation*. Maryknoll, NY: Orbis Books, 1973.

Gutiérrez Alea, Tomás. *Dialéctica del espectador*. Havana: Unión de Escritores y Artistas de Cuba, 1982.

Gutiérrez-Albilla, Julián Daniel. "Picturing the Beggars in Luis Buñuel's 'Viridiana': A Perverse Appropriation of Leonardo Da Vinci's 'Last Supper.'" *Journal of Romance Studies* 5 (2005): 59–73.

Hagan, John, and Ronit Dinovitzer. "Collateral Consequences of Imprisonment for Children, Communities, and Prisoners." *Crime and Justice* 26 (1999): 121–62.

Häkkinen, Sakari. "Developing Methods for Poverty Studies." *Diaconia* 4 (2013): 122–42.

Hale, Jane. "Framing the Unframable: Samuel Beckett and Francis Bacon." *Samuel Beckett Today/Aujourd'hui* 2 (1993): 95–102.

Hall, Stuart. "Cultural Studies and Its Theoretical Legacies." Pages 277–94 in *Cultural Studies*. Edited by Lawrence Grossberg, Cary Nelson, and Paula A. Treichler. New York: Routledge, 1992.

———. "Race, Culture, and Communications: Looking Backward and Forward at Cultural Studies." *Rethinking Marxism* 5 (2009): 10–18.

Halperin, David M. *How To Be Gay*. Cambridge: Harvard University Press, 2012.

———. *Saint Foucault: Towards a Gay Hagiography*. New York: Oxford University Press, 1995.

Hammill, Graham L. *Sexuality and Form: Caravaggio, Marlowe, and Bacon*. Chicago: University of Chicago Press, 2000.

Harley, Felicity. "Crucifixion in Roman Antiquity: The State of the Field." *JECS* 27 (2019): 303–23.

Harvey, David. "From Space to Place and Back Again: Reflections on the Condition of Postmodernity." Pages 3–29 in *Mapping the Futures: Local Cultures, Global Change*. Edited by Jon Bird, Barry Curtis, Tim Putnam, and Lisa Tickner. New York: Routledge, 2016.

Hatina, Thomas R. "Who Will See 'The Kingdom of God Coming with Power' in Mark 9,1—Protagonists or Antagonists?" *Bib* 86 (2005): 20–34.

Havard, John C. "Typological Rhetoric of Tomás Gutiérrez Alea's *La última cena*." *Hipertexto* 7 (2008): 58–67.

Hawthorn, T. "The Gerasene Demoniac: A Diagnosis." *ExpTim* 66 (1954–1955): 79–80.
Hayes, Tom. "A Jouissance beyond the Phallus: Juno, Saint Teresa, Bernini, Lacan." *American Imago* 56 (1999): 331–55.
Hays, Richard. *Echoes of Scripture in the Letters of Paul*. New Haven: Yale University Press, 1989.
Hedrick, Charles W. "Paul's Conversion/Call: A Comparative Analysis of the Three Reports in Acts." *JBL* 100 (1981): 415–32.
Heil, John Paul. "The Narrative Strategy and Pragmatics of the Temple Theme in Mark." *CBQ* 59 (1997): 76–100.
Hellwig, Monika. *Whose Experience Counts in Theological Reflection?* The 1982 Père Marquette Theology Lecture. Milwaukee: Marquette University Press, 1982.
Henao Castro, Andrés Fabián. "Ontological Captivity: Toward a Black Radical Deconstruction of Being." *Differences* 32 (2021): 85–113.
Henderson, Suzanne Watts. "'If Anyone Hungers…': An Integrated Reading of 1 Cor 11.17–34." *NTS* 48 (2002): 195–208.
Hengel, Martin. *Crucifixion in the Ancient World and the Folly of the Message of the Cross*. Philadelphia: Fortress, 1978.
Hernández, Juan Antonio. "Multitud, devenires y éxodo: La última cena de Tomás Gutiérrez Alea." *Revista Iberoamericana* 69.205 (2003): 839–48.
Hernando, Victoria, et al. "HIV Infection in Migrant Populations in the European Union and European Economic Area in 2007–2012: An Epidemic on the Move." *Journal of Acquired Immune Deficiency Syndromes* 70.2 (2015): 204–11.
Heyward, Carter. "Lamenting the Loss of Love: A Response to Colin Gran.," *JRE* 24 (1996): 23–28.
Hidalgo, Jacqueline M. *Revelation in Aztlán: Scriptures, Utopias, and the Chicano Movement*. New York: Palgrave Macmillan, 2016.
Hoad, Neville Wallace. *African Intimacies: Race, Homosexuality, and Globalization*. Minneapolis: University of Minnesota Press, 2007.
Hobbs, Robert. "Yinka Shonibare Mbe: The Politics of Representation." Pages 24–37 in *Yinka Shonibare Mbe*. Edited by Rachel Kent. Munich: Prestel, 2008.
Hodge, Caroline Johnson. "Apostle to the Gentiles: Constructions of Paul's Identity." *BibInt* 13 (2005): 270–88
———. *If Sons, Then Heirs: A Study of Kinship and Ethnicity in the Letters of Paul*. New York: Oxford University Press, 2007.

Hofius, Otfried. "Die Erzählung von der Fußwaschung Jesu: Joh 13,1–11 als narratives Christuszeugnis." *ZKT* 106 (2009): 156–76.
Hoke, Jimmy. *Feminism, Queerness, Affect, and Romans: Under God?* ECL 30. Atlanta: SBL Press, 2021.
Hollander, John. *The Figure of Echo: A Mode of Allusion in Milton and After*. Berkeley: University of California Press, 1981.
Hollenbach, Paul. "Jesus, Demoniacs, and Public Authorities: A Sociohistorical Study." *JAAR* 49 (1981): 567–88.
Hollywood, Amy M. *Sensible Ecstasy: Mysticism, Sexual Difference, and the Demands of History*. Chicago: University of Chicago Press, 2002.
Hong, Yan, et al. "Rural-to-Urban Migrants and the HIV Epidemic in China." *AIDS and Behavior* 10 (2006): 421–30.
Horrell, David G. "Paul, Inclusion and Whiteness: Particularizing Interpretation." *JSNT* 40 (2017): 123–47.
Horsley, Richard A. *Hearing the Whole Story: The Politics of Plot in Mark's Gospel*. Louisville: Westminster John Knox, 2001.
Horst, Pieter W. van der. "Eros." *DDD*, 304–6.
Huebner, Daniel R. "Anachronism: The Queer Pragmatics of Understanding the Past in the Present." *The American Sociologist* 52 (2021): 740–61.
Huffer, Lynne. *Mad for Foucault: Rethinking the Foundations of Queer Theory*. New York: Columbia University Press, 2010.
Hultgren, Arland J. "The Johannine Footwashing as a Symbol of Eschatological Hospitality." *NTS* 28 (1982): 539–46.
Humphreys, Colin J. *The Mystery of the Last Supper: Reconstructing the Final Days of Jesus*. Cambridge: Cambridge University Press, 2011.
Hunt, Steven A. "The Roman Soldiers at Jesus' Arrest: 'You are Dust, and to Dust You Shall Return.'" Pages 554–67 in *Character Studies in the Fourth Gospel: Narrative Approaches to Seventy Figures*. Edited by John Steven A. Hunt and Donald Francois Tolmie. WUNT 314. Tübingen: Mohr Siebeck 2013.
Hurtado, Larry W. "Convert, Apostate or Apostle to the Nations: The 'Conversion' of Paul in Recent Scholarship." *SR* 22 (1993): 273–84.
Hylton, Richard. "Yinka Shonibare: Dressing Down." *Third Text* 12.46 (2008): 101–3.
Iñiguez, Isabel. "Construimos teología de la liberación desde las nuevas resistencias y esperanzas." Pages 173–83 in *La fuerza de los pequeños: Hacer teología de la liberación desde las nuevas resistencias y esperan-*

zas. Edited by Francisco Aquino Júnior, Geraldina Céspedes, and Alejandro Ortiz Cotte. Montevideo: Fundación Amerindia, 2020.

Irigaray, Luce. *Speculum of the Other Woman*. Ithaca, NY: Cornell University Press, 1985.

Isiorhovoja, Osbert Uyovwieyovwe, Godwin Omegwe, and Sylvester Ese Ibomhen. "Quest for Africentric Biblical Reading among African Christians." *KIU Journal of Humanities* 8 (2023): 257–63. https://doi.org/10.58709/niujhu.v8i2.1676.

Jackson, Howard M. "The Death of Jesus in Mark and the Miracle from the Cross." *NTS* 33 (1987): 16–37.

Jackson, Timothy P. *Love Disconsoled: Meditations on Christian Charity*. Cambridge: Cambridge University Press, 1999.

———. *Political Agape: Christian Love and Liberal Democracy*. Grand Rapids: Eerdmans, 2015.

———. *The Priority of Love: Christian Charity and Social Justice*. Princeton: Princeton University Press, 2003.

Jackson, Zakiyyah Imam. *Becoming Human: Matter and Meaning in an Antiblack World*. New York: New York University Press, 2021.

Jacob, Sharon. *Reading Mary alongside Indian Surrogate Mothers*. New York: Palgrave Macmillan, 2015.

Jamison, Kay R. *An Unquiet Mind*. New York: Knopf, 1995.

Jefferson, Tony. *Resistance through Rituals: Youth Subcultures in Post-War Britain*. London: Routledge, 2002.

Jennings, Mark A. "The Veil and the High Priestly Robes of the Incarnation: Understanding the Context of Heb 10:20." *PRSt* 37 (2010): 85–97.

Jennings, Willie James. *The Christian Imagination: Theology and the Origins of Race*. New Haven: Yale University Press, 2010.

Jensen, Robin. *The Substance of Things Seen: Art, Faith, and the Christian Community*. Grand Rapids: Eerdmans, 2004.

Jeong, Mark. "The Collapse of Society in Luke 23: A Thucydidean Take on Jesus' Passion." *NTS* 67 (2021): 317–35.

Jewett, Robert. "The Agape Meal: A Sacramental Model for Ministry Drawn from Romans 13:8," *AJBI* 33 (2007): 73–92.

———. *Romans: A Commentary*. Hermeneia. Minneapolis: Fortress, 2007.

Joe, Sean. "Analyzing Mass Incarceration." *Science* 374.65 (2021): 237.

John, Helen C. "Conversations in Context: Cross-Cultural (Grassroots) Biblical Interpretation Groups Challenging Western-Centric (Professional) Biblical Interpretation." *BibInt* 27 (2019): 36–68.

———. "Legion in a 'Living Landscape': Contextual Bible Study as Disruptive Tool (Luke 8:26–39 Interpreted in Owamboland, Namibia)." *ExpTim* 128 (2017): 313–24.

Johnson, Luke Timothy. *The Gospel of Luke*. Collegeville, MN: Liturgical Press, 1991.

Johnson, Luke Timothy, and Daniel J. Harrington. *The Acts of the Apostles*. Collegeville, MN: Liturgical Press, 1992.

Jordan, Mark. *The Ethics of Sex*. Malden, MA: Blackwell, 2002.

Joseph, Simon J. *Jesus and the Temple: The Crucifixion in Its Jewish Context*. Cambridge: Cambridge University Press, 2018.

Katz, Jonathan. *The Invention of Heterosexuality*. Chicago: University of Chicago Press, 2014.

Keenan, James. *The Works of Mercy: The Heart of Catholicism*. Plymouth, UK: Rowman & Littlefield, 2008.

Keith, Chris. "The Role of the Cross in the Composition of the Markan Crucifixion Narrative." *Stone-Campbell Journal* 9 (2006): 61–75.

Kelly, Kevin J., and Karen Birdsall. "The Effects of National and International HIV/AIDS Funding and Governance Mechanisms on the Development of Civil-Society Responses to HIV/AIDS in East and Southern Africa." *AIDS Care* 22.2 (2010): 1580–87.

Kelly, Shawn, *Race, Ideology and the Formation of Modern Biblical Scholarship*. London: Routledge, 2002.

———. *Racializing Jesus: Race, Ideology, and the Formation of Modern Biblical Scholarship*. London: Routledge, 2005.

Kelly, Thomas M. *Theology at the Void: The Retrieval of Experience*. Notre Dame, IN: University of Notre Dame Press, 2002.

Kilgore, James William. *Understanding Mass Incarceration: A People's Guide to the Key Civil Rights Struggle of Our Time*. New York: New Press, 2015.

Kim, Doosuk. "Intertextuality and New Testament Studies." *CurBR* 20 (2022): 238–60. https://doi.org/10.1177/1476993X221100993.

Kim, Jean Kyoung. *Woman and Nation: An Intercontextual Reading of the Gospel of John from a Postcolonial Feminist Perspective*. BibInt 69. Leiden: Brill, 2004.

Kimondo, Stephen Simon. *The Gospel of Mark and the Roman-Jewish War of 66–70 CE: Jesus' Story as a Contrast to the Events of the War*. Eugene, OR: Wipf & Stock, 2019.

Kinder, Marsha. *Blood Cinema: The Reconstruction of National Identity in Spain*. Berkeley: University of California Press, 1993.

Kingsmill, Edmee. *The Song of Songs and the Eros of God: A Study in Biblical Intertextuality*. Oxford: Oxford University Press, 2009.

Kireopoulos, Antonios, Mitzi Budde, and Matthew D. Lundberg, eds. *Thinking Theologically about Mass Incarceration: Biblical Foundations and Justice Imperatives*. Mahwah, NJ: Paulist, 2017.

Kitzberger, Ingrid Rosa. *Autobiographical Biblical Criticism: Between Text and Self*. Leiden: Deo, 2002.

———. "Love and Footwashing: John 13:1–20 and Luke 7:36–50 Read Intertextually." *BibInt* 2 (1994): 190–205.

Klingbeil, Gerald A. "When Action Collides with Meaning: Ritual, Biblical Theology, and the New Testament Lord's Supper." *Neot* 50 (2016): 423–39.

Klinghardt, Matthias. "Legionsschweine in Gerasa: Lokalkolorit und historischer Hintergrund von Mk 5,1–20." *ZNW* 98 (2007): 28–48.

Klinken, Adriaan S. van, and Masiiwa Ragies Gunda. "Taking Up the Cudgels against Gay Rights? Trends and Trajectories in African Christian Theologies on Homosexuality." *Journal of Homosexuality* 59 (2012): 114–38.

Kloppenborg, John S. "*Evocatio Deorum* and the Date of Mark." *JBL* 124 (2005): 419–50.

Koskenniemi, Erkki, Kirsi Nisula, and Jorma Toppari. "Wine Mixed with Myrrh (Mark 15.23) and Crurifragium (John 19.31–32): Two Details of the Passion Narratives." *JSNT* 27 (2005): 379–91.

Kotrosits, Maia. *How Things Feel: Biblical Studies, Affect Theory, and the (Im)Personal*. Leiden: Brill, 2016.

———. "Queer Persistence: On Death, History, and Longing for Endings." Pages 133–44 in *Sexual Disorientations: Queer Temporalities, Affects, Theologies*. Edited by Kent L. Brintnall, Joseph A. Marchal, and Stephen D. Moore. New York: Fordham University Press, 2018.

Kötting, Bernhard. "Fußwaschung." *RAC* 8:743–77.

Kowalski, Beate. "'Was ist Wahrheit?' (Joh 18,38a): Zur literarischen und theologischen Funktion der Pilatusfrage in der Johannespassion." Pages 201–27 in *Im Geist und in der Wahrheit: Studien zum Johannesevangelium und zur Offenbarung des Johannes sowie andere Beiträge*. Edited by Konrad Huber. NTA 52. Münster: Aschendorff Verlag 2008.

Kristeva, Julia. *The Kristeva Reader*. Edited by Toril Moil. New York: Columbia University Press, 1986.

Krüger, René. "Teología bíblica contextual en América Latina." *Acta Poética* 31 (2010): 185–207. https://doi.org/10.19130/iifl.ap.2010.2.351.

Kuecker, Aaron J. "'You Will Be Children of the Most High': An Inquiry into Luke's Narrative Account of Theosis." *Journal of Theological Interpretation* 8 (2014): 213–28.

Kupers, Terry Allen. *Solitary: The Insider Story of Supermax Isolation and How We Can Abolish It.* Berkeley: University of California Press, 2017.

Lamoreaux, Jason T. "Ritual Negotiation in 1 Corinthians: Pauline Authority and the Corinthian Community." *Neot* 50 (2016): 397–422.

Landes, Paula Fredriksen. *Augustine on Romans: Propositions from the Epistle to the Romans and Unfinished Commentary on the Epistle to the Romans.* SBLTT 23. Chico, CA: Scholars Press, 1982.

Lanzendörfer, Tim, and Mathias Nilges. "Literary Studies after Postcritique: An Introduction." *Amerikastudien/American Studies* 64 (2019): 491–513. https://doi.org/10.33675/AMST/2019/4/4.

Latour, Bruno. "Why Has Critique Run Out of Steam? From Matters of Fact to Matters of Concern." *Critical Inquiry* 30 (2004): 225–48.

Lau, Markus. "Die Legio X Fretensis und der Besessene von Gerasa: Anmerkungen zur Zahlenangabe 'ungefähr Zweitausend' (Mark 5,13)." *Bib* 88 (2007): 351–64.

Lawson, R. P., trans. *The Song of Songs: Commentary and Homilies*, ACW. Westminster, MD: Newman, 1957.

Leonard, Ellen. "Experience as a Source for Theology." Pages 44–61 in *Proceedings of the Annual Convention.* Edited by Catholic Theological Society of America. Washington, DC: Catholic Theological Society of America, 1988.

Levi, Primo. *The Drowned and the Saved.* Translated by Raymond Rosenthal. New York: Random House, 1989.

———. *Survival in Auschwitz and the Reawakening: Two Memories.* Translated by Marion Wiesel. New York: Hill & Wang, 2006.

Levinas, Emmanuel. *Totality and Infinity: An Essay on Exteriority.* Translated by Alphonso Lingis. Pittsburgh: Duquesne University Press, 1969.

Liem, Marieke, and Robert J. Sampson. *After Life Imprisonment: Reentry in the Era of Mass Incarceration.* New York: New York University Press, 2016.

Liew, Tat-siong Benny. *Politics of Parousia: Reading Mark Inter(con)textually.* BibInt 42. Leiden: Brill, 1999.

———. "What Has Been Done? What Can We Learn? Racial/Ethnic Minority Readings of the Bible in the United States." Pages 307–36 in *The Future of the Biblical Past: Envisioning Biblical Studies on a Global Key.*

Edited by Fernando F. Segovia and Roland Boer. SemeiaSt 66. Atlanta: Society of Biblical Literature, 2012.

———. *What Is Asian American Biblical Hermeneutics? Reading the New Testament*. Honolulu: University of Hawai'i Press; Los Angeles: UCLA Asian American Studies Center, 2008.

Lin, Yii-Jan. "Who Is the Text? The Gendered and Racialized New Testament." Pages 137–56 in *The Oxford Handbook of New Testament, Gender, and Sexuality*. Edited by Benjamin H. Dunning. Oxford: Oxford University Press, 2019.

Liu, Shao-hua. *Passage to Manhood: Youth Migration, Heroin, and AIDS in Southwest China*. Stanford, CA: Stanford University Press, 2011.

Löfstedt, Torsten. "Jesus the Angry Exorcist: On the Connection between Healing and Strong Emotions in the Gospels." *SEÅ* 81 (2016): 113–26.

Lofton, Kathryn. "Everything Queer?" Pages 195–204 in *Queer Christianities: Lived Religion in Transgressive Forms*. Edited by Kathleen T. Talvacchia, Mark Larrimore, and Michael F. Pettinger. New York: New York University Press.

Lohse, Wolfram. "Die Fußwaschung (Joh 13, 1–20): Eine Geschichte ihrer Deutung." Diss., Erlangen, 1967.

Lomax, Tamura. *Jezebel Unhinged: Loosing the Black Female Body in Religion and Culture*. Durham, NC: Duke University Press, 2018.

Lozada, Francisco, Jr. "New Testament Interpretation in the United States: A Perspective from a Cultural Observer." Pages 209–25 in *Reading the New Testament in the Manifold Contexts of a Globalized World: Exegetical Perspectives*. Edited by Eve-Marie Becker, Jens Herzer, Angela Standhartinger, and Florian Wilk. Neutestamentliche Entwürfe zur Theologie 32. Tübingen: Francke, 2022. https://doi.org/10.24053/9783772057656.

———. *Toward a Latino/a Biblical Interpretation*. RBS 91. Atlanta: SBL Press, 2017.

Lugones, María. "Methodological Notes toward a Decolonial Feminism." Pages 68–86 in *Decolonizing Epistemologies: Latina/o Theology and Philosophy*. Edited by Ada María Isasi-Díaz and Eduardo Mendieta. New York: Fordham University Press, 2011.

Luz, Ulrich. *Matthew 21–28: A Commentary*. Hermeneia. Minneapolis: Fortress, 2005.

Lynch, James P., and William J. Sabol. "Prison Use and Social Control." Pages 7–44 in *Policies, Processes, and Decisions of the Criminal Justice*

System: Criminal Justice 2000. Edited by Julie Horney. Washington, DC: National Institute of Justice, 2000.

Lyons, William John. "Hope for a Troubled Discipline? Contributions to New Testament Studies from Reception History." *JSNT* 33 (2010): 207–20.

———. *Joseph of Arimathea: A Study in Reception History*. Oxford: Oxford University Press, 2014.

Mackendrick, Karmen. *Counterpleasures*. Albany: State University of New York Press, 1999.

Maclean, Ian. *The Renaissance Notion of Woman: A Study in the Fortunes of Scholasticism and Medical Science in European Intellectual Life*. Cambridge: Cambridge University Press, 1980.

Maldonado-Torres, Nelson. "Descolonización y el giro decolonial." *Tabula Rasa* 9 (2008): 61–72.

———. "On the Coloniality of Being: Contributions to the Development of a Concept." *Cultural Studies* 21 (2007): 240–70.

———. "Race, Religion, and Ethics in the Modern/Colonial World." *Journal of Religious Ethics* 42 (2014): 691–711.

———. "Secularism and Religion in the Modern Colonial World-System: From Secular Postcoloniality to Postsecular Transmodernity." Pages 533–80 in *Coloniality at Large: Latin America and the Postcolonial Debate*. Edited by Mabel Moraña, Enrique Dussel, and Carlos A. Jáuregui. Durham, NC: Duke University Press, 2008.

Manent, Pierre. *Metamorphoses of the City: On the Western Dynamic*. Translated by Marc LePain. Cambridge: Harvard University Press, 2013.

Mannermaa, Tuomo, and Kirsi Irmeli Stjerna, eds. *Two Kinds of Love: Martin Luther's Religious World*. Minneapolis: Fortress, 2010.

Marchal, Joseph A. *Appalling Bodies: Queer Figures before and after Paul's Letters*. Oxford: Oxford University Press, 2020.

———. *Hierarchy, Unity, and Imitation: A Feminist Rhetorical Analysis of Power Dynamics in Paul's Letter to the Philippians*. AcBib 24. Atlanta: Society of Biblical Literature, 2006.

———. "'Making History' Queerly: Touches across Time through a Biblical Behind." *BibInt* 19 (2011): 376–81.

———. *Philippians: Historical Problems, Hierarchical Visions, Hysterical Anxieties*. Sheffield: Sheffield Phoenix, 2014.

Marcus, Joel. "Crucifixion as Parodic Exaltation." *JBL* 125 (2006): 73–87.

———. *Mark 8–16: A New Translation with Introduction and Commentary*. AYB 27A. New Haven: Yale University Press, 2009.
Marcuse, Herbert. *Eros and Civilization: A Philosophical Inquiry into Freud*. Boston: Beacon, 1966.
Mariategui, José Carlos. *Siete ensayos de interpretación de la realidad Peruana*. Barcelona: Linkgua ediciones, 1928.
Marion, Jean-Luc. *The Erotic Phenomenon*. Chicago: University of Chicago Press, 2007.
Markusse, Gabi, and Paul Middleton. *Salvation in the Gospel of Mark: The Death of Jesus and the Path of Discipleship*. Eugene, OR: Pickwick, 2018.
Martin, Dale B. "Heterosexism and the Interpretation of Romans 1:18–32." *BibInt* 3 (1995): 332–55.
———. *Sex and the Single Savior: Gender and Sexuality in Biblical Interpretation*. Louisville: Westminster John Knox, 2006.
———. *Slavery as Salvation: The Metaphor of Slavery in Pauline Christianity*. New Haven: Yale University Press, 1990.
Martin, Richard T. "Ideology, Deviance, and Authority in the Gospel of Matthew: The Political Functioning of Performative Writing." *Literature and Theology* 10 (1996): 20–32.
Martin-Márquez, Susan. "Coloniality and the Trappings of Modernity in 'Viridiana' and 'The Hand in the Trap.'" *Cinema Journal* (2011): 96–114.
Martínez Herranz, Amparo. *La España de Viridiana*. Zaragoza: Prensas de la Universidad de Zaragoza, 2013.
Matera, Frank J. "Ethics for the Kingdom of God: The Gospel according to Mark." *Louvain Studies* 20 (1995): 187–200.
———. *New Testament Ethics: The Legacies of Jesus and Paul*. Louisville: Westminster John Knox, 1996.
Mathew, Bincy. *The Johannine Footwashing as the Sign of Perfect Love*. WUNT 464. Tübingen: Mohr Siebeck, 2018.
Matson, Mark A. "To Serve as Slave: Footwashing as Paradigmatic Status Reversal." Pages 113–31 in *One in Christ Jesus: Essays on Early Christianity and "All That Jazz," in Honor of S. Scott Bartchy*. Edited by David L. Matson and K. C. Richardson. Eugene, OR: Wipf and Stock, 2014.
Mbembe, Achille. *Necropolitics*. Durham, NC: Duke University Press, 2019.
McGowan, Andrew. *Ascetic Eucharists: Food and Drink in Early Christian Ritual Meals*. Oxford: Clarendon, 1999.
———. "The Myth of the 'Lord's Supper': Paul's Eucharistic Meal Terminology and Its Ancient Reception." *CBQ* (2015): 503–21.

McKinlay, Judith E. "Sarah and Hagar: What Have I to Do with Them?" Pages 159–77 in *Her Master's Tools? Feminist and Postcolonial Engagements of Historical-critical Discourse*. Edited by Caroline Vander Stichele and Todd Penner. GPBS 9. Atlanta: Society of Biblical Literature, 2005.

McKinzie, Gregory. "The Symbolism of Divine Presence in Mark 15:33–39." *ResQ* 60 (2018): 219–21.

McKnight, Scot, and Nijay Gupta. *The State of New Testament Studies: A Survey of Recent Research*. Grand Rapids: Baker Academic, 2019.

McRae, Rachel M. "Eating with Honor: The Corinthian Lord's Supper in Light of Voluntary Association Meal Practices." *JBL* 130 (2011): 165–81.

Medina, José. *The Epistemology of Resistance: Gender and Racial Oppression, Epistemic Injustice, and Resistant Imaginations*. New York: New York University Press, 2013.

Meganck, Tine, Sabine van Sprang, Inga Rossi-Schrimpf, and Marie-Andrée Lambert. "Rubens on the Human Figure: Theory, Practice and Metaphysics." Pages 52–64 in *Rubens on the Human Figure: Theory, Practice and Metaphysics*. Edited by Joost vander Auwera. Tielt: Lannoo, 2007.

Mendieta, Eduardo. "Imperial Somatics and Genealogies of Religion: How We Never Became Secular." Pages 235–50 in *Postcolonial Philosophy of Religion*. Edited by Purushottama Bilimoria and Andrew B. Irvine. Berlin: Springer, 2009.

Mendoza, Breny. *Ensayos de crítica feminista en nuestra America*. Mexico: Herder, 2014.

Menéndez-Antuña, Luis. "Bible and Sexuality Studies." In *The Oxford Handbook of the Bible in Latin and Latinx America*. Edited by Fernando F. Segovia and Ahida Pilarski. Oxford: Oxford University Press, forthcoming.

———. "Black Lives Matter and Gospel Hermeneutics: Political Life and Social Death in the Gospel of Luke." *CurTM* 45.4 (2018): 29–34.

———. "Is There a Room for Queer Desires in the House of Biblical Scholarship? A Methodological Reflection on Queer Desires in the Context of Contemporary New Testament Studies." *BibInt* 23 (2015): 399–427.

———. "Of Social Death and Solitary Confinement: The Political Life of a Gerasene (Luke 8:26–39)." *JBL* 138 (2019): 643–64.

Menon, Madhavi. *Indifference to Difference: On Queer Universalism*. Minneapolis: University of Minnesota Press, 2015.

Mercer, Kobena. *Travel and See Black Diaspora Art Practices since the 1980s*. Durham, NC: Duke University Press, 2016.
Merleau-Ponty, Maurice. *Phenomenology of Perception*. London: Routledge, 2005.
Metropolitan Museum of Art. *Dutch and Flemish Paintings from the Hermitage*. New York: Metropolitan Museum of Art, 1988.
Metzger, James A. *Consumption and Wealth in Luke's Travel Narrative*. BibInt 88. Leiden: Brill, 2007.
Metzner, Jeffrey L., and Jamie Fellner. "Solitary Confinement and Mental Illness in U.S. Prisons: A Challenge for Medical Ethics." *Journal of the American Academy of Psychiatry and the Law* 38 (2011): 104–8.
Mignolo, Walter D. *The Darker Side of Western Modernity: Global Futures, Decolonial Options*. Durham, NC: Duke University Press, 2011.
———. *The Politics of Decolonial Investigations*. Durham, NC: Duke University Press, 2021.
Mignolo, Walter, and Catherine E. Walsh. *On Decoloniality: Concepts, Analytics, and Praxis*. Durham, NC: Duke University Press, 2018.
Miller, Jacques-Alain ed. *The Seminar of Jacques Lacan, Book XX: Encore, on Femininity Sexuality, the Limits of Love and Knowledge 1972–1973*. New York: Norton, 1998.
Miller, Julie B. "Rapt by God: The Rhetoric of Rape in Medieval Mystical Literature." Pages 235–53 in *The Subjective Eye: Essays in Culture, Religion, and Gender in Honor of Margaret R. Miles*. Edited by Margaret R. Miles, Richard Valantasis, Deborah J. Haynes, James D. Smith, and Janet F. Carlson. Eugene, OR: Pickwick, 2006.
Moffitt, David M. "Unveiling Jesus' Flesh: A Fresh Assessment of the Relationship between the Veil and Jesus' Flesh in Hebrews 10:20." *PRSt* 37 (2010): 71–84.
Moloney, Francis J. *A Body Broken for a Broken People: Eucharist in the New Testament*. Melbourne: Collins Dove, 1990.
———. "Εἰς Τέλος (v. 1) as the Hermeneutical Key to John 13:1–38." *Salesianum* 76 (2014): 27–46.
———. "John 21 and the Johannine Story. Pages 237–51 in *Anatomies of Narrative Criticism: The Past, Present, and Futures of the Fourth Gospel as Literature*. Edited by Tom Thatcher and Stephen D. Moore. RBS 55. Atlanta: Society of Biblical Literature, 2008.
———. *Love in the Gospel of John: An Exegetical, Theological, and Literary Study*. Grand Rapids: Baker, 2013.
———. "A Sacramental Reading of John 13:1–38." *CBQ* 53 (1991): 237–56.

———. "The Structure and Message of John 13:1–38." *ABR* 34 [1986]: 1–16.

Moore, Stephen D. "Between Birmingham and Jerusalem: Cultural Studies and Biblical Studies." *Semeia* 82 (1998): 1–32.

———. *God's Beauty Parlor: And Other Queer Spaces in and around the Bible*. Stanford, CA: Stanford University Press, 2001.

———. "A Modest Manifesto for New Testament Literary Criticism: How to Interface with a Literary Studies Field That Is Postliterary, Posttheoretical, and Postmethodological." Pages 355–72 in *The Bible in Theory: Critical and Postcritical Essays*. RBS 57. Atlanta: Society of Biblical Literature, 2010.

Moore, Stephen D., and Yvonne Sherwood. *The Invention of the Biblical Scholar: A Critical Manifesto*. Minneapolis: Fortress, 2011.

Moreno Fraginals, Manuel. *The Sugarmill: The Socioeconomic Complex of Sugar in Cuba, 1760–1860*. Translated by Cedric Belfrage. New York: Monthly Review Press, 1976.

Morgan, Jon. "Visitors, Gatekeepers and Receptionists: Reflections on the Shape of Biblical Studies and the Role of Reception History." Pages 61–76 in *Reception History and Biblical Studies: Theory and Practice*. Edited by Emma England and John Lyons. London: Bloomsbury T&T Clark, 2015.

Morris, Leon. *Luke: An Introduction and Commentary*. TNTC. Nottingham: Inter-Varsity Press, 2008.

Moser, Antonio. "Sexualidad." Pages 107–24 in *Mysterium liberationis: Conceptos fundamentales de la teología de la liberación*. Edited by Ignacio Ellacuría and Jon Sobrino. Madrid: Editorial Trotta, 1990.

Moss, Candida. *God's Ghostwriters: Enslaved Christians and the Making of the Bible*. London: Harper Collins, 2024.

———. "The Secretary: Enslaved Workers, Stenography, and the Production of Early Christian Literature." *JTS* 71 (2023): 20–56.

Motyer, Stephen. "The Rending of the Veil: A Markan Pentecost?" *NTS* 33 (1987): 155–57.

Moxnes, Halvor. *The Economy of the Kingdom: Social Conflict and Economic Relations in Luke's Gospel*. Eugene, OR: Wipf & Stock, 1997.

Moyise, Steve. "Intertextuality and Historical Approaches to the Use of Scripture in the New Testament." Pages 23–32 in *Reading the Bible Intertextually*. Edited by Richard B. Hays, Stefan Alkier, and Leroy A. Huizenga. Waco, TX: Baylor University Press, 2009.

Mpolo, Aimé Mpevo. "Sexualité et résistance aux envoyés en Mc 5,1–6,29: Analyse structurelle et transtextualité." *Science et Sprit* 66 (2014): 243–67.

Muizelaar, Klaske, and Derek L. Phillips. *Picturing Men and Women in the Dutch Golden Age: Paintings and People in Historical Perspective*. New Haven: Yale University Press, 2003.

Mullett, Michael A. *The Catholic Reformation*. London: Routledge, 1999.

Musser, Amber Jamilla. *Sensational Flesh: Race, Power, and Masochism*. New York: New York University Press, 2014.

Myles, Robert J. *The Homeless Jesus in the Gospel of Matthew*. Sheffield: Sheffield Phoenix, 2014.

Nadella, Raj. "The Ambivalent Pilate: Reverse Mimicry in Matthew's Gospel." *Bangalore Theological Forum* 45 (2013): 56–65.

Nagle, Brendan. "Aristotle and Arius Didymus on Household and πόλις." *Rheinisches Museum für Philologie* 145 (2002): 198–223.

Nasrallah, Laura S. *Archaeology and the Letters of Paul*. Oxford: Oxford University Press, 2019.

———. "The Work of Nails: Religion, Mediterranean Antiquity, and Contemporary Black Art." *JAAR* 90 (2022): 356–76.

Neyrey, Jerome H. "The Footwashing in John 13:6–11: Transformation Ritual or Ceremony?" Pages 198–213 in *The Social World of the First Christians: Essays in Honor of Wayne A. Meeks*. Edited by L. Michael White and O. Larry Yarbrough. Minneapolis: Fortress, 1995.

Nguyen, Tan Hoang. *A View from the Bottom: Asian American Masculinity and Sexual Representation*. Durham, NC: Duke University Press, 2014.

Nickelsburg, George W. E. "The Genre and Function of the Markan Passion Narrative." *HTR* 73 (1980): 153–84.

Niemand, Christoph. "Was bedeutet die Fusswaschung: Sklavenarbeit oder Liebesdienst? Kulturkundliches als Auslegungshilfe für Joh 13,6–8." *PzB* 3 (1994): 115–27.

Nikolopoulos, Georgios, Michail Arvanitis, Aikaterini Masgala, and Dimitra Paraskeva. "Migration and HIV Epidemic in Greece." *The European Journal of Public Health* 15.3 (2005): 296–99.

Nisula, Timo. *Augustine and the Functions of Concupiscentia*. Leiden: Brill, 2012.

Nobus, Dany. "The Sculptural Iconography of Feminine Jouissance: Lacan's Reading of Bernini's Saint Teresa in Ecstasy." *The Comparatist* 39 (2015): 22–46.

Nori, Franziska, and Barbara Dawson, eds. *Francis Bacon and the Existential Condition in Contemporary Art*. Ostfildern: Hatje Catz, 2013.

Ntozi, J. P., and Samuel Zirimenya. "Changes in Household Composition and Family Structure during the AIDS Epidemic in Uganda." *The Continuing African HIV/AIDS Epidemic* (1999): 193–209.

Nygren, Anders. *Agape and Eros: A Study of the Christian Idea of Love*. Translated by A. G. Hebert and Philip S. Watson. London: SPCK, 1932.

Odets, Walt. *In the Shadow of the Epidemic: Being HIV-Negative in the Age of AIDS*. Durham, NC: Duke University Press, 1995.

O'Kane, Martin. *Painting the Text: The Artist as Biblical Interpreter*. Sheffield: Sheffield Phoenix, 2007.

Okantey, Peter Carlos. "Jesus, the Originator of Servant Leadership: A Narrational Texture Analysis of John 13:1–17." *Journal of Biblical Theology* 5 (2022): 250–59.

Oliver Torelló, Juan Carlos, and Lino Cabezas Gelabert. "La imagen del crucificado en Salvador Dalí, José María Sert y Juan de la Cruz: Hipótesis de realización del dibujo del monasterio de la Encarnación de Ávila." *Locus Amoenus* 14 (2016): 215–32.

Oord, Thomas J. *The Nature of Love: A Theology*. St. Louis: Chalice, 2010.

Oropeza, B. J. "New Studies in Textual Interplay: An Introduction." Pages 3–8 in *New Studies in Textual Interplay*. Edited by Craig A. Evans, B. J. Oropeza, and Paul Sloan. LNTS 632. London: Bloomsbury, 2020.

Ostrow, Steven F. "Caravaggio's Angels." Pages 123–48 in *Caravaggio's Angels*. Edited by Lorenzo Pericolo and David M. Stone. Farnham: Ashgate, 2014.

Outka, Gene. "Theocentric Agape and the Self: An Asymmetrical Affirmation in Response to Colin Grant's Either/Or." *JRE* 24 (1996): 35–42.

Park, Rohun. "Revisiting the Parable of the Prodigal Son for Decolonization: Luke's Reconfiguration of Oikos in 15:11–32." *BibInt* 17 (2009): 507–20.

Park, Wongi. "Multiracial Biblical Studies." *JBL* 140 (2021): 435–59.

Parker, Angela N. *If God Still Breathes, Why Can't I? Black Lives Matter and Biblical Authority*. Grand Rapids: Eerdmans, 2021.

Parker, Holt N. "The Teratogenic Grid." Pages 47–65 in *Roman Sexualities*. Edited by Judith P. Hallett and Marilyn B. Skinner. Princeton: Princeton University Press, 1997.

Pattillo, Mary, David Weiman, and Bruce Western, eds. *Imprisoning America: The Social Effects of Mass Incarceration*. New York: Russell Sage, 2004.

Patterson, Amy S., Marian Burchardt, and Louise Mubanda Rasmussen. *The Politics and Anti-politics of Social Movements: Religion and AIDS in Africa.* London: Routledge, 2016.

Patterson, Orlando. *Slavery and Social Death: A Comparative Study.* Cambridge: Harvard University Press, 1982.

Paul, Herman. "The Postcritical Turn: Unravelling the Meaning of 'Post' and 'Turn.'" Pages 305–24 in *Writing the History of the Humanities: Questions, Themes and Approaches.* Edited by Herman Paul. London: Bloomsbury, 2022.

Pearson, Brook W. R. "Method, Metaphor and Mammaries: The Ideology of Feminist New Testament Criticism." Pages 226–39 in *Religion and Sexuality.* Edited by Michael A. Hayes, Wendy J. Porter, and David Tombs. Sheffield: Sheffield Academic, 1998.

Pendergrass, Taylor, and Mateo Hoke, eds. *Six by Ten: Stories from Solitary.* Chicago: Haymarket, 2018.

Penner, Todd, and Davina C. Lopez. *De-introducing the New Testament: Texts, Worlds, Methods, Stories.* Chichester: Wiley-Blackwell, 2015.

Penney, James. *After Queer Theory: The Limits of Sexual Politics.* London: Pluto, 2014.

Peppiat, Michael. *Francis Bacon: Anatomy of an Enigma.* New York: Farrar, Straus & Giroux 1997.

———. *Francis Bacon in Your Blood: A Memoir.* London: Bloomsbury, 2015.

Perpich, Diane. "From the Caress to the Word: Transcendence and the Feminine in the Philosophy of Emmanuel Levinas." Pages 28–52 in *Feminist Interpretations of Emmanuel Levinas.* Edited by Tina Chanter. University Park: Pennsylvania State University Press, 2001.

Petro, Anthony M. *After the Wrath of God: AIDS, Sexuality, and American Religion.* Oxford: Oxford University Press, 2015.

Philo. *On Abraham, On Joseph, On Moses.* Translated by F. H. Colson. LCL. Cambridge: Harvard University Press, 1935.

Pieper, Josef. *Faith, Hope, Love.* San Francisco: Ignatius Press, 1997.

Pippin, Tina. *Death and Desire: The Rhetoric of Gender in the Apocalypse of John.* Eugene, OR: Wipf & Stock, 2021.

———. "Eros and the End: Reading for Gender in the Apocalypse of John." *Semeia* 59 (1992): 193–210.

Pitre, Brant. *Jesus and the Last Supper.* Grand Rapids: Eerdmans, 2015.

Pixley, Jorge V., and Clodovis Boff. *The Bible, the Church and the Poor.* Theology and Liberation. Maryknoll, NY: Orbis Books, 1989.

Poirier, John C. "Jesus as an Elijianic Figure in Luke 4:16–30." *CBQ* 69 (2007): 349–63.

Poplutz, Uta. "Das Drama der Passion: Eine Analyse der Prozesserzählung Joh 18,28–19,16a unter Berücksichtigung dramentheoretischer Gesichtspunkte." Pages 769–82 in *The Death of Jesus in the Fourth Gospel*. Edited by Gilbert van Belle. BETL 200. Leuven: Leuven University Press 2007.

Prince, Deborah Thompson. "Picturing Saul's Vision on the Road to Damascus: A Question of Authority." *BibInt* 25 (2017): 364–98.

Przybylski, Benno. *Righteousness in Matthew and His World of Thought*. Cambridge: Cambridge University Press, 1980.

Punt, Jeremy. "New Testament Interpretation, Interpretive Interests, and Ideology: Methodological Deficits amidst South African Methodolomania?" *Scriptura* 65 (1998): 123–52.

Quijano, Aníbal. "Coloniality of Power, Eurocentrism, and Latin America." *Nepantla: Views from the South* 1 (2000): 533–80.

———. *Ensayos en torno a la colonialidad del poder*. Buenos Aires: Ediciones del Signo, 2019.

Rahmsdorf, Olivia. "'You Shall Not Wash My Feet εἰς τὸν αἰῶνα' (John 13.8): Time and Ethics in Peter's Interactions with Jesus in the Johannine Narrative." *JSNT* 41 (June 2019): 458–77.

Rahner, Karl. *Foundations of Christian Faith: An Introduction to the Idea of Christianity*. New York: Crossroad, 1982.

Rambo, Shelly. *Spirit and Trauma: A Theology of Remaining*. Louisville: Westminster John Knox, 2010.

Rancière, Jacques. *Hatred of Democracy*. London: Verso, 2014.

Raphael, Steven, and Michael A. Stoll, eds. *Do Prisons Make Us Safer? The Benefits and Costs of the Prison Boom*. New York: Russell Sage, 2009.

Reed, Esther D. "Refugee Rights and State Sovereignty: Theological Perspectives on the Ethics of Territorial Borders." *Journal for the Society of Christian Ethics* 30 (2010): 59–78.

Reventlow, Henning Graf, and William Farmer. *Biblical Studies and the Shifting of Paradigms, 1850–1914*. JSOTSup 192. Sheffield: Sheffield Academic, 1995.

Rhoads, David M. *Reading Mark: Engaging the Gospel*. Minneapolis: Fortress, 2004.

Rhodes, Lorna A. *Total Confinement: Madness and Reason in the Maximum Security Prison*. Berkeley: University of California Press, 2004.

Rice, Peter. "The Rhetoric of Luke's Passion: Luke's Use of Common-Place to Amplify the Guilt of Jerusalem's Leaders in Jesus' Death." *BibInt* 21 (2013): 355–76.
Richardson, Michael. *Gestures of Testimony: Torture, Trauma, and Affect in Literature*. New York: Bloomsbury, 2016.
Riera, Emilio. "Viridiana." Pages 218–25 in *The World of Luis Buñuel*. Edited by Julio Mellen. New York: Oxford University Press, 1986.
Ringe, Christophe. *Necropolitics: The Religious Crisis of Mass Incarceration in America*. Lanham, MD: Lexington Books, 2020.
Rivera, Mayra. *Poetics of the Flesh*. Durham, NC: Duke University Press, 2015.
———. *The Touch of Transcendence: A Postcolonial Theology of God*. Louisville: Westminster John Knox, 2007.
Rivera Zambrano, Jennifer. "Pintar las fuerzas: Deleuze y Nietzsche en la pintura de Francis Bacon." *Cuestiones de Filosofía* 16 (2014): 28–40.
Rivera-Fuentes, Consuelo, and Lynda Birke. "Talking with/in Pain: Reflections on Bodies under Torture." *Women's Studies International Forum* 24 (2001): 653–68.
Roberts, Suzanne. "Contexts of Charity in the Middle Ages: Religious, Social, and Civic." Pages 24–53 in *Contexts of Charity in the Middle Ages: Religious, Social, and Civic*. Edited by Jerome B. Schneewind. Bloomington: Indiana University Press, 1996.
Robinson, Brandon Andrew. "Doing Sexual Responsibility: HIV, Risk Discourses, Trust, and Gay Men Interacting Online." *Sociological Perspectives* 61 (2018): 383–98.
Rodman, Gilbert. *Why Cultural Studies?* Chichester: Wiley-Blackwell, 2014.
Rodríguez, José L. "Contamination and Transformation: A Kristevan Reading of Luis Buñuel's *Viridiana*." *Studies in Hispanic Cinema* 1 (2005): 169–80,
Rodríguez Gómez, Federico. "Francis Bacon: Notas sobre la carnalidad." *Investigaciones Fenomenológicas* 2 (2010): 399–410.
Rohrbaugh, Richard L. "The Pre-industrial City in Luke-Acts." Pages 129–43 in *The Social World of Luke-Acts: Models for Interpretation*. Edited by Jerome H. Neyrey. Peabody, MA: Hendrickson,1991.
Romero Losacco, José. *Pensar distinto, pensar de(s)colonial*. Caracas: Editorial El Perro y la Rana, 2021.
Rosenblum, Robert. "Caritas Romana after 1760; Some Romantic Lactations." Pages 46–63 in *Woman as Sex Object: Studies in Erotic Art*.

Edited by Thomas B. Hess and Linda Nochlin. New York: Newsweek, 1972.

Rosenthal, Lisa. *Gender, Politics, and Allegory in the Art of Rubens*. New York: Cambridge University Press, 2005.

Rotheram-Borus, M. J., D. Flannery, E. Rice, and P. Lester. "Families Living with HIV." *AIDS Care* 17.8 (2005): 978–87.

Rowe, Mark. *God's Kingdom and God's Son: The Background to Mark's Christology from Concepts of Kingship in the Psalms*. Leiden: Brill, 2002.

Royalty, Robert M. *The Streets of Heaven: The Ideology of Wealth in the Apocalypse of John*. Macon, GA: Mercer University Press, 1998.

Royster, Paula D. *Decolonizing Arts-Based Methodologies: Researching the African Diaspora*. Leiden: Brill, 2021.

Rubin, Gayle S. "Thinking Sex: Notes for a Radical Theory of the Politics of Sexuality." Pages 143–78 in *Culture, Society and Sexuality*. Edited by Richard Parker and Peter Aggleton. London: Routledge, 2006.

Rubin, Miri. *Mother of God: A History of the Virgin Mary*. New Haven: Yale University Press, 2009.

Rueda, Carolina. "Mise en abyme, parodia y violencia en La ultima cena de Tomás Gutiérrez Alea." *Apuntes Hispánicos* 9 (2008): 17–26.

Runesson, Anna. *Exegesis in the Making: Postcolonialism and New Testament Studies*. BibInt 103. Leiden: Brill, 2010.

Runions, Erin. *The Babylon Complex: Theopolitical Fantasies of War, Sex, and Sovereignty*. New York: Fordham University Press, 2014.

Russell, John. *Francis Bacon*. London: Thames & Hudson, 1993.

Ryan, Michael. "Introduction to the Encyclopedia of Literary and Cultural Theory." Pages xiii–xx in vol. 1 of *The Encyclopedia of Literary and Cultural Theory*. Edited by Michael Ryan. 3 vols. Chichester: Wiley-Blackwell, 2011.

Salter, Gregory. *Art and Masculinity in Post-war Britain: Reconstructing Home*. London: Routledge, 2020.

Samuelsson, Gunnar. *Crucifixion in Antiquity: An Inquiry into the Background of the New Testament Terminology of Crucifixion*. WUNT 310. Tübingen: Mohr Siebeck, 2011.

Sánchez Rodríguez, Gabriel. "Viridiana: La perversión de la miseria." *Comunicación y Hombre* (2016): 191–207.

Sánchez-Biosca, Vicente. "Escenas de liturgia y perversión en la obra de Buñuel." *Archivos de la Filmoteca: Valencia: Filmoteca de la Generalitat Valenciana* 35 (2000): 8–25

———. "El intertexto religioso en Viridiana (Luis Buñuel)." *Intertextualitat i recepció* 11 (1998): 135–43.
Santos, Boaventura de Sousa. *The End of the Cognitive Empire*. Durham, NC: Duke University Press, 2018.
———. *Epistemologies of the South: Justice against Epistemicide*. Boulder, CO: Paradigm, 2014.
Sawyer, John F. A. *Sacred Languages and Sacred Texts: Religion in the First Christian Centuries*. London: Routledge, 1999.
Scarry, Elaine. *The Body in Pain: The Making and Unmaking of the World*. Oxford: Oxford University Press, 1987.
Schmied, Virginia, and Deborah Lupton. "Blurring the Boundaries: Breastfeeding and Maternal Subjectivity." Pages 15–31 in *Abjectly Boundless: Boundaries, Bodies and Health Work*. Edited by Trudy Rudge and Dave Holmes. Farnham: Ashgate, 2010.
Schnackenburg, Rudolf. *The Gospel of Matthew*. Grand Rapids: Eerdmans, 2002.
Schneiders, Sandra M. "The Foot Washing (John 13:1–20): An Experiment in Hermeneutics." *CBQ* 43 (1981): 76–92.
Schoenfeld, Heather. *Building the Prison State: Race and the Politics of Mass Incarceration*. Chicago Series in Law and Society. Chicago: University of Chicago Press, 2018.
Schroeder, Paul A. *Tomás Gutiérrez Alea: The Dialectics of a Filmmaker*. New York: Routledge, 2016.
Schüssler Fiorenza, Elisabeth. "Changing the Paradigms: Toward a Feminist Future of the Biblical Past." Pages 289–306 in *The Future of the Biblical Past: Envisioning Biblical Studies on a Global Key*. Edited by Fernando F. Segovia and Roland Boer. SemeiaSt 66. Atlanta: Society of Biblical Literature, 2012.
———. *Democratizing Biblical Studies: Toward an Emancipatory Educational Space*. Louisville: Westminster John Knox, 2009.
———. *Rhetoric and Ethic: The Politics of Biblical Studies*. Minneapolis: Fortress, 1999.
———. *Wisdom Ways: Introducing Feminist Biblical Interpretation*. Maryknoll, NY: Orbis Books, 2001.
Schüssler Fiorenza, Elisabeth, and Kent Harold Richards, eds. *Transforming Graduate Biblical Education: Ethos and Discipline*. GPBS 10. Atlanta: Society of Biblical Literature, 2010.
Schwartzberg, Steven. *A Crisis of Meaning How Gay Men Are Making Sense of AIDS*. New York: Oxford University Press, 1996.

Scott, Darieck. *Extravagant Abjection: Blackness, Power, and Sexuality in the African American Literary Imagination*. New York: New York University Press, 2010.

Sedgwick, Eve Kosofsky. "Paranoid Reading and Reparative Reading, or, You're So Paranoid, You Probably Think This Essay Is about You." Pages 123–52 in *Touching Feeling: Affect, Pedagogy, Performativity*. Durham, NC: Duke University Press, 2003.

Seesengood, Robert Paul. *Competing Identities: The Athlete and the Gladiator in Early Christianity*. New York: T&T Clark, 2006.

Segovia, Fernando F. "'And They Began to Speak in Other Tongues': Competing Modes of Discourse in Contemporary Biblical Criticism." Pages 1–32 in *Social Location and Biblical Interpretation in the United States*. Vol. 1 of *Reading from This Place*. Edited by Fernando F. Segovia and Mary Ann Tolbert. Minneapolis: Fortress, 1995.

———. "Criticism in Critical Times: Reflections on Vision and Task." *JBL* 134 (2015): 6–29.

———. "Cultural Criticism: Expanding the Scope of Biblical Criticism." Pages 307–36 in *The Future of the Biblical Past: Envisioning Biblical Studies on a Global Key*. Edited by Fernando F. Segovia and Roland Boer. SemeiaSt 66. Atlanta: Society of Biblical Literature, 2012.

———. *Decolonizing Biblical Studies: A View from the Margins*. Maryknoll, NY: Orbis Books, 2000.

———. "John 13:1–20, The Footwashing in the Johannine Tradition." *ZNW* 73 (2009): 31–51.

Seo, Pyung Soo. *Luke's Jesus in the Roman Empire and the Emperor in the Gospel of Luke*. Eugene, OR: Pickwick, 2015.

Shaner, Katherine A. "The Danger of Singular Saviors: Women, Slaves, and Jesus's Disturbance in the Temple (Mark 11:15–19)." *JBL* 140 (2021): 39–61.

———. *Enslaved Leadership in Early Christianity*. New York: Oxford University Press, 2018.

Shaw, J. F., trans. *On Christian Doctrine: St. Augustine*. Mineola, NY: Dover, 2012.

Shaw, Stacey A., and Nabila El-Bassel. "The Influence of Religion on Sexual HIV Risk." *AIDS and Behavior* 18 (2014): 1569–94.

Sheppard, Beth M. *The Craft of History and the Study of the New Testament*. RBS 60. Atlanta: Society of Biblical Literature, 2012.

Shults, LeRon, and Jan-Olav Henriksen, eds. *Saving Desire: The Seduction of Christian Theology*. Grand Rapids: Eerdmans, 2011.

Sielke, Sabine. "Phallic Mother." Page 432 in *Encyclopedia of Feminist Literary Theory*. Edited by Elizabeth Kowalewski-Wallace. New York: Garland, 1997.
Simon, Samuel. *A Postcolonial Reading of Mark's Story of Jesus*. LNTS 340. London: T&T Clark, 2007.
Sloyan, Gerard Stephen. *The Crucifixion of Jesus: History, Myth, Faith*. Minneapolis: Fortress, 1995.
Smith, Julia H., and Alan Whiteside. "The History of AIDS Exceptionalism." *Journal of the International AIDS Society* 13.1 (2010): 1–8.
Smith, Mitzi J., and Yung Suk Kim. *Toward Decentering the New Testament: A Reintroduction*. Eugene, OR: Cascade, 2018.
Smith, Paul, ed. *The Renewal of Cultural Studies*. Philadelphia: Temple University Press, 2011.
Smith, Terence V. *Petrine Controversies in Early Christianity: Attitudes toward Peter in Christian Writing of the First Two Centuries*. WUNT 15. Tübingen: Mohr Siebeck, 1985.
Sneed, Roger A. *Representations of Homosexuality: Black Liberation Theology and Cultural Criticism*. Basingstoke: Palgrave Macmillan, 2010.
Soble, Alan. *The Structure of Love*. New Haven: Yale University Press, 1990.
Sobrino, Jon. *Jesus in Latin America*. Eugene, OR: Wipf & Stock, 2004.
———. *No Salvation outside the Poor: Prophetic-Utopian Essays*. Maryknoll, NY: Orbis Books, 2008.
———. *The True Church and the Poor*. Maryknoll, NY: Orbis Books, 1984.
———. *Witnesses to the Kingdom: The Martyrs of El Salvador and the Crucified Peoples*. Maryknoll, NY: Orbis Books, 2003.
Söding, Thomas. "Die Macht der Wahrheit und das Reich der Freiheit: Zur johanneischen Deutung des Pilatus-Prozesses (Joh 18,28–19,16)." *ZTK* 93 (1996): 35–58.
Sontag, Susan. *Regarding the Pain of Others*. London: Penguin, 2019.
Spicq, Ceslas. *Agape in the New Testament*. St. Louis: Herder, 1963.
Spurlin, William J. *Imperialism within the Margins: Queer Representation and the Politics of Culture in Southern Africa*. New York: Palgrave Macmillan, 2006.
Steinberg, Leo. *The Sexuality of Christ in Renaissance Art and in Modern Oblivion*. New York: Pantheon, 1984.
Sterling, Gregory E. "*Mors philosophi*: The Death of Jesus in Luke." *HTR* 94 (2001): 383–402.
Stevens, Mark, and Annalyn Swan. *Francis Bacon: Revelations*. New York: Knopf, 2020.

Stewart, Alistair C. *Breaking Bread: The Emergence of Eucharist and Agape in Early Christian Communities*. Grand Rapids: Eerdmans, 2023.

Stockton, Kathryn Bond. *Beautiful Bottom, Beautiful Shame: Where "Black" Meets "Queer."* Durham, NC: Duke University Press, 2006.

Stone, Ken. "Bibles That Matter: Biblical Theology and Queer Performativity." *BTB* 38 (2008): 14–25.

Strange, James F. "Tombs, the New Testament and the Archaeology of Religion." *RevExp* 106 (2009): 399–419.

Straumann, Benajamin. "*Oikeiosis* and *Appetitus Societatis*: Hugo Grotius' Ciceronian Argument for Natural Law and Just War." *Grotiana* 24–25 (2003–2004): 41–66.

Strecker, George. *Der Weg der Gerechtigkeit: Untersuchung zur Theologie des Matthäus*. Göttingen: Vanderhoeck & Ruprecht, 1971.

Sugirtharajah, R. S. *Exploring Postcolonial Biblical Criticism: History, Method, Practice*. Chichester: Wiley-Blackwell, 2012.

Suh, Joong Suk. "Das Weltgericht und di Matthäische Gemeinde." *NovT* 48 (2006): 217–33.

Sundt, Catherine. "Religion and Power: The Appropriation of Da Vinci's *The Last Supper* in *Viridiana* and *L'última cena*." *Romance Notes* 49 (2009): 71–79.

Susser, Ida. *AIDS, Sex, and Culture: Global Politics and Survival in Southern Africa*. Chichester: Wiley, 2011.

Szkredka, Slawomir. *Sinners and Sinfulness in Luke: A Study of Direct and Indirect References in the Initial Episodes of Jesus/ Activity*. WUNT 434. Tübingen: Mohr Siebeck, 2017.

Talvacchia, Kathleen T. "Disrupting the Theory-Practice Binary." Pages 184–94 in *Queer Christianities: Lived Religion in Transgressive Forms*. Edited by Michael F. Pettinger, Kathleen Talvacchia, and Mark Larrimore. New York: New York University Press, 2015.

Támez, Elsa. *Bajo un cielo sin estrellas: Lecturas y meditaciones bíblicas*. Sabnilla: Departamento Ecuménico de Investigaciones, 2001.

Theobald, Michael. "Gattungswandel in der johanneischen Passionserzählung: Die Verhöre Jesu durch Pilatus (Johannes 18,33–38; 19,8–12) im Licht der *Acta Isidori* und anderer Prozessdialoge." Pages 447–83 in *Studies in the Gospel of John and Its Christology*. Edited by Joseph Verheyden, Geert Van Oyen, Michael Labahn, and Reimund Bieringer. BETL 265. Leuven: Peeters 2014.

Thomas, John C. *Footwashing in John 13 and the Johannine Community*. JSNTSup 61. Sheffield: JSOT Press, 1991.

Thomas, Owen C. "Theology and Experience." *HTR* 78 (1985): 179–201.
Thompson, Marianne M. "'His Own Received Him Not': Jesus Washes the Feet of His Disciples." Pages 258–73 in *The Art of Reading the Scripture*. Edited by Ellen F. Davis and Richard B. Hays. Grand Rapids: Eerdmans, 2003.
Tin, Louis-Georges. *The Invention of Heterosexual Culture*. Cambridge: MIT Press, 2012.
Toensing, Holly Joan. "Living among the Tombs: Society, Mental Illness, and Self-Destruction in Mark 5:1–20. Pages 131–43 in *This Abled Body: Rethinking Disabilities in Biblical Studies*. Edited by Hector Avalos, Sarah J. Melcher, and Jeremy Schipper. SemeiaSt 55. Atlanta: Society of Biblical Literature, 2007.
Tombs, David. "Honor, Shame, and Conquest: Male Identity, Sexual Violence, and the Body Politic." *Journal of Hispanic/Latino Theology* 9 (2002): 21–40.
———. "Prisoner Abuse: From Abu Ghraib to *The Passion of the Christ*." Pages 175–201 in *Religion and the Politics of Peace and Conflict*. Edited by Linda Hogan and Dylan Lee Lerhke. Eugene, OR: Pickwick, 2009.
Tombs, David, and Jayme R. Reaves. "#MeToo Jesus: Naming Jesus as a Victim of Sexual Abuse." *International Journal of Public Theology* 13 (2019): 387–412.
Tomkins, Silvan. *Shame and Its Sisters: A Silvan Tomkins Reader*. Edited by Eve Kosofsky Sedgwick and Adam Frank. Durham, NC: Duke University Press, 1971.
Tonstad, Linn Marie. "The Limits of Inclusion: Queer Theology and its Others." *Theology & Sexuality* 21 (2015): 1–19.
Tops, Thomas. "Transforming Historical Objectivism into Historical Hermeneutics: From 'Historical Illness' to Properly Lived Historicality." *Neue Zeitschrift für Systematische Theologie und Religionsphilosophie* 61 (2019): 490–515.
Townes, Emilie Maureen. *Womanist Ethics and the Cultural Production of Evil*. Basingstoke: Palgrave Macmillan, 2007.
Townsley, Jeramy. "Paul, the Goddess Religions, and Queer Sects: Romans 1:23–28." *JBL* 130 (2011): 707–28.
Tracy, David. "The Divided Consciousness of Augustine on Eros." Pages 91–106 in *Erotikon: Essays on Eros, Ancient and Modern*. Edited by Shadi Bartsch and Thomas Bartscherer. Chicago: University of Chicago Press, 2005.

Tuhkanen, Mikko. *Leo Bersani: Queer Theory and Beyond*. Albany: SUNY Press, 2014.

Twelftree, Graham. "Deliverance and Exorcism in the New Testament." Pages 45–68 in *Exorcism and Deliverance: Multi-disciplinary Studies*. Edited by William K. Kay and Robin A. Parry. Milton Keynes: Paternoster, 2011.

Ulansey, David. "The Heavenly Veil Torn: Mark's Cosmic *Inclusio*." *JBL* 110 (1991): 123–25.

Vaage, Leif E. "An Other Home: Discipleship in Mark as Domestic Asceticism." *CBQ* 71 (2009): 741–61.

Vacek, Edward Collin. "Love, Christian and Diverse: A Response to Colin Grant." *JRE* 24 (1996) 29–34.

———. *Love, Human and Divine: The Heart of Christian Ethics*. Washington, DC: Georgetown University Press, 1994.

Valdés, Hernán. *Tejas verdes: Diario de un campo de concentración en Chile*. Barcelona: Laia, 1974.

Van Oyen, Geert, and Patty Van Cappellen. "Mark 15:34 and the Sitz im Leben of the Real Reader." *ETL* 91 (2015): 569–99.

Vander Stichele, Caroline. "The Head of John and Its Reception or How to Conceptualize 'Reception History.'" Pages 79–93 in *Reception History and Biblical Studies*. Edited by Emma England and John Lyons. London: Bloomsbury T&T Clark, 2015.

Vander Stichele, Caroline, and Todd Penner. "Mastering the Tools or Retooling the Masters? The Legacy of Historical-Critical Discourse." Pages 1–30 in *Her Master's Tools? Feminist and Postcolonial Engagements of Historical-Critical Discourse*. Edited by Caroline Vander Stichele and Todd Penner. GPBS 9. Atlanta: Society of Biblical Literature, 2005.

Vargas, Alicia. "Who Ministers to Whom: Matthew 25:31–46 and Prison Ministry." *Dialog* 52 (2013): 128–37.

Velden, Nina Müller van. "When Gender Performance Is Not Straightforward: Feet, Masculinity and Power in John 13:1–11." *Neot* 53 (2019): 291–309.

Verburg, Winfried. *Passion als Tragödie? Die literarische Gattung der antiken Tragödie als Gestaltungsprinzip der Johannespassion*. SBS 182. Stuttgart: Verlag Katholisches Bibelwerk 1999.

Vigil, José María, and Leonardo Boff. *La opción por los pobres*. Presencia Teológica. Santander: Sal Terrae, 1991.

———. ¿Qué es optar por los pobres? Evangelio con rostro Latinoamericano. Santa Fé de Bogotá: Ediciones Paulinas, 1994.
Vigil, María López, Jon Sobrino, and Rafael Díaz-Salazar. *La matanza de los pobres: Vida en medio de la muerte en El Salvador*. Madrid: HOAC, 1993.
Wachsmuth, Curt, and Otto Hense, eds. *Ioannis Stobaei Anthologium*. 5 vols. Berlin: Weidmann, 1884.
Wachtel, Klaus, and Michael W. Holmes, eds. *The Textual History of the Greek New Testament: Changing Views in Contemporary Research*. TCS 8. Atlanta: Society of Biblical Literature, 2011.
Wadell, Paul J. *The Primacy of Love: An Introduction to the Ethics of Thomas Aquinas*. New York: Paulist, 1992.
Wakefield, Sara, and Christopher Uggen. "Incarceration and Stratification." *Annual Review of Sociology* 36 (2010): 387–406.
Walatka, Todd. "Principle of Mercy: Jon Sobrino and the Catholic Theological Tradition." *TS* 77 (2016): 96–117.
Wardle, Timothy. "Mark, the Jerusalem Temple and Jewish Sectarianism: Why Geographical Proximity Matters in Determining the Provenance of Mark." *NTS* 62 (2016): 60–78.
Warner, Michael. "Introduction." Pages vii–xxxi in *Fear of a Queer Planet: Queer Politics and Social Theory*. Edited by Michael Warner. Minneapolis: University of Minnesota Press, 1993.
———. *The Trouble with Normal: Sex, Politics, and the Ethics of Queer Life*. New York: Free Press, 1999.
Warren, Calvin. *Ontological Terror: Blackness, Nihilism, and Emancipation*. Durham, NC: Duke University Press, 2018.
Washington, Harold C., Susan Lochrie, and Pamela Thimmes, eds. *Escaping Eden: New Feminist Perspectives on the Bible*. BibSem 65. Sheffield: Sheffield Academic, 1998.
Waters, Kenneth L. "Jesus and the Passover in Mark 14:1–12: A Chronological Confusion?" *Studia Biblica Slovaca* 12 (2022): 180–210.
Watt, Jan G. van der. "The Meaning of Jesus Washing the Feet of His Disciples (John 13)." *Neot* 51 (2017): 25–39.
Watts, Galen, and Sharday Morusinjohn. "Can Critical Religion Play by Its Own Rules? Why There Must Be More Ways to Be 'Critical' in the Study of Religion." *JAAR* 90 (2022): 1–18.
Weber, Kathleen. "The Image of Sheep and Goats in Matthew 25:31–46." *CGQ* 59 (1997): 657–78.

Weheliye, Alexander G. *Habeas Viscus: Racializing Assemblages, Biopolitics, and Black Feminist Theories of the Human.* Durham, NC: Duke University Press, 2014.

Weine, Stevan M. *Testimony after Catastrophe: Narrating the Traumas of Political Violence.* Evanston, IL: Northwestern University Press, 2006.

Weiss, Margot Danielle. *Techniques of Pleasure: BDSM and the Circuits of Sexuality.* Durham, NC: Duke University Press, 2011.

Wenkel, David H. *Jesus' Crucifixion Beatings and the Book of Proverbs.* London: Springer, 2018.

West, Dennis. "Esclavitud y cine en Cuba: El caso de La última cena." Pages 157–70 in *Tomás Gutiérrez Alea: Poesía y revolución.* Edited by Tomás Gutiérrez Alea. Gran Canaria: Filmoteca Canaria, 1994.

Western, Bruce. *Homeward: Life in the Year after Prison.* New York: Russell Sage Foundation, 2018.

———. *Punishment and Inequality in America.* New York: Russell Sage, 2006.

Western, Bruce, Anthony A. Braga, Jaclyn Davis, and Catherine Sirois. "Stress and Hardship after Prison." *American Journal of Sociology* 120 (2015): 1512–47.

Whitaker, Robyn. "A Failed Spectacle: The Role of the Crowd in Luke 23." *BibInt* 25 (2017): 399–416.

———. "Rebuke or Recall? Rethinking the Role of Peter in Mark's Gospel?" *CBQ* 75 (2013): 666–82.

White, Heather R. *Reforming Sodom: Protestants and the Rise of Gay Rights.* Chapel Hill: University of North Carolina Press, 2015.

Whittaker, Andrea M. "Living with HIV: Resistance by Positive People." *Medical Anthropology Quarterly* 6 (1992): 385–90.

Wiarda, Timothy. "Peter as Peter in the Gospel of Mark," *NTS* 45 (1999): 19–37.

Wiebe, Gregory David. "The Demonic Phenomena of Mark's 'Legion': Evaluating Postcolonial Understandings of Demon Possession." Pages 189–212 in *Exegesis in the Making: Postcolonialism and New Testament Studies,* by Anna Runesson. BibInt 103. Leiden: Brill, 2011.

Wildeman, Christopher, and Bruce Western. "Incarceration in Fragile Families." *Future of Children* 20 (2010): 157–77.

Williams, Ritva H. "The Mother of Jesus at Cana: A Social-Science Interpretation of John 2:1–2." *CBQ* 59 (1997): 679–92.

Wilson, Brittany E. "The Blinding of Paul and the Power of God: Masculinity, Sight, and Self-Control." *JBL* 133 (2014): 367–86.

Wilson, Carol Bakker. *For I Was Hungry and You Gave Me Food: Pragmatics of Food Access in the Gospel of Matthew*. Eugene, OR: Pickwick, 2014.

Wimbush, Vincent L. *Black Flesh Matters: Essays on Runagate Interpretation*. Lanham, MD: Lexington/Fortress Academic, 2022.

———. "Signifying on the Fetish: Mapping a New Critical Orientation." Pages 337–348 in *The Future of the Biblical Past: Envisioning Biblical Studies on a Global Key*. Edited by Fernando F. Segovia and Roland Boer. SemeiaSt 66. Atlanta: Society of Biblical Literature, 2012.

———, ed. *Theorizing Scriptures: New Critical Orientations to a Cultural Phenomenon*. New Brunswick: Rutgers University Press, 2008.

———. *White Men's Magic: Scripturalization as Slavery*. Oxford: Oxford University Press, 2012.

Winn, Adam. "The Good News of Isaiah and Rome in Mark 1:1." Pages 95–108 in *New Studies in Textual Interplay*. Edited by Craig A. Evans, B. J. Oropeza, and Paul Sloan. London: Bloomsbury, 2020.

Winterer, Caroline. *The Mirror of Antiquity: American Women and the Classical Tradition, 1750–1900*. Ithaca, NY: Cornell University Press, 2007.

Witherington, Ben, III. *Making a Meal of It: Rethinking the Theology of the Lord's Supper*. Waco, TX: Baylor University Press, 2007.

Wolter, Michael. *The Gospel according to Luke: Volume I (Luke 1–9)*. Waco, TX: Baylor University Press, 2016.

Yalom, Marilyn. *A History of the Breast*. New York: Knopf, 1997.

Young, Stephen L. "Let's Take the Text Seriously." *Method and Theory in the Study of Religion* 32 (2020): 328–63.

Yountae, An. *The Coloniality of the Secular: Race, Religion, and Poetics of World-Making*. Durham, NC: Duke University Press, 2024.

———. "Decolonial Theory of Religion: Race, Coloniality, and Secularity in the Americas." *JAAR* 88 (2020): 947–80.

Zabus, Chantal. *Out in Africa: Same-Sex Desire in Sub-Saharan Literatures and Cultures*. Suffolk: Currey, 2013.

Zeki, Semir, and Tomohiro Ishizu. "The 'Visual Shock' of Francis Bacon: An Essay in Neuroesthetics." *Frontiers in Human Neuroscience* 7 (2013): art. 850. https://doi.org/10.3389/fnhum.2013.00850.

Zournazi, Mary. *Hope: New Philosophies for Change*. New York: Routledge, 2003.

Zumstein, Jean. *Kreative Erinnerung: Relecture und Auslegung im Johannesevangelium*. 2nd ed. ATANT 84. Zürich: Theologischer Verlag 2004.

ANCIENT SOURCES INDEX

Hebrew Bible

1 Samuel
  25:41 — 162

Psalms
  69:22 — 125

Isaiah
  58:7 — 76
  65:4 — 152

Ancient Jewish Writers

Josephus, *Jewish Antiquities*
  17.354–355 — 110
  18.1–10 — 110
  19.157 — 150
  26–27 — 110

Josephus, *Jewish War*
  2.75 — 110
  2.167 — 110
  2.241 — 110
  2.253 — 110
  2.305–308 — 110
  5.449 — 110
  5.451 — 110–11

Philo, *De Iosepho*
  8.38–39 — 151–52

Philo, *In Flaccum*
  95 — 150

Second Testament

Matthew
  8:28–34 — 136
  14:19 — 163
  15:36 — 163
  25:31–46 — 65–95, 137
  26:17–30 — 161
  26:22 — 161
  26:26 — 163
  26:47–27:56 — 125
  27:46 — 125
  27:52 — 125

Mark
  1:1 — 57, 113
  1:10–11 — 115
  1:16 — 113–14
  1:23 — 152
  1:24 — 155
  3:11 — 152
  3:14 — 114
  3:16 — 114
  3:19 — 114
  5:5 — 140–41, 149
  5:7 — 155
  5:8 — 149
  5:33 — 152
  6:41 — 163
  6:49 — 152
  7:25 — 152
  8:6 — 163
  8:22–26 — 113–14
  8:34–9:2 — 114
  9:12 — 122

Mark (*continued*)

9:31	114	6:47	153
10:28	113	7:7	153
10:32–33	114	8:1	149, 153
11:1–21	114–16	8:4	149–50, 152
11:27–34	116	8:11	153
12:1–12	116	8:26–39	129–160
13:2	115	8:40	150
13:5	116	8:47	152
13:9–12	114, 121	9:16	163
13:14	116	9:26	153
13:26	116, 121	9:35	154–55
13:31	121	9:38–39	150
14:1–21	114, 116, 161	9:52	150
14:22	163	9:58	150
14:41	114	10:38	150
14:43	107, 111	10:39	153
14:50	111, 114	11:27	154
14:53	107, 111	11:28	153
14:54	111	11:37–52	150
14:55–56	118	12:10	153
14:58	111, 115	12:52–53	151
14:61	111	14:26	151
14:62	111, 116	15:11–32	151
14:65	107	16:2	153
14:67	114	17:13	154
14:70	114	19:5	150
14:72	114	20:3	153
15:1–39	97–127	22:1–6	161
		22:7–39	161
		22:19	163

Luke

		23:9	153
1:2	153	23:23	154
1:38	217	24:17	153
1:76	156	23:45	125
3:4	153	23:46	124
3:22	154–5	24:29–30	150
4:18	150		
4:22	153	John	
4:27	150	6:11	163
4:31–36	151	6:51c–58	163
4:33	150, 152, 154–55	10:10	167
4:38	150	13:1	195, 197
5:1	153	13:1–37	115–116, 161–189
5:17	150	14:15	162
5:27–29	150	14:21	162

14:23	162	27.2	150
14:24	162	79.2	150
15:12	162		
15:17	162	Polybius, *Histories*	
19:11	125	3.82.8	150
19:30	125		
19:34	163	Valerius Maximus, *Facta et Dicta Memorabilia*	

Acts

		5.4	74, 78, 89
2:18	217		
3:2	151		
4:29	217		
6:12	150		
8:3	217		
9:1–8	191–225		
13–14	217		
16:6–10	218		
16:17	217–18		
19:29	150		
20:19	217–18		
20:22	218		
22:4–5	217		
24:25	217		
26:9–11	217		
26:24–25	217		
27:17–36	150, 217		

Greco-Roman Literature

Cicero, *De finibus*
   3.63   153

Cicero, *De officiis*
   1.50   154

Cicero, *De legibus*
   1.22   154
   1.32   154

Dio Chrysostom, *Kingship Orations*
   4   152

Dionysius of Halicarnassus, *Roman Antiquities*
   6.26   150

MODERN AUTHORS INDEX

Abbott, Jack Henry	129, 139	Bazzana, Giovanni B.	147
Abogunrin, Samuel O.	151	Beal, Timothy K.	58–59, 202
Ådna, Jostein	118	Beavis, Mary Ann	162
Aernie, Jeffrey W.	105	Becker, Eve-Marie	32, 54
Agamben, Giorgio	135	Beckford, Robert	150
Aguero, Eduardo Emilio	167	Beedon, David K.	130
Aguilar Chiu, José Enrique	105, 117	Behar, Olga	120
Aichele, George	2, 41	Benéitez Rodríguez, Manuel	126
Alexander, Claire	40	Berdini, Paolo	89, 204
Alexander, Michelle	137	Berger, Dan	137
Allison, Dale C. Jr.	125	Berlant, Lauren	90–91
Althaus-Reid, Marcela	28, 65–68, 196, 199	Bersani, Leo	87, 198, 205–216, 222
		Berthier, Nancy	173
Anderson, Gary A.	75	Bérubé, Michael	52
Anderson, Janice Capel	34, 51	Best, Ernest	113
Ángel Ferrando, Miguel	9	Birke, Lynda	120
Ankrah, Maxine	192	Black, Fiona C.	31
Anzaldúa, Gloria	220	Boehler, Genilma	66
Apata, Temidayo	192	Boer, Roland	14, 233
Aquinas, Thomas	68	Boff, Leonardo	10, 28, 75
Arcadi, James	162	Bonavía, Pablo	29
Arendt, Hannah	69	Bond, Helen	104, 127
Arya, Rina	156–57	Bor, Robert	192
Augustine	68–72	Bose, Joerg	142
Avalos, Hector	7	Boyarin, Jonathan	233
Bailey, Randall C.	15	Braga, Anthony A.	158
Bal, Mieke	60, 202	Brandon, S. G. F.	116
Ballengee, Jennifer R.	105	Brett, Mark G.	42
Barclay, John	49	Brintnall, Kent L.	199, 213, 216, 222
Barmania, Sima	192	Brown, Vincent	137
Barr, James	71	Bruner, Frederick Dale	77
Barreto, Eric D.	13	Buckhanon Crowder, Stephanie	230
Barthes, Roland	55	Budde, Mitzi	130
Bartholomew, Craig	7	Buell, Denise Kimber	15
Bauckham, Richard	113, 166–68	Burchardt, Marian	193

Burkett, Delbert Royce	3	Craghan, John F.	159
Burnaby, John	70	Crook, Zeba	14
Burrus, Virginia	68–69, 94–95	Crosby, Christina	158
Butler, Judith	24	Crossan, John	14
Byron, John	218	Crossley, James G.	202
Califia, Pat	92	Crowder, Stephanie Buckhanon	230
Campbell, William S.	105	Cruz, Jon	50–51
Capánaga, Victorino	70	Culpepper, Alan R.	165
Careri, Giovanni	212	Cupples, Julie	18
Carey, Greg	13	Dashke, Dereck	121
Carr, David McLain	68	Davidson, Steed	6
Carroll, John T.	153	Davies, Philip R.	31
Carroll, Margaret D.	84, 86	Davis, Jaclyn	158
Carter, Warren	148, 159	Davis, Oliver	198, 223–24
Caruth, Cathy	119	Dawes, James	119
Casaldáliga, Pedro	75	Dawson, Barbara	156
Casassus, Juan	123	Dean, Tim	93, 198, 202–224
Casella, Jean	158	Deane, Kevin D.	192
Caserio, Robert L.	209	Decena, Carlos Ulises	65
Castelli, Elizabeth A.	219	Deering, Kathleen N.	192
Castillo, José	10, 28	Deleuze, Gilles	61, 145
Castro-Gómez, Santiago	18	Denbeaux, Mark	98
Cavadini, John C.	68	Derrida, Jacques	24, 71–72, 207
Chacón, Luis	155	Destro, Adriana	151, 169
Chambers, Samuel A.	153	Di Cesare, Donatella	123
Chance, J. Bradley	115, 122	Diebold-Scheuermann, Carola	125
Chapman, David W.	104	Dijk, Rijk van	193
Chare, Nicholas	156	Dijkhuizen, Petra	189
Charles, Ronald	162	Dilger, Hansjörg	193
Choi, Jin Young	62, 155	Dinkler, Michal Beth	36–37, 112–14, 153
Claassens, Juliana	54		
Clark-Soles, Jaime	164, 167	Dinovitzer, Ronit	130
Clear, Todd R.	130	Domínguez, Ana Lidia M.	121
Clum, John	45	Dormeyer, Detlev	126
Collins, John J.	13	Douglass, Frederick	50
Coloe, Mary	168	Dowd, Sharyn E.	105, 113
Comaroff, Jean	18	Driggers, Ira Brent	115
Comaroff, John L.	18	Dube, Musa W.	7, 194–95
Comfort, Megan	130	Dubler, Joshua	130
Cone, James	107	Dunning, Benjamin	91
Cook, Granger	104	Dussel, Enrique	18, 75
Cooke, Bernard	200	Dutoit, Ulysse	87, 209–213
Cooper, Kate	151	Eisenman, Stephen F.	97–99
Córdova Quero, Hugo	167	El-Bassel, Nabila	193
Couldry, Nick	47	Elliott, Dyan	83

Elliott, John H.	152	Ghannam, Jess	98
Eribon, Didier	196	Gibson, David	166
Erzen, Tanya	130	Gillman, Laura	46
Escobar, Arturo	18	Glancy, Jennifer A.	104, 162
Ese Ibomhen, Sylvester	9	Goldman, Eleanor	192
Eubank, Nathan	105	Goldstein, Warren	233
Euler, Alida	125	González Faus, José Ignacio	10, 28
Evans, C. Stephen	7	Grant, Colin	70
Evora, Jose Antoni	173	Grassian, Stuart	140
Exum, J. Cheryl	37, 89	Gray, Sherman	76–77
Fabre, Jean-Philippe	149	Green, Joel B.	149, 153, 155
Falkoff, Marc	97	Gregg, Melissa	47
Fanon, Frantz	147–48, 173	Grindheim, Sigurd	77
Farmer, Paul	192	Grosfoguel, Ramón	1, 5, 8, 18
Farmer, William	7	Grossberg, Lawrence	41, 43–44, 48
Febus Perez, Beatriz	66	Guattari, Félix	61
Fellner, Jamie	131	Guebara, Ivone	28
Felski, Rita	10–11, 31, 35, 51	Guenther, Lisa	138–40, 148
Feník, Juraj	168	Guijarro Oporto, Santiago	162
Ferrando, Miguel Ángel	9	Gunda, Masiiwa Ragies	195
Fifield, Peter	157	Gundry, Robert H.	76
Finaldi, Gabriele	100	Gupta, Nijay	3
Fiorani, Flavio	174	Gurtner, Daniel M.	117, 122
Foltz, Mary C.	198	Guth, Christine	160
Foucault, Michel	8, 24, 73, 91–92, 118, 132, 138, 195–96, 207, 213, 218	Gutiérrez Alea, Tomás	173
		Gutiérrez Gustavo	24, 28, 66–67, 75
Fraginals, Manuel Moreno	161, 169–71	Gutiérrez-Albilla, Julián Daniel	176
France, R. T.	112	Habermas, Jürgen	26
Franco, Konrad	132	Hagan, John	130
Fredrick, David	218	Häkkinen, Sakari	55
Freeman, Elizabeth	74, 202	Hale, Jane	157
Freud, Sigmund	71, 224	Hall, Stuart	45, 47–48, 50
Fricker, Miranda	9	Halperin, David	44–45, 91–92, 195
Frost, Natasha	130	Hammill, Graham L.	209
Frye, David L.	18	Harley, Felicity	104–105
Fuller, Samuel	132	Harrington, Daniel J.	217
Furey, Constance M.	200, 202	Harvey, David	50
García Olivo, Pedro	180–81	Hatina, Thomas R.	112
García Ruiz, Alicia	178, 180	Havard, John	172
Garrison, William Lloyd	50	Hawthorn, T.	159
Gates, Henry Louis Jr.	55	Hayes, Tom	85
Geddert, Timothy	117	Hays, Richard	56
Gelabert, Lino Cabezas	100	Healy, Mary	7
Gelpi, D. L.	199	Hedrick, Charles W.	216
Georgia, Allan	105	Heil, John Paul	116

Hellwig, Monika	199	Joe, Sean	130
Henao Castro, Andrés Fabían	160	John, Helen C.	41, 159
Henderson, Suzanne Watts	189	Johnson, Luke Timothy	149, 153, 217
Hengel, Martin	104, 124, 127	Johnston, Deborah	192
Henriksen, Jan-Olav	69	Jordan, Mark	74
Hernández, Juan Antonio	174	Joseph, Simon J.	104
Hernando, Victoria	192	Katz, Jonathan	194
Heyward, Carter	70	Keenan, James	75
Hidalgo, Jacqueline M.	6, 33, 52	Keith, Chris	105
Hoad, Neville Wallace	194	Keller, Catherine	68–69
Hobbs, Robert	182–83	Kelly, Kevin J.	192
Hodge, Caroline Johnson	49	Kelly, Shawn	7, 42
Hofius, Otfried	166	Kelly, Thomas M.	199
Hoke, Jimmy	91	Kilgore, James William	130
Hoke, Mateo	159	Kim, Doosuk	56
Hollander, John	56	Kim, Jean Kyoung	54
Hollenbach, Paul	148	Kim, Yung Suk	3
Hollywood, Amy M.	85	Kimondo, Stephen Simon	104
Holmes, Michael W.	53	Kinder, Marsha	178
Hong, Yan	192	King, Rebekka	233
Horrell, David G.	107	Kingsmill, Edmee	68
Horsley, Richard	148	Kireopoulos, Antonios	130
Horst, Pieter W. van der	68	Kitzberger, Ingrid Rosa	31, 168
Huebner, Daniel R.	24	Klingbeil, Gerald A.	164
Huffer, Lynne	196	Klinghardt, Matthias	148
Hultgren, Arland J.	166	Klinken, Andriaan S. van	195
Humphreys, Colin J.	162	Kloppenborg, John S.	116
Hunt, Steven A.	126	Koskenniemi, Erkki	124
Hurtado, Larry W.	216	Kotrosits, Maia	54, 199
Hylton, Richard	184	Kötting, Bernhard	166
Iñiguez, Isabel	29	Kowalski, Beate	126
Irigaray, Luce,	85–86, 212, 220–21	Kristeva, Julia	55
Ishizu, Tomohiro	157	Krüger, René	9
Isiorhovoja, Osbert Uyovwieyovwe	9	Kuecker, Aaron	218
Jackson, Howard M.	117	Kupers, Terry Allen	132, 137
Jackson, Timothy P.	68, 70–72, 83	Lacan, Jacques	85–86, 212
Jackson, Zakiyyah Imam	160	Lambert, Marie-Andrée	79
Jacob, Sharon	52–53	Lamoreaux, Jason T.	189
Jamison, Kay R.	140, 157	Landes, Paula Fredriksen	218
Jefferson, Tony	44	Lanzendörfer, Tim	11
Jennings, Mark A.	122	Lapko, Róbert	168
Jennings, Willie James	137	Latour, Bruno	11
Jensen, Robin	89	Lau, Markus	148
Jeong, Mark	124	Leonard, Ellen	199
Jewett, Robert.	164	Levi, Primo	119

Levinas, Emmanuel	142, 219–22	McRae, Rachel M.	189
Liem, Marieke	158	Medina, José	107
Liew, Tat-Siong Benny	6, 14–15, 54	Meganck, Tine	79
Lin, Yii-Jan	21	Mendieta, Eduwardo	23
Liu, Shao-hua	192	Mendoza, Breny	67
Lloyd, Vincent W.	130	Menéndez-Antuña, Luis	12, 67, 112, 121, 137, 196
Lochrie, Susan	42		
Löfstedt, Torsten	160	Menon, Madhavi	32, 184–85
Lofton, Kathryn	203	Mercer, Kobena	188
Lohse, Wolfram	166	Merleau-Ponty, Maurice	141
Lomax, Tamura	44–46	Metzger, James A.	134
Lopez, Davina C.	3	Metzner, Jeffrey L.	131
Losier, Tossaint	137	Middleton, Paul	112
Lozada, Francisco	32, 38	Mignolo, Walter D.	2, 18
Lugones, María	67	Miller, Jacques-Alain	85
Lundberg, Matthew D.	130	Miller, Julie B.	211
Lupton, Deborah	85	Miller, Riva	192
Luther, Martin	70	Miscall, Peter	2
Luz, Ulrich	76	Moffitt, David M.	122
Lynch, James P.	130	Moloney, Francis	163, 165, 168
Lyons, William	59–60, 202	Moore, Stephen D.	7, 10–11, 14, 23, 33, 36–37, 39, 51, 68, 94–95, 107, 195, 218, 222
Mackendrick, Karmen	92		
Maclean, Ian	82		
Maldonado-Torres, Nelson	18, 23–26, 173	Moraga, Cherríe	220
		Moreno Fraginals, Manuel	161, 169–71
Manent, Pierre	153	Morgan, Jon	60
Mannermaa, Tuomo	70	Morris, Leon	153
Marchal, Joseph A	91, 195, 219	Morusinjohn, Sharday	24
Marcus, Joel	105, 114	Moser, Antonio	65
Marcuse, Herbert	71	Moss, Candida	162
Mariategui, José Carlos	24–25	Motyer, Stephen	117
Marion, Jean-Luc	72	Moxnes, Halvor	148, 151
Markusse, Gabi	112	Moyise, Steve	56
Martin-Márquez, Susan	179	Mpolo, Aimé Mpevo	159
Martin, Dale	74, 194–95, 218	Mubanda Rasmussen, Louise	193
Martin, Richard T.	42	Muizelaar, Klaske	84
Martínez Herranz, Amparo	175	Mullett, Michael A.	87
Matera, Frank J.	77, 112	Musser, Amber Jamilla	203
Mathew, Bincy	116–117	Myles, Robert J.	150
Matson, Mark A.	116	Nadella, Raj	125
Mbembe, Achille	7, 132–33	Nagle, Brendan	151
McGowan, Andrew	163–164	Nasrallah, Laura Salah	58, 162
McKinlay, Judith	57	Neyrey, Jerome H.	168
McKinzie, Gregory	117	Nguyen, Tan Hoang	198, 203
McKnight, Scot	3	Nickelsburg, George W. E.	105

Niemand, Christoph	167–68	Poplutz, Uta	125
Nikolopoulos, Georgios	192	Prince, Deborah Thompson	219
Nilges, Mathias	11	Przybylski, Benno	77
Nisula, Kirsi	124	Punt, Jeremy	42
Nisula, Timo	69	Quijano, Aníbal	18, 23, 25
Nobus, Dany	212	Rae, Murray	7
Nori, Franziska	156	Rahmsdorf, Olivia	168
Ntozi, J. P.	192	Rahner, Karl	200
Nygren, Anders	70–71	Rambo, Shelly	126
O'Kane, Martin	89	Rancière, Jacques	223–24
Odets, Walt	191	Raphael, Steven	130
Okantey, Peter Carlos	168	Rasing, Thera	193
Oliver Torelló, Juan Carlos	100	Reaves, Jayme R.	106
Omegwe, Godin	9	Reed, Esther	75
Oord, Thomas J.	70	Reiss, Michael J.	192
Oropeza, B. J.	55–57	Reiter, Keramet	132
Ostrow, Steven F.	87	Reventlow, Henning Graf	7
Outka, Gene	70	Rhoads, David M.	104
Oyen, Geert	105	Rhodes, Lorna A.	142
Park, Rohun	151	Rice, Peter	124
Park, Wongi	4, 8, 14–17, 22	Richards, Kent Harold	33
Parker, Angela	62, 230	Richardson, Michael	121
Parker, Holt N.	218	Ridgeway, James	158
Parkhurst, Justin O.	192	Riera, Emilio	177
Patler, Caitlin	132	Ringe, Christoper	130
Patterson, Amy S.	193	Rivera Zambrano, Jennifer	145
Patterson, Orlando	133, 136–37, 148	Rivera-Fuentes, Consuelo	120
Pattillo, Mary	130	Rivera, Mayra	199, 220–22
Paul, Herman	11	Roberts, Suzanne	75
Pearson, Brook W. R.	42	Robinson, Brandon Andrew	193
Pendergrass, Taylor	158	Rodman, Gilbert	40
Penner Lopez, Todd C.	2–3	Rodríguez Gómez, Federico	157
Penney, James	203	Rodríguez, José L.	177
Peppiat, Michael	142, 156	Rodríguez, M. Benéitex	126
Pérez Galdós, Benito	175	Rohrbaugh, Richard L.	149
Perez, Beatriz Febus	66	Romero, Losacco José	18
Perpich, Diane	221	Rosenblum, Robert	79, 83, 86
Pesce, Mauro	151, 169	Rosenthal, Lisa	81–82
Petro, Anthony	193–94	Rossi-Schrimpf, Inga	79
Phillips, Derek L.	84	Rotheram-Borus, M. J	192
Pieper, Josef	70	Rowe, Mark	112
Pippin, Tina	41	Royalty, Robert M.	42
Pitre, Brant	162	Royster, Paula D.	18
Pixley, Jorge	10, 28	Rubin, Gayle	224
Poirier, John C.	150	Rubin, Miri,	83

Rueda, Carolina	173	Smith, Julia	192
Ruiz, García	180	Smith, Mitzi J.	3
Runesson, Anna	2	Smith, Paul	57–58
Runions, Erin	52	Smith, Terence V.	113
Russell, John	156	Sneed, Roger A.	46
Ryan, Michel	36	Soble, Alan	71
Sabol, William J.	130	Sobrino, Jon	9–10, 66–67, 75, 107
Said, Edward	26	Söding, Thomas	126
Salter, Gregory	100	Sontag, Susan	127
Sampson, Robert J.	158	Spicq, Ceslas	70
Samuelsson, Gunnar	104, 124	Spivak, Gayatri Chakravorty	24, 26
Sánchez Rodríguez, Gabriel	180	Sprang, Sabine van	79
Sánchez-Biosca, Vicente	176, 178	Spronk, Klaas	54
Santos, Boaventura de Sousa	5, 12, 17–19	Spurlin, William J.	195
		Staley, Jeffrey L.	31
Sawyer, John F. A.	58	Steinberg, Leo	100
Scarry, Elaine	103, 106, 108–11, 117–19, 123, 126	Sterling, Gregory E.	125
		Stevens, Mark	142
Schmied, Virginia	85	Stewart, Alistair C.	164
Schnabel, Eckhard J.	104	Stjerna, Kirsi Irmeli	70
Schnackenburg, Rudolf	76	Stockton, Kathryn Bond	198
Schneiders, Sandra M.	169	Stoll, Michael A.	130
Schoenfeld, Heather	130	Stone, Ken	7
Schroeder, Paul	173–174	Strange, James F.	152
Schüssler Fiorenza, Elisabeth	2, 4, 7, 14–15, 33, 39, 51, 57	Straumann, Benjamin	154
		Strecker, George	77
Schwartz, David	48	Struthers Malbon, Elizabeth	105
Schwartzberg, Steven	191	Sugirtharajah, R. S.	7
Scott, Darieck	198, 203	Suh, Joong Suk	76–77
Sedgwick, Eve Kosofsky	11	Sundt, Catherine	176
Seesengood, Robert Paul	31	Susser, Ida	192
Segovia, Fernando F.	7, 14–15, 37–42, 61–62, 107, 165, 187, 200	Swan, Annalyn	142
		Szkredka, Slawomir	149
Seo, Pyung Soo	153	Talvacchia, Kathleen T.	200–201
Shaner, Katherine	23, 162	Tamayo, Juan José	28
Shaw, Stacey A.	193	Támez, Elsa	28–30
Sheppard, Beth M.	54	Theobald, Michael	125
Sherwood, Yvonne	7, 10, 11, 23, 33, 107	Thimmes, Pamela	42
Shourd, Sarah	158	Thomas, John C.	165–66
Shults, LeRon	69	Thomas, Owen C.	200
Sielke, Sabine,	82	Thompson, Marianne M.	166
Simon, Samuel	105	Tin, Louis-Georges	194
Sirois, Catherine	158	Toensing, Holly Joan	159
Sloyan, Garard Stephen	105	Tombs, David,	42, 106, 127
Smith, Abraham	39, 51	Tomkins, Silvan	85

Tonstad, Linn Marie	203	Whiteside, Alan	192
Toppari, Jorma	124	Whittaker, Andrea M.	192
Tops, Thomas	36	Wiarda, Timothy	113
Townes, Emilie	51	Wiebe, Gregory	148
Townsley, Jeramy	11	Wildeman, Christopher	130
Tracy, David.	69	Williams, Raymond	46
Tuhkanen, Mikko	216	Williams, Ritva H.	155
Twelftree, Graham	159	Wilson, Brittany E.	216–18, 222
Uggen, Christopher	130	Wilson, Carol Bakker	76
Ulansey, David	122	Wimbush, Vincent L.	6–7, 17, 31
Vaage, Leif E.	112–13	Winn, Adam	57
Vacek, Edward Collin	68, 70	Winterer, Caroline	86
Valdés, Hernán	103	Witherington, Ben, III	163
Van Alphen, Ernst	142–46	Wolter, Michael	149–50
Van Cappellen, Patty	105	Yalom, Marilyn,	83
Vander Stichele, Caroline	2, 60–61	Young, Stephen L.	48–50
Vargas, Alicia	77	Yountae, An	24–25, 232
Vattimo, Gianni	26	Zabus, Chantal	195
Velden, Nina Müller van	168	Zeki, Semir	157
Verburg, Winfried	125	Zirimenya, Samuel	192
Vigil, José María	10, 75	Zournazi, Mary	47
Vigil, María López	10	Zubaydah, Abu	98
Wachtel, Klaus	53	Zumstein, Jean	126
Wadell, Paul J.	68		
Wakefield, Sara	130		
Walatka, Todd	75		
Walsh, Catherine E.	18		
Walsh, Richard	2		
Wardle, Timothy	117		
Warner, Michael	73, 90–91, 203		
Warren, Calvin	160		
Washington, Harold C.	42		
Waters, Kenneth L.	162		
Watt, Jan Gabriël van der	168		
Watts, Galen	24		
Weber, Kathleen	77		
Weheliye, Alexander	133		
Weiman, David	130		
Weine, Stevan M.	119		
Weiss, Margot Daniell	91, 94		
Wenkel, David H.	104		
West, Dennis	171		
Western, Bruce	130, 158		
Whitaker, Robyn	113–14, 124		
White, Heather R.	194		

SUBJECT INDEX

(anti)identarianism, 11–12, 32, 184–186, 197–8, 209, 222–225, 230–31
abolition. *See* carceral system
Abu Ghraib, 97–99
abyssal line, 12, 17–26, 29, 32–34, 36, 46, 56, 132–4, 191, 225, 227–31
academy, the, 5, 15, 21, 26, 29, 33, 39, 48
affect theory, 84–87
agape, 65–74, 77–78 83–95, 162–64, 183, 187–88
agape meal. *See* Last Supper
AIDS. *See* HIV
Alea, Tomás Gutiérrez, 169–89
allotriosis, 141, 154
anachronism, 24, 93, 107, 183, 231
analgesic literary strategies, 124–25
apocalypticism, 115, 121
art studies, 2, 36, 41, 54, 57–61, 79–95, 98–103, 136, 142–47, 157, 169–89, 204, 208, 210–23
Augustine, 68–72
Bacon, Francis, 103, 135–36, 142–46, 156–57
barebacking, 198–224
Bernini, Gian Lorenzo, 211–215, 222
biblical exceptionalism, 41
biblical studies, 1–32, 35–50, 54, 62, 106, 194–200, 218
Black liberation theology, 11, 17, 28, 45–46, 50–55, 62, 100, 107, 133, 181–87, 195, 227
breastfeeding, 73–103
Buñuel, Luis, 169, 174–189
cannibalism, 174
capitalism. *See* Marxism
Caravaggio, Michelangelo Merisi da, 60–61, 86–89, 199–225
carceral system, 31, 37, 41, 129–34, 258, 229
caritas, 66–95
Catholicism, 75, 170, 174–78, 187, 196
citizenship, 2, 228–29
coloniality. *See* postcolonial critique
concupiscence, 68–70, 220
conversion, 207
  of Paul, 199–218, 222, 225
Conversion on the Way to Damascus, The. *See* Caravaggio, Michelangelo Merisi da
crucifixion. *See also* Dalí, Salvador; Souza, Francis Newton; Bacon, Francis
  of Jesus, 99–147, 166, 176
  Roman, 104, 127
cruising, 199–222
cultural studies, 2–20, 27, 31, 33–34, 35–63, 65, 86, 145–46, 163, 169, 179, 184, 189, 202–204, 228–33
cupiditas, 69–71
Dalí, Salvador, 100–103
decentering, 40–41, 49, 127, 209, 228
decolonialism. *See* postcolonial critique
democracy, 26, 41, 47, 51–52, 98, 223–24, 228–29
democratization. *See* democracy
disability studies, 9, 158–60, 203, 230
discipleship, 76, 112–17, 167, 203
disgust, 86, 92, 175
ecotheology, 21, 28–29, 229
Ecstasy of Saint Teresa. *See* Bernini, Gian Lorenzo

Enlightenment, 10, 179, 183, 184
enslavement 50, 62, 53, 133–38, 160–78, 187, 189, 227
  Atlantic Slave Trade, 86, 137, 187
  Greco Roman slavery, 99, 116, 162
epistemicide, 12, 14–22, 40, 62
Epistemologies of the South, 5, 12–34, 232
epistemology, 16, 19, 20, 22, 28, 30, 107, 231
  in crisis, 1–5, 9, 15, 19, 31–32, 36–27
eros, 63–95, 183, 219, 220
erotohistoriography, 74, 79, 85, 87, 90, 95, 202, 204, 205
ethics, 5, 13, 19, 22, 27, 28–31, 46, 57, 62, 66–71, 73–77, 89, 94–95, 105–9, 114–15, 118, 126–27, 130, 142, 165–69, 180, 187–88, 194, 197, 203–8, 210, 216, 219–22, 227–33
Eucharist. *See* Last Supper
exegesis, 6, 9–10, 13, 23, 26, 29, 37, 53, 68, 174, 197
extractavist methodologies, 5, 21–23
fantasy, 94
femininity, 81–85, 120, 181, 199, 206, 210. *See also* sex
feminism, 2, 7, 14–15, 28, 42, 46, 55, 57, 67, 82, 94, 120, 187, 195, 206, 221, 230, 232. *See also* womanism
fetish. *See* S&M
fetishization, 6, 60
footwashing, 162–188
fucking. *See* sex
gaze, 46, 60, 80, 84–86, 92, 94, 98, 134, 146, 163, 178, 195, 209–11
Gemma Augustea, 99
gender, 8, 11–12, 34, 45–46, 65–67, 81, 82, 84–86, 91–92, 148, 152, 168, 178–79, 181, 183–87, 197–98, 206–9, 213, 218, 229. *See also* masculinity; femininity; queer theory
genealogies, 2–3, 7–8, 12, 13, 16, 18, 118, 196
Global North, 3–22, 27, 29, 31, 33–34, 40, 66, 75, 107, 132, 193, 195, 196–98, 223

Global South, 3–22, 24, 26, 27–34, 35, 40, 67, 75, 132, 195, 197, 225. *See also* Epistemologies of the South; abyssal line
globalization, 47, 181–82
Greco-Roman world, 12, 44, 56, 60, 104, 127, 166–67, 189, 216–217
guilds. *See* academy, the
Hellenism 49, 152
hegemony, 2–6, 9, 24, 26–27, 35, 40, 45, 48–49, 51, 167
hermeneutic of suspicion, 45, 41, 51
high-theory, 8, 24
historicism, 2–34, 35–38, 40–41, 44, 47–51, 57–62, 74, 194, 229, 231–32
historiography, 1–6, 9–12, 53–54, 58–60, 74, 187, 195–96, 204, 227, 230
HIV, 31, 41, 93, 191–225, 227, 229
ideological criticism, 13, 22, 27–28, 37, 39, 41, 50–52, 86, 107, 134, 169, 187–89, 227
imprisonment. *See* carceral system
incarceration. *See* carceral system
inter(con)textuality, 34, 54–63, 68, 73–74, 78, 90, 106, 133, 189, 200–203, 230
Jesus, 66–67, 74–77, 83, 99, 103–118, 121–27, 148–56, 161–74, 216–17, 219. *See also* crucifixion; footwashing
jouissance, 84–85, 87, 92, 94, 212–215
Judaism, 25, 28, 49, 56, 164, 166, 167, 189
kingdom of God, 112–113, 151
lactation. *See* breastfeeding
La última cena. *See* Alea, Tomás Gutiérrez
Last Supper, 161–89
Last Supper Exploded. *See* Shonibare, Yinka
Latin America, 5, 9–12, 18, 20, 27–32, 66, 106, 107, 194, 196–97
liberation theology, 8, 12, 27–33, 46, 62, 65–68, 75–76, 107, 195–196
literary theory/criticism, 3, 7, 10–11, 24, 31, 33–34, 35–37, 45–46, 50–60, 65, 74, 103–109, 111–12, 115, 117–19, 121, 122–27, 135, 147, 157, 159, 162, 167, 196, 202–4, 228–29

logos, 153–54
Marxism, 8, 17, 22, 25, 28, 43, 51–52, 67, 137, 173–74, 178, 182, 185, 187, 198, 229
masculinity, 81–82, 119, 206, 210, 215–18. *See also* sex
modernity, 12, 17–27, 39, 60, 196, 232
monoracialism. *See* whiteness
Mujerista theology, 230
multiculturalism. *See* cultural studies
multiracialism, 8, 16–17, 22, 27, 32
objectivism, 4–5, 7, 10, 12, 17–20, 22–23, 27–28, 30, 32, 35, 50, 62, 107, 231
oikeiosis/oikos, 141, 151–55, 159
oppression, 22, 41, 46, 52, 53, 99, 100, 112, 148, 170, 188
paganism, 70, 76
pain. *See* torture
Paul, 12, 49, 199–225. *See also* conversion
Pero and Cimon, 79–95. *See also* Rubens, Peter Paul; Sauco, Max
phallus, 81, 82, 86, 210–215
phenomenology, 41, 72, 106, 107–8, 129–30, 134, 136–42, 147, 157, 159–60, 200
polis, 135, 138, 148–49, 152, 156
postabyssal. *See* abyssal line
postcolonial critique, 4–12, 17–30, 41, 50–55, 62, 67, 100, 132, 135, 147–50, 159–60, 161–89, 194, 196, 198, 227, 229, 231–32
postmodernity, 12–13, 17, 24, 26–27, 39, 42, 50, 59, 60, 136
presentism, 6–7, 11–12, 38, 232
preteritism, 6–7, 9–12, 231
protectionism, 48–50
psychoanalysis, 176, 195, 215. *See also* phallus
queer theory, 7–12, 44–51, 65–95, 185, 197, 193, 195–225, 227, 230, 232
race, 9, 17, 22–23, 46, 147, 183–85, 203
ratio and oratio, 67, 154
reception history, 36, 39, 51, 53–63, 77, 89, 113, 174, 177, 179, 202, 215, 232

Roman Charity. See Rubens, Peter Paul; Caravaggio, Michelangelo Merisi da; Sauco, Max
Rubens, Peter Paul, 73–74, 78–95
S&M, 73–74, 78, 84, 90–95, 178, 212–213
sacraments 75, 163, 165, 188. *See also* Last Supper
Sauco, Max, 92–93
Saul. *See* Paul
scientifism, 10, 17–18, 22, 28, 30, 32, 35, 62, 194, 231
secularism, 4, 12, 17–18, 22–28, 30, 231
seven virtues, 75
Seven Works of Mercy. See Caravaggio, Michelangelo Merisi da
sex. *See also* masculinity; femininity; queer theory
   as act, 69, 73, 175–176, 183, 193–225
   as identity, 11–12, 46, 65–100, 178, 183, 193–225
   sexuality, 11–12, 45–46, 65–100, 184–85, 191–225
Shonibare, Yinka, 181–89
slavery. *See* enslavement
social death, 121, 129–60, 164. *See also* enslavement
sociology of knowledge, 5, 8, 19, 27
solitary confinement, 44, 62, 99, 129–60, 227–28
Souza, Francis Newton, 100–103, 129
subject/object/Other relationship, 9, 20–21, 54, 55–62, 65, 68, 72, 75, 91, 98–100, 123, 133–34, 137–48, 154–58, 167, 170, 180, 196, 198, 200, 202–15, 219–23, 231
submission, 69, 82, 90, 145, 162, 171, 199, 207–22
subversion, 34, 43, 55, 178
suicide, 97, 131, 176, 179
Supreme Court, 227–28, 230
taboo, 94. *See also* psychoanalysis
temple, the, 110–18, 122–23
top/bottom, 90–95, 202, 206–10, 214, 216–19

torture, 41, 62, 94, 97–127, 132–33, 143, 158, 165, 170, 173, 227. *See also* solitary confinement
totalitarianism, 30
utopia, 3, 27–38, 46, 63, 71, 110, 113, 207
Viridiana, see Buñuel, Luis
visual studies. *See* art studies
voyeurism, 79, 91, 94, 178. *See also* gaze.
whiteness, 4, 8, 15–17, 19, 22–23, 26–27, 30, 32, 55, 107, 132, 183, 231
womanism, 46, 51, 230. *See also* Black liberation theology

www.ingramcontent.com/pod-product-compliance
Lightning Source LLC
Chambersburg PA
CBHW051210300426
44116CB00006B/508